FinTech Development for Financial Inclusiveness

Muhammad Anshari
Universiti Brunei Darussalam, Brunei

Mohamad Nabil Almunawar
Universiti Brunei Darussalam, Brunei

Masairol Masri
Universiti Brunei Darussalam, Brunei

IGI Global
PUBLISHER of TIMELY KNOWLEDGE

A volume in the Advances in Finance, Accounting, and Economics (AFAE) Book Series

Published in the United States of America by
IGI Global
Business Science Reference (an imprint of IGI Global)
701 E. Chocolate Avenue
Hershey PA, USA 17033
Tel: 717-533-8845
Fax: 717-533-8661
E-mail: cust@igi-global.com
Web site: http://www.igi-global.com

Library of Congress Cataloging-in-Publication Data

Names: Anshari, Muhammad, 1977- editor. | Almunawar, Mohammad Nabil, 1960- editor. | Masri, Masairol, 1974- editor.

Title: FinTech development for financial inclusiveness / Muhammad Anshari, Mohammad Nabil Almunawar, and Masairol Masri, editor.

Description: Hershey, PA : Business Science Reference, [2022] | Includes bibliographical references and index. | Summary: "This book highlights how FinTech supports the availability and equality of opportunities to access financial services for individuals and businesses to take advantage of affordable, and timely financial products and services by featuring conceptual, case studies, recent development, best practices, comparative assessment, business processes, as well as strategies and outputs in studies of FinTech from multiple domains of knowledge"-- Provided by publisher.

Identifiers: LCCN 2021031964 (print) | LCCN 2021031965 (ebook) | ISBN 9781799884477 (hardcover) | ISBN 9781799884484 (paperback) | ISBN 9781799884491 (ebook)

Subjects: LCSH: Finance--Technological innovations. | Financial services industry--Technological innovations. | Financial institutions--Technological innovations.

Classification: LCC HG173 .F537 2022 (print) | LCC HG173 (ebook) | DDC 332.0285--dc23

LC record available at https://lccn.loc.gov/2021031964

LC ebook record available at https://lccn.loc.gov/2021031965

This book is published in the IGI Global book series Advances in Finance, Accounting, and Economics (AFAE) (ISSN: 2327-5677; eISSN: 2327-5685)

British Cataloguing in Publication Data
A Cataloguing in Publication record for this book is available from the British Library.

Advances in Finance, Accounting, and Economics (AFAE) Book Series

Ahmed Driouchi
Al Akhawayn University, Morocco

ISSN:2327-5677
EISSN:2327-5685

Mission

In our changing economic and business environment, it is important to consider the financial changes occurring internationally as well as within individual organizations and business environments. Understanding these changes as well as the factors that influence them is crucial in preparing for our financial future and ensuring economic sustainability and growth.

The **Advances in Finance, Accounting, and Economics (AFAE)** book series aims to publish comprehensive and informative titles in all areas of economics and economic theory, finance, and accounting to assist in advancing the available knowledge and providing for further research development in these dynamic fields.

Coverage

- Economics of Agriculture and Biotechnology
- Development Economics
- E-Accounting
- Health Economics
- International Economics
- Risk Analysis and Management
- Economic Indices and Quantitative Economic Methods
- Economic Theory
- Evidence-Based Studies
- Comparative Accounting Systems

IGI Global is currently accepting manuscripts for publication within this series. To submit a proposal for a volume in this series, please contact our Acquisition Editors at Acquisitions@igi-global.com or visit: http://www.igi-global.com/publish/.

The Advances in Finance, Accounting, and Economics (AFAE) Book Series (ISSN 2327-5677) is published by IGI Global, 701 E. Chocolate Avenue, Hershey, PA 17033-1240, USA, www.igi-global.com. This series is composed of titles available for purchase individually; each title is edited to be contextually exclusive from any other title within the series. For pricing and ordering information please visit http://www.igi-global.com/book-series/advances-finance-accounting-economics/73685. Postmaster: Send all address changes to above address.

Titles in this Series

For a list of additional titles in this series, please visit: http://www.igi-global.com/book-series/advances-finance-accounting-economics/73685

Handbook of Research on Changing World Economic Order in the Post-Pandemic Period
Sushanta Kumar Mahapatra (IBS Hyderabad, The ICFAI Foundation for Higher Education, India) and Vishal Sarin (Lovely Professional University, India)
Business Science Reference • © 2022 • 470pp • H/C (ISBN: 9781799868965) • US $295.00

Handbook of Research on Developing Circular, Digital, and Green Economies in Asia
Patricia Ordóñez de Pablos (The University of Oviedo, Spain)
Business Science Reference • © 2022 • 521pp • H/C (ISBN: 9781799886785) • US $225.00

Handbook of Research on Climate Change and the Sustainable Financial Sector
Odunayo Magret Olarewaju (Durban University of Technology, South Africa) and Idris Olayiwola Ganiyu (University of KwaZulu-Natal, South Africa)
Business Science Reference • © 2021 • 573pp • H/C (ISBN: 9781799879671) • US $295.00

CSR and Management Accounting Challenges in a Time of Global Crises
Ionica Oncioiu (Titu Maiorescu University, Romania)
Business Science Reference • © 2021 • 278pp • H/C (ISBN: 9781799880691) • US $215.00

Impact of Global Issues on International Trade
Ahu Coşkun Özer (Marmara University, Turkey)
Business Science Reference • © 2021 • 291pp • H/C (ISBN: 9781799883142) • US $215.00

Handbook of Research on the Empirical Aspects of Strategic Trade Negotiations and Management
Nuno Crespo (ISCTE – Instituto Universitário de Lisboa, Portugal) and Nadia Simoes (ISCTE – Instituto Universitário de Lisboa, Portugal)
Business Science Reference • © 2021 • 446pp • H/C (ISBN: 9781799875680) • US $265.00

Handbook of Research on Financial Management During Economic Downturn and Recovery
Nuno Miguel Teixeira (Center for Research in Business and Administration, School of Business Sciences, Polytechnic Institute of Setúbal, Portugal) and Inês Lisboa (CARME, School of Management and Technology, Polytechnic of Leiria, Portugal)
Business Science Reference • © 2021 • 566pp • H/C (ISBN: 9781799866435) • US $295.00

IGI Global
PUBLISHER of TIMELY KNOWLEDGE

701 East Chocolate Avenue, Hershey, PA 17033, USA
Tel: 717-533-8845 x100 • Fax: 717-533-8661
E-Mail: cust@igi-global.com • www.igi-global.com

Editorial Advisory Board

Table of Contents

Detailed Table of Contents

For a very long period of time, financial inclusion researchers have been addressing the barriers that prevent unprivileged people from accessing and using financial services. Financial exclusion is an underlying social problem that dates from the creation of the first financial system. Without the access to the banking and financial infrastructures, the unbanked are perpetuating a vicious cycle of poverty. Blockchain is leading this transformation of allowing unbanked and underbanked people to have access and interact with the finance industry. The promise of a digital economy is starting to take shape, as financial technology (FinTech) companies are evolving the concept of democratization of access. Decentralized finance (DeFi) is expanding the possibilities of financial technology by creating an ecosystem based on transparency, accessibility, and efficiency. We are witnessing a paradigm shift for most of the financial services which are remodeling the accessibility and usability of these services, addressing the excluded and underserved population.

Financial technology has emerged as a game-changer to complement and enhance how the Millennial and Generation Z conduct transactions. Responding to calls of prior research, this study used the unified theory of acceptance and use of technology (UTAUT) to understand how performance expectancy and effort expectancy factors influence consumers' intention to use financial technology. Performance expectancy (PE) and effort expectancy (EE) were investigated as exogenous variables towards the intention to use financial technology (FinTech) that act as endogenous variables in this study. The authors collected 284

Millennial and Generation Z respondents and analysed the data using PLS-SEM. The result from the study's structural model suggested that FinTech continuance use intention was dependent on performance expectancy and effort expectancy on engaging with young vibrant consumers and establishing attractive FinTech elements. In addition, Millennial and Generation Z consumers with a high-performance expectancy were found to emphasize FinTech components in the engagement process.

Siti NurulJannah Rosli, Universiti Brunei Darussalam, Brunei
Muhammad Anshari, Universiti Brunei Darussalam, Brunei
Mohammad Nabil Almunawar, Universiti Brunei Darussalam, Brunei
Masairol Masri, Universiti Brunei Darussalam, Brunei

Digital wallet is expanding largely driven by the evolution of internet and smartphone penetration. Numerous digital wallet providers have risen in many countries including Brunei Darussalam. However, the level of adoption is still low, and cashless society is still far from an expected target. There's no magic formula in deploying a guaranteed successful digital wallet, but developing a digital wallet ecosystem that is tailored to the local markets will be expected to increase digital culture and cashless society. The research assesses the existing digital wallet ecosystem, then analyses the extent of compatibility of local market demand. Furthermore, it introduces an improved digital wallet ecosystem model in order to support financial inclusion achieved through a holistic digital wallet ecosystem. The chapter also examines external factors that contribute to the digital wallet ecosystem's width of usage.

Mia Fithriyah, Indonesia Open University, Indonesia
Masairol Masri, Universiti Brunei Darussalam, Brunei
Mohammad Nabil Almunawar, Universiti Brunei Darussalam, Brunei
Muhammad Anshari, Universiti Brunei Darussalam, Brunei

Despite the increasing adoption of financial technology (FinTech) and the need for secure payment methods, mobile payments as a mode of settling daily business transactions have not received sufficient attention. To date, several business actors prefer to use conventional money payment modes. However, it is apparent that the need for a more effective payment method today is considered as a basic necessity, considering the current complexity of consumers and the negative effect of COVID-19. Moreover, the crisis raised a wave of apprehension over a large number of business actors, particularly small and medium-size enterprises (SMEs). The literature search indicated that the government should implement the correct policy to help create an acceptable environment for financial transactions for both the user and providers. It is also necessary to ensure that client security and privacy rights are protected during the mobile payment transactions.

In Indonesia after the Asian financial crisis of 1997–1998, wide reforms were carried out, and "inclusive" economic development were adopted. One component of inclusive economic development is "financial inclusion." This implies an absence of barriers that might deter micro, small, and medium enterprises (MSMEs) from obtaining financial services. However, the portion of bank credit received by MSMEs is still small. Therefore, financial technology (FinTech) is welcome as an alternative source of funding for MSMEs. This chapter discusses three related issues, namely financial inclusion, MSMEs, and P2P lending. It concludes that Indonesia still has a long way to go to achieve full financial inclusion. This chapter suggests that with the presence of P2P lending, the number of MSMEs, especially MSEs, in Indonesia that have access to formal financing will increase. Even though aggregate data are not available, the interviews with a small number of owners of MSEs who received P2P loans suggest that the presence of P2P lending companies give some benefits for MSEs.

How the future financial industry is going to be reshaped by technological innovations is now a concern. Financial technology (FinTech), a much-discussed topic around the globe, is changing the overall financial system. The trend is not an exception in developing countries like Bangladesh. In this chapter, the authors aim to explore the current state of FinTech in Bangladesh in light with the possible challenges for growth, opportunities, and future prospects. The growth of FinTech helps a large percentage of people to become banked or has given possible access to formal finance. For having access to finance, high rate of mobile phone penetration, smooth mobile internet access, and high cost of access to formal finance are some factors that have enhanced FinTech penetration in Bangladesh for the past few years. In line with the given prospects, there are problems too. Therefore, using an in-depth study, this research addresses those issues, provides recommendations, and looks for possible solutions for the smooth operation of FinTech in Bangladesh.

The Indonesian Population Census 2020 reported that the majority of Indonesia's population is in the productive age group and dominated by Generation Z (27.94%). As the generation that currently dominates the population, Generation Z's characteristics are important to learn. They are the future. Generation Z has the potency to accelerate Indonesia's financial inclusion through digitalization because they are adaptable to technology. Responding to the survey results which put Generation Z in Indonesia in the first rank for the levels of happiness and religious awareness, a survey was conducted for Islamic financial technology literacy to find out how they face challenges as well as opportunities in digital era to be in line with religious values and may accelerate financial inclusion. The great potential of Generation Z for technology as well as religious awareness in turn will support financial inclusion towards inclusive development in Indonesia. Hence, this chapter will describe the survey results of digital financial knowledge and behavior of Generation Z in Indonesia.

The COVID-19 pandemic has changed people's digital behavior and caused giant leaps in various digital businesses. SMEs face various challenging factors in the transformation of their business into a digital ecosystem. Currently, Indonesia is the country with the fastest-growing digital economy and FinTech in ASEAN. Fintech plays a vital role in the digital economy, especially helping SMEs go digital and accelerate their business performance, such as venture capital financing, digital payment services, and financial arrangements. However, the role of fintech has not been maximized in increasing financial inclusion. There are still various obstacles and challenges such as technology adoption, financial literacy, digital literacy, financial inclusion, and fintech inclusion, and various program efforts from all stakeholders to bring SMEs into the digital ecosystem. Without cooperation, increasing financial literacy and financial inclusion and fintech inclusion will be challenging to achieve.

FinTech provides more inclusive financial services for individual users and companies. China, with the highest penetration rate of online payment around the world, enables individual users to enjoy in-depth inclusive lending services. This chapter will portray and assess FinTech's adoption, challenges, and its potentials to China. Based on previous literature, the characteristics of FinTech in China and the roles of government in promoting FinTech to Chinese business will be discussed. This chapter will also select cases from Hangzhou and the Greater Bay Area in order to analyze the opportunities and challenges for Chinese companies integrating FinTech into its business operations.

Chapter 10

Heru Susanto, University of Technology Brunei, Brunei & National Research and Innovation Agency, Indonesia & Tunghai University, Taiwan
Fahmi Ibrahim, University of Technology Brunei, Brunei
Rodiah, Department of Informatics, Gunadarma University, Indonesia
Didi Rosiyadi, National Research and Innovation Agency, Indonesia
Desi Setiana, University of Brunei Darussalam, Brunei & Ministry of Law and Human Rights, Indonesia
Alifya Kayla Shafa Susanto, Department of Information Security, School of Computing and Informatics, University of Technology Brunei, Brunei
Nicolas Kusuma, Department of Informatics, Gunadarma University, Indonesia
Iwan Setiawan, National Research and Innovation Agency, Indonesia

Financial technology (FinTech) as part of financial inlcussion changes conventional business models to be information technology minded. The presence of FinTech in the wider community makes it easy for access to financial service products and transactions and payment systems more practically, efficiently, and economically. Unfortunately, as the security risk in transacting increases, cyber security in the financial services industry and FinTech service providers is considered a major target by cybercriminals. This study proposed a security management approach through hybrid blockchain method implemented through flask framework and encryption to protect transaction data. The results are promising. Referring to accuracy, this study successfully reduces data leakage and misuse of personal data and financial data in FinTechs.

Chapter 11

Yeoul Hwangbo, Asian Study Society, South Korea

The challenge over most countries has been legislating related acts and regulations on global electronic commerce taxation, but they have not implemented the consumption tax system for global electronic commerce so far. Consumer payment tax (CPT) is based on fintech and thereby proposed so that consumers can pay the consumption taxes to related taxation office of the countries in accordance with consumer country's jurisdiction principle, considering the CPT is assessed to satisfy most of the electronic commerce taxation criteria and has the potential to be applied to electronic commerce.

Chapter 12

Heru Susanto, University of Technology Brunei, Brunei & National Research and Innovation Agency, Indonesia & Tunghai University, Taiwan
Nurul Mardhiah, Department of Management, School of Business, University of Technology Brunei, Brunei
Alifya Kayla Shafa Susanto, Department of Information Security, School of Computing and Informatics, University of Technology Brunei, Brunei

In recent years, the number of financial technology players and users have increased at a significant rate due to the rapid technological advancement in financial technology. While smart devices are providing more useful features to users, they have also made it possible for cyber threats to migrate from desktops to smart devices. Thus, it is important for smart device users to be aware that their device could be exposed to cyber threats and that users could protect their devices by employing data-centric cyber security measures. This study reveals how financial technology business model responded to the breach phenomenon by employing data-centric protection approaches. The result is very interesting. Data-centric security is very needed as it is capable of protecting data as a whole. It provides a gapless protection, meaning to say, the data are encrypted and classified wherever it moves. With persistent protection and cross-platform operability, data-centric security will eliminate gaps and keep data protected.

Foreword

FinTech (financial technology) is a portmanteau term that alludes to the creative and innovative use of smart mobile devices to develop and supply financial services and products, resulting in a new way of delivering financial services. FinTech is one of the most recent advancements in the finance business. It has grown at a rapid pace in recent years. It provides low-cost, high-quality services in a financially sustainable setting.

The term financial inclusiveness refers to anybody and everyone having easy accessibility to financial products and services. FinTech has made a big contribution to financial inclusion. The goal of financial inclusion is to reduce the number of people who do not have access to the funds. As a result, it is expected that in the future, everybody will have access to financial services. To improve community welfare, those financial services should be of high quality, secure, and affordable to everyone. Financial services must be tailored to people's needs and must fulfill very few simple criteria. Furthermore, safe financial services are built to keep people's rights and responsibilities from the vulnerabilities that the services potentially cause.

FinTech Development for Financial Inclusiveness is a timely book that documents research findings and expert perspectives from academics, professionals, financial advisers, and policymakers on a variety of multi-disciplinary issues and challenges that the financial business is experiencing as a result of the current rapid pace of innovative technology. Chapters in the book document the FinTech's experts their views and initiate discussion on a range of FinTech's development and achievements in supporting financial inclusiveness.

The book showcase FinTech experts' insights and encourage discussion on a multitude of FinTech advancements and accomplishments in promoting financial inclusion. I applaud the editors of Universiti Brunei Darussalam School of Business and Economics (UBDSBE) for taking the significant step of compiling this important book, which provides conceptual understanding and shares practical experience that will help governments, practitioners, and the general public understand the prospects and challenges of disruptive innovations. I am optimistic that the research presented in this book will contribute in the development of new business models, applications, processes, products, or services with a meaningful impact on financial markets and institutions, as well as financial service provision.

Masairol Masri
School of Business and Economics, Universiti Brunei Darussalam, Brunei

Preface

Utilizing ICT to deliver financial services as well as creating new financial products and services accessible through the Web/Apps has attracted much attention lately and it has marched to a new area called Financial Technology (FinTech), which can be considered as a disruptive innovation in financial sectors. Many innovations have been created in FinTech, and some of them are disruptive innovations that threaten the existing players in the financial industry. FinTech is now widely used around the world. Eventually, FinTech will either disrupt or complement existing financial services (Anshari et al., 2019a). The role of financial services in the financial industry is vitally important. As technology evolves, the delivery of the services is being shifted from traditional delivery systems to innovative delivery systems that heavily use information and communication technology (ICT) to serve the public in much better ways.

FinTech innovations have led to new business models, applications, processes, or products that affect financial markets and institutions and the provision of financial services. FinTech includes five major areas which are finance and investment, operations and risk management, payments and infrastructure, data security and monetization, and customer interface. It covers many types of financial services such as crowdfunding, money transfer, loan, Peer-to-Peer (P2P) lending, asset management, mobile payment, and fundraising.

Financial Inclusiveness refers to an effort to make financial services and products to be easily available and affordable to anyone irrespective of personal net worth or company size. Financial inclusion aims to create a strong, functional, diverse, efficient and flexible financial system in order to establish a market-driven, productive and competitive economy. Hence, financial inclusion attempted to eliminate barriers that exclude individuals from engaging with the financial sector services (Anshari et al., 2019b). So why are people outside of the system? In the context of financial exclusion, it refers to accessible, affordable and relevant financial solutions for all individuals, regardless of their nationality, gender, race or religion (Popescu, 2022).

The book *FinTech Development for Financial Inclusiveness* is expected to become a major literature and reference for FinTech development, especially in promoting financial inclusion, featuring conceptual, case studies, recent development, best practices, comparative assessment, business processes, as well as strategies and outputs in studies of FinTech from multiple domains of knowledge. To ensure the quality, each chapter in this book was reviewed in two rounds. Readers are likely to be academicians and students who can use chapters in this book for their references on the latest development of financial technology, researchers academia to gain perspective of disruptive innovation in the financial sector, government organizations who interested in the field of FinTech, business owners who need to understand the phenomenon of FinTech, technopreneurs who seek innovative ideas on FinTech, financial & banking practitioners who need to understand recent development of FinTech, policymakers who need to understand the major core of FinTech and Financial Inclusiveneness, and also general public who seek information the emergence of FinTech.

The book covers a wide range of topics from Overview of FinTech, FinTech as Decentralized Finance (DeFi) for Financial Inclusion, FinTech as Future Game-Changer, Digital Wallet Ecosystem, Financial Inclusion & SMEs, Digital Financial Knowledge, and FinTech's security, both in the Asia region and in several specific countries such as Bangladesh, Brunei Darussalam, China, Japan, Indonesia, Romania, and Malaysia. The book includes 12 chapters that address the recent FinTech development in promoting Financial Inclusiveness with respect to process, strategies, challenges, lessons learnt, as well as outcomes. The following is the summary of each chapter.

Chapter 1, titled "Understanding FinTech and Decentralized Finance (DeFi) for Financial Inclusion," by Andrei Dragos Popescu (Finance, University of Craiova, Romania & SCX Holdings Pte. Ltd, Singapore), stated that for a very long period of time, financial inclusion researchers have been addressing the barriers that prevent unprivileged people from accessing and using financial services. Financial exclusion is an underlying social problem that dates from the creation of the first financial system. Without access to the banking and financial infrastructures, the unbanked are perpetuating a vicious cycle of poverty. Blockchain is leading this transformation of allowing unbanked and underbanked people to have access and interact with the finance industry. The promise of a digital economy is starting to take shape, as Financial Technology (FinTech) companies are evolving the concept of democratization of access. Decentralized Finance (DeFi) is expanding the possibilities of financial technology by creating an ecosystem based on transparency, accessibility and efficiency. We are witnessing a paradigm shift for most of the financial services which are remodeling the accessibility and usability of these services, addressing the excluded and underserved population.

Chapter 2, titled "Financial Technology as a Future Game-Changer," by Nelson Lajuni (Universiti Malaysia Sabah, Malaysia), Avnner Chardles Wellfren (Universiti Malaysia Sabah, Malaysia), Noraini binti Abdullah (Universiti Malaysia Sabah, Malaysia), and Salumah binti Nain (Universiti Malaysia Sabah, Malaysia), stated that FinTech has emerged as a game-changer to complement and enhance how the millennial and Generation Z conduct transactions. Responding to calls of prior research, this study used the Unified Theory of Acceptance and Use of Technology (UTAUT) to understand how performance expectancy and effort expectancy factors influence consumers' intention to use financial technology. Performance expectancy (PE) and effort expectancy (EE) were investigated as exogenous variables towards the intention to use financial technology (FinTech) that act as endogenous variables in this study. We collected 284 millennial and Generation Z respondents and analysed the data using PLS-SEM. The result from the study's structural model suggested that FinTech continuance use intention was dependent on performance expectancy and effort expectancy on engaging with young vibrant consumers and establishing attractive FinTech elements. In addition, millennial and Generation Z consumers with a high-performance expectancy were found to emphasize FinTech components in the engagement process.

Chapter 3, titled "Digital Wallet Ecosystem in Promoting Financial Inclusion," by Siti NurulJannah Rosli (Universiti Brunei Darussalam), Muhammad Anshari (Universiti Brunei Darussalam, Brunei Darussalam), Mohammad Nabil Almunawar (Universiti Brunei Darussalam, Brunei Darussalam), and Masairol Masri (Universiti Brunei Darussalam, Brunei Darussalam), affirms that Digital wallet is expanding largely driven by the evolution of Internet and smartphone penetration. Numerous digital wallet providers have risen in many countries including Brunei Darussalam. However, the level of adoption is still low and a cashless society is still far from an expected target. There's no magic formula in deploying a guaranteed successful digital wallet but developing a digital wallet ecosystem that is tailored to the local markets will be expected to increase digital culture and a cashless society. The research assesses the existing digital wallet ecosystem, then analyse the extent of compatibility of local market demand. Furthermore, it introduces an improved digital wallet ecosystem model in order to support financial inclusion that can be achieved through a holistic digital wallet ecosystem. The paper also examines external factors that contribute to the digital wallet ecosystem's width of usage.

Chapter 4, titled "Financial Inclusion and Mobile Payment to Empower Small and Medium-Sized Enterprises: Post-COVID-19 Business Strategy," by Mia Fithriyah (Indonesia Open University, Indonesia), Masairol Masri (Universiti Brunei Darussalam, Brunei Darussalam), Mohammad Nabil Almunawar (Universiti Brunei Darussalam, Brunei Darussalam), and Muhammad Anshari (Universiti Brunei Darussalam, Brunei Darussalam), states that despite the increasing adoption of Financial Technology (FinTech), and the need for secure payment methods, mobile payments as a mode of settling daily business transactions have not received sufficient attention. To date, several business actors prefer to use conventional money payment modes. However, it is apparent that the need for a more effective payment method today is considered a basic necessity, considering the current complexity of consumers and the negative effect of COVID-19. Moreover, the crisis raised a wave of apprehension over a large number of business actors, particularly Small and Medium-size Enterprises (SMEs). The literature search indicated that the government should implement the correct policy to help create an acceptable environment for financial transactions for both the user and providers. It is also necessary to ensure that clients' security and privacy rights are protected during mobile payments transactions.

Chapter 5, titled "Financial Inclusion, P2P Lending, and MSMEs: Evidence From Indonesia," by Tulus T.H. Tambunan (Universitas Trisakti, Indonesia), discusses in Indonesia after the Asian financial crisis of 1997–1998 wide reforms have been carried out and "inclusive" economic development has been adopted. One component of inclusive economic development is "financial inclusion". This implies an absence of barriers that might deter micro, small and medium enterprises (MSMEs) from obtaining financial services. However, the portion of bank credit received by MSMEs is still small. Therefore, financial technology (fintech) is welcome, as an alternative source of funding for MSMEs. This chapter discusses three related issues, namely financial inclusion, MSMEs, and P2P lending. It concludes that Indonesia still has a long way to go to achieve full financial inclusion. This chapter suggests that with the presence of P2P lending, the number of MSMEs, especially MSEs, in Indonesia that have access to formal financing will increase. Even though aggregate data are not available, the interviews with a small number of owners of MSEs who (ever) received P2P loans suggest that the presence of P2P lending companies do give some benefits for MSEs.

Chapter 6, titled "An Overview of FinTech in Bangladesh: Problems and Prospects," by Sheikh Abu Taher (Jahangirnagar University, Bangladesh) and Masatsugu Tsuji (Faculty of Economics, Kobe International University, Japan), states that how the future financial industry is going to reshape by technological innovations. Financial technology (FinTech), a much-discussed topic around the globe, is changing the overall financial system. The trend is not an exception in developing countries like Bangladesh too. In this chapter, the authors aim to explore the current state of FinTech in Bangladesh in light with the possible challenges for growth, opportunities, and future prospects. The growth of FinTech helps a large percentage of people to become banked or has given possible access to formal finance. Having access to finance, a high rate of mobile phone penetration, smooth mobile internet access and a high cost of access to formal finance are some factors that enhance FinTech penetration in Bangladesh for the past few years. In line with the given prospects, there are problems that remain too. Therefore, using an in-depth study, this research addresses those issues, provide recommendations and look for a possible solution for the smooth operation of FinTech in Bangladesh.

Chapter 7, titled "Digital Financial Knowledge and Behavior of Generation Z in Indonesia: A Survey of Islamic FinTech Literacy Toward Digital Financial Inclusion," by Khairunnisa Musari (Kiai Haji Achmad Siddiq State Islamic University, Indonesia), and Sutan Emir Hidayat (Gunadarma University and National Committee for Islamic Economy & Finance, Indonesia), investigates that the majority of Indonesia's population is in the productive age group and dominated by Generation Z (27.94%). As the generation that currently dominates the population, Generation Z's characters are important to be learned. They are the future. Generation Z has the potency to accelerate Indonesia's financial inclusion through digitalization because they are adaptable to technology. Responding to the survey results which put Generation Z in Indonesia in the first rank for the levels of happiness and religious awareness, then a survey was conducted for Islamic financial technology literacy to find out how they face challenges as well as opportunities in the digital era to be in line with religious values and may accelerate financial inclusion. The great potential of Generation Z for technology as well as religious awareness, in turn, will support financial inclusion towards inclusive development in Indonesia. Hence, this chapter will describe the survey results of digital financial knowledge and behavior of Generation Z in Indonesia.

Chapter 8, titled "The challenges of FinTech Inclusion and Digitization of SMEs in Indonesia," by Syafrizal Helmi Situmorang (Universitas Sumatera Utara, Indonesia), explores that the COVID-19 pandemic has changed people's digital behavior and caused giant leaps in various digital businesses. SMEs face various challenging factors in the transformation of their business into a digital ecosystem. Currently, Indonesia is the country with the fastest-growing digital economy and FinTech in ASEAN. Fintech plays a vital role in the digital economy, especially helping SMEs go digital and accelerate their business performance, such as venture capital financing, digital payment services, and financial arrangements. However, the role of fintech has not been maximized in increasing financial inclusion. There are still various obstacles and challenges such as technology adoption, financial literacy, digital literacy, financial inclusion, and Fintech inclusion. Various program efforts from all stakeholders to bring SMEs into the digital ecosystem. Without cooperation, increasing financial literacy and financial inclusion, and fintech inclusion will be challenging to achieve.

Chapter 9, titled "How the Development of FinTech Can Bolster Financial Inclusion Under an Era of Disruptive Innovation? Cases Study on China," by Poshan Yu (Soochow University, China), Chenghai Li (Independent Researcher, China), Michael Sampat (Independent Researcher, China), and Zuozhang Chen (Soochow University, China), states that FinTech provides more inclusive financial services for individual users and companies. China, with the highest penetration rate of online payment around the world, enables individual users to enjoy in-depth inclusive lending services. This chapter will portray and assess FinTech's adoption, challenges, and its potentials to China. Based on previous literature, the characteristics of FinTech in China and the roles of government in promoting FinTech to Chinese business will be discussed. This chapter will also select cases from Hangzhou and the Greater Bay Area, in order to analyze the opportunities and challenges for Chinese companies integrating FinTech into its business operations.

Chapter 10, titled "Securing Financial Inclusiveness Adoption of Blockchain FinTech Compliance," by Heru Susanto (Tunghai University, Taiwan; LIPI, Indonesia; and University of Technology Brunei, Brunei Darussalam), Fahmi Ibrahim (University of Technology Brunei, Brunei Darussalam), Rodiah Rodiah (Gunadarma University, Indonesia), Didi Rosiyadi, Informatics (Indonesian Institute of Sciences, Indonesia), Desi Setiana (University of Brunei Darussalam, Brunei Darussalam), Alifya Kayla Shafa

Susanto (University of Technology Brunei, Brunei Darussalam), Akbari Indra Basuki (Informatics, LIPI, Indonesia), and Iwan Setiawan (Indonesian Institute of Sciences, Indonesia), explores FinTech as part of financial inclusion changes conventional business models to be information technology minded. The presence of FinTech in the wider community makes it easy access to financial service products; transactions, and payment systems more practically, efficiently and economically. Unfortunately, the security risk in transacting increases, cyber security in the financial services industry and FinTech service providers is considered a major target by cybercriminals. Leakage and misuse of personal data and financial data by irresponsible parties, and the lack of public knowledge about the processes that occur within FinTech. This study proposed a security management approach through a hybrid blockchain method that implemented through flask framework and encryption, to protect transaction data, which the accuracy determined based on the parameters of the user data sent. The results are promising. Refer to accuracy, this study successfully reduces data leakage and misuse of personal data and financial data at FinTech.

Chapter 11, titled "Government Challenges Over Global Electronic Commerce Using FinTech: Design of Consumer Payment Tax (CPT) System," by Yeoul Hwangbo (Asian Study Society & Tashkent University, Uzbekistan), examines the challenge over most countries have been legislating related acts and regulations on global electronic commerce taxation, but they have not implemented the consumption tax system for global electronic commerce so far, Consumer Payment Tax (CPT) is based on fintech and thereby proposed so that consumers can pay the consumption taxes to related taxation office of the countries in accordance with consumer country's jurisdiction principle, considering the CPT is assessed to satisfy most of the electronic commerce taxation criteria and has the potential to been applied to electronic commerce.

Finally, Chapter 12, titled "Crafting Strategies of Security Breaches: How Digital Ecosystem Works in Data-Centric," by Heru Susanto (University of Technology Brunei, Brunei Darussalam), Nurul Mardhiah (University of Technology Brunei, Brunei Darussalam), Alifya Kayla Shafa Susanto (University of Technology Brunei, Brunei Darussalam), discusses several approaches taken by government and agencies on cyber security in Brunei such as in terms of technical, and management include legal, organizational, education and awareness as well as collaboration. Then, compare approaches regarding cyber security between Brunei and other countries, namely Indonesia and Malaysia. It also focuses on several ways to protect individuals or organizations from becoming a victim on this digital platform, and cyber threats include types and impact.

After the summaries of the chapters included in the book, the book portrays and assesses FinTech Development for Financial Inclusiveness's overview, adoption, challenges, and future directions. The emphasis of the book is on quality, research-based studies which contribute to theory, lessons learnt and best practices, critical understanding and policy formulation on FinTech. We hope you all find them useful and interesting for research, teaching, and policy studies.

Thank you,

Muhammad Anshari
Universiti Brunei Darussalam, Brunei

Mohammad Nabil Almunawar
Universiti Brunei Darussalam, Brunei

Masairol Masri
Universiti Brunei Darussalam, Brunei

REFERENCES

Anshari, M., Almunawar, M. N., & Masri, M. (2019a). Financial Technology and Disruptive Innovation in Business. *International Journal of Asian Business and Information Management, 12*(3).

Anshari, M., Almunawar, M. N., Masri, M., & Hamdan, M. (2019b). *Digital Marketplace and FinTech to Support Agriculture Sustainability. Energy Procedia, 156C*, 234–238.

Popescu, A. D. (2022). *Understanding FinTech and Decentralized Finance (DeFi) for Financial Inclusion*. IGI Global.

Acknowledgment

The editors would like to acknowledge the help of all the people involved in this project and, more specifically, to the authors and reviewers that took part in the review process. Without their support, this book would not have become a reality. The editors wish also to acknowledge the valuable supports of UBD School of Business & Economics (UBDSBE).

Muhammad Anshari
Universiti Brunei Darussalam, Brunei

Mohammad Nabil Almunawar
Universiti Brunei Darussalam, Brunei

Masairol Masri
Universiti Brunei Darussalam, Brunei

Chapter 1
Understanding FinTech and Decentralized Finance (DeFi) for Financial Inclusion

Andrei Dragos Popescu
https://orcid.org/0000-0002-9048-3055
University of Craiova, Romania & SCX Holdings Pte. Ltd., Singapore

ABSTRACT

For a very long period of time, financial inclusion researchers have been addressing the barriers that prevent unprivileged people from accessing and using financial services. Financial exclusion is an underlying social problem that dates from the creation of the first financial system. Without the access to the banking and financial infrastructures, the unbanked are perpetuating a vicious cycle of poverty. Blockchain is leading this transformation of allowing unbanked and underbanked people to have access and interact with the finance industry. The promise of a digital economy is starting to take shape, as financial technology (FinTech) companies are evolving the concept of democratization of access. Decentralized finance (DeFi) is expanding the possibilities of financial technology by creating an ecosystem based on transparency, accessibility, and efficiency. We are witnessing a paradigm shift for most of the financial services which are remodeling the accessibility and usability of these services, addressing the excluded and underserved population.

INTRODUCTION

FinTech sits at the intersection of Finance and Technology and this concept relies directly to financial inclusion as it explores opportunities of using software and digital platforms to deliver financial services to consumers. It is an impactful concept as it harnesses mobile technology, big data analytics and blockchain to provide services to individuals in ways that are more convenient, accessible and intuitive.

We will be looking at FinTech as a convergence of technologies used to support novel banking concepts and to enable innovative financial services as they are dramatically changing the financial landscape.

DOI: 10.4018/978-1-7998-8447-7.ch001

The aim of this chapter is to understand the basics, along with the philosophy, of what Financial Technology (FinTech) is achieving in terms of innovation, automatization, digitization, blockchain and the power of Decentralized Finance (DeFi) that has spurred from this novel approach of technology driven services.

FinTech matters for financial inclusion because is the developing force for new tools and technologies to provide greater access to financial services, achieving efficiency across an area of products that need to be more affordable.

The use of technology in the recent period has become more pervasive, impacting all areas of the financial services supply chain: from payments and remittances to asset management. A wide range of non-financial actors are emerging and playing an ever-increasing role in offering innovative financial products.

We have identified three dimensions where technology can be impactful and transform the prospect of financial inclusion: the first one is overcoming the limited banking infrastructure of the financial sector; the second dimension is to take technology seriously as an enabler of accelerated growth which brings us to the third dimension where technology has the potential to be leveraged beyond the financial services themselves to a range of applications that can truly empower people.

With any great leap forward, great gaps are generated that are left behind.

Here we need to address, improve and scale a series of factors which play important roles: the regulatory frameworks which need to be open and enabling; identification infrastructures that need to be accessible and verifiable in real time; data communication infrastructures that need to be reliable, accessible and affordable; technology infrastructures that need to be interoperable and with seamless interfaces; merchant infrastructures that need to be pervasive; and a financial literacy & consumer protection infrastructure that needs to be inclusive.

An enabling regulatory environment can help facilitate interoperability, so people can join more services and engage with others across different networks, which help these services reach scale and provide more functionalities for consumers.

Phenomenal advancements in technology come with a social element of change that we need to understand and embrace, while we retrain and retool individuals. As we move forward, with great innovation and implementations comes great responsibility and we need to ensure that any social environmental change is sustainable and we address inclusivity as part of the agenda in this process. Therefore, what is needed is to reinvent this space for sustainability to reach the points of inclusiveness, taking advantage of the opportunities and possibilities for everyone to benefit from FinTech solutions.

We are envisioning a world where we have a fully connected economy that is driven by neutral, transparent and open financial services, with a clear focus on inclusiveness and where everyone speaks the same financial language. This is the promise of Decentralized Finance or DeFi, which refers to the shift from traditional centralized financial systems to peer-to-peer finance enabled by blockchain-based technology.

Universal financial access is not such a utopic idea because of the advancements in blockchain and DeFi implementations. The technology is available and will require some collaboration efforts between governments, regulators, legacy financial institutions, innovators and enablers. By fostering blockchain technology with extended capabilities to access DeFi, everyone is well positioned to improve their overall financial involvement.

So why are people outside of the system? In the context of financial exclusion, we need to refer to accessible, affordable and relevant financial solutions for all individuals, regardless of their nationality, gender, race or religion.

When we think about the unbanked, or the underbanked, the main problem that we need to assess is what record do they have? What data do we have and what type of data can they generate? We need to have good consumer credit histories to be able to score individuals so that they can have access to credit lines. When you do not have the established credit data infrastructure, then you have to look at the mix of data sources that you have so that you can provide an alternative way to score.

The good news is that virtually everybody now leaves a digital footprint somewhere, so for the first time we move from a place where there was a scarcity of data into a surplus of data. Financial technology firms can use that data to begin building a trust equation.

We can collect and analyze data using different forms of financial technology, like alternative credit scoring and algorithms that leverage social networks to find areas and opportunities for private sector entities to assist the underserved customers.

FinTech can have a number of potential benefits: it can increase speed, enhance customer choice and ensure accessibility. In this way, consumers will get more choices and better-target services with keener prices, SMEs will be able to access new credit and financial services which will result in a more inclusive ecosystem with people better connected and more informed about finance and access to financial services.

These innovations are a real opportunity for the world as it leads financial inclusion, making it affordable and reachable for those disadvantaged in society.

Research Methodology

In order to properly assess financial inclusion and to identify novel and innovative solutions, we should start from the premise of understanding financial exclusion. The concept of financial exclusion relates to the social status of an individual which is proliferating a well know cycle that involves: inadequate financial education, lack of awareness about financial services, lack of credit history, lack of valid identification instruments, and the financial dependency on family & friends. A result of this vicious cycle is the exclusion from any type of activity by the gatekeepers of the traditional financial system.

Although FinTechs are exploring solutions in eliminating some of the gatekeepers and intermediaries in the process chains, they are still acting as centralized access points. We are tackling this problem from the perspective of Decentralized Finance (DeFi), where we are envisioning an ecosystem of decentralized applications (dApps) & protocols that leverage the same philosophy.

We are using a qualitative approach to analyze and vet the proper solutions and infrastructures, in order to find the best scenarios of inclusiveness from a decentralized finance stand-point. This research will analyses the novel characteristics of FinTech and DeFi, intending to offer an overview of the ways in which it impacts financial inclusion.

This chapter aims to contribute to the larger goal of providing viable solutions for financial inclusiveness, identifying disruptive innovations and applications by means of technology convergence.

THE DEMOCRATIZATION OF ACCESS

In order to access the economic system, we need to lower the bridge that provides additional opportunities for upwards mobility and improved economic outcomes for people.

The goals for building this bridge should focus on the ability to accumulate long-term wealth & savings, having safe & affordable means to make everyday payments, having access to credit and insurance for a proper hedge against key risks.

Financial inclusion has many facets, but the most important facet comes down to being counted and included.

One of the most accepted definition of FinTech is the innovative use of technology in the design, development and delivery of financial products and services (Popescu AD., 2020b). When we look at some of the innovations that are happening in the FinTech space, we can certainly identify some really effective tools to achieve some of the needed results.

The main target of the FinTech approach is to scale up the ecosystem from a cash economy towards a digital one, for better accountability and efficiency. It is a simple approach with the possibility of a big impact.

Digital transformation is imperative for the financial services industry to remain competitive and achieve longevity in the market (Hazik M., Hassnian A., 2019).

The innovative frontier that FinTechs opened, is still embedded within the traditional financial infrastructure (Lynn T. et al., 2019). The drive to improve accessibility and delivery of financial services has lowered the friction points for transaction costs, lending requirements and investment gateways. As technology democratized lending and payment channels, it is no wonder that acquisition costs per client is becoming more affordable via digital channels.

In the same manner the internet helped democratize the access to information around the world, Blockchain and Distributed Ledger Technology (DLT) can help democratize the access to financial services. It is important to acknowledge the role of this technology as it will facilitate and optimize the entry gateway for the excluded population.

The use of blockchain-based technologies can reduce the burden of compliance for FinTechs and other traditional financial institutions, who are struggling to keep up with the increasing cost of client acquisition. Blockchain along with Distributed Ledger Technology, helps emerging markets leapfrog from an outdated and costly environment towards a more efficient and balanced one (Treiblmaier H., Clohessy T., 2020).

The usage of blockchain-based technology is a seamless way to access, manage and move capital. Most of the successful FinTech companies in the world, realized the potential of this technology and are streamlining services developed on top of this novel infrastructure.

As we accelerate the FinTech adoption, we are including more people in the ecosystem and that leads to a greater economic participation. Facilitating this financial access lays the foundation to economic prosperity for a lot of the participants. Digital inclusion and acceleration of adoption are the key success factors.

Digital financial inclusion can be a catalyst for equitable development and economic growth. What is required, is to identify the delicate balance of technology convergence to achieve the best outcomes.

Financial Identity

For a better understanding of the financial exclusion, we need to address an important factor which brings everything to the basics: Financial Identity.

FinTech is revamping the way we define identity as our digital footprint is being constructed by the social interactions we are developing via our internet connected/mobile devices. This new form of digital identity is becoming a foundation layer in a digital environment that will be useful towards a financial identity.

This is where blockchain can be most relevant for the underserved, making them and their transactions visible and allowing the opportunity to access this data when they need to.

This new approach will improve financial health and builds momentum for a fully digital financial history, much needed from a credit scoring perspective. Providing a novel credit scoring architecture based on a digital footprint is vital in shrinking the information gap for more efficient financial inclusion processes.

In today's socioeconomic environment, one of the biggest market inefficiencies is the insufficient access to an open and fair credit infrastructure (Popescu AD., 2019). A result of this problem is an unproductive system that does not generate any financial history records for almost 68% of adults worldwide (World Bank, 2018). This information gap intensifies financial inequalities and spins other socioeconomic issues in a vicious cycle. A resolution for the lack of credit infrastructure can have both, a financial and a social impact, as the implementations rely on the participation, adoption and competitiveness of FinTech companies.

This trap, that was thoroughly researched, is referred to as the Credit Conundrum. The lack of credit history is a result of the fact that to have one, you need to have access to credit in the first place, and for access to credit you are required to provide credit and transactions history.

Figure 1. The Credit Conundrum

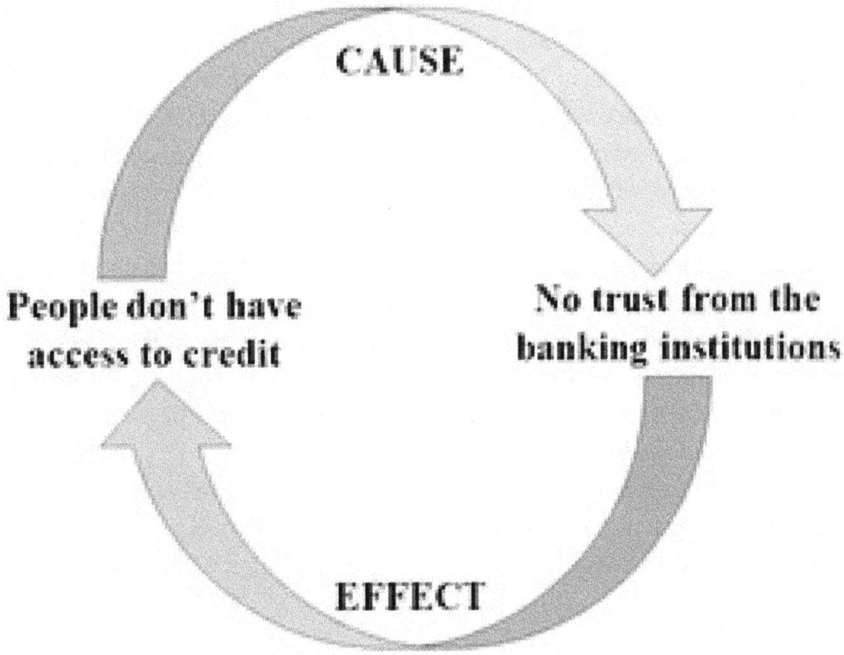

The only solution to break this cycle is for the consumers to find the proper financial institutions which are willing to lend them, without asking for formal credit history. This type of solutions are being developed by innovative FinTech companies which aggregate data into digital financial identities, that can provide all the information required to offer consumers the chance for their first loan. In this manner the vicious cycle of the credit conundrum can be broken.

The credit conundrum has a direct correlation to what blockchain-based technologies are bringing in this equation, which is trust. The concept of this conundrum is important to understand, not because people without credit history are not creditworthy, but because they cannot demonstrate their creditworthiness.

Financial Identity as a Service (FiDaaS) is basically an infrastructure that can enable the creation, utilization and distribution of digital financial identities.

The concept of Financial Identity as a Service is getting a lot of traction as these alternative credit identities open a new world of financial opportunities for underbanked consumers. Over 80% of adults worldwide use mobile phones for different transactions, generating data that FiDaaS can process to predict and utilize in credit decisions. When consumers lack sufficient credit history, financial institutions typically have no choice but to turn them away. The concept of FiDaaS arms financial institutions with the insights they need to increase the addressable market for financial services, attracting new customers, while managing lending risk (Juvo, 2021).

The incentive to implement a system like this is significant as the processing and managing of data for financial decisions is a critical component within any value chain. Having easy and undisputable access to one's financial footprint is critical to unlocking access to microcredit and other financial products (Lauer J., 2017). Having ownership of the data, along with the ability of being able to pull the data when its needed and knowing that these records cannot be disputed, is one of the biggest promise of blockchain and distributed ledger technology.

DECENTRALIZED FINANCE AND INCLUSIVENESS

Despite a century of innovations, the financial system is far from being perfect. Settlement of stocks, bonds and other financial instruments takes days to clear and requires a massive amount of human capital involved in the process. Massive inefficiencies that come at a very high cost, when it comes to international banking and remittance services, along with privileged/inequal access to financial services, have as result, billions of unbanked people across the globe. The whole financial infrastructure consists of siloed systems built with proprietary technologies and algorithms that each company has to develop from scratch.

The beautiful user interfaces provided by FinTech companies only cover the fact that the financial system is built on old and inefficient foundations. Something that seems to be instant for the user can take days to fully process behind the scene. On top of that, the backbone of the financial system has not evolved much since the mainframe computers were introduced (Wewege L., Thomsett M. C., 2019). This is exactly why we need something new, something better that can address some of these problems and this is where Decentralized Finance (DeFi) comes into play.

FinTech companies understood very fast the value proposition of decentralization and are making agile steps in implementing decentralized solutions in their workflows. This translation and conversion of services within a decentralized environment is a progression approach towards efficiency and optimization. A new model for an alternative financial system is being built by means of novel technologies with hope of a drastic reduction in inequality and unfair distribution of resources.

Decentralization matters as DeFi allows us to use some of the inherent attributes of blockchain technology to completely reinvent finance, so we can conduct financial transactions without any centralized intermediaries (Popescu AD., 2020c). Unlike centralized entities that have an office and employees, DeFi platforms operate using blockchain smart contracts, which are basically contracts that are written in code. If the conditions quoted in the contract are met, then the payout or consequences are automatically executed. Basically, the contract is fulfilled without any human intervention. Such smart contracts are fully transparent and available to anyone to inspect.

Instead of relying on old and inefficient infrastructure, DeFi leverages the power of cryptography, decentralization and blockchain to build a new financial system:

- A system that can provide access to well-known financial services, such as payments, lending, borrowing and trading in a more efficient, fair and open way;
- Efficient as all operations are settled almost immediately. It does not matter that counterparties may be in completely different geographic locations with different laws and regulations;
- Most of the DeFi protocols can operate with no or minimal human involvement;
- Fair, as all services are completely transparent and censorship resistant;
- Permisionless, as everyone with a browser, smartphone and an internet connection can access them. There is no document verification, no need to provide income statements, regardless of nationality or race, as everyone is treated in the exact same way;
- Censorship resistant, as no other party can deny access to the services. Even multiple bad actors cannot change the rules of an adequately decentralized system;
- Open, as everyone can build a new DeFi application, participate and contribute to the ecosystem.

Decentralized Finance comes with an alternative approach of interpretation for the financial systems. The way of how DeFi is operating, is impacting the whole structure of the financial system at a macroeconomic level. The core concept of DeFi is of an open financial system that operates flawlessly without intermediaries (Metwaly A. H. W., Metwaly A. W., 2021). The power incentive of such an ecosystem is designed by smart contracts that can translate all operations of the traditional finance world. Envision the banking infrastructure along with services like insurance, borrowing, lending and crediting that is mirrored in an open, transparent, trustworthy and censorship resistant digital environment.

The cornerstones of any efficient financial system are the processes of borrowing and lending. DeFi protocols enabled these processes on a large scale between the participants of the ecosystem without any intermediaries, by developing an automatic price discovery system for the interest rates by means of supply and demand.

The beauty of this solution is that these protocols are focusing on inclusiveness, as there are no restrictions whatsoever. Anybody can interact and access these decentralized applications (dApps), with any amount, at any time and from anywhere.

The main divergence with regards to the traditional finance is that loans in DeFi are commonly secured by over-collateralization. Projects like Compound (2021) are driving the hype for this type of processes, but new projects like AAVE (2021) are developing and enabling uncollateralized loans as a new concept.

Compound is an algorithmic, autonomous interest rate protocol built for developers, to unlock a universe of open financial applications.

AAVE is a decentralized non-custodial liquidity market protocol where users can participate as depositors or borrowers. Depositors provide liquidity to the market to earn a passive income, while borrowers are able to borrow in an over-collateralized (perpetually) or under-collateralized (one-block liquidity) fashion (AAVE, 2021).

Synthetix is the backbone for derivatives trading in DeFi, allowing anyone, anywhere to gain on-chain exposure to a vast range of assets (Synthetix, 2021). Many platforms, projects, and interfaces are already using the derivatives liquidity enabled by Synthetix.

Yearn Finance is a project that developed a suite of products, for and within Decentralized Finance (DeFi), that provides lending aggregation, yield generation, and insurance on the Ethereum blockchain. The protocol is maintained by various independent developers and is governed by YFI token holders (Yearn Finance, 2021). yBorrow is a new concept under development which is focusing on an internal tool enabling credit delegation for smart contract to smart contract lending.

Nexus Mutual uses the power of blockchain technology so people can share risk together, eliminating the need for an insurance company (Nexus Mutual, 2021). An innovative concept of sharing that translates a collective experience regarding alternative risk by means of smart contracts. A powerful concept which is getting a lot of traction and is bridging different protocols across the ecosystem that can benefit from the participation.

Uniswap is a decentralized trading protocol that is guaranteeing liquidity for the users and other dApps within the DeFi sphere (Uniswap, 2021). The Uniswap protocol empowers developers, liquidity providers and traders to participate in a financial marketplace that is open and accessible to all.

The protocol can be used for trading and is designed to eliminate trusted intermediaries and unnecessary forms of rent extraction. This process allows fast and efficient swapping of tokens.

In contrast to traditional finance, new applications can leverage the existing protocols and build on top of the existing solutions. All of the above can be achieved in a transparent environment via the blockchain infrastructure. This propriety is called composability and is a feature of design wherein the various components of a system can be easily connected to form any number of satisfying results or even other concepts (Popescu AD., 2020a). Because of this feature, DeFi was easily described as "The Lego of Finance".

Trading volume, number of outstanding loans, total debt and other metrics can be reliably checked on the blockchain by means of smart contracts. Even better, these numbers cannot be tampered with.

With the settlement of different assets measured in seconds, instead of days, the counterparty risk is dramatically reduced.

As every record is publicly available on the blockchain, accounting verticals are super easy and can be completely automated. This can dramatically reduce the human capital needed for an equal access to novel financial services.

A DeFi protocol does not care who you are, it just follows predefined rules that are exactly the same for every participant.

All of these services have been accomplished with impressive speed and the concept of DeFi is expanding exponentially, as FinTech companies are taking advantage of the use cases and aggregation of services they can promote.

What we are witnessing is the rapid evolution of a new global open financial system that everyone can have access to, and from which none is excluded.

Maturity Stages of DeFi

Stage 1 – Facilitation of Payments and Exchanges

The evolution of the crypto assets ecosystem (Arslanian H., Fischer F., 2019) started with the implementations of the centralized exchanges and wallet providers. The business models scaled up quickly as these concepts represented the main entry point to the financial digital assets space.

Because of these concepts and the applications developed around them, the efficient value transfers between parties could be performed, without any other intermediaries or traditional finance players. This represented the first stage of the evolution as it enabled the financial digital assets to fulfill some basic functions of a financial environment, namely the exchange of assets and facilitations of payments.

Stage 2 – Facilitation of Digital Assets Flow

The missing link for the next step, was to facilitate the flows of funds for savers and borrowers. All these elements started to be built with a speed rarely seen and the structure of an advanced financial system started to take shape. These functions evolved with the introduction of stablecoins, the appearance of Decentralized Exchanges (DEX) and the borrowing & lending protocols.

All these dApps were the necessary platforms to facilitate the managing and moving of capital flows between savers and borrowers.

Stage 3 – Acknowledgement

The third stage of the maturity process was established when the competition with traditional financial institutions started and the rules of the decentralized environment were acknowledged.

Traditional finance laws and regulations do not apply in this new digital environment and cannot be enforced. This is seen as a major advantage in comparison with the highly regulated traditional finance space, as it allows DeFi participants to act, respond and adapt more agilely for optimization and efficiency purposes.

We are addressing here the adoption speed, as DeFi established itself as a highly scalable and a fast execution global ecosystem.

As stated above, DeFi is permisionless, which is one of the most important attribute in order to provide viable options for the users that cannot access banking or other financial services. The ecosystem grew exponentially and adapted to the required use cases in order to provide the best inclusive services for everyone.

From Tokenization to Monetization

Blockchain and Distributed Ledger Technology represents the enabler for universal participation into this novel secure, transparent and emerging financial system (Arslanian H., Fischer F., 2019).

As DeFi grows exponentially, the concepts that are operating within this space are becoming influential disruptors in the financial space. Bridges from traditional finance to DeFi are being built to create real-world solutions for real-world challenges, especially in the areas of payments, remittances, lending, insurance and investments.

The process of tokenization, opened the ability to link the real-word with the digital one. This new term describes a link between tokens, which are developed on top of DLT/blockchain-based technology, and real-world assets. A direct result of this asset-backed tokens is an improved market liquidity. These procedures have a great impact for the acceptance of assets with low liquidity, such as real-estate and art.

The innovation of the tokenization process comes from the fact that it enables the splitting of assets into parts and allows investors to control and manage only a fraction of the asset. This is important as it grants low-income earners the opportunity to participate in the investment sphere for goods or services that were out of reach, due to the high acquisition costs involved.

From the financial inclusion perspective, the tokenization process is adding a number of notable advantages.

One important property worth mentioning is the ability to reach a global investors market for the issuers. The costing factor with regards to every aspect of the investment and trading procedures, makes all of these micro investments feasible (Tan L.J., 2020). This is how the barriers to investments, that allow the participation towards savings, are lowered.

A perfect example for the tokenization model that addresses financial inclusion is "The Cow Token". Lay R. (2018) is describing in his whitepaper how a blockchain based architecture represents a solution to tokenize livestock. The poor are much richer than they think, as all they need is a solution to unlock their economic potential. Sentinel Chain is deploying a B2B marketplace for financial services accepting the use of livestock as collateral, through the process of tokenization. The Sentinel Chain addresses two main issues to be solved in order to allow the asset tokenization of livestock. First, the creation of a process that transforms livestock from "dead capital" to a fungible asset with a transparent and clear defined value. Second, the creation of an open and transparent marketplace that connects the unbanked to the network of global financial providers.

Decentralized applications and protocols are uniting themselves in a suite of tools for a tokenized world.

The advent of tokenization offers a multitude of ways to boost financial inclusion and make sustainable wealth creation accessible and feasible.

The innovation that we are seeing today in FinTech, along with all subsets of blockchain technology and digital assets has created a reality that allows financial inclusion in ways that could never have been imagined before.

CONCLUSION

An important transition is taking place, as most of the global connected citizens are getting accommodated with the user-friendly interfaces of the platforms, applications and other emerging technologies, which are promoted by FinTech companies. This transition is happening, even though the traditional financial infrastructure is expanding and improving.

Blockchain has been one of the most impactful technologies in the FinTech space. Most notably, it has catalyzed the democratization of finance. Customers are empowered to manage and hold their own money without a bank or any other financial intermediary. People that were previously excluded from our financial systems can not only participate in the financial system, but they can also own their finances and start a new financial journey in a way they were never able to do. This shift goes against all the traditional notions of finance and completely disrupts the role a bank plays in personal finance.

A traditional bank can pick and choose its clients, it can decide to work only with the ones that will be the most profitable or exclude clients from certain regions. DeFi platforms are open to anyone with a basic internet connection and access to digital assets. This is seen by proponents of DeFi as another example of how blockchain technology can help in promoting financial inclusion and providing access to financial services to anyone, regardless of their wealth, status, location, gender, race or religion.

FinTech companies, along with DeFi, are experiencing a dynamic growth and represent a natural progression in the evolution of how people interact with money. This natural evolution may even change the fundamental way we interact with financial products, as the amount of innovative dApps and emerging technologies, which are being implemented, are truly disruptive.

We believe that these new modern financial services are just an extension, and even a reiteration, of the traditional finance products, but this is also a stepping stone towards the development of a new inclusive financial world.

The platforms developed by Financial Technology companies represent the new era of innovation in finance and created a real competitive environment for services like investing, banking and payment networks.

Our approach for this chapter, comes from the perspective of adoption for cutting-edge financial products that remove intermediaries, put consumers in control of their finances, promote incentive models to reward participation and empower communities. This notion of DeFi has been very well assimilated by FinTech companies and creates the perfect environment for financial inclusion as it addresses most of the hurdles that have been thoroughly researched.

Like with all other big technological improvements, they often happen gradually, then suddenly we will probably see some of the incumbents, trying to tap into the possibilities and opportunities of DeFi.

Although DeFi presents us with a unique value proposition, it comes with its own challenges.

We are still in early days of adoption & development of such an ecosystem and the risks involved are directly proportional with the vision and mission.

Despite its novel vision, the DeFi sphere is still complicated and, for the time being, quite hard to use. The interaction process of protocols is not very intuitive and some of them require some specialized skillsets. These issues are predominant for the reason that most of the dApps, protocols and platforms were not developed based on what the users want/need, but rather on what is available to the developers (C. Russo, 2020). Other risks and challenges are related to fraud, volatility, usability and regulatory uncertainty.

It is also very important not to get into the extreme side of technology dependency. Solutions should not depend on sophisticated and expensive devices as the penetration and adoption scenarios will suffer.

Despite the challenges, DeFi is a 0 to 1 innovation.

Sorting out some of these challenges is just a matter of time.

All of the above is laying out the foundation for a new architecture of a financial environment on which financial inclusion can thrive. The attributes of Decentralized Finance define the perfect environment for financial inclusion and foster all the right principles for it to grow.

Eventually, through innovation and the adoption of disruptive technologies, we can surely envision a future where financial inclusion is the expectation, rather than the exception. As we continue to witness a new generation of entrepreneurs building real-world solutions that are designed to enable a brighter future, we can expect to see the development of even more sophisticated financial solutions built for a more inclusive digital asset driven economy.

DeFi is currently the best option available for providing the unbanked with access to financial services, and in doing so, helping to lift millions of people out of poverty. Making the technology easily accessible is the first step toward achieving these goals.

REFERENCES

AAVE. (2021). *The Liquidity Protocol.* Available at https://aave.com/

Arslanian, H., & Fischer, F. (2019). The Future of Finance: The Impact of FinTech, AI, and Crypto on Financial Services. Springer International Publishing. doi:10.1007/978-3-030-14533-0

Compound Finance. (2021). Available at https://compound.finance

Hazik, M., & Hassnian, A. (2019). Blockchain, Fintech, and Islamic Finance. In Building the Future in the New Islamic Digital Economy. Publisher de Gruyter.

Juvo. (2021). *Building Financial Identities for 4 Billion People Globally.* Available at https://www.juvo.com/

Lauer, J. (2017). Creditworthy: A History of Consumer Surveillance and Financial Identity in America. Columbia Studies in the History of U.S. Capitalism.

Lay, R. (2018). *Sentinel Chain - The World's First Global Marketplace for Financial Inclusion Services.* Available at https://infocorp.io/Cow-Token-A-Local-Blockchain-UseCase.pdf

Lynn, T., Mooney, J. G., Rosati, P., & Cummins, M. (2019). Disrupting Finance: FinTech and Strategy in the 21st Century. Palgrave Studies in Digital Business & Enabling Technologies, 121-130. doi:10.1007/978-3-030-02330-0_8

Metwaly, A. H. W., & Metwaly, A. W. (2021). *Stake Hodler Capitalism: Blockchain and DeFi.* Decentralized Finance.

Nexus Mutual. (2021). *Get covered against smart contract failure & exchange hacks.* Available at https://nexusmutual.io/

Popescu, A. D. (2019). Empowering Financial Inclusion through FinTech. *Social Sciences and Education Research Review*, *6*(2), 198–215.

Popescu, A. D. (2020a). Decentralized Finance – The Lego of Finance. *Social Sciences and Education Research Review*, *7*(1), 321–348.

Popescu, A. D. (2020b). *Financial Technology (FinTech) as a Driver for Financial Digital Assets.* Ovidius University Annals, Economic Sciences Series.

Popescu AD. (2020c). Transitions and concepts within Decentralized Finance (Defi) Space. *Research Terminals In The Social Sciences.*

Russo, C. (2020). *The Defiant: Money Legos Aren't Fitting Right (But They Could).* Available at https://thedefiant.substack.com/p/money-legos-arent-fitting-right-but-ac9

Synthetix. (2021). *The Derivatives Liquidity Protocol*. Available at https://synthetix.io/

Tan, L. J. (2020). Economics and Math of Token Engineering and DeFi: Fundamentals of Token Economics. Economics Design.

Teigland, R., Siri, S., Larsson, A., Puertas, A.M., & Bogusz, C.I. (2018). The Rise And Development Of FinTech: Accounts Of Disruption From Sweden And Beyond. *Routledge International Studies In Money And Banking*, 88 – 90.

Treiblmaier, H., & Clohessy, T. (2020). *Blockchain and Distributed Ledger Technology Use Cases: Applications and Lessons Learned*. Springer International Publishing. doi:10.1007/978-3-030-44337-5

Uniswap. (2021). *Uniswap Protocol - Swap, earn, and build on the leading decentralized crypto trading protocol*. Available at https://uniswap.org/

Wewege, L., & Thomsett, M. C. (2019). *The Digital Banking Revolution: How Fintech Companies Are Transforming the Retail Banking Industry Through Disruptive Financial Innovation*. De Gruyter. doi:10.1515/9781547401598

World Bank Group. (2018). *The Global Findex Database – Measuring Financial Inclusion and the FinTech Revolution*. Available at https://globalfindex.worldbank.org/

Yearn Finance. (2021). Available at https://yearn.finance

Chapter 2
Financial Technology as a Future Game-Changer

Nelson Lajuni
Universiti Malaysia Sabah, Malaysia

Avnner Chardles Wellfren
Universiti Malaysia Sabah, Malaysia

Noraini Binti Abdullah
Universiti Malaysia Sabah, Malaysia

Salumah Binti Nain
Universiti Malaysia Sabah, Malaysia

ABSTRACT

Financial technology has emerged as a game-changer to complement and enhance how the Millennial and Generation Z conduct transactions. Responding to calls of prior research, this study used the unified theory of acceptance and use of technology (UTAUT) to understand how performance expectancy and effort expectancy factors influence consumers' intention to use financial technology. Performance expectancy (PE) and effort expectancy (EE) were investigated as exogenous variables towards the intention to use financial technology (FinTech) that act as endogenous variables in this study. The authors collected 284 Millennial and Generation Z respondents and analysed the data using PLS-SEM. The result from the study's structural model suggested that FinTech continuance use intention was dependent on performance expectancy and effort expectancy on engaging with young vibrant consumers and establishing attractive FinTech elements. In addition, Millennial and Generation Z consumers with a high-performance expectancy were found to emphasize FinTech components in the engagement process.

INTRODUCTION

FinTech (Financial Technology) refers to the use of technology to deliver financial services that offer solutions to customers' problems. The revolution in financial services touted by FinTech drew most of

DOI: 10.4018/978-1-7998-8447-7.ch002

the stakeholders e.g., banks, policymakers, and customers. Every stakeholder has a huge impact on the sector, which shows several possibilities to satisfy customer needs and expectations (Hochstein, 2015). Banks are one of the key drivers of the country's economy since they provide extensive financial records and background information on customers. The rapid use of technology in financial services had helped in fostering the growth of FinTech, as e-banking services (Kaushal & Ghosh, 2016).

FinTech is a relatively recent digital change in the financial services business. Fintech was at the forefront of this disruption, introducing new ideas in financial services and raising worldwide awareness of the business. Furthermore, it prompted customers to seek out services that were easy to use, real-time, and available 24 hours a day, seven days a week (Arner et al, 2016). Researchers and financial specialists are interested in this sort of study because obvious financial indicators demonstrate that non-banking financial institutions have a detrimental influence on conventional banks' income. Recent investigations have uncovered an unexpected fact: FinTech providers account for 24 percent of banks' income. Moreover, banks invested significant resources into determining the causes of this income loss and clients' withdrawal from conventional banking services (Strandvik et al., 2018).

FinTech is not just about digitizing financial services; it encompasses a variety of business and industry concepts. As numerous researchers have noted, in addition to other FinTech innovations, big data enables new and diversified ways of conducting business by emphasizing the quality of decision-making processes, timeliness, and, of course, cost. Additionally, when neural technology is combined with big data analytics, businesses can intercept bureaucracy along the line of business processes, simplifying complex decision-making (Nicoletti, 2017). Other advances, such as robo-advisory in investing and financial planning, as well as the emergence of new digital asset values: cryptocurrency, undoubtedly expand the worldwide meaning of FinTech. Robo-advisory has been promoted as a replacement for human advisors in financial services, particularly during the current Covid-19 pandemic, which has compelled the entire industry toward digital implementation (Uhl & Rohner, 2018). On the other hand, cryptocurrency is a fundamentally digital asset that possesses many of the same characteristics as traditional investment assets but is valued differently (Liu & Tsyvinski, 2021). The buzz surrounding cryptocurrency's quick rise in value in recent years has become a new big headline for numerous magazines and articles, including Bloomberg, Forbes, Reuters, and Yahoo Finance. As we can see, though FinTech's impact is still relatively new, its emergence has certainly caught off traditional financial players such as banks, mutual funds, and governments, who believe FinTech is much too early.

The critical question, however, is why now? By addressing this question, we can gain a better understanding of the global perspective on FinTech and its future projections. According to (Schindler, 2017)'s research paper, the scholar argues that the concept of supply and demand has fueled financial innovation and necessitated the development of FinTech. On the supply side, technology has undoubtedly been the primary driver, as evidenced by the famous automated teller machine (ATM) as its pioneer innovation. However, the 2008 financial crisis in major countries also served as a wake-up call, by weakening regulation and security of established financial institutions and economies. On the demand side, a diverse range of financial products and services compete for the attention of a population that is changing demographically, with a young generation that is eager and hungry for informative technology as a part of their daily lives. The World Bank and IMF expressed similar sentiments in a recent report, describing FinTech as an opportunity to address the fragility of the traditional financial system (World Bank, 2019). Around the world, regions such as Africa Sub-Saharan, Asia, Europe, the Middle East, and Latin America have embraced the World Bank's call for accelerated adoption of FinTech, while also working to create an enabling environment globally. Bloomberg reports that the involvement of global financial behemoths such as JP Morgan Chase & Co., Ant Group Co., and Walmart Inc demonstrates a high level of interest in the global market (Jennifer, 2021)

However, FinTech is not all rainbows and sunshine, as booing from the other part of financial demonstrates that the concepts are far from perfect for global implementation. Currently, FinTech has taken the financial system by surprise, and while adoption has accelerated, a sizable portion of the financial system remains unprepared. For instance, it has been demonstrated that consumer concerns and risks regarding cybersecurity have an effect on consumer intent and usage (Cojoianu et al., 2020; Stewart & Jürjens, 2018). Due to the fact that FinTech relies on information technology to connect transaction and processing data, it also acts as a gateway for malicious intruders who may hack all the way to a consumer's or financial institution's privacy data. On the other hand, cryptocurrency is viewed as a high-risk investment due to its volatility, lack of regulation, and vulnerability to inflationary pressures (Sydney & Vildana, 2021). The convergence of cryptocurrency and information technology has resulted in the rise of the dark marketplace, a virtual hub for illegal activity such as money laundering, drug trafficking, and a variety of other outlawed activities (Foley et al., 2019). Similarly, individuals lack legal protection if a FinTech platform, such as robo-advisory, provides incorrect input and advice to clients (Lightbourne, 2017). These are just a few of the impediments to the industry's efforts to fertilize FinTech growth.

To mitigate the problem, the government and financial institutions are addressing it. Latest developments in the use of "sandboxes," a controlled environment used to evaluate a policy or solution to a particular issue, have yielded encouraging results (World Bank, 2019). Across regions, several sandboxes pursue distinct aims, including legislation, crypto asset development, and payment and settlement. The World Bank concluded that FinTech is appropriately aligned and is making inroads internationally as planned, despite hurdles in balancing competing policy agendas, foundation infrastructure restrictions, limited financial and monetary stability, and, ultimately, cyber security (World Bank, 2019). In other words, the message from global nations is that FinTech is manageable and under control. Hence, this interpretation is absolutely good news for established financial institutions that are concerned about being supplanted by FinTech firms (Cole et al., 2019). Plus, current major financial businesses have amassed a wealth of resources, enabling them to capitalize on FinTech opportunities simply by merging, investing directly, or even purchasing the entire FinTech-based company (Dranev et al., 2019). For the consumer, as new generations enter the job market, FinTech presents an excellent opportunity for researchers to expand domain knowledge while also improving FinTech in ways that benefit consumers' daily financial activities.

Millennials and Gen Z are early adopters of FinTech services, and this emphasizes the significance of moving quickly into FinTech; because of this, FinTech services are critical for banks, since Millennials and Gen Z are the key drivers for this process (Meola, 2017). UTAUT (Unified Theory of Acceptance and Use of Technology) demonstrated that Millennials and Gen Z are the most receptive to technology, and this means that financial services of firms, banks, and FinTech providers must take advantage of this knowledge to drive new FinTech services like e-banking and mobile banking into the digital channels that Millennials and Gen Z are using (Brodmann et al, 2018; Berraies et al., 2017). Thus, this study aims to investigate the performance expectancy and effort expectancy influence on the intention to use FinTech. It is critical and vital to understand the reasons that inspire consumers to accept new emerging high-risk technology, since this technology, though dangerous, is expected to provide significant value to consumers (Chang et al., 2016). Numerous previous researches have examined various determinants that contribute to customers' adoption of FinTech services (Chen et al., 2015; Kim et al., 2016; Ryu, 2018; Stewart & Jürjens, 2018; Pinochet et al., 2019).

FINTECH DEVELOPMENT IN MALAYSIA

FinTech's potential to act as an economic and social catalyst through technological advancements has undoubtedly piqued many people's interest. By facilitating consumer access to a variety of financial services, it has enabled consumers to do so as easily as using a smartphone. FinTech has been at the forefront of the region's transformation, spreading awareness to every corner of the globe. Malaysia, without a doubt, is not an exception. Malaysia's population will reach 32.7 million by 2020, with approximately 15.9 million people in the labor force, bringing Malaysia's contribution to GDP from the digital economy to approximately 20 per cent, up from 19.1 per cent in 2019 (FinTech News Malaysia, 2021) Previously, optimism for FinTech development and adoption in Malaysia was fueled by the improvement in the digital sector. Let us not forget, however, that global movement restrictions and closed international borders in 2020 as a result of a health crisis will undoubtedly have an impact on Malaysia's economy and social life. Malaysia's GDP, in fact, is expected to contract by 5.6 per cent in 2020. Tracking government, financial institution, and international collaboration progress makes it much easier to monitor and address FinTech issues in order to further mobilize the FinTech industry's evolution.

According to a report, internet banking will grow by approximately 100 percent in 2020, reaching its highest level in a decade. Long-term government plans such as MyDIGITAL, a national initiative to transform Malaysia from a manufacturing-based economy to a digitally-driven and digital economy leader among peers, have accelerated the transition from universal 4G coverage to significantly faster and more affordable 5G connectivity for the entire population (Economic Planning Unit, 2021; FinTech News Malaysia, 2021). This ambition is backed up by targets such as credit card ownership of 30 per cent, debit card ownership of 143 per cent, online banking penetration of 112.5 per cent, and a banked population of 95 per cent by 2020. Again, as a result of the pandemic, consumers, the majority of whom are millennial, have accelerated the adoption of mobile banking for everyday use. Additionally, the government's distribution of rebates or stimuli to the vulnerable population during pandemics contributes to the current positive momentum. FinTech adoption has benefited from the increasing popularity of social media platforms, which will account for approximately 86 per cent of the total population in January 2021. Malaysia has made such strides that it is now ranked higher than 139 other countries and first among Asian countries by the World Economic Forum (FinTech News Malaysia, 2021).

According to the above figure, the top three category FinTech companies by market share are payment, e-wallet, and lending companies, accounting for 20 percent, 15 percent, and 14 percent of the market, respectively. The primary theme shared by the top three categories has always been online payment, which is why it is worth highlighting in this study. Internet banking is the most widely used digital payment method, according to rigorous analysis. Indeed, e-money accounted for 29 percent of total payment transactions, while internet banking accounted for 88 percent of total transaction value. A sizable portion of those transactions are conducted via mobile banking. In 2020, total mobile transaction value will reach RM 460 billion, up from RM 200 billion in the previous year. Since 2019, the increasing number of digital businesses applying for licenses has also increased the industry's capacity to reach such peak numbers.

Malaysia is obviously anticipating issues and challenges that will arise as a result of the rapid adoption of FinTech waves. As a result, Bank Negara Malaysia (BNM) has developed several major assessment themes to ascertain applicant requirements. BNM is evaluating risk management and compliance capabilities, transformative technology, robust customer analytics, financial strength, and Shariah expertise (FinTech News Malaysia, 2021). Malaysia has made significant strides in laying the regulatory groundwork for future digital finance. Bursa Malaysia Berhad, Malaysia's stock exchange, has established Bursa RegSub and Securities Commission Malaysia in 2020 to facilitate consumer distribution of investment assets, financial products, and services. This quickly resulted in the establishment of additional FinTech features such as e-KYC, digital assets, lending, and digital banking before the year's end.

Figure 1. Framework Model
Source: Malaysia FinTech Report (2021)

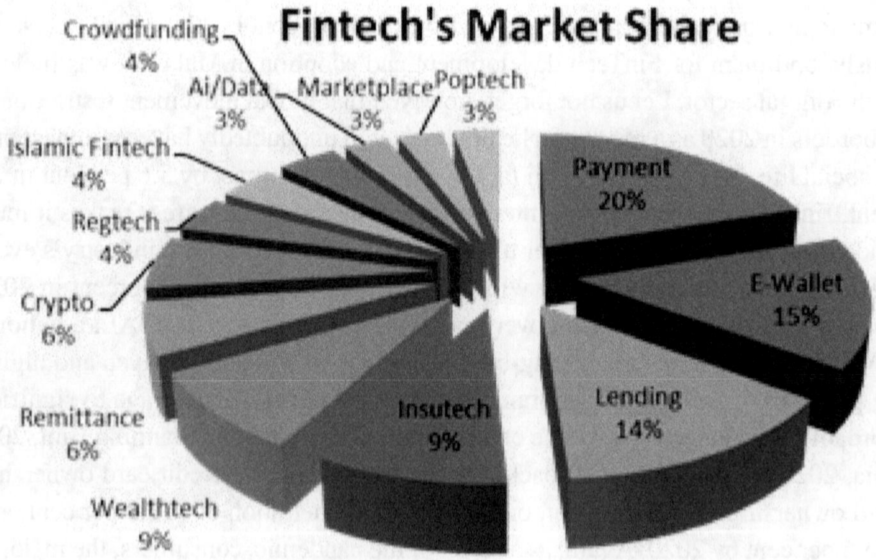

Government policy and response have been designed in accordance with the nation's infrastructure with consumer demand. This presents an opportunity for well-known companies such as GHL, Boost, Grabpay, and Paypal to enter the FinTech domain, having already aggressively tapped into Malaysia's new business industry. Not only business, but also academic research in Malaysia has increased in recent years, indicating the importance of FinTech as a source of knowledge. For example, Foroughi et al. (2019), Mohd Thas Thaker et al. (2019), and Rehman and Shaikh (2020) have all conducted studies on mobile banking intention and adoption. Other researchers have concentrated on the use of electronic wallets (Abdullah et al., 2020; Aji et al., 2020; Alam et al., 2021; Andrew et al., 2019). Not only has prior research contributed new knowledge and findings to the development of FinTech, but it has also inspired authors to conduct a more critical examination of the FinTech adoption in Malaysia.

Performance Expectancy

According to Venkatesh et al. (2003), performance expectancy (PE) is defined as an individual's belief that by utilizing the system, he or she will improve job performance. Venkatesh et al. (2003) further elaborate on the concept by stating that various strengths have varying effects on consumer behavioral intentions. For example, Loureiro et al. (2018) discovered that in the context of a retail website, the information and technology, as well as the consumer's prior experience, all positively influence an individual's satisfaction. As a result, this reaffirms their commitment to website usage and may even satisfy them to the point of recommending it to other consumers. Other researchers, such as Ryu and Fortenberry (2021), concentrate on omnichannel and performance expectations. Due to social and economic constraints caused by the pandemic, many retailers conduct business both online and offline. One critical point is that omni-channel enables consumers to gather information not only through websites but also through physical observation (e.g., showrooming), allowing consumers to confirm their initial assessment based on online information and then properly evaluate the goods' quality of state (Johnson & Ramirez, 2020). A thorough examination of prior findings, the quality and quantity of information, reveals that it is critical in determining the ideal PE. In general, other research indicates that PE is significantly more significant and influential on behavioral intention than other variables (Venkatesh et al., 2003; Kim-Soon et al., 2015; Zainol et al., 2017).

Effort Expectancy

Venkatesh et al. (2003) define effort expectancy (EE) as the degree of ease associated with system use, incorporating the concepts of perceived ease of use, complexity, and ease of use. Naturally, there are numerous ways to interpret these concepts. Yaseen and El (2018), for example, concluded that EE has a positive correlation with behavioral intention to use e-banking services. According to the findings, consumers prefer to learn about e-banking and navigate around financial services online easily, aided by the amplification provided by mobile phone usage. However, the authors assert that, in comparison to older generations, a higher level of EE is observed among the younger generation, which was an early adopter of e-banking. Even in social networking apps, Chua et al. (2018) found that the younger generation has a similar EE level. Additionally, the system's simplicity encourages consumers to use it more frequently. When a system requires extensive training or a complex function, it discourages initial and continued use. On the one hand, Najib et al. (2021) investigate EE through the lens of small food enterprises adopting FinTech. Contrary to consumer perceptions, small food businesses appear to be unaffected by EE's FinTech adoption. A portion of the explanation is that small businesses lack abundant resources, necessitating a different approach than e-banking or social media networking. That is, EE should be investigated in a manner consistent with the nature of consumer usage in the first place. Nonetheless, an abundance of academic research demonstrating the relevance of EE on FinTech adoption continues to grow (Senyo & Osabutey, 2020; Singh et al., 2020).

DEVELOPMENT OF FRAMEWORK MODEL

The model was painstakingly created after exhaustive examinations of the available literature on this subject. Indeed, the tools employed in this research were mostly adopted and adapted to fit the research's setting. As shown in Figure 2, we developed two hypotheses to test the suggested research model.

H_1: Performance Expectancy has a positive influence on intention to use FinTech
H_2: Effort Expectancy has a positive influence on intention to use FinTech.

Figure 2. Framework Model

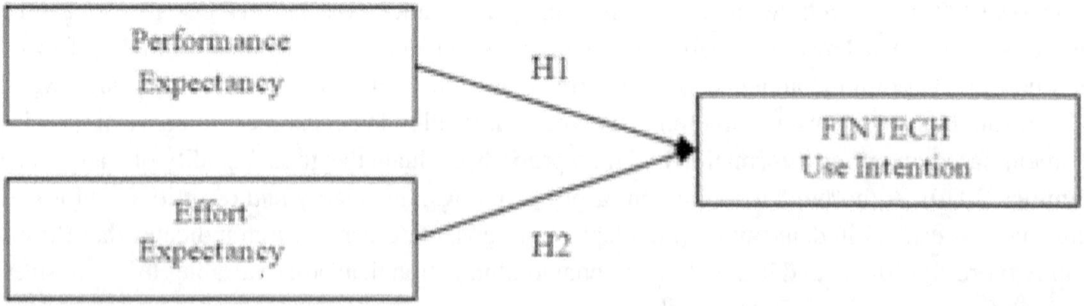

Research Methodology

To guarantee that the acquired data were genuine and that the sample characteristics matched the study's purpose, a non-probability purposive sampling methodology was used. The questionnaire was utilized as a tool to collect pertinent data from the respondents for this investigation. Respondents were asked to rate their level of agreement or disagreement with each set of statements on a 5-point Likert scale. The study's target audience was made up of millennial and generation Z customers.

G*power 3.0 analysis was used to calculate sample size (Faul et al., 2007). With the effect size of f-square 0.15, error pro-0.05, power Gf 0.95, and two evaluated predictors, G-Power analysis software was used. A minimum sample size of 107 respondents was required for this investigation. Data was gathered by using an online approach and a field survey. Three hundred fifty (350) surveys were given out, however, only three hundred eleven (311) hotels responded within six months, representing an 88.9% response rate. 27 of the 311 questionnaires received were discarded, leaving 284 that could be used in the final analysis (81.14 percent response rate). Multiple items were used to explore the structures (see Figure 1), and the data was then analyzed using SmartPLS 3.3.3 (Ringle et al., 2015) to evaluate the hypotheses.

DATA ANALYSIS AND RESULTS

In this study, we select respondents from millennial and Generation Z consumers by looking at how performance expectancy and effort expectancy relate to the FinTech use intention. Most respondents are between 26-33 (42.3%) followed by 18-25 (31.7%) and 34-41 (26.1%) years old. The majority who participated were females (70.4%) and the remaining 29.6 percent were males. In term of education level, most respondents are degree holders with 65.5 percent followed by those with Sijil Pelajaran Malaysia (SPM/O-Level) and Sijil Tinggi Pelajaran Malaysia/A-Level/ Diploma holders made up 31.7 per cent. On the other hand, those holding master degrees are around 2.8 per cent. Meanwhile, the majority or 30.3 percent earned less than RM1000 per month followed by those who earned RM2501-RM4000 (24.6%), RM1001-RM2500 (23.9%), and those who earned RM4001-RM5500 made up 12 per cent. Another 9.1 percent earned above RM5500. In this study, married couples made up 33.8 per cent of the total respondents but the majority were single of 66.2 per cent.

Table 1. Respondent Profile

Age	Frequency	Percent
18-25	90	31.7
26-33	120	42.3
34-41	74	26.1
Gender	**Frequency**	**Percent**
Male	84	29.6
Female	200	70.4
Education	**Frequency**	**Percent**
SPM/O-Level	14	4.9
STPM/A-Level/Diploma	76	26.8
Degree	186	65.5
Master	8	2.8
Income (RM)	**Frequency**	**Percent**
< 1000	86	30.3
1001-2500	68	23.9
2501-4000	70	24.6
4001-5500	34	12.0
5501-7000	12	4.2
7001-8500	4	1.4
8501-10000	8	2.8
10001-11500	2	.7
Total	284	100.0
Marital	**Frequency**	**Percent**
Single	188	66.2
Married	96	33.8
Total	284	100.0

Measurement Model

Cronbach's alpha (CA), composite reliability (CR), and convergent validity testing results are shown in Table 2 and Figure 2 (graphical depiction of Table 2). The result shows that the construct (or variable under examination) has a high level of internal consistency (Roldán & Sánchez-Franco, 2012) as well as enough average variance extracted (AVE) to support convergent validity (Hair et al., 2017). Indicators measuring effort expectancy (EE), intention to use FinTech (IFIN), and performance expectancy (PE) constructs achieve satisfactory loadings value higher than 0.708 (Hair et al., 2017).

Table 2. Measurement Model Assessment

Construct	Item	Loadings	CA	CR	AVE
EE	EE1	0.887	0.948	0.960	0.828
	EE2	0.905			
	EE3	0.935			
	EE4	0.917			
	EE5	0.906			
IFIN	IFIN1	0.912	0.946	0.961	0.861
	IFIN2	0.957			
	IFIN3	0.930			
	IFIN4	0.912			
PE	PE2	0.901	0.931	0.951	0.829
	PE3	0.895			
	PE4	0.914			
	PE1	0.932			

*No item was deleted as loading Composite Reliability > .708 (Hair et al., 2017)

Figure 3. Model Assessment

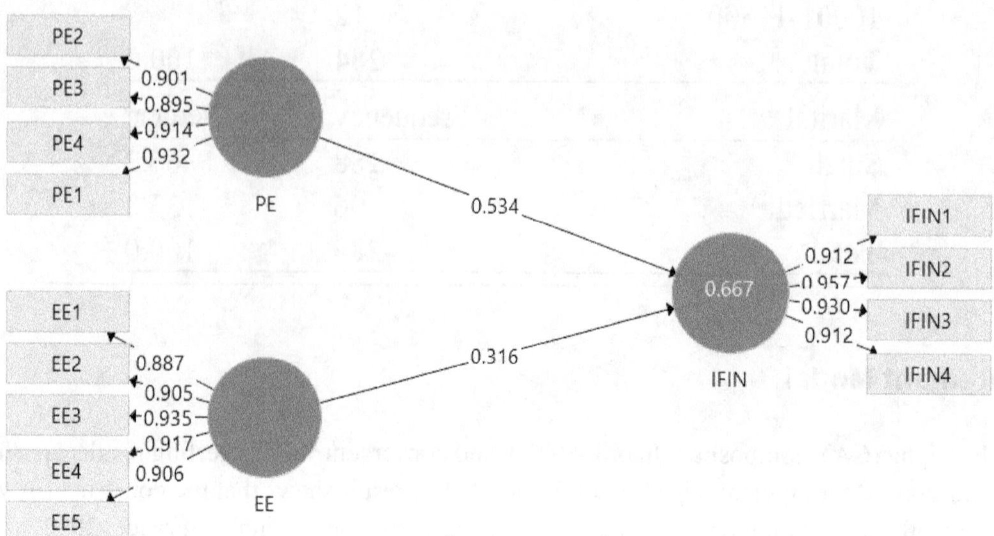

The Cronbach's alpha (CA) value for the EE = 0.938 and the composite reliability (CR) value was 0.940 implying that the EE possesses high internal consistency. Next, IFIN and PE were also revealed to have high internal consistency with Cronbach's alpha (CA) values for the IFIN and PE were 0.916 and 0.931. Meanwhile, the composite reliability (CR) values were 0.921 and 0.941 respectively. In a similar vein, the EE, IFIN, and PE also indicate that convergent satisfaction validity with the average variance extracted (AVE) values for EE, IFIN, and PE were higher than the threshold value of 0.5, demonstrating that the indicators could explain more than 50 per cent of the constructs' variance.

Discriminant Validity

Table 3 displays the HTMT criterion to evaluate discriminant validity (Ringle et al., 2018). In assessing discriminant validity, this study applies Henseler's (2015) heterotrait-monotrait ratio of correlations criterion. The result specifies that discriminant validity is well-established at HTMT0.85 (Diamantopoulos & Siguaw, 2006), which implies that the discriminant validity issue is of no concern. The findings indicated that it is appropriate to proceed with the structural model assessment to test the study's hypotheses, as there is no issue of multicollinearity between indicators loaded on different constructs in the outer model.

Table 3. HTMT Criterion

	EE	IFIN	PE
EE			
IFIN	0.802		
PE	0.888	0.847	

Criteria: Discriminant validity is established at HTMT0.90 (Gold et al., 2001)
Note: (EE) Effort Expectancy, (IFIN) Intention to use FINTECH,
(PE) Performance Expectancy

Structural Model Assessment

Table 5 demonstrates the assessment of the path coefficients, which is represented by Beta values for each path relationship. A 5000-bootstrap resampling of data was conducted to test the hypotheses (Hair et al., 2017). The results for path coefficients indicate that both constructs Performance expectancy (PE) and effort expectancy (EE) have a positive influence on the intention to use financial technology (FinTech).

Table 4 and Figure 4 (graphical illustration of Structural Modelling) depicts the path coefficient assessment. The results indicate all three proposed relationships are significant. Specifically, the study found support for H_1 (PE → IFIN, $\beta = 0.534$, $p < 0.000$, LLCI = 0.355, ULCI = 0.691) and H_2 (EE → IFIN, $\beta = 0.316$, $p < 0.001$, LLCI = 0.149, ULCI = 0.486).

Table 4. Path Coefficients Assessment

Direct Effect	Beta	S.E.	t-value	p-value	LLCI	ULCI	Decision
H1: PE -> IFIN	0.534	0.102	5.208	0.000	0.355	0.691	Supported
H2: EE -> IFIN	0.316	0.103	3.082	0.001	0.149	0.486	Supported

Note: $*p<0.05$, $**p<0.01$, Bias Corrected, LL=Lower Limit, UL=Upper Limit
p-value of 0.01, 0.05 (Hair et al., 2017)

Figure 4. Path Coefficients

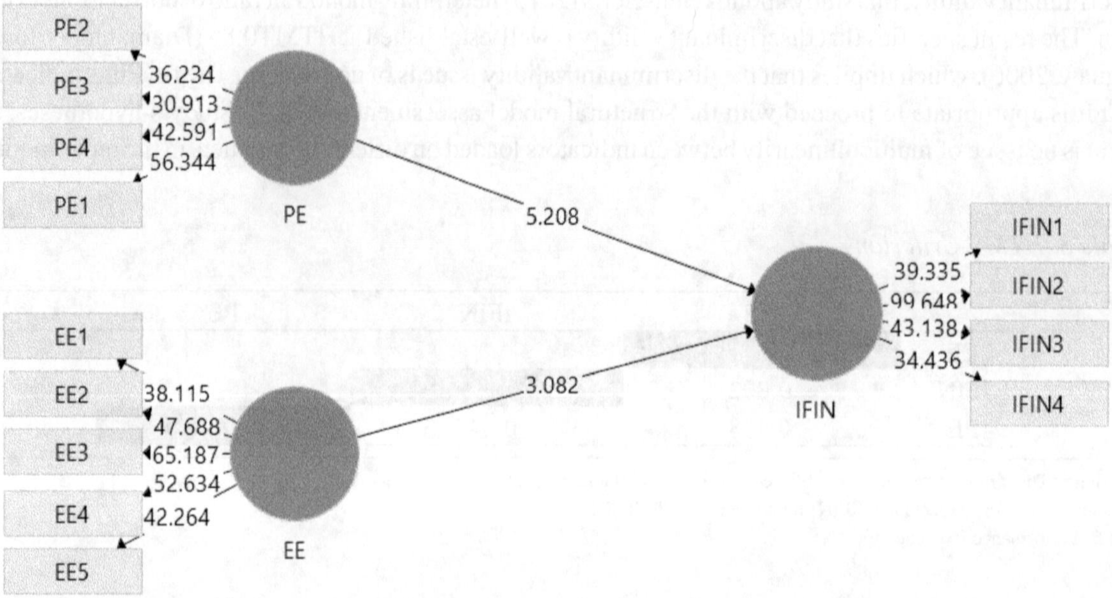

Model Quality Assessment

The model's quality assessment is shown in Table 5. At 0.257, H1 (PE IFIN) has a moderate effect size f^2 on the IFIN value (Cohen, 1988). H2 (EE IFIN) on the other hand, with an impact size of 0.090, shows a minor influence on IFIN. The R^2 coefficient of determination, which demonstrates whether the PE and EE can explain IFIN, indicates that there are considerable effects (Chin, 1998). The R^2 value of 0.667 indicates that the PE and EE could account for a significant portion of IFIN.

In addition, the multi-collinearity of indicators is evaluated. All construct indicators meet the VIF values, and they are consistently below the threshold values of 5.0 (Hair et al., 2014) and 3.3 (Diamantopoulos and Siguaw, 2006; Kock & Lynn 2012). As a result, it can be inferred that collinearity concerns do not approach critical levels in any of the constructs, indicating that estimating the PLS path model is not a problem. The predictive relevant values of PE IFIN and EE IFIN were 0.564, as shown by Q^2 utilizing the blindfolding approach (Hair et al., 2017), showing that the constructs (PE and EE) could predict IFIN significantly.

Table 5. Model Quality Assessment

Direct Effect	f^2	R^2	VIF	Q^2
H1: PE -> IFIN	0.257	0.667	3.130	0.564
H2: EE -> IFIN	0.090		3.130	

f2 ≥ 0.35 consider Substantial (Cohen, 1988)
R2 ≥ 0.26 consider Substantial (Cohen, 1989)
VIF ≤ 3.3 (Diamantopoulos & Siguaw, 2006)
Q2 > 0.00 consider large (Hair, 2017)
$0.02 \leq Q^2 < 0.15$: weak predictive power
$0.15 \leq Q^2 < 0.35$: moderate predictive power
$Q^2 \geq 0.35$: strong predictive power

Table 6. Result of PLSpredict

Construct	Items	PLS-RMSE	MAE	Q^2_predict	LM-RMSE	MAE	Q^2_predict	PLS-LM RMSE	MAE	Q^2_predict	Predict Power
FINTECH Use Intention	IFIN2	0.748	0.510	0.575	0.785	0.537	0.531	-0.037	-0.027	0.044	High
	IFIN1	0.681	0.449	0.638	0.705	0.438	0.612	-0.024	0.011	0.026	
	IFIN4	0.857	0.614	0.480	0.892	0.629	0.437	-0.035	-0.015	0.043	
	IFIN3	0.776	0.574	0.549	0.806	0.594	0.514	-0.030	-0.020	0.035	

The prediction relevance of the endogenous constructs was investigated using the PLS predict approach (Shmueli et al., 2019). (FinTech uses intention). Table 7 shows that all FinTech Use Intention indicators showed lower prediction error (RMSE and MAE) than the linear model (LM), indicating that FinTech Use Intention had strong predictive power (Shmueli et al., 2019).

DISCUSSION

This study investigates whether Performance Expectancy (PE) and Effort Expectancy (EE) are associated with FinTech use intention. The path coefficients results revealed both hypotheses to be supported. Specifically, (H_1) the PE has a positive influence on intention to use FinTech. This finding affirmed the study by Venkatesh et al., 2003; Kim-Soon et al., 2015; Zainol et al., 2017) that FinTech users desire a simple, straightforward, and expedient performance process and environment for FinTech services. For example, consumers prefer mobile banking services because they may provide a faster service. Regardless of their level of education, users are more likely to complete a simple task using more complex technology than they are to complete a complex task using less complex technology. When new technologies become available, people may be hesitant to use them because they have a limited amount of time to learn how to use them. If mobile banking is to be accepted by users, it must be perceived as a more convenient and faster method of conducting online transactions than the traditional brick and mortar.

Given the importance of performance expectancy in influencing the intention to use FinTech services, special attention must be paid to the design of simple-to-use, useful, and reliable systems.

In a similar vein, H_2 affirmed a positive influence of EE towards FinTech use intention. This study confirmed previous findings by Wang and Liao (2007) that discovered effort expectancy has a significant effect on the customer's intention to use FinTech services. Additionally, Chua et al. (2018) highlighted that the younger generation has a comparable effort expectancy level compared to other generations. The ease with which the system operates encourages consumers to use it more frequently. This is most likely due to the state of current technology, which is user-friendly and easy for youth to use. The majority of users are adaptable to technological changes, and developers of online transaction platforms recognize the importance of effort expectancy by emphasizing a user-friendly online platform system.

From a theoretical standpoint, this research has aided in broadening our understanding of the factors influencing intention to use FinTech services from the perspectives of Generation Z and Millennial users, as well as the future prospects of other generations not yet users. The research's primary theoretical contribution is the extension of UTAUT and assessing the model in the context of Generation Z and Millennial users' intentions to use FinTech in Malaysia. From a managerial standpoint, the findings of this research will be extremely beneficial for FinTech players and policymakers in Malaysia as a tool for determining the success of the intention and, consequently, the adoption of FinTech services. The findings of this study suggest that in order to increase adoption of FinTech services, they must also develop a belief in the performance and effort expectations of FinTech platforms. Additionally, they can assist their current and prospective users by organizing awareness campaigns and providing incentives as a token of appreciation.

Finally, the relevant authorities especially the government and the FinTech players must expand financial inclusion and access by helping to ensure that communities have access to high-quality financial services. FinTech enables market players to reach out to the unbanked and underinsured, while also promoting positive social and economic outcomes. Stakeholders must ensure that financial services are efficient and robust, which makes enabling technologies and solutions like real-time payments, open application programming interfaces, and blockchain particularly appealing. By stimulating competition, the government can foster healthy competition and thus foster the development of a sustainable and effective industry, with many citing new FinTech players as a catalyst for competitive change. Governments want to ensure the overall stability of the financial services system by managing emerging bubbles and potential system risks and by finding ways to support technologies that provide a clearer view of emerging risk areas, as well as better risk and compliance management.

CONCLUSION AND RECOMENDATION

Malaysia's government should prioritize modifying and harmonizing existing regulatory frameworks and enacting new legislation to fill identified gaps. This should be accomplished through engagement with FinTech startups and the broader financial services community to develop an understanding of current trends, uses, and risks associated with emerging technologies. The government must then ensure that they are better educated about the complexities of FinTech innovation by collaborating with other governments and organizations to conduct research and gain additional insights. Finally, the government must devise mechanisms for allowing experimentation while ensuring sector stability, such as through the establishment of sandboxes and hackathons.

The research examined Millennials and Gen Z, the two major players in FinTech's development. In FinTech services and applications, both generations exhibit a higher degree of expertise and knowledge than previous generations (Carlin et al., 2017). FinTech appeals to Generation Z and Millennials because of its openness, simplicity of usage, and flexibility. The financial services sector has long been criticized for its use of jargon. The internet has facilitated the growth of portals that have increased public awareness of the sector. Another reason why Gen Zs and Millennials are interested in FinTech is that it is becoming more integrated. In summary, FinTech has advanced the financial services sector tremendously. It has enabled more individuals to engage with financial services than ever before and is beginning to alter behavioral patterns as well.

The researchers suggested that governments and FinTech companies utilize incentives to get consumers to utilize their electronic banking services. FinTech businesses have a lucrative segment that aligns with their business strategies; Gen Zs and Millennials are regarded as the primary target demographics due to the fact that one-third of them lack bank accounts or banking expertise in comparison to previous generations in Malaysia. Banks and financial institutions could play a significant role in this competition to acquire this unbanked segment; they could offer virtual accounts to this segment via e-wallet services, which must be user-friendly and simple to use in order to grow the targeted customer base and provide the required services.

Future study should focus on other approaches e.g., conducting Partial Least Square-Multigroup Analysis to examine whether income level, gender, different group of generations influences the intention or decision to use FinTech. Other researchers could also consider applying a qualitative approach to understand further reasons why different groups of generations have different levels of acceptance towards changes or, in extreme cases, refuse towards intention/decision to use FinTech. While FinTech provides customers with improved services and experiences, FinTech players need to note that trust is equally critical.

Financial inclusion has been identified as a marker of sound money management (Demirguc-Kunt et al., 2017). In the same vein, FinTech has been hailed as a modern means of increasing financial inclusion among the millennial generation through the provision of digital features (Allen et al., 2016; Ozili, 2018). We are regret that this study missed the opportunity to address this issue. Therefore, future research also may include financial inclusion and other variables that will offer fresh insights into the intention/decision to adopt FinTech.

ACKNOWLEDGMENT

The authors would like to thank Universiti Malaysia Sabah for providing research funding as well as the resources needed to complete this study. The Centre for Research and Innovation (PPI) at Universiti Malaysia Sabah is supporting this research, which is sponsored by Skim Dana NIC (SDN) (Project code: SDN0055-2019) which was led by Dr Nelson Lajuni.

REFERENCES

Abdullah, N., Redzuan, F., & Daud, N. A. (2020). E-wallet: Factors influencing user acceptance towards cashless society in Malaysia among public universities. *Indonesian Journal of Electrical Engineering and Computer Science*, *20*(1), 67–74. doi:10.11591/ijeecs.v20.i1.pp67-74

Aji, H. M., Berakon, I., & Md Husin, M. (2020). COVID-19 and e-wallet usage intention: A multigroup analysis between Indonesia and Malaysia. *Cogent Business & Management*, *7*(1), 1804181. doi:10.1080/23311975.2020.1804181

Alam, M. M., Awawdeh, A. E., & Muhamad, A. I. Bin. (2021). Using e-wallet for business process development: challenges and prospects in Malaysia. *Business Process Management Journal*.

Allen, F., Demirguc-Kunt, A., Klapper, L., & Martinez Peria, M. S. (2016). The foundations of financial inclusion: Understanding ownership and use of formal accounts. *Journal of Financial Intermediation*, *27*(4), 1–30. doi:10.1016/j.jfi.2015.12.003

Andrew, J. V., Ambad, A. S. N., & Tan, K. E. (2019). A Model of Factors Influencing Consumers' Intention to Use e-Wallet System in Malaysia: A Systematic Review. *Malaysian Journal of Business and Economics*, *6*(2), 2289–8018.

Carlin, B., Olafsson, A., & Pagel, M. (2017). *Fintech adoption across generations: Financial fitness in the information age (No. w23798)*. National Bureau of Economic Research.

Chang, Y., Wong, S. F., Lee, H., & Jeong, S. P. (2016, August). What motivates Chinese consumers to adopt FinTech services: a regulatory focus theory. In Proceedings of the 18th annual international conference on electronic commerce: *E*-commerce in smart connected world (pp. 1-3). Academic Press.

Chen, D., Lou, H., & Van Slyke, C. (2015). Toward an understanding of online lending intentions: Evidence from a survey in China. *Communications of the Association for Information Systems*, *36*(1), 17. doi:10.17705/1CAIS.03617

Chin, W. W. (1998). Issues and opinion on structural equation modeling. *Management Information Systems Quarterly*, (March), vii–xvi.

Cojoianu, T. F., Clark, G. L., Hoepner, A. G. F., Pažitka, V., & Wójcik, D. (2020). Fin vs. tech: Are trust and knowledge creation key ingredients in fintech start-up emergence and financing? *Small Business Economics*. Advance online publication. doi:10.100711187-020-00367-3

Demirguc-Kunt, A., Klapper, L., & Singer, D. (2017). Financial Inclusion and Inclusive Growth: A Review of Recent Empirical Evidence. *Financial Inclusion and Inclusive Growth: A Review of Recent Empirical Evidence*.

Diamantopoulos, A., & Siguaw, J. A. (2006). Formative versus reflective indicators in organizational measure development: A comparison and empirical illustration. *British Journal of Management*, *17*(4), 263–282. doi:10.1111/j.1467-8551.2006.00500.x

Dranev, Y., Frolova, K., & Ochirova, E. (2019). The impact of fintech M&A on stock returns. *Research in International Business and Finance*, *48*(February), 353–364. doi:10.1016/j.ribaf.2019.01.012

Economic Planning Unit. (2021). *Malaysia Digital Economy Blueprint*. https://www.epu.gov.my/sites/default/files/2021-02 malaysia-digital-economy-blueprint.pdf

Emmanuel, C., Otley, D., & Merchant, K. (1990). *Accounting for management control*. Academic Press.

Faul, F., Erdfelder, E., Lang, A.-G., & Buchner, A. (2007). G*Power 3. A flexible statistical power analysis program for the social, behavioral, and biomedical sciences. *Behavior Research Methods, 39*(2), 175–191. doi:10.3758/BF03193146 PMID:17695343

Fintech News Malaysia. (2021). *Malaysia FinTech Report 2021*. https://de.statista.com/statistik/studie/id/44591/dokument/fintech-report/

Foley, S., Karlsen, J. R., & Putnins, T. J. (2019). Sex, Drugs, and Bitcoin: How Much Illegal Activity Is Financed through Cryptocurrencies? *Review of Financial Studies, 32*(5), 1798–1853. doi:10.1093/rfs/hhz015

Foroughi, B., Iranmanesh, M., & Hyun, S. S. (2019). Understanding the determinants of mobile banking continuance usage intention. *Journal of Enterprise Information Management, 32*(6), 1015–1033. doi:10.1108/JEIM-10-2018-0237

Hair, J. F., Hult, G. T. M., Ringle, C. M., & Sarstedt, M. (2014). *A Primer on Partial Least Squares Structural Equation Modeling (PLS-SEM)*. Sage Publications.

Hair, J. F., Hult, G. T. M., Ringle, C. M., Sarstedt, M., & Thiele, K. O. (2017). Mirror, mirror on the wall: A comparative evaluation of composite-based structural equation modeling methods. *Journal of the Academy of Marketing Science, 45*(5), 616–632. doi:10.100711747-017-0517-x

Hayduk, L. A., & Littvay, L. (2012). Should researchers use single indicators, best indicators, or multiple indicators in structural equation models? *BMC Medical Research Methodology, 12*(159), 159. doi:10.1186/1471-2288-12-159 PMID:23088287

Henseler, J., Ringle, C. M., & Sarstedt, M. (2015). A new criterion for assessing discriminant validity in variance-based structural equation modeling. *Journal of the Academy of Marketing Science, 43*(1), 115–135. doi:10.100711747-014-0403-8

Jennifer, S. (2021). *Why Fintech Battles Ahead Are About More Than Banks*. https://www.bloomberg.com/news/articles/2021-03-02/why-fintech-battles-ahead-are-about-more-than-banks-quicktake

Kim, Y., Choi, J., Park, Y. J., & Yeon, J. (2016). The adoption of mobile payment services for "Fintech". *International Journal of Applied Engineering Research: IJAER, 11*(2), 1058–1061.

Klassen, R. D., & Whybark, D. C. (1999). Environmental management in operations: The selection of environmental technologies. *Decision Sciences, 30*(3), 601–631. doi:10.1111/j.1540-5915.1999.tb00900.x

Kock, N., & Lynn, G. (2012). Lateral collinearity and misleading results in variance-based SEM: An illustration and recommendations. *Journal of the Association for Information Systems, 13*(7), 546–580. doi:10.17705/1jais.00302

Lightbourne, J. (2017). Algorithms & Fiduciaries: Existing and proposed regulatory approaches to artificially intelligent financial Planners. *Duke Law Journal, 67*(3), 651–679.

Liu, Y., & Tsyvinski, A. (2021). Risks and Returns of Cryptocurrency. *Review of Financial Studies, 34*(6), 2689–2727. doi:10.1093/rfs/hhaa113

Mohd Thas Thaker, M. A., Allah Pitchay, A. B., Mohd Thas Thaker, H. B., & Amin, M. F. B. (2019). Factors influencing consumers' adoption of Islamic mobile banking services in Malaysia: An approach of partial least squares (PLS). *Journal of Islamic Marketing*, *10*(4), 1037–1056. doi:10.1108/JIMA-04-2018-0065

Nicoletti, B. (2017). *The Future of FinTech*. Springer International Publishing. doi:10.1007/978-3-319-51415-4

Ozili, P. K. (2018). Impact of digital finance on financial inclusion and stability. *Borsa Istanbul Review*, *18*(4), 329–340. doi:10.1016/j.bir.2017.12.003

Pinochet, L. H. C., Diogo, G. T., Lopes, E. L., Herrero, E., & Bueno, R. L. P. (2019). Propensity of contracting loans services from FinTech's in Brazil. *International Journal of Bank Marketing*.

Rehman, Z. U., & Shaikh, F. A. (2020). Critical Factors Influencing the Behavioral Intention of Consumers towards Mobile Banking in Malaysia. *Engineering, Technology &. Applied Scientific Research*, *10*(1), 5265–5269.

Ringle, C., Wende, S., & Will, A. (2015). *SmartPLS 3.3.3*. http://www.smartpls.com

Ringle, C., Wende, S., & Will, A. (2018). Partial least squares structural equation modeling in HRM research. *International Journal of Human Resource Management*, *31*(1), 1–27.

Roldán, J. L., & Sánchez-Franco, M. J. (2012). Variance-based structural equation modeling: Guidelines for using partial least squares. In M. Mora, O. Gelman, A. L. Steenkamp, & M. Raisinghani (Eds.), *Research methodologies, innovations and philosophies in software systems engineering and information systems* (pp. 193–221). IGI Global. doi:10.4018/978-1-4666-0179-6.ch010

Ryu, H. S. (2018). What makes users willing or hesitant to use Fintech?: The moderating effect of user type. *Industrial Management & Data Systems*, *118*(3), 541–569. doi:10.1108/IMDS-07-2017-0325

Schindler, J. (2017). FinTech and Financial Innovation: Drivers and Depth. *Finance and Economics Discussion Series, 2017*(081).

Shmueli, G., Sarstedt, M., Hair, J. F., Cheah, J. H., Ting, H., Vaithilingam, S., & Ringle, C. M. (2019). Predictive model assessment in PLS-SEM: Guidelines for using PLSpredict. *European Journal of Marketing*, *53*(11), 2322–2347. doi:10.1108/EJM-02-2019-0189

Stewart, H., & Jürjens, J. (2018). Data security and consumer trust in FinTech innovation in Germany. *Information & Computer Security*, *26*(1), 109–128. doi:10.1108/ICS-06-2017-0039

Sydney, M., & Vildana, H. (2021). *Wall Street Asks If Bitcoin Can Ever Replace Fiat Currencies*. https://www.bloomberg.com/news/articles/2021-06-13/wall-street-asks-if-bitcoin-can-ever-replace-fiat-currencies

Uhl, M. W., & Rohner, P. (2018). Robo-Advisors versus Traditional Investment Advisors: An Unequal Game. *The Journal of Wealth Management*, *21*(1), 44–50. doi:10.3905/jwm.2018.21.1.044

World Bank. (2019). *Fintech: The experience so far- executive Summary*. https://documents.worldbank.org/curated/en/130201561082549144/Fintech-The-Experience-so-Far-Executive-Summary

Chapter 3
Digital Wallet Ecosystem in Promoting Financial Inclusion

Siti NurulJannah Rosli
Universiti Brunei Darussalam, Brunei

Muhammad Anshari
https://orcid.org/0000-0002-8160-6682
Universiti Brunei Darussalam, Brunei

Mohammad Nabil Almunawar
https://orcid.org/0000-0001-5296-2576
Universiti Brunei Darussalam, Brunei

Masairol Masri
Universiti Brunei Darussalam, Brunei

ABSTRACT

Digital wallet is expanding largely driven by the evolution of internet and smartphone penetration. Numerous digital wallet providers have risen in many countries including Brunei Darussalam. However, the level of adoption is still low, and cashless society is still far from an expected target. There's no magic formula in deploying a guaranteed successful digital wallet, but developing a digital wallet ecosystem that is tailored to the local markets will be expected to increase digital culture and cashless society. The research assesses the existing digital wallet ecosystem, then analyses the extent of compatibility of local market demand. Furthermore, it introduces an improved digital wallet ecosystem model in order to support financial inclusion achieved through a holistic digital wallet ecosystem. The chapter also examines external factors that contribute to the digital wallet ecosystem's width of usage.

INTRODUCTION

The growth in information communication technology (ICT) has created a surge of progressive technologies that has affected many sectors including financial services. These technologies have produced many

DOI: 10.4018/978-1-7998-8447-7.ch003

disruptive innovations that are said to be the driver in reconstructing business processes and creating new business models including in the financial services industry. The recent developments in ICT have deeply revolutionised the financial service industry where this new set of technologies has played an important role in introducing FinTech, a coalescence of the word, financial and technology. FinTech redesigned a particular segment in a financial system's value chain to alleviate the network between banks and their clients (Omarini, 2018, p.98). Areas such as digital crowdfunding, mobile payments, crypto currencies and peer-to-peer (P2P) are categorized as FinTech (Schindler, 2017; Sugiantoro et al., 2020).

FinTech began to influence our daily lives, through facilitating the process of payments and services and providing the essentials infrastructure for the financial institution's operation. It allows the organization and modernization of financial services and at the same time benefits the customers by the efficiency and convenience that offers them access to efficient services through their smartphones (Anshari, 2020; Ahad et al., 2017). Generally, FinTech are seen as the tools and concepts for financial services delivery channels, which are through the means of internet connectivity and the encompassing adoptions of smartphone technology applied in financial sectors that aids business in managing their financial operations (Kim et. al, 2015; Hamdan & Anshari, 2020).

The rise of FinTech in the global financial market has transformed traditional credit and debit card payment into a digital transaction and digital payment, which, for instance, initiates the changes in the payment system. These transitions are also urged by the growing trends in culture including cashless payments. According to de Almeida et al. (2018), using cash to perform transactions is troublesome to consumers due to the back and forth journey to the Automated Teller Machine (ATM). This repetitive action of withdrawing money is because the limited amount of cash that consumers are able to carry and that forces them to limit their spending. Moreover, cash can be cumbersome and hence pose a threat to consumers of losing the wallet or having it stolen. Apart from that the fourth industrial revolution also took part in the development of the Internet and the formation of e-commerce. Hence, these fostered digitalization by introducing consumers with an array of e-payment choices such as credit and debit cards, electronic and digital or mobile wallets, electronic cash and contactless payment method (Chern, 2018; Anshari et al., 2019).

The phenomenon of FinTech has widespread across continents and become popular both in developed and developing countries as the success comes from the integration between ICT and finance to address real-life needs (Anshari et al., 2021a, Hamdan et al., 2020). It is apparent that ASEAN is one of the region's leading the FinTech boom considering the exponential growth of its Internet economy. The progressive use of smartphones and Internet by the population is one of the factors that contributed to the noticeable growth of the FinTech industry in ASEAN countries. Thus, this align with the recent 51st ASEAN Foreign Ministers' Meeting (AMM) in Singapore which aimed to build an "Innovation and Resilience" with its focal point on "utilizing disruptive digital technologies through both harnessing opportunities and managing challenges coming from it" as ASEAN citizens need to be future-ready as well as fitted-out with skills in order to cultivate capabilities towards smart cities (ASEAN, 2018).

Moreover, digital disruption has led to the increase in the number of global digital wallet users in two years. Between 2017 and 2019, digital wallet users globally soared from 500 million to 2.1 billion where 70% are from China and India alone (De Sartiges et al., 2020). In fact, China has long been a dominator in the mobile economy attributed by its strong FinTech firms that enables to accelerate digital culture especially cashless payment to be prevalent across the country. However, in recent years, Southeast Asia has ascended and challenged the status quo (Anshari et al., 2020a). The rise of mobile wallets drives the mobile economy in the region resulting in an enhanced economic growth and vigorous smartphone penetration, hence outperforming China. The numerous e-wallets services provided by significant market players such as banks, consumer FinTech firms, ride sharing firms, and telecommunications companies has also largely contributed to the outstanding performance of the region. Along with that, both under banked and unbanked individuals in Southeast Asia have acquired the accessibility to financial services via e-wallets through their smartphones (Tech in Asia, 2019).

In addition, ASEAN has a total value of digital payments transaction of US$73 billion in 2018 and it is expected to double by 2023 (Chen et al., 2020). For instance, it can be said that digital culture is the new norm in ASEAN, thus, supported by e-Conomy SEA 2019 report, South-east Asia adoption of digital payment has reached its peak, where it is expected to surpass US$1 trillion by 2025 (Google et al., 2019).

On the other hand, in light to realizing Brunei 'Wawasan 2035', a robust and advanced financial service sector is seen as a vital component in this evolution, to provide liquidity needed for commerce and trade. One of the goals stated in the financial sectors blueprint, is, to address financial services as the enabler for Brunei economic diversification growth (Autoriti Monetori Brunei Darussalam, 2016). Indeed, more and more digital initiatives and innovation arises in Brunei notably the digital wallets boom, which align with the digital masterplan 2025 where DEC Brunei Darussalam., (2020), mentioned that in preparing Brunei adoptions of digital wallet economy, ICT infrastructure are to be upgraded to enhance readiness in delivering flawless digital services that will enrich official, commercial and personal transactions convenience (DEC Brunei Darussalam, 2020).

Aforementioned, digital wallets are a type of FinTech in the form of applications operated primarily through smartphones. It enables individuals to convert from a traditional into a digital monetary system (Tech in Asia, 2019). According to Tech in Asia. (2019), the digital wallets user percentage in ASEAN countries surpassed the global average percentage of 37% with Thailand at 47%, Malaysia at 42%, The Philippines at 40% and Vietnam at 39%. Moreover, the digital wallet used in these ASEAN countries are not limited to food delivery and transportation services only, but also purchases ranging from the grocery stores to hawker stands (De Sartiges., 2019). Now this raises the question to what extent are the comprehensions of the digital wallet ecosystem in Brunei.

This study is expected to contribute in providing a better understanding of the digital digital wallets ecosystem especially in Brunei Darussalam's context. A particular attention is given to the development of the digital wallet ecosystem to ensure that digital wallet services are able to help develop the Brunei economy to flourish, through a feasible and seamless financial system. This research may help developers in upgrading the current digital wallet ecosystem.

The rise in digital wallet service providers is growing significantly, however, despite this growth, the acceptance and usage of digital wallets in Brunei are considered slow compared to other ASEAN countries. This research has identified the inadequacy and lack of localization in its digital wallet ecosystem components as the main problem in this poor adoption of digital wallet in Brunei. What factors contribute to a robust digital wallet ecosystem in Brunei? And what are the internal and external factors in designing the most fitting digital wallet ecosystem in Brunei?

LITERATURE REVIEW

FinTech

Financial Technology (FinTech) can be defined as the innovations of the financial sectors associated with the technology that enabled disintermediation in a business model. This improves the financial process of a firm and further eases the operation in creating and delivering product and services, consumer's privacy and law and regulations enforcement. For instance, provide a new medium for entrepreneurships that breed opportunities and growth (Dhar and Stein, 2017; Al-Mudimigh, & Anshari, 2020)

Digital Wallet

According to Jain and Singhal (2020), digital wallets are a server-based wallet that allows the electronic mode of transaction to take place, thus, enabling customers to purchase and conduct payment online through various electronic devices. Additionally, it is the subset of electronic banking and an extension of internet banking with an upgraded function and characteristics (Laukkanen, and Passanen, 2008)" (p. 540). Hence, cashless payment transactions can be completed at any participating merchant's location.

Function

Consumers' daily transactions are made easy by means of digital wallet applications and its all-inclusive features that can be accessed through digital devices, which include smartphones, tablets and computers (Anshari et al., 2020b). A digital wallet is not only functioned as another mode of payment, it is a digital device with built-in real wallet content and behaviour. It has the ability in storing data of consumer information including payment credit card data and shipping address details. Other than that, it is also able to store loyalty cards, gift cards, insurance cards and more (Anshari et al., 2021b).

On top of that, digital wallets provided consumers with selections of different types of payment within the wallet application to perform transactions such as paying merchants online, in-app or in-store. Therefore, can be used to purchase from e-commerce sites, collect rewards, and more. Whilst the funding of the wallet payment may come from a debit or credit card, prepaid card, bank account, e-money account, virtual currency, or any other store of value.

These digital wallet software applications are equipped with a high level of security where credential provisioning will occur during enrollment of users into the application, such as identity check where verification of user ID and password will take place for wallet access. Moreover the encrypted transactions authentication hides the actual credit card information used to make payment, for instance, protected consumers from risks (Peterson & Wezel, 2016).

Type of Digital Wallet

As stated by Kanimozhi, & Kamatchi, 2017), digital wallet can be categorized into three types, which are the open digital wallets, semi-closed digital wallets and closed digital wallets.

- Open digital wallets refers to the wallet issued by the banks that permits cash withdrawal from ATMs. It was also used to purchase goods and services including financial services like funds transfer at any card accepting merchant locations.
- Semi-closed digital wallets are the wallet issued by telecom companies that can be used for purchase of goods and services and transfers money to other users that uses the same digital wallet platform. The drawbacks of this system are the prohibition towards the users from cash withdrawal.
- Closed digital wallets are the digital wallet that was issued by independent wallet companies that can be used for purchase of goods and services such as amazon and grab.

Technology

The two most popular built-in technologies in digital wallets are NFCs and QR codes. NFCs or Near-field communication is a technology that enables short range wireless connection that aids digital wallets to complete transactions. Consumers of digital wallets can simply tap their phones onto a compatible POS (Point of scale) terminal to make payment (Chandler, 2020; Anshari et al., 2022). QR Codes or also known as quick response is a two-dimensional code that generally has black squares pattern arranged in a square-shaped white background. These codes can be read by imaging devices such as smartphones. These codes are usually placed on various products and store checkouts. Digital wallet users can then easily scan the code displayed by phone camera or compatible QR codes scan app to make payment (Gundaniya, 2020).

Challenges

As cited from Balan (2006), the three key challenges of a digital wallet are mass market appeal, stakeholder dynamics and compelling user experience.

Mass-Market Appeal

In order to increase in market demand and leverage economies of scale, it is important to ensure the mass market appeal. Thus the digital wallet needs to be relatable with the market it serves in order to receive a positive response and user perception on the application and its features. One of the ways to intensify the mass market appeal, is through making digital wallets usable in daily needs of making transactions. These require assistance from financial institutions, retailers and government bodies to provide the digital wallet with support for both point of sale transactions and peer-to-peer transactions between individuals. The challenges in this operation are in coordinating the stakeholders (Thani & Anshari, 2020).

Stakeholder Dynamics

Cooperation of multiple stakeholders such as banks, retailers, regulatory bodies and consumers are needed in the implementation of a successful digital wallet. The difficulties in fulfilling multiple stakeholders business and strategic goals make it a challenge to deploy the digital wallet.

Compelling User Experience

The design and concept of a digital wallet must correspond to consumers' demand especially in its usage. This includes the simplicity in the digital wallet used to complete the task at hand, which can be delivered through a straightforward cognitive load put on the user. Additionally, the functionality of a digital wallet must be compatible with the market culture it serves by fulfilling the core expectations of the certain market. Besides that, functionality of a digital wallet includes the storage, transactions and the security of the application.

Digital Ecosystems

The further expansion of web development has led to the advent of dual environments that people live in, which is ecological environments and digital environments. There is no longer just a world of physically connected economy but also digitally networked economy. Chang & West (2006) cited that this shift in economy has initiated the open, dynamic and network collaborative environment in organization operation that is called as digital ecosystems as a replacement to the traditional close wall organizational operations.

Digital ecosystems can be defined as the compositions of digital entities that are interconnected among each in a self-organizing, scalable and sustainable system. These entities may include groups of enterprises, technology, people and things, where the interactions occur among these entities leads to the stimulation of information, boost system utility, and gain benefits (Li et al., 2012, p. 118).

Furthermore, the digital ecosystem has reshaped how businesses are carried out. For instance, in business perspective, the concept of a digital ecosystem serves as a smart and responsive environment embodied with data and processes. By employing computerized space and tools into the system, it acts as a platform that connects brands with their customers. Essentially, it will revolutionize the entire aspects of life especially in making routines more efficient. In this case, the components of digital ecosystems are service providers, trading partners, suppliers, customers, applications and all related technologies (Zangre, 2018).

The presence of the digital ecosystem in business has fostered the collaboration between the organization and customers as interoperability is the key to the success of the digital ecosystem. Hence, the collaborative manners between the stakeholders will help achieve commercial gains, improved services, generate value, gain profits and drive innovation. One of the commonly known examples for the digital ecosystem is the banking application, where it is used in the integrations of online banking services including mobile wallet, digital passbook and expense manager (Samiya, 2020).

Digital Wallet Ecosystem

The ecosystem for a digital wallet consists of different aspects such as multiple stakeholders, various business models, the technical infrastructure and security and legal framework. However in this research study, the stakeholders involved will be emphasized especially the role of consumers, merchants and banks in enabling ubiquitous use of the payment proposition and financial inclusion.

Consumers

According to Karavellas (2013), consumers appear to be a major influence in determining the success of a digital wallet ecosystem as they're responsible for generating value for the other stakeholders. Thus, their choices and decision making define the success or failures of a digital wallet ecosystem and further help in designing strategic management that would be implemented by stakeholders.

Merchants

They also stated that, merchants make up one of the two ends in monetary transactions typically with consumers. It has a prominent role in the digital wallet ecosystem as it will define the range of services provided and consumer's willingness to adopt the digital wallet. For example, banks, post offices, transportation service providers and retailers. For instance, with these available merchants in the ecosystem, digital wallets are capable of bringing services such as payments for movie tickets, taxi, retail, utilities, e-commerce, health, education and e-delivery.

Banks

Furthermore, it also mentions that banks act as a depository institution offering numerous different banking services thereby optimizing their financial assets. Generally, banks in the ecosystem enable seamless end-to-end interaction through embedding payments in the platform. This allows a cohesive and frictionless user experience between all aspects of the digital wallet ecosystem. Hence, due to its control towards the global payment network, banks have become a crucial component of the ecosystem as it will be the basis for the execution of digital wallets.

FinTech and Financial Inclusion

Financial Inclusion refers to an effort to make financial services and products to be easily available and affordable to a more of the world's population, such as individuals and business irrespective of their personal net worth or company size. Financial inclusion aims to create a strong, functional, diverse, efficient and flexible financial system in order to establish a market-driven, productive and competitive economy. Hence, financial inclusion, attempted to eliminate barriers that exclude individuals from engaging with the financial sector services. One of the ways to achieve inclusive finance is through the advancement of FinTech such as digital wallets that enable digital transactions by using solely a smartphone (Dev, 2006).

Digital Economy in Brunei Darussalam

In the past few years Brunei has been progressing towards realizing its Brunei Vision 2035, which is a development framework and visionary approach by His Majesty to build well-educated and highly skilled citizens. This is in line with developing a dynamic and sustainable economy with an income per capita that is comparable to other top nations across the globe. This vision consisted of 13 key components to achieve the above-mentioned goals, which, one of it, is the implementation of Information Technology (IT) throughout the country. (Wong. J, n.d.). For instance, this widespread enforcement of IT mechanism would enable a seamless flow of information across the government, citizens and business, thus, allowing greater transparency and greater insights for decision making.

As a matter of fact, Brunei is tech savvy with the opportunities to expand beyond its current status as mentioned in the Digital in 2019 Global Overview report from Hootsuite, the internet penetration in Brunei stood at 95% in 2020 (Kemp, 2020). In addition to that, it was reported that 99% of the country's population owned a smartphone, where mobile penetration in Brunei Darussalam was at 131.9% in 2019 (AITI, 2019). Looking at the number portrayed, there is no doubt that the country has an active increase in digital activity.

Digital Wallets in Brunei

Wasil (2020) stated that the founding of the regulatory guideline and FinTech Unit established by Autoriti Monetari Brunei Darussalam (AMBD) in 2017 has resulted in several companies strongly venturing into the financial tech domains. This has contributed to an increase in Brunei based digital payment solutions where firms and startups keenly move towards transforming Brunei to become cashless as a culture. A number of these notable FinTech solutions mainly in a form of digital wallet that are available in Brunei are such as BIBD NEXGEN Wallet, Progresif Pay, BruPay and Pocket.

BIBD NEXGEN Wallet

BIBD was among the first financial institutions to initiate branchless banking services, which allows implementation of digital technologies to enable larger digital audience expansion beyond the banking sector industry. In 2012, Bank Islam Brunei Darussalam (BIBD) introduced the customers with the nation's first cashless mobile payment solution that is incorporated in their BIBD mobile application as added services. It gives customers access to numerous banking services such as account viewing, transaction, money transfers and others through smartphones and tablets (Unsworth, 2012).

In 2018, BIBD launched QuickPay services; a digital payment solution, which enables customers to scan QR codes using their BIBD mobile app to make payments. Businesses can display the code online or printed (Wong, 2020).

While, in 2019, BIBD introduced the first NFCs (Near field communication) technology where it syncs up users debit or virtual cards to the wallet, hence, acts a substitute whereby users are able to make payment transactions with their smartphones at any MasterCard or Visa terminal within the country or abroad without carrying their debit cards. NFCs allow offline function with up to $100 for each five transactions made while unlimited transactions with an Internet connection (Wong, 2018).

On top of that, BIBD NEXGEN wallet offers the most stretched banking services in Brunei that can be directly accessed from a smartphone. This service includes, online payment, money transfer, utilities online payment and generating PIN for cardless cash withdrawals at BIBD ATMs (BIBD, n.d.).

Progresif Pay

Progresif Pay is Brunei's owned digital wallet introduced in 2018 developed by Progresif Cellular Sdn Bhd through their collaboration with BIBD. Similar to popular digital wallet apps like China's Alipay, Progresif Pay allows consumers and businesses to carry out cashless transactions with their smartphones, however is exclusively offered to Progresif phone line users only. Moreover, it also enables bills payment, money transfer to friends and family, shop online and send money abroad securely. Progresif Pay also aims to achieve financial inclusion of the nations where it enables parents to send allowances to their children of age 15 years and above while business can use it for paying staff wages. This benefits both the underbanked and unbanked population of the country (James, 2018).

BruPay

BruPay is a digital wallet platform that eliminates the need to open a specific bank account or specific phone line to get access to digital financial solutions as several financial institutions are integrated within the apps. At the meantime only BIBD and Baiduri bank users are able to deposit money directly to the digital wallet as well as the cash counter at the BruPay's office. Moreover, transactions on BruPay can be made using the QR codes or by keying in the recipient's phone number and thus, payments will be sent directly to a merchant's profile. BruPay also offers an online marketplace in their applications enabling businesses to list and sell their products or services without any registration fees. For instance, merchants can also track their sales and generate their performance report by signing up for the 'back office' system in BruPay. Furthermore, BruPay's unique selling point is disabling transaction fees for any purchases or money transfer from one BruPay user to another, however, withdrawing money from the platform will be charged (Wong, 2019).

Pocket

Pocket is introduced by ThreeG Media as Brunei's first digital wallet applications that can link to multiple cards. It was launched at the end of 2019, with the aim to be a cashless payment gateway suited to local markets' lifestyle. It is known for their unique features of being able to accommodate up to three Visa or MasterCard's from different banks within the apps. Thus, Pocket acts as a digital debit or credit card, instead of performing the tedious process of money transfer between a digital wallet and bank account. Users are then able to make payment transactions either through a "scan and pay" method where users can just scan QR codes displayed on the store counter or through remote payment by using the 'Biller function' that works similarly to bank transfer. On top of that, the value-added services in the apps include membership and deals. Moreover, both tourists and foreign workers are able to use Pocket apps by using Brunei's phone line number and international bank card that supports Visa and MasterCard (Zin, 2020).

Developing Digital Ecosystem of a Digital Wallet in Brunei

Brunei's digital wallet and payment solutions are being adopted at a tremendous rate however the adoption is still low to transform Brunei into a cashless society. Therefore, more work still needs to be done if Brunei's wants to be on par with other ASEAN countries. For instance, a good solution is to develop a digital wallet ecosystem that supports customers in today's digitally connected lifestyle. In this research a robust and extensive digital wallet ecosystem model is introduced focusing on the seamless service delivery among citizens, businesses and government agencies.

Proposed Digital Wallet Ecosystem Model

The figure below are a digital wallet ecosystem designed exclusively for Brunei's market delivering full suites of services, consumer-focused, tailored to local market, end to end experience to drive broad consumer adoption of digital wallets and mobile payments in the nations.

As seen from the figure, the ecosystem are situated in one digital wallet provider that house peer-to peer lending services and merchants ranging from, retailers, postal service, transportation service, and banks. For instance with this merchants and features embraced in a digital wallet, consumers are able to pay for essential daily products and services namely, entertainments such as movie tickets, transport services such as darts, shopping, utilities, e-commerce, e-delivery such as Gamma, health, education, hotel, restaurants and petrol.

Figure 1. Digital Ecosystems for Digital Wallet in Brunei
Source: Authors' Compilation, 2020

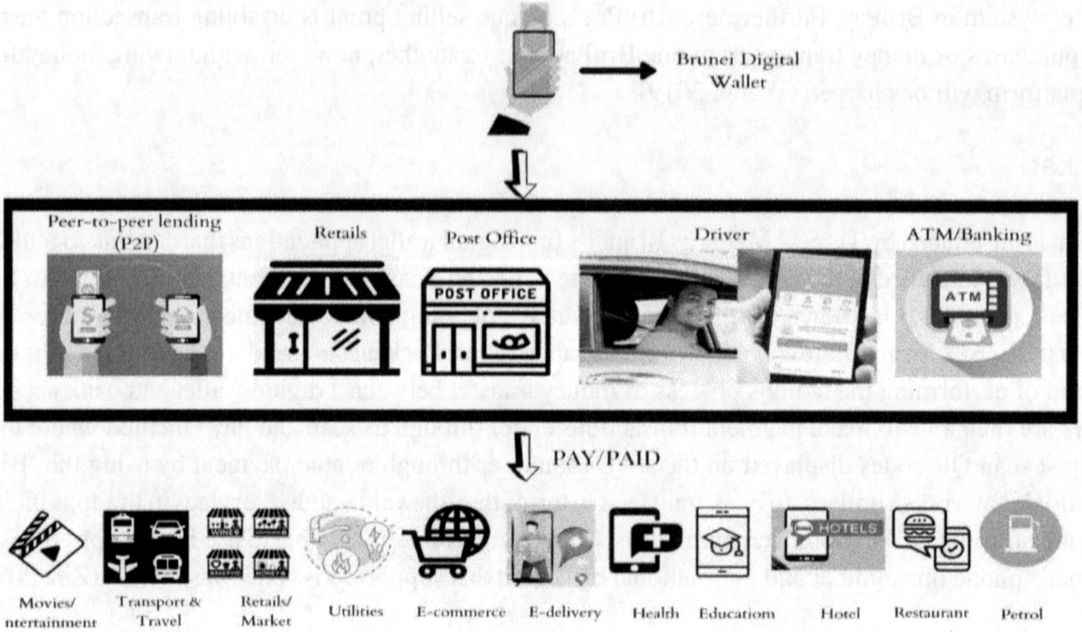

METHODOLOGY

This research gathers data through quantitative method approach whereby surveys were distributed to the targeted consumers. Surveys were created using Google forms and administered through social media, emails, and messenger apps particularly WhatsApp messenger. There are two main requirements to be eligible to answer this survey, which is, a citizen of Brunei Darussalam and must be from millennial generation; any individuals of age ranging from 18 to 40 years old. The question in this survey surround the issues mentioned in the literature review and the proposed digital wallets ecosystem model, which are based on participants experiences and expectations in digital wallets. Every components related to the digital wallet ecosystem will be touched in the survey. This survey consisted of 9 sections with a total of 52 questions. There are 4 sections to be solely answers by a digital wallet user and 1 section to be solely answers by a non-digital wallet users.

The data collected through this survey are for the purpose of developing knowledge and establish understanding on the topic of research. Data analysis will be done and concluded by the use of Microsoft excels.

RESULTS

There were 54.8% of the age between 21 to 25 years old, and 19.2% were of age between 25 to 30 years old, 13.5% were of age between 18 to 20 years old and 12.5% were of age between 30 to 40 years old. In addition, majority of the respondents were female which 77.9%, while male respondents were only 19.2%. The other 2.9% respondents prefer not to tell. For education level, 49.5% from respondents were a degree holder, 19.4% respondents were a level certificate holder and 12.6% were a diploma holder. The other 18.5% were respondents ranging from master to PhD.

For employment status, 34.6% of the respondents are employed, 7.7% are self-employed, 2.9% respondents are a part-timer and 1.9% are interning. While 45.2% are still studying and 7.7% are unemployed. Access to banking services; almost all of the respondents owned a bank account, which is 97.1%, while the other 2.9% do not have a bank account. Monthly income; around 42% earns in between $350 to $1500 per month, 38% earns less than $350 and 20% earns more than $1500.

Use smartphone for payment; all of the respondents have access or own a smartphone. 89.4% respondents are using smartphone for payments whereas 10.6% did not use their smartphone for payment.

Payment method preference; More than half of the total respondents which are 56.7% preferred cashless payments method, while 43.3% still preferred to use cash for payment.

Access to digital wallet account and application; respondents who preferred cashless payment, only 57.6% own a digital wallet whereas and 42.4% do not own a digital wallet.

Digital wallet usage; respondents who preferred cashless payment, 59.3% have used a digital wallet while 40.7% respondents never use a digital wallet.

User Experience of Digital Wallet

Frequency of using digital wallet; respondents who have used a digital wallet, 5.7% use it all the time, 34.3% use it few times in a week, 45.7% use it few times in a months and 14.3% rarely use it.

Familiarity to local or Brunei-owned digital wallet application; majority of these digital wallet users, uses BIBD NEXGEN wallet which is 88.6%. While 14.3% uses Pocket wallet, 5.7% uses Apple pay, 2.9% of respondents uses BruPay, 2.9% uses Baiduri Bank Digital personal.

User preferences on local digital wallet; majority of the respondents preferred BIBD NEXGEN wallet which is 88.6%, followed by Pocket which preferred by 8.6% of respondents, 5.7% preferred Apple Pay.

Reasoning behind user preferences; the most important factor that lead to the preferences are the digital wallet is easy to use claimed by 97.5% of the respondents. The second factor is the variations of benefits provided in the digital wallet as claimed by 42.9% of the respondents.

Type of transaction made in the local digital wallet; money transfer is the most popular transaction in a digital wallet at 62.9%.

Rating for user experience on the local digital wallet; On a scale 1 to 5, 1 being very dissatisfied and 5 being very satisfied, 45.7% of the respondents rated 5 for their experience of using local's digital wallet. While only 5.7% respondents rated 1.

Rate on local digital wallet usability; on a scale 1 to 5, 5 being very easy and 1 being very difficult, 51.4% of respondents rated 5 for the ease of use aspects of the local digital wallet, while only 5.7% of respondents rated 2.

Rate on local digital wallet convenience; on a scale 1 to 5, 1 being very inconvenient and 5 being very convenient, 54.3% of respondents rated 4 for the convenience of local digital wallet while only 8.6% respondents rated 2.

User Experience in The Aspects of Merchants

Peer-to-peer lending (P2P) services availability; According to 25.7% of digital wallet users, P2P services are available in the local digital wallet, however 60% are unsure about the availability of P2P services in any local digital wallet services, while 14.3% claims there are no such services available.

Availability of digital wallet services in local post office; According to 8.6% of respondents, post offices uses local digital wallet, however 51.4% are unsure about the availability the adoption of post office in any local digital wallet services, while 40% claims there are no such services available.

Availability of digital wallet services at local retailers; according to 82.9% of digital wallet users, the local digital wallet service are available through the nation's retailers shop, however 14.3% of digital wallets users are unsure about the availability of digital wallet services at local retailers, while 2.9% of digital wallet users claims there are no such services available.

Availability of digital wallet services in local bank; according to 74.3% of digital wallet users, the local digital wallet service are available through the nation's banks, however 17.1% are unsure about the availability of digital wallet services at local banks, while 8.6% claims there are no such services available.

Availability of digital wallet services in local transportation merchants; according to 28.6% of digital wallet users, the local digital wallet service are available through the nation's transportation merchants, however 54.3% are unsure about the availability of digital wallet services at any transportation merchants, while 17.1% claims there are no such services available.

User satisfaction on choices of merchants in local digital wallet; on a scale 1 to 5, 5 being very satisfied and 1 being very unsatisfied, most digital wallet users rated their satisfaction in selections of merchants 3 and 4 each at 40%.

Local market demand in selection of services and vendors in digital wallet application; on a scale 1 to 5, 5 being strongly agreed and 1 being strongly disagreed, most digital wallets users' participants rated 4 which are at 34.3%.

User Experience in The Aspects of Services

Satisfaction in choices of services provided; on a scale 1 to 5, 5 being very satisfied and 1 being very unsatisfied, most digital wallets users' participants rate 3 and 4 each at 31.4%.

Satisfaction in the number of services available; on a scale 1 to 5, 5 being very satisfied and 1 being very unsatisfied, most digital wallets users' participants' rate 2 for selections of services available which is at 31.4%.

Compatibility of local lifestyle with the variation of services in local digital wallet; on a scale 1 to 5, 5 being strongly agree and 1 being strongly disagree, most digital wallets users participants rate 2 for availability of services that cam cater to the nations lifestyles which is at 37.1%.

Developing Digital Wallet Ecosystem from The Perspective of Digital Wallet User

User knowledge on digital wallet functionality; majority of the digital wallets users are fully aware of the functionality of a digital wallet which is at 68.6% of digital wallets users.

Obstacles faced by digital wallet user; the most voted barriers in performing digital wallets transactions is the poor internet connection which votes by 94.3% that followed by the unavailability of digital wallet service in all merchants votes by 74.3%.

Sustainability of current digital wallet ecosystem; a total of 42.9% (15 respondents) would still use the local digital wallet regardless of the stagnant improvement given in the services. While 42.9% (15 respondents) remains neutral in their usage of digital wallets and 14.3% (5 respondents) will unlikely to continue using the digital wallet.

Digital wallet merchant's demands by the local market; all of the stated services are demanded by local market with and addition towards using digital wallets in hotels, tourist's area and hospitals. 60% rated 5 as in strongly agree for the digital wallets in Brunei to adopt merchants listed above.

Local market demands on services in digital wallet; 71.4% of digital wallets users claimed that all of the stated services are essentials to cater to the nation's lifestyle. On a scale 1 to 5, 54.3% rate 5 as in strongly agree that the services above should be incorporated in any local digital wallets.

Sustainability of proposed digital wallet ecosystem model; on a scale 1 to 5, 65.7% (23 digital wallet users) will definitely use the digital wallets services given that the services above are included.

Developing Digital Wallet Ecosystem from Non-Digital Wallet Users Perspective

Familiarity to local digital wallet; 69.9% of respondents have come across local digital wallets while the other 30.4% have not come cross any local digital wallets. While, BIBD NEXGEN wallet being the most popular digital wallets known by non-digital wallet users at 65.4%.

Reasoning of not using digital wallet; the most voted reasons on why digital wallets are not adopted by these participants are firstly, do not have enough knowledge about digital wallet at 53.6%, followed by safety and security issue at 52.2%.

Obstacles in using cash as mode of payment; long queue in ATM and back and forth journey to ATM are the most voted obstacles of a cash payment at 63.8% and 62.3% respectively. On a scale 1 to 5, 5 being willing to use and 1 being not willing to use, most non digital wallets users voted 3 in their willingness to adopt digital wallet given the obstacles above are solve which is at 34.8% while only 26.1% willing to use digital wallet given obstacles above are solved.

Knowledge on digital wallet functionality; only 30.4% of non-digital wallet users are fully aware of the functionality of a digital wallet while, 43.5% are unsure and 26.1% does not fully understand the functionality of a digital wallet.

Digital wallet service and vendors demands by the local market; the local market demands all of the services. On a scale 1 to 5, 5 being willing to use and 1 being not willing to use, most non digital wallet users at 37.5% voted 3 as their willingness to use the digital wallets given the above merchants are provided.

Local market demands on participative merchants in digital wallet; the availability of all stated services are essentials to cater to the Bruneian lifestyle. Willingness to use digital wallet considering the chosen services are available. 37.7% rate 5 and 36.2% rate 4 for their willingness to use the digital wallets given that the stated services above are included.

Financial Inclusion

Role of digital wallet compared to other payments method; there are 56.7% claimed that digital wallet are only and alternative choice to cash payments. The degree of digital wallet influence in transforming Brunei to "cashless society" shows majority of the respondents rate between 2 to 4 for the statement "Digital wallet in Brunei, has successfully transform Brunei into a cashless society.

Influence of holistic digital wallet ecosystem to drive financial inclusion; on a scale 1 to 5, 5 being strongly agree and 1 being strongly disagree, majority of respondents' rate 3 and 4 in supporting the proposed digital wallet ecosystem model in boosting financial inclusion within the nation.

Other external factors that influence the successfulness of a digital wallet ecosystem; most of them voted supports from the government, private and public sectors commitment and approval from authorities as the other factors that contributes to the successfulness to a digital wallets.

DISCUSSION

The purpose of this study is to determine the local market demands in a digital wallet and to test the compatibility of the proposed digital wallet ecosystem model towards the said market. Furthermore, to analyze the other external factors that contributes to the success of a digital wallet ecosystem as well as investigating whether financial inclusion can be accomplished. An important implication of these findings is that it will drive a better understanding in tackling digital technologies adoption in a specific market, especially a digital wallet. The surveys are distributed towards a specific group which is the millennial generation this is because according to the Department of Economics Planning and Development, the youths total population in Brunei which are those of age 15 to 40 years old are 194,100 (Scoop, 2019) and more than half of the e-commerce users in Brunei are millennial as stated by the AITI study where they founded the 76% of Bruneians who uses e-commerce to shop or pay bills were mainly comprises of millennial generation (Huzair, 2018).

To deduce, that a digital ecosystem of digital wallets has a positive impact on its acceptance and adoption throughout the nations, different factors are to be taken into account such as mass market appeal, compelling users' experience, financial inclusion promotion, and other external factors. These factors play a significant role in determining whether the all-embracing proposed digital wallet ecosystem model provides a seamless operation for consumers, commerce and governments.

Market appeal

For digital wallets, mass market appeal is a fundamental factor for it to succeed. This is to ensure there is widespread consumer adoption, however, consumers are known to have fear for its security especially with how their data is stored, secured or used. In order to make digital wallet more appealing, it has to be supported by its ecosystem that adopts a holistic approach intended to foster end-to-end interaction of commerce and customers. Hence, it is necessary for a digital wallet ecosystem in reducing complexity and creating a straightforward system. Moreover, the digital wallet ecosystem must designed a digital wallet that is convenient for consumers and commerce such as linking up to three cards in one digital wallet reduce the complicated process of money transfer between a digital wallet and banks and hence act as digital debit and credit card, in fact, this tactics are pursued by one of Brunei digital wallet called 'Pocket'.

Other than that, the digital wallet ecosystem needs to include the essential daily products and services of the local markets. This is to increase the usability of the digital wallet in everyday use. In this research paper, the merchants preferred by Brunei local markets are peer-to-peer lending solutions, banks and ATM services, postal services, retailers and transportation services. According to the findings, the merchants in Brunei's digital wallet are mainly made up of retailers where up to 82.9% of the digital wallet users' respondents claims the availability of local retailers in the digital wallet. Thus, would result in consumers to use digital wallets merely for retail payments and disregard the other useful functions of a digital wallet. Thereby, the other services such as banks and ATM services and P2P lending solutions does not efficiently use in digital wallets.

Additionally, digital wallets in Brunei have yet to venture towards including transportation service merchants and post office merchants. This inefficient use of digital wallet and the unavailability of merchants highly demanded by the local market will result in limited market penetration and hence lack the ecosystem-wide approach of the digital wallets.

Compelling user experiences

The proposed digital wallet ecosystem, encourage the payment services that is needed by the local market. These payment services need to be included in entertainments payment, transportation payments, retail payment, utilities payment, e-commerce payment, e-delivery payment, health payment, education payment, hotel payment, restaurants payment and petrol payment. Among these payment services Brunei digital wallet only support retail payment, some utilities payment, health payment, restaurants payment and petrol payment. Thus it needs more merchants to participate to widen the selections of payment services in Brunei digital wallet ecosystem.

However, payments do not defines a digital wallets services by itself, but it also needs to include value-added services such as loyalty, rewards and membership programmes. Moreover, to enhance consumer's experiences, increase in consumer's engagement through a personalized communication tools to foster interactions between consumers and commerce within the digital wallet ecosystem.

Moreover, these payments are not functional without the seamless technology which is NFCs and QR codes. Hence the availability of this technology will assist the cashless and contactless payment in the payment processes without this technology, the digital wallet can only support remote and online payment. While with these technology, digital wallet is able to aid payments even during offline mode.

Financial inclusion promotion

A critically designed digital wallet ecosystem could promote a financial inclusion economy. Hence, other than merchants and services in the ecosystem, technology and system of the digital wallet must support in eliminating barriers towards financial services for under banked and unbanked users. These can be found in ProgresifPay and BruPay where Progresif Pay only requires phone line to access to its digital wallet while in BruPay individuals can directly went to the their office to top up their digital wallet account.

External factors

External factors also plays a role in digital wallet ecosystem in terms of ensuring it to succeed. According to the findings, more than half of the non-digital wallet users are not fully aware of the functionality of a digital wallet where 43.5% are unsure and 26.1% does not fully understand the functionality of a digital wallet. This lack of knowledge in digital wallet services encourage stakeholders to market the digital wallet in by conveying the services provided and tutorial of using the digital wallets. BIBD NEXGEN wallet has been keen in educating its customers about the function of its digital wallet through their YouTube channel and hence resulted in the huge number of users chose BIBD NEXGEN wallet as their everyday digital wallet where 88.6% of digital wallet users preferred BIBD NEXGEN wallet compared to the other three Brunei's digital wallet. This is due to the creation of familiarity through the constant marketing and customer engagement through marketing of BIBD NEXGEN wallet.

Furthermore, supports from the government, private and public sectors commitment and approval from authorities are also important in order to create an all-embracing digital wallet ecosystem. While, some limitations from the study were identified that lacking research references that has been done surrounding the topic of FinTech and digital wallets in Brunei. Furthermore, the possibility of respondents that answers the survey halfheartedly with no intention to fully commit to the study of the research that will disrupt the data collected and respondents do not have enough understanding of the research topic.

CONCLUSION

A digital wallet ecosystem in Brunei requires the diverse, valuable content and a robust and flexible technological platform that can support promotions of merchants and services within the digital wallet applications. External factors must also support the ecosystem in order to maintain sustainable growth in the long run across multiple areas. In addition, consumer-focused services will encourage adoption and it is essential for the ecosystem to scale. Lastly, incorporations of high in demand of merchants and services of the local market, as well as technology that enable seamless operations for both and online transactions will ensure the digital wallet ecosystem to strive by fully catering the nations lifestyles.

REFERENCES

Ahad, A. D., Anshari, M., & Razzaq, A. (2017). Domestication of smartphones among adolescents in Brunei darussalam. *International Journal of Cyber Behavior, Psychology and Learning*, *7*(4), 26–39. doi:10.4018/IJCBPL.2017100103

Al-Mudimigh, A., & Anshari, M. (2020). Financial technology and innovative financial inclusion. In *Financial technology and disruptive innovation in ASEAN* (pp. 119–129). IGI Global.

Anshari, M. (2020, March). Workforce mapping of fourth industrial revolution: Optimization to identity. *Journal of Physics: Conference Series, 1477*(7), 072023. doi:10.1088/1742-6596/1477/7/072023

Anshari, M., Almunawar, M. N., & Masri, M. (2020a). An overview of financial technology in Indonesia. *Financial technology and disruptive innovation in ASEAN*, 216-224.

Anshari, M., Almunawar, M. N., & Masri, M. (2020b). Financial Technology and Disruptive Innovation in Business: Concept and Application. *International Journal of Asian Business and Information Management, 11*(4), 29–43. doi:10.4018/IJABIM.2020100103

Anshari, M., Almunawar, M. N., & Masri, M. (2022). Financial Technology Ecosystem in Promoting a Healthy Lifestyle. In *Emerging Ecosystem-Centric Business Models for Sustainable Value Creation* (pp. 159–169). IGI Global. doi:10.4018/978-1-7998-4843-1.ch007

Anshari, M., Almunawar, M. N., Masri, M., & Hamdan, M. (2019). Digital marketplace and FinTech to support agriculture sustainability. *Energy Procedia, 156*, 234–238. doi:10.1016/j.egypro.2018.11.134

Anshari, M., Almunawar, M. N., Masri, M., & Hrdy, M. (2021b). Financial Technology with AI-Enabled and Ethical Challenges. *Society*, 1–7.

Anshari, M., Arine, M. A., Nurhidayah, N., Aziyah, H., & Salleh, M. H. A. (2021a). Factors influencing individual in adopting eWallet. *Journal of Financial Services Marketing, 26*(1), 10–23. doi:10.105741264-020-00079-5

Autoriti Monetori Brunei Darussalam. (2016). *Brunei Darussalam financial sector blueprint, 2016-2025* [Slides]. AMBD. https://www.ambd.gov.bn/SiteAssets/financial-sector-blueprint/Final%20Sector%20 Blueprint%202016%20-%202025%20FINAL.pdf

Balan, R. K., Ramasubbu, N., & Tayi, G. K. (2006). *Digital wallet: Requirements and challenges.* Singapore Management University and SUNY at Albany.

BIBD. (n.d.). *BIBD NEXGEN wallet.* http://www.bibd.com.bn/personal/digitalbanking/nexgen-mobile/

Chandler, N. (2020, July 27). *How digital wallets work.* HowStuffWorks. https://electronics.howstuffworks.com/gadgets/high-tech-gadgets/digital-wallet.htm

Chang, E., & West, M. (2006). Digital Ecosystems A Next Generation of the Collaborative Environment. *iiWAS, 214*, 3-24.

Chen, L., & Kimura, F. (2020). *E-commerce Connectivity in ASEAN.* Academic Press.

De Sartiges, D., Aparna, B., Justine, T., & Patrick, W. (2020, May 20). *Southeast Asian Consumers Are Driving a Digital Payment Revolution.* Boston Consulting Group (BCG). Retrieved from https://www.bcg.com/publications/2020/southeast-asian-consumers-digital-payment-revolutions

Dev, S. M. (2006). Financial inclusion: Issues and challenges. *Economic and Political Weekly*, •••, 4310–4313.

Drive the Country's Economic Progress. (n.d.). Retrieved from http://www.information

Google, Temasek, & Bain & Company. (2019). *e-Conomy SEA 2019: Swipe up and to the right: Southeast Asia's $100 billion internet economy*. Retrieved from https://www.blog.google/documents/47/SEA_Internet_Economy_Report_2019.pdfgov.bn/Publication%20listsPDF/Brunei%20Darussalam%20Newsletter/2020/BDN%20JUL%202020.pdf

Gundaniya, N. (2020, February 5). *Everything you need to know about QR code payments*. Digital Finance Solutions, Ewallet Payment System, Wallet App Development. https://www.digipay.guru/blog/everything-you-need-to-know-about-qr-code-payments/

Hamdan, M., & Anshari, M. (2020). Paving the Way for the Development of FinTech Initiatives in ASEAN. In *Financial technology and disruptive innovation in ASEAN* (pp. 80–107). IGI Global. doi:10.4018/978-1-5225-9183-2.ch004

Hamdan, M., Chen, C. K., & Anshari, M. (2020, November). Decision Aid in Budgeting Systems for Small & Medium Enterprises. In *2020 International Conference on Decision Aid Sciences and Application (DASA)* (pp. 253-257). IEEE. 10.1109/DASA51403.2020.9317018

Hazair, H. (2018, November 18). *Local e-wallet BruPay banks on millennials, merchant-friendly features*. The Scoop. https://thescoop.co/2018/11/14/local-e-wallet-brupay-banks-on-millennials-merchant-friendly-features/

James, K. (2018, May 15). *Progresif launches brunei's first mobilwallet*. The World News. https://theworldnews.net/bn-news/progresif-launches-brunei-s-first-mobile-wallet

Karavellas, T. (2013). *Towards a Universal Mobile Payments System* (Master's thesis).

Li, W., Badr, Y., & Biennier, F. (2012). Digital ecosystems. *Proceedings of the International Conference on Management of Emergent Digital EcoSystems - MEDES'12*, 118–119. https://www.researchgate.net/publication/262330068_Digital_ecosystems_Challenges_and_prospects

Omarini, A. E. (2018). *FinTech and the future of the payment landscape: the mobile wallet ecosystem. A challenge for retail banks?* Academic Press.

Samiya, T. M. (2020, January). *A preview of digital ecosystem & engagement through gaming in the context of bangladesh, robi axiata ltd*. BRAC University. http://dspace.bracu.ac.bd/xmlui/bitstream/handle/10361/14008/15104161_BBA.pdf?sequence=1

Scoop, T. (2019, September 10). *Calling all youths: 'We need your input for the national youth policy.'* The Scoop. https://thescoop.co/2018/12/20/calling-all-youths-we-need-your-input-for-the-national-youth-policy/#:%7E:text=According%20to%20the%20Department%20of,Youth%20Congress%20in%20February%202019

Sugiantoro, B., Anshari, M., & Sudrajat, D. (2020, June). Developing Framework for Web Based e-Commerce: Secure-SDLC. *Journal of Physics: Conference Series, 1566*(1), 012020. doi:10.1088/1742-6596/1566/1/012020

Tech in Asia. (2019, November 5). *The future of Southeast Asia's mobile wallets. Tech in - Connecting Asia's Startup Ecosystem*. https://www.techinasia.com/future-southeast-asias-mobile-wallets

Thani, F. A., & Anshari, M. (2020). Maximizing Smartcard for Public Usage: PDCA and Root Cause Analysis. *International Journal of Asian Business and Information Management, 11*(2), 121–132. doi:10.4018/IJABIM.2020040108

The 51st AMM and related meetings. (2018). *ASEAN.* Retrieved from https://asean.org/wp-content/uploads/2018/08/PM-Remarks-Transcript.pdf

Unsworth, A. (2012, December 12). *First m-banking platform in brunei.* Mobile Payments World. https://www.mobilepaymentsworld.com/first-m-banking-platform-in-brunei-2/

Wasil, W. (2020, April 18). Brunei moving closer towards smart nation, digital economy – the bruneian. *The Bruneian News.* https://www.thebruneian.news/brunei-moving-closer-towards-smart-nation-digital-economy

Wong, A. (2018, December 15). *BIBD introducing brunei's first NFC mobile payment in january.* Biz Brunei. https://www.bizbrunei.com/2018/12/bibd-nexgen-wallet-introducing-bruneis-first-nfc-mobile-payment-in-january/

Wong, A. (2019, November 3). *BruPay launches: No transaction or registration fees.* Biz Brunei. https://www.bizbrunei.com/2018/11/brupay-launches-no-transaction-registration-fees/

Wong, A. (2020, November 13). *Scan and pay: BIBD QuickPay enables cashless payment using QR codes.* Biz Brunei. https://www.bizbrunei.com/2018/08/scan-and-pay-bibd-quickpay-enables-cashless-payment-using-qr-codes/

Zin, A. (2020, July 27). *Cashless payments straight out of your pocket – the bruneian.* The Bruneian News. https://www.thebruneian.news/cashless-payments-straight-out-of-your-pocket

Chapter 4
Financial Inclusion and Mobile Payment to Empower Small and Medium-Sized Enterprises:
Post-COVID-19 Business Strategy

Mia Fithriyah
Indonesia Open University, Indonesia

Masairol Masri
Universiti Brunei Darussalam, Brunei

Mohammad Nabil Almunawar
https://orcid.org/0000-0001-5296-2576
Universiti Brunei Darussalam, Brunei

Muhammad Anshari
https://orcid.org/0000-0002-8160-6682
Universiti Brunei Darussalam, Brunei

ABSTRACT

Despite the increasing adoption of financial technology (FinTech) and the need for secure payment methods, mobile payments as a mode of settling daily business transactions have not received sufficient attention. To date, several business actors prefer to use conventional money payment modes. However, it is apparent that the need for a more effective payment method today is considered as a basic necessity, considering the current complexity of consumers and the negative effect of COVID-19. Moreover, the crisis raised a wave of apprehension over a large number of business actors, particularly small and medium-size enterprises (SMEs). The literature search indicated that the government should implement the correct policy to help create an acceptable environment for financial transactions for both the user and providers. It is also necessary to ensure that client security and privacy rights are protected during the mobile payment transactions.

DOI: 10.4018/978-1-7998-8447-7.ch004

INTRODUCTION

As compared to large companies, SMEs has very limited access to funding which might potentially have a negative impact on their business operation. With the shockwave of Covid-19 pandemic, SMEs are experiencing limited cash buffers resulting in higher dependence on bank financing and limited access to new credit lines. This is further worsen with shrinking revenues which could trigger income shortages and eventually negatively impact their operation (Pierre et al, 2020). The potential vulnerability of SMEs to the COVID-19 shock is a significant concern for policymakers everywhere. Much literature has emerged to investigate the factors that convoluted the SMEs during the outbreak. In addition to that, various studies suggested on strategies that could contribute in maintaining the operational continuity of SMEs. One of the breakthrough that has aloft during Covid-19 is FinTech payments. FinTech has ease the access of finance between buyers and sellers without the need to have a face-to-face dealing. The literature has also shown that mobile payments has contributed significantly to the economic development where it has provided easy access to finance and simplified transactions at individuals and businesses level (Coffie et al, 2020).

With the advancement in IT technology, various Fintech technologies integrating finance and technology were being developed. This is mainly due to rapidly growing online market and supply of mobile devices. Thus, this has increase the scale of mobile Fintech payment service that enables easy online and off-line payment. To some extent, FinTech services for SMEs claimed to resolve the payment, settlement, investment, and financing challenges of SMEs (Coffie et al, 2020). This trend started in 2013. The market research company, Gartner predicted that the average annual growth of the global mobile payment market size has reached up to 38% within five years. Furthermore, by 2016 the world's non-cash transaction volumes grew by 8.9% and increase by 10.1% with only a year (Kang, 2018).

LITERATURE REVIEW

Financial Technology (FinTech) and Financial Inclusion

Financial Technology (FinTech) is an industry made up of companies employ technology in transforming financial systems by delivering various financial products and services (Coffie et al, 2020). It is a breakthrough to promise accessible, affordable, and secure financial products and services for individuals and businesses. FinTech's existence in the financial service sector allows financial service providers to offer a wide range of new services that remove intermediaries and administrative layers to make transactions more effective and less prone to error (Cumming et al, 2018). Besides, FinTech is an online platform that differs from traditional funding channels. Most obvious is that there is a huge growth of mobile banking that allows customers to perform a wide range of transactions online. Furthermore, FinTech remarkably facilitates quicker network of access to financial services to the entire transaction services, from checking financial status, making payments, withdrawing, transferring funds, etc.

Financially, SMEs need an impactful breakthrough in payment transactions to survive during the pandemic. Several studies stated that FinTech resolves payment and settlement bottlenecks through collaboration with traditional financial institutions. The adoption of FinTech successfully mitigates the failures of traditional financial institutions. It significantly supports individuals and SMEs to access bank accounts and undertake various transactions remotely (Drasch et al, 2018). FinTech services delivered via mobile phones make up for the infrastructural deficiencies restricting the delivery of financial products and services mainly to rural communities (Demirgüç-Kunt et al, 2020).

FinTech Payment Mobile Payment (M-Payment)

On payment aspects, FinTech payment is another crucial trend of development for SMEs. More and more companies have developed payment related solutions for their customers. According to the data from the Starbucks company's Q3 financial report stated that mobile payments increased to 30% of transactions in U.S. company-operated stores (Leong & Sung, 2018). Thus, FinTech payments allow users for a seamless e-payment process, focusing on improving convenience, efficiency, traceability, and security (McWaters, 2015; Kim et al, 2010; Barkhordari, 2016).

FinTech Payment by means of mobile devices are something that common in supporting people's everyday life. The data indicated that four out of five people are dependent on shopping through mobile phones. However, the adoption of mobile payment (m-payment) services has remained lethargic. In 2015, a study found that while 52% of people are "extremely aware" of m-payment services, only 18% reported using these services routinely (Silbert, 2015).

The various types of m-payment referred to mobile money, mobile money transfer, and mobile wallet. They operated under financial regulation with the digital process. M-payment can be utilized in various payments for goods, services, and bills/invoices. It uses mobile devices (such as mobile phones, smartphones, or personal digital assistants) and wireless communication technologies (Ericlee & Evanson, 2014).

M-payment offers a wide range of transaction services and being adopted worldwide in many ways. In developing countries, m-payment solutions have been deployed to extend financial services to the unbanked community. In fact, according to financial access report, 50% of the world's adult population has no access to bank institution. This community includes the Small Medium-size Enterprises (SMEs) actors, where they often use micropayments and non-legal financial agents to corroborate their financial issue (Ericlee & Evanson, 2014; Al-Mudimigh & Anshari, 2020).

M-payments in developing countries have attracted public and private funding organizations such as the Bill and Melinda Gates Foundation, USAID, and MercyCorps. The combined market for all m-payments was projected to reach more than $600B globally by 2014. However, M-payments as a way of completing daily business transactions have still not received enough attention. Conventional money payment modes continue to be used today (Halim et al., 2021). The reasons for this varies among countries. One of them lies in the host country's macroeconomic environment and government policies and regulations, such as overvalued currency and currency controls, high tariffs and taxes, and slow and expensive licensing processes for financial institutions.

M-Payment Transaction Method

Compared to conventional payment tools, the power of mobile payments can be seen via its ease of use, comprehensive coverage, timeliness and security concerns, transfer fees, and other additional services such as SMS as measures of effectiveness (Ericlee & Evanson, 2014). Mobile devices can be used to access and utilize mobile payment services to pay bills and invoices. Furthermore, it allow the users to connect to a server, perform authentication and authorization, make mobile payment, and subsequently confirm the completed transaction (Antovski & Gusev, 2003). To better understand the detail payment model with m-payment system, it is important to understand the whole process of this mode of financial transaction.

Based on figure 1, financial payment service system with m-payment is connected to existing financial institutions with IT technology-based digital payment infrastructure. As a result, all user payment data is fully recorded by financial institutions, and users can access payments independently from the financial institution's system (Anshari et al., 2020; Mulyani et al., 2019a). The advantage offered by mobile payment is that it offers a payment method that is much more flexible and convenient than traditional payment services. A practical and straightforward side is also presented where all transaction processes are connected between various financial institutions. In addition, users can take advantage of various financial institutions' payment services with a single payment method. For instance, if a user has entered several bank accounts and card information on a FinTech payment service, they can experience a diverse transaction experience as desired because FinTech payment service providers can customize payment services for the needs of users and merchants. Thus, m-payment service comprises all technologies offered to the user as well as all tasks conducted by the payment service providers to carry out payment transactions (Kang, 2018; Hamdan & Anshari, 2020).

Figure 1. M-payment infrastructure in Fintech environment
Source: Kang (2018)

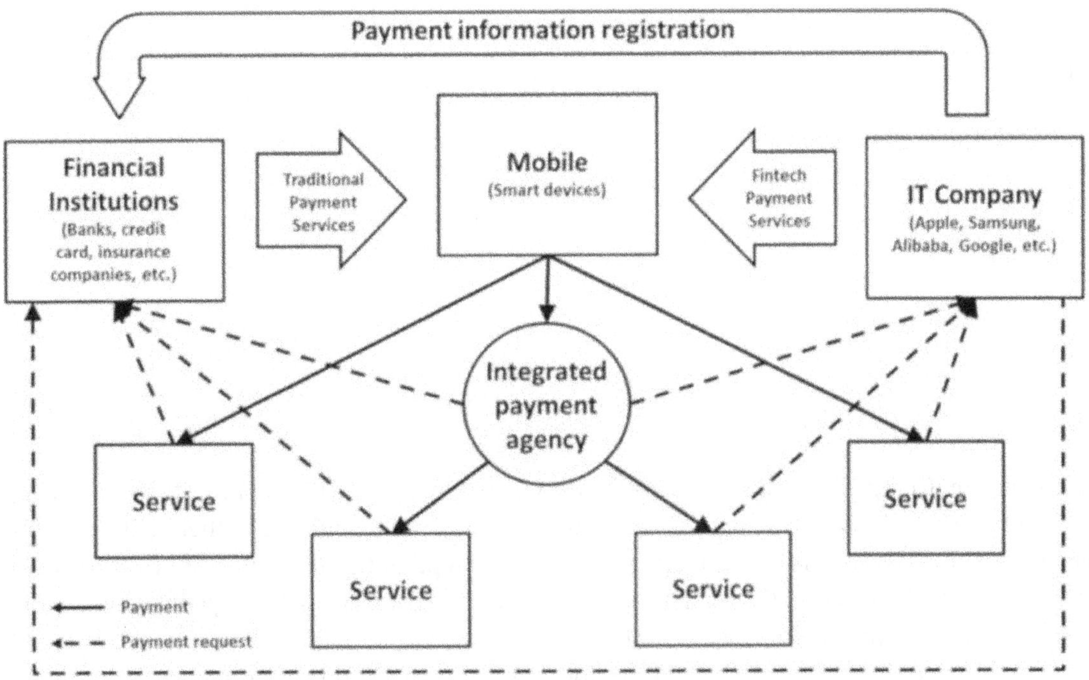

Mobile Payment System Characteristics

Mobile technology as the basis of the system is a broad category that addresses all devices, protocols, and infrastructures that permit one to communicate and exchange data with other individuals or systems anywhere and anytime (Lim, 2007). As m-payment proliferate in importance, it is necessary to identify specific system characteristics. Concerning m-payment, the unique attributes include mobility and reachability, compatibility, convenience, perceive ease of use and perceive of usefulness (Ding, Ijima, & Ho, 2004; Anshari et al., 2021a). Mobility implies that users can carry cell phones or other mobile devices to conduct transactions from anywhere within a mobile network area (Au & Kauffman, 2008; Ding et al., 2004; Anshari et al., 2021b). The reachability of mobile devices makes it possible for people to be contacted anytime and anywhere and provides users with the choice to limit their reachability to particular people or times (Kim, 2010). It is also labeled the benefits provided by m-payment as "anytime and anywhere computing" and defined the two most common dimensions of mobility – independence of time and place. The temporal and spatial dimensions of mobility broaden computing capacity and allow, in principle, access to information, communication, and services anywhere and anytime (Au & Kauffman, 2008). Other than that, reachability means easy to be contacted anytime and anywhere (Au & Kauffman, 2008; Ng-Kruelle et al, 2002; Ondrus & Pigneur, 2006). This feature renders m-payment users reachable by m-payment service providers.

Figure 2. M-payment System Characteristic
Source: Ding, Ijima & Ho (2004)

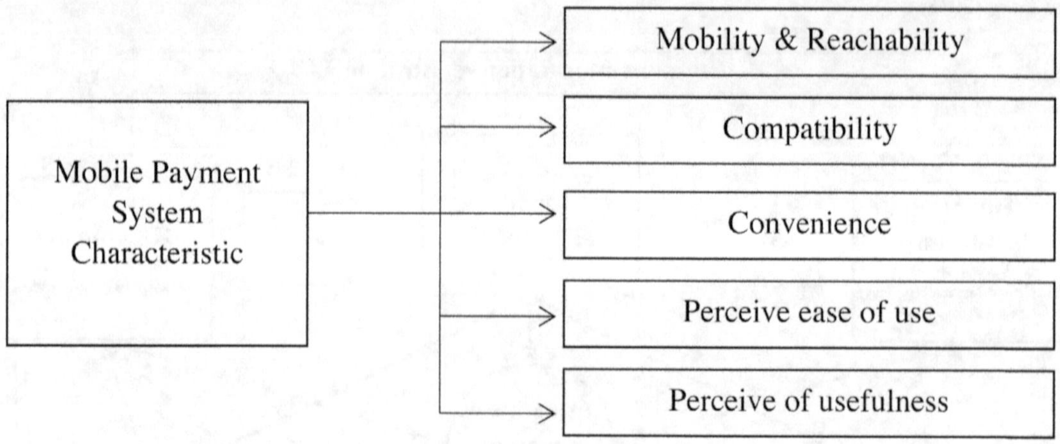

Furthermore, Compatibility described as the answer to the user's needs and lifestyles. It is also perceived usefulness and ease of use that can be assumed to be parallel with each other, and together with compatibility, they are the most significant indicators of adoption (Mallat, Rossi, & Tuunainen, 2006; Anshari et al., 2019). Besides, Convenience is promised to make life easier for people and ameliorate the difficulty of everyday tasks (Obe & Balogu, 2007; Ahad et al., 2017). Convenience is related to the elements generating time and place utility for users (Clarke, 2001). Convenience is nothing but a combination of time and place utilities, which are principal characteristics of m-payment. In addition, perceive ease of use means that m-payment must be easy to learn and easy to use where it positively affects both the perceived usefulness and intention to use (Kim, 2010; Mulyani et al., 2019b). Finally, the perceived usefulness of the system indicated that users would use m-payment systems when they find the system useful for their transaction needs or financial issues (Au & Kauffman, 2008; Mallat, 2007; Ondrus & Pigneur, 2006; Hasmawati et al., 2020).

Methodology

This study contains element of exploratory research and use secondary data to support the comprehensive study about post-Covid19 financial business strategy for SMEs with m-payment model. It builds on recent reviews of m-payment, FinTech, Financial Inclusion, and SMEs. It employed a rigorous approach and transparent to search the relevant literatures, selected publications for inclusion according to textual data using structured thematic forms and synthesized the data using a systematic approach-featuring summary of data analytic and theme comparisons. A systematic literature review (SLR) was conducted on Google Scholar and the Scopus bibliographic database by specifying the inclusion criteria that were used to select articles using the keywords 'mobile payment (m-payment)', 'Financial Technology (FinTech)', 'Financial Inclusion', and 'Small Medium-size Enterprises (SMEs)'. The study chose only English-language articles published in peer-reviewed journals and reliable sources. After removing duplicates and articles beyond the scope of this study, these articles were reviewed to extract to get themes. The themes were then derived by considering the generic nature of the discussion and recommendations.

DISCUSSION

Mobile payments have offered such as tenants a more effective method of paying rent which has a greater reach, and therefore the unbanked are well catered for, more convenient and timely, easy to use are among other benefits. The literature studied also reveals that SMEs using m-payment services in Cameroon has higher profitability as it provides funding opportunities (Talom & Tengeh, 2020). Another study has also shown the positive impact of mobile-based money transfers in Kenya farming community. The study reveals that mobile money services provide easy access for farmers and can be replicated in SMEs (Kirui et al, 2013). Study by Davis (1989) and Ganciu & Andrei (2019), investigated the perceived usefulness and ease of using financial transactions with technology and diffusion of technology has been the primary theoretical foundation for studies of technology diffusion in the past and recent literature. Thus, it can be suggested that specific characteristics of m-payment services can drive diffusion in SMEs.

Meanwhile, another study has explored the success factors in the adoption of m-payment dependable upon the ability of SME CEOs to consider all possible outcomes of deployed technology that can be affected by education level, age, and gender (Hamdan et al., 2020). Theory of planned behavior (TPB) applied discusses that the characteristics of SMEs CEOs as the basis for the decision to deploy FinTech payment services in sub-regions (Ajzen, 1991). Most of SMEs across sub-Saharan Africa covers up to more than 85% of all businesses dominated with m-payment which involving for economic growth (Quartey et al., 2017). This shows the importance of m-payment services in driving economic development for SMEs. Thus, the positive opportunities for SMEs when adopting M-payment transaction can thematically be categorized as in Table 1.

Although m-payments are more effective than conventional methods, this study found that m-payments also facing several challenges primarily caused by the novelty of mobile technology. A study by Kim et al. (2010) showed that users with highly innovative characteristics found m-payment to be easy to use. M-payment users with significant m-payment knowledge do not have difficulty in adapting to m-payment. It is noted that among the four system characteristics, reachability is the most critical predictor of perceived ease of use and perceived usefulness. Compared to traditional offline payment, the growth opportunities of m-payment overflow. As telecommunications technologies progresses, m-payment service providers can magnify these system characteristics without additional costs by taking advantage of the declining cost of technologies, thus resulting in more prominent adoption by users (Kim et al, 2010).

Table 1. Positive opportunities for SMEs when adopting M-payment

	Opportunities
Innovative & Attractiveness	M-payment offered tenants a more effective method of paying
Assurance	M-payment more convenient and timely
Simplicity	M-payment easy to use and adopt
Accessibility	M-payment provide easy access
Financial Inclusion	M-payment services can drive financial diffusion in SMEs

Source: Authors' Compilation, 2021

CONCLUSION

As were are approaching the Post COVID-19, to effectively assist SMEs and preventing an increase in their failure rates, relevant stakeholders such as the m-payment providers, government, and SMEs Actors (m-payment users) need rethink and re-evaluate their policies/directions to ensure m-payment flourishes for betterment of the SMEs community. With regards to the m-payment providers, m-payment must explicitly communicate the mobile payment operations to government authorities to ensure transparency. In addition, the there is a need for a standard administrative rates and efficient transfer payment process to merchants once transaction is completed. Secondly, the government need to strengthen their policies aimed at creating a safe environment while conducting financial transactions. Thus, it is imperative to closely monitor and protect the user's security and privacy rights. Finally, for the SMEs actors (m-payment users) to be more knowledgeable on m-payment utilization. However, this can be assisted by the m-payment provider by providing a more concise and simplified business processes. This is to avoid misunderstandings in the event of a dispute or intricacy in the future.

REFERENCES

Ahad, A. D., Anshari, M., & Razzaq, A. (2017). Domestication of smartphones among adolescents in Brunei darussalam. *International Journal of Cyber Behavior, Psychology and Learning*, *7*(4), 26–39. doi:10.4018/IJCBPL.2017100103

Ajzen, I. (1991). The theory of planned behavior. *Organizational Behavior and Human Decision Processes*, *50*(2), 179–211. doi:10.1016/0749-5978(91)90020-T

Al-Mudimigh, A., & Anshari, M. (2020). Financial technology and innovative financial inclusion. In *Financial technology and disruptive innovation in ASEAN* (pp. 119–129). IGI Global.

Anshari, M., Almunawar, M. N., & Masri, M. (2020). Financial Technology and Disruptive Innovation in Business: Concept and Application. *International Journal of Asian Business and Information Management, 11*(4), 29–43. doi:10.4018/IJABIM.2020100103

Anshari, M., Almunawar, M. N., Masri, M., & Hamdan, M. (2019). Digital marketplace and FinTech to support agriculture sustainability. *Energy Procedia, 156*, 234–238. doi:10.1016/j.egypro.2018.11.134

Anshari, M., Almunawar, M. N., Masri, M., & Hrdy, M. (2021). Financial Technology with AI-Enabled and Ethical Challenges. *Society*, 1–7.

Anshari, M., Arine, M. A., Nurhidayah, N., Aziyah, H., & Salleh, M. H. A. (2021). Factors influencing individual in adopting eWallet. *Journal of Financial Services Marketing, 26*(1), 10–23. doi:10.105741264-020-00079-5

Antovski, L., & Gusev, M. (2003). *M-Payments.* Paper presented at the 25th International Conference of Information Technology Interfaces, Cavtat, Croatia.

Au, Y. A., & Kauffman, R. J. (2008). The economics of mobile payments: Understanding stakeholder issues for an emerging financial technology application. *Electronic Commerce Research and Applications, 7*(2), 141–164. doi:10.1016/j.elerap.2006.12.004

Barkhordari, M., Nourollah, Z., Mashayekhi, H., Mashayekhi, Y., & Ahangar, M. (2016). Factors influencing adoption of e-payment systems: An empirical study on Iranian customers. *Information Systems and e-Business Management, 15*(1), 89–116. doi:10.100710257-016-0311-1

Clarke, I. (2001). Emerging value propositions for M-commerce. *The Journal of Business Strategy, 18*(2), 133–149.

Coffie, C. P. K., Hongjiang, Z., Mensah, I. A., Kiconco, R., & Simon, A. E. O. (2020). Determinants of FinTech payment services diffusion by SMEs in Sub-Saharan Africa: Evidence from Ghana. *Information Technology for Development*, 1–22. doi:10.1080/02681102.2020.1840324

Cumming, D., & Hornuf, L. (2018). The Economics of Crowdfunding. Fintech and the Financing of SMEs and Entrepreneurs: From Crowdfunding to Marketplace Lending. doi:10.1007/978-3-319-66119-3

Davis, F. D. (1989). Perceived usefulness, perceived ease of use, and user acceptance of information technology. *Management Information Systems Quarterly, 13*(3), 319–340. doi:10.2307/249008

Demirgüç-Kunt, A., Klapper, L., Singer, D., Ansar, S., & Hess, J. (2020). The global Findex Database 2017: Measuring financial inclusion and opportunities to expand access to and use of financial services. *The World Bank Economic Review, 34*(Supplement_1), S2–S8. Advance online publication. doi:10.1093/wber/lhz013

Ding, X., Ijima, J., & Ho, S. (2004). *Unique features of mobile commerce. Tokyo 152- 8552.* Graduate School of Decision Science and Technology, TITECH.

Drasch, B. J., Schweizer, A., & Urbach, N. (2018). Integrating the 'troublemakers': A taxonomy for cooperation between banks and fintechs. *Journal of Economics and Business, 100*(March), 1–17. doi:10.1016/j.jeconbus.2018.04.002

Ericlee, N. M., & Evanson, M. N. (2014). *Effectiveness of Mobile payment services among SMEs: experiences from SMEs in Ongata Rongai Township of Kajiando County in Kenya*. International Research Journal of Business and Management – IRJBM.

Ganciu, M. R., & Andrei, N. (2019). Using technology acceptance model to adopt Intelligent Banking. *FAIMA Business & Management Journal, 7*(4), 13–23. https:search.proquest.com/openview/56b6c584 8dd1b5891876bc4cae0f856d/1? pq-origsite=gscholar&cbl=2037693

Gourinchas, Kalemli-Özcan, Penciakova, & Sander. (2020). *Covid-19 And Sme Failures, Nber Working Paper Series*. National Bureau of Economic Research.

Halim, N. A. R. A., Hashim, N. F. A., Alek, S. K. A., Asmali, K. N., Rosli, R., & Anshari, M. (2021). BeUsin: Savings and Investment Platform. In Handbook of Research on Innovation and Development of E-Commerce and E-Business in ASEAN (pp. 526-548). IGI Global.

Hamdan, M., & Anshari, M. (2020). Paving the Way for the Development of FinTech Initiatives in ASEAN. In *Financial technology and disruptive innovation in ASEAN* (pp. 80–107). IGI Global. doi:10.4018/978-1-5225-9183-2.ch004

Hamdan, M., Jaidin, J. H., Fithriyah, M., & Anshari, M. (2020, December). E-Learning in Time of Covid-19 Pandemic: Challenges & Experiences. In *2020 Sixth International Conference on e-Learning (econf)* (pp. 12-16). IEEE. 10.1109/econf51404.2020.9385507

Hasmawati, F., Samiha, Y. T., Razzaq, A., & Anshari, M. (2020). Understanding Nomophobia Among Digital Natives: Characteristics And Challenges. *Journal of Critical Reviews, 7*(13), 122–131.

Kang, J. (2018). Mobile payment in Fintech environment: trends, security challenges, and services. *Human-Centric Computing and Information Sciences, 8*(1), 32. doi:10.1186/s13673-018-0155-4

Kim & Mirusmonov. (2010). *An empirical examination of factors influencing the intention to use mobile payment*. doi:10.1016/j.chb.2009.10.013

Kim, C., Tao, W., Shin, N., & Kim, K.-S. (2010). An empirical study of customers' perceptions of security and trust in e-payment systems. *Electronic Commerce Research and Applications, 9*(1), 84–95. doi:10.1016/j.elerap.2009.04.014

Kirui, O. K., Okello, J. J., Nyikal, R. A., & Njiraini, G. W. (2013). Impact of mobile phone-based money transfer services in agriculture: Evidence from Kenya. *Zeitschrift für Ausländische Landwirtschaft, 52*(2), 141–162. doi:10.4018/jictrda.2012010101

Leong, K., & Sung, A. (2018). FinTech (Financial Technology): What is It and How to Use Technologies to Create Business Value in Fintech Way? *International Journal of Innovation, Management and Technology, 9*(2), 74–78. doi:10.18178/ijimt.2018.9.2.791

Lim, A. S. (2007). Inter-consortia battles in mobile payments standardization. *Electronic Commerce Research and Applications, 2*(2), 15–23.

Mallat, N. (2007). Exploring consumer adoption of mobile payments – A qualitative study. *The Journal of Strategic Information Systems, 16*(4), 413–432. doi:10.1016/j.jsis.2007.08.001

Mallat, N., Rossi, M., & Tuunainen, V. K. (2006). The impact of use situation and mobility on the acceptance of mobile ticketing services. *Proceedings of the 39th Hawaii international conference on system sciences*. 10.1109/HICSS.2006.472

McWaters, R. (2015). *The future of financial services: How disruptive innovations are reshaping the way financial services are structured, provisioned and consumed*. World Economic Forum.

Mulyani, M. A., Razzaq, A., Ridho, S. L. Z., & Anshari, M. (2019b, October). Smartphone and Mobile Learning to Support Experiential Learning. In *2019 International Conference on Electrical Engineering and Computer Science (ICECOS)* (pp. 6-9). IEEE. 10.1109/ICECOS47637.2019.8984501

Mulyani, M. A., Razzaq, A., Sumardi, W. H., & Anshari, M. (2019a, August). Smartphone Adoption in Mobile Learning Scenario. In *2019 International Conference on Information Management and Technology (ICIMTech)* (Vol. 1, pp. 208-211). IEEE. 10.1109/ICIMTech.2019.8843755

Ng-Kruelle, G., Swatman, P. A., Rebme, D. S., & Hampe, J. F. (2002). The price of convenience. Privacy and mobile commerce. *Quarterly Journal of Electronic Commerce*, *3*(3), 273–285.

Obe, O. O., & Balogu, V. F. (2007). Practice, trends and challenges of mobile commerce in Nigeria. *Information Technology Journal*, *6*(3), 448–456. doi:10.3923/itj.2007.448.456

Ondrus, J., & Pigneur, Y. (2006). Towards a holistic analysis of mobile payments: A multiple perspectives approach. *Electronic Commerce Research and Applications*, *5*(3), 246–257. doi:10.1016/j.elerap.2005.09.003

Quartey, P., Turkson, E., Abor, J. Y., & Iddrisu, A. M. (2017). Financing the growth of SMEs in Africa: What are the constraints to SME financing within ECOWAS? *Review of Development Finance*, *7*(1), 18–28. doi:10.1016/j.rdf.2017.03.001

Razzaq, A., Samiha, Y. T., & Anshari, M. (2018). Smartphone habits and behaviors in supporting students self-efficacy. *International Journal of Emerging Technologies in Learning*, *13*(2), 94. doi:10.3991/ijet.v13i02.7685

Silbert, S. (2015). *How Mobile Payments Will Grow in 2016*. Retrieved June 13, 2021, from www.fortune.com

Talom, F. S. G., & Tengeh, R. K. (2020). The impact of mobile money on the financial performance of the SMEs in Douala, Cameroon. *Sustainability*, *12*(1), 183. doi:10.3390u12010183

Chapter 5
Financial Inclusion, P2P Lending, and MSMEs:
Evidence From Indonesia

Tulus Tambunan
Center for Industry, SME, and Business Competition Studies, Universitas Trisakti, Indonesia

ABSTRACT

In Indonesia after the Asian financial crisis of 1997–1998, wide reforms were carried out, and "inclusive" economic development were adopted. One component of inclusive economic development is "financial inclusion." This implies an absence of barriers that might deter micro, small, and medium enterprises (MSMEs) from obtaining financial services. However, the portion of bank credit received by MSMEs is still small. Therefore, financial technology (FinTech) is welcome as an alternative source of funding for MSMEs. This chapter discusses three related issues, namely financial inclusion, MSMEs, and P2P lending. It concludes that Indonesia still has a long way to go to achieve full financial inclusion. This chapter suggests that with the presence of P2P lending, the number of MSMEs, especially MSEs, in Indonesia that have access to formal financing will increase. Even though aggregate data are not available, the interviews with a small number of owners of MSEs who received P2P loans suggest that the presence of P2P lending companies give some benefits for MSEs.

INTRODUCTION

During the so-called "New Order" era (1966-1998) Indonesia experienced a rapid economic development and an annual growth rate of between 6 and 8 percent. The regime reduced the poverty rate in the country through rural economic development based on agricultural modernization and industrialization. With these achievements, Indonesia was called one of the "Asian Tigers," along with Malaysia and Thailand (World Bank, 1993; Krugman, 1994). However, this economic performance at the macro level hid some problems because the development strategy implemented had created inefficiencies and market distortions. Indonesia suffered from high economic costs and a widening gap in income levels. During the New Order era, the development process was exclusive, affecting only certain areas, such

DOI: 10.4018/978-1-7998-8447-7.ch005

as Java, and certain groups in society, namely those deemed important by policy makers (Booth and McCawley, 1981; Hill, 1994).

The 1997-1998 Asian financial crisis hit Indonesia hard. It was the most severe economic crisis Indonesia has ever seen since the country's independence in 1945. It caused an economic recession in 1998, with a growth rate of -13 percent. Following Indonesia's recovery from recession, the country has undergone a major transformation. It has initiated extensive institutional changes and has become one of the most dynamic democracies in the region. From a social and economic perspective, Indonesia has also seen a lot of progress (Tambunan, 2015).

Broad reforms have been carried out in all areas including economic, social and political, and a new development strategy, namely "inclusive" economic development and growth, has been adopted. In this inclusive development, the Indonesian government has adopted a three-track strategy, namely "pro-growth", "pro-job", and "pro-poor". This strategy is considered important for Indonesia because strong economic growth after the 1998 crisis has not completely eliminated poverty and even inequality tends to widen (Pukuh and Widyasthika, 2017).

An important element of "inclusive" development is financial inclusion, which means broad access to financial services. This implies the absence of price and non-price barriers that might prevent people from obtaining financial services. Currently, more and more institutions are paying attention to the issue of financial inclusion. At the G20 Toronto Summit held in June 2010, global leaders pledged to support financial inclusion to empower the roughly one-third of the world's population who still live in poverty (OECD, 2010). Financial inclusion has also been integrated into the 2015 Association of Southeast Asian Nations (ASEAN) Economic Community Blueprint (ASEAN, 2015).

For Indonesia, there are strong reasons to adopt financial inclusion as a new national development policy goal, considering (i) poverty and the gap between poor and non-poor are still serious problems; (ii) the financial sector is highly concentrated, i.e. dominated by banks (most profitable, with low levels of intermediation), with a growing capital market, although still concentrated in a few large companies, and with low penetration of pension funds., insurance, and other non-bank financial institutions; and (iii) only a small part of the total Indonesian population has access to banking services. One concrete action taken was the launch of the National Strategy for Financial Inclusion, in December 2010, by Bank Indonesia (BI), Indonesia's central bank (Tambunan, 2015). Since then, the government and monetary authorities, such as BI and the Financial Services Authority (OJK) have had many high-level discussions on financial inclusion, focusing on how to provide better access to banking services. They realized that the main problem was information asymmetry between supply (banks) and demand (especially for the poor) information on financial inclusion (Hadad 2010).

As in many other countries, micro, small and medium enterprises (MSMEs) play an important role in economic development in Indonesia. Moreover, because they are very labor intensive and account for about 99 percent of the total number of companies and 97 percent of the total employment, while large enterprises (LEs) are only one and three percent respectively. MSMEs, especially micro and small enterprises (MSEs) are very important for job creation, poverty alleviation, and reduction of inequality in income distribution and economic development between regions. Therefore, the development of these companies has become part of the poverty alleviation policy in the country. However, these companies face many obstacles that made it difficult for them to develop or even survive, and limited access to funding from formal sources was the most serious. This problem has long been recognized by the Indonesian government, therefore, since the 'New Order' era (1970) until now, the emphasis on MSME policies has been on MSME funding. The first time the government launched a credit scheme specifically designed for MSMEs was in 1971, followed by many other credit schemes in the 1980s and 1990s (Tambunan, 2018). In 2007, the government launched a public guarantee credit scheme, known as Kredit Usaha Rakyat (or KUR), specifically for MSEs who do not have access to commercial banks due to a lack of valuable assets as collateral.

However, data from BI shows that the portion of bank credit received by MSMEs is still small. Therefore, the existence of financial technology (FinTech) companies that are growing rapidly in Indonesia since the last few years is very welcome, because this new way of financing through online is considered to be a good alternative source of funding for MSMEs, especially MSEs. FinTech is an innovation in the financial services industry that utilizes technology. Among many FinTech-based products, peer-to-peer (P2P) lending is the most important for MSEs. It provides an online marketplace suitable for investors, which can be individuals, multi-finance companies or even banks, who wish to invest and MSEs who wish to borrow. Thus, given the failure of many banks to provide adequate loans to MSMEs, especially MSEs, the emergence of P2P lending offers significant opportunities (Joseph, 2019; Shofawati, 2019; Nurohman et al,, 2021). Especially during the Covid-19 pandemic, P2P lending can help MSMEs in Indonesia to survive (Wardhani, 2020).

This study aims to discuss the implementation of financial inclusion and examine the latest developments of online-based P2P lending and its importance, especially for MSEs as an alternative source of financing in Indonesia. This is a descriptive research that analyzes secondary and primary data. Primary data were collected from: (i) a survey of 60 respondents, namely 30 MSME owners and 30 managers/directors of P2P lending companies, of which a total of 40 respondents considered useful (i.e. 10 MSMEs and 30 P2P), and (ii) a series of focus group discussions (FGD) with selected P2P companies. The results of this study show that the number of MSMEs continues to grow despite facing various obstacles with limited access to funding as the most serious. Although commercial banks are required by the government to extend credit to MSMEs, the percentage of total commercial credit to these businesses is still very small. Therefore, as suggested by the survey findings, the emergence of P2P is important as an alternative source of funding for MSEs. and banks are the main investors in P2P lending companies. To the author's knowledge, this is the first study ever conducted, at least in Indonesia. It takes stock of empirical evidence in the literature through the lens of MSME owners.

FINANCIAL INCLUSION

Inclusive economic development was used in the academic literature for the first time in 1998 but became an integral part of the literature only starting in 2008. According to Ali and Zhuang (2007), Ali and Son (2007), and Rauniyar and Kanbur (2010), the term "inclusive economic development" does not have a widely accepted definition. The concept clearly includes inclusion and economic development, and views inclusion as both a process and an end. Sen (1999), Sachs (2004), Ali and Son (2007), and Rauniyar and Kanbur (2010) emphasize that inclusive economic development is economic growth coupled with equal distribution of economic opportunities. It focuses on creating economic opportunities and making them accessible to everyone in society at all levels, not just the poor. Similarly, inclusive economic growth is growth that emphasizes that economic opportunities created by economic growth are freely available to all, including the poor (Tambunan, 2015).

Financial inclusion is one of the key elements of inclusive economic development. The term financial inclusion became popular in the early 2000s, stemming from a research finding which shows that poverty is a direct result of financial exclusion. Since then, financial inclusion has been adopted by governments in many developing countries as an effective strategy for alleviating poverty by providing public services to all members of society, including the poor, women and youth in urban and rural areas (including relatively remote areas). These public services include access to bank facilities for credit and saving, insurance and pensions (Babajide et al., 2015). An inclusive financial system enables easy broad-based access to financial services by making customized financial products available at affordable prices without strict documentation, especially for the poor or other disadvantaged groups in the economy. Without an inclusive financial system, the poor will depend on their limited savings and especially the MSE run mainly by poor rural households will not have the opportunity to grow or even to survive because they have to rely on their limited capital due to their limitations. limited income (Babajide et al., 2015).

Access to Bank Account

The most frequently used indicator to measure the level of financial inclusion is the percentage of the adult population who has an account in the formal financial sector. Based on the 2017 Global Financial Inclusion Index database from the World Bank (Demirgüç-Kunt, et al. 2018), as can be seen in Table 1, the largest member country was Singapore, followed by Thailand and Malaysia (Table 1). Despite being the largest country in Southeast Asia (ASEAN) in terms of economy, size and population, Indonesia is not the largest member country with respect to total bank account holders. To a certain extent, this has to do with poverty which is still one of the socio-economic problems faced by the country. Other causes are because many households in rural areas are located far from the bank location and the low level of financial literacy, especially among the poor. So, with this indicator, the conclusion is that the level of financial inclusion in Indonesia is still relatively low. So, with this indicator, the conclusion is that the level of financial inclusion in Indonesia is still relatively low.

Table 1. Share of the Adult Population with a Bank Account in the Formal Financial Sector in ASEAN, 2017

Member states	Account ownership		
	Adults with an account (%)	Gap between men and women (percentage points)*	Gap between richer and poorer (percentage points)
Cambodia	22	-	12
Indonesia	49	-5	20
Lao PDR	29	-6	19
Malaysia	85	5	8
Myanmar	26	-	6
Philippines	34	-9	27
Singapore	98	-	-
Thailand	82	4	7
Vietnam	31	-	18

Note: * a negative value indicates that a larger share of women than men have an account.
Source: Global Findex database (Demirgüç-Kunt, et al. 2018).

In addition, Table 2 shows statistics regarding the use of bank accounts by the adult population (aged 15 years and over) in Indonesia. As can be seen, when compared to the average East Asia and Pacific and lower middle-income countries, the implementation of financial inclusion in Indonesia is still far from satisfactory. For example, the number of account holders by adults who are in the poorest 40 percent reached only 22.2 percent in 2014. In fact, this group is one of the main targets for implementing financial inclusion in Indonesia. Other key indicators are savings and credit. It was revealed that total savings at financial institutions in 2014 was only around 26.6 percent, a slight increase from 15.3 percent in 2011, and total loans were smaller at 13.1 percent in 2014, also a small increase from 8.5 percent in. 2011. The implementation of an inclusive financial system aims to provide access for all members of society, including the poor, to formal financial institutions to save their money or/and to borrow money.

Table 2. Select Indicators of Financial Inclusion in Indonesia, 2014 (% age 15+)

Description	Indonesia	East Asia & Pacific	Lower middle income
Account			
All adults	36.1	69.0	42.7
Women	37.5	67.0	36.3
Adults belonging to the poorest 40%	22.2	60.9	33.2
Young adults	35.2	60.7	34.7
Adults living in rural areas	28.7	64.5	40.0
Financial Institution Accounts			
All adults	35.9	68.8	41.8
All adults 2011	19.6	55.1	28.7
Mobile Accounts			
All adults	0.4	0.4	2.5
Access to Financial Institutions			
Has debit card	25.9	42.9	21.2
Has debit card 2011	10.5	34.7	10.1
ATM is the main mode of withdrawal (% with an account)	70.9	53.3	42.4
ATM is the main mode of withdrawal (% with an account) 2011	51.1	37.0	28.1
Use of Account in the Past Year			
Used an account to receive wages	6.6	15.1	5.6
Used an account to receive government transfers	3.0	8.1	3.3
Used an account to receive to pay utility bills	3.9	11.8	3.1
Other Digital Payments in the Past Year			
Used a Debit Card to make Payments	8.5	14.8	9.6
Used a Credit Card to make Payments	1.1	10.8	2.8
Used the Internet to Pay bills or make purchases	5.1	15.6	2.6
Savings in the Past Year			
Saved at a Financial Institution	26.6	36.5	14.8
Saved at a Financial Institution 2011	15.3	28.5	11.1
Credit in the Past Year			
Borrowed from a Financial Institution	13.1	11.0	7.5
Borrowed from a Financial Institution 2011	8.5	8.6	7.3

Source: World Bank. Financial Inclusion Data: Indonesia (https://datatopics.worldbank.org/financialinclusion/country/indonesia).

Credit for Households

Another important indicator of financial inclusion is public access to credit from formal financial institutions.

In Indonesia, of all five bank groups that provide credit to households and businesses in various schemes, namely commercial bank, state-owned bank, Bank Perkreditan Rakyat (BPR), Bank Pembangunan Daerah (BPD), and Bank Rakyat Indonesia (BRI) are the main financial institutions that provide microfinance to households (for example, housing (mortgage) loans, vehicle loans, and other consumer loans) and to businesses. BPR is also known as a people's credit bank or a rural bank or a second-tier bank to serve MSMEs, low-income groups, and/or poor households. BPD is a regional or a provincial development bank owned by the provincial government that has the same legal form as a commercial bank. BRI has various credit schemes, including microcredit known as Kredit Umum Pedesaan (KUPEDES), distributed through all BRI Unit Desa (village branches of BRI). It is a general-purpose rural loan scheme with competitive interest rates. It offers loans (working capital and investment) to those who fulfil the requirements in all economic sectors, from businesses in agriculture, trade, industry, and services, to individual borrowers who require loans for education, house renovation, purchase of vehicles, etc. Figure 1 shows the trend for outstanding loans and loans for businesses and households (HH) allocated by commercial banks, rural banks, and other banks. Unfortunately, data on microcredit is not available (Tambunan, 2015).

Figure 1. Outstanding Total, Consumption and Business Loans (in Rupiah and Foreign Currencies) of all Banks, 2016–2021 (IDR billion)
Source: Bank Indonesia (https://www.bi.go.id/id/statistik/ekonomi-keuangan/seki/Default.aspx)

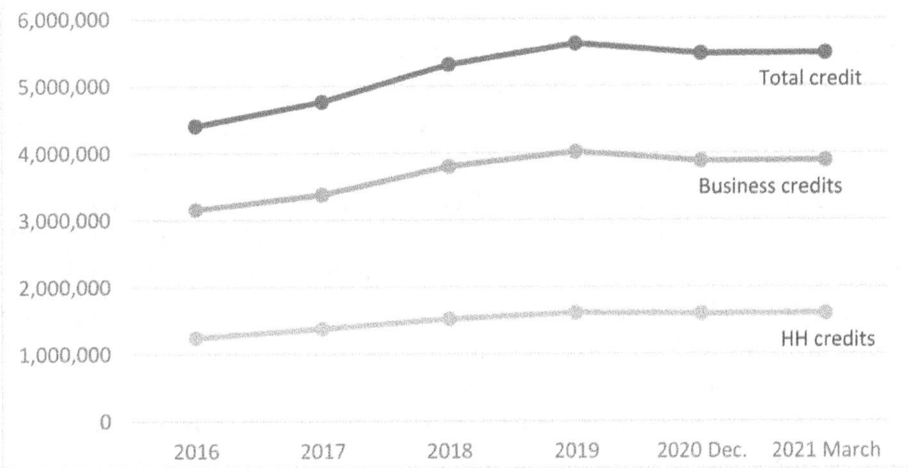

It can be seen that the growth of HH loans shows a positive trend although the average per year is relatively slow, and most of the banking loans in Indonesia are still dominated by business loans. In 2016 the share of HH in commercial loans was recorded at only about 28 percent and in March 2021 it only increased slightly to 29.5 percent. The HH loan is intended primarily for the purchase of a house, flat or apartment, purchase of a car or motorcycle, purchase of a shophouse or home office.

At least in theory, it can be assumed that there are many factors that directly and indirectly affect the growth of family/HH credit loans, including the lack of people who know or understand banking system and service facilities, especially those related to credit, people who are aware of existing credit schemes, and people's real income that affects their consumption patterns. Even though Indonesia is much better off than, say 50 years ago and the poverty rate continues to decline every year, the majority of the population is still from the low-income group. As said before, one of the important targets of implementing financial inclusion is to open full access for households, especially those from low-income or poor groups, to banking services, including loans.

Credit for MSMEs

As in other countries, in Indonesia, MSMEs have an important role because of their potential contribution to improving income distribution, job creation, poverty reduction, industrial development, rural development, and export growth. Their number is very large, slightly more than 99 percent of the total enterprises in the country, and especially MSEs are widespread throughout rural areas and therefore they may have a special "local" meaning for the rural economy. Moreover, the majority of MSEs in Indonesia are mostly agriculture-based activities. Therefore, the government's efforts to support these companies can also be considered as an effort, indirectly, to support the agricultural sector.

According to data from the State Ministry of Cooperatives and SMEs (Menegkop & UKM) and the Central Statistics Agency (BPS), in 1997 there were around 39.765 million MSMEs or about 99.8 percent of the total business entities in Indonesia. The number of MSMEs grows every year, except in 1998, when the 1997-98 Asian financial crisis hit Indonesia. The crisis caused the rupiah exchange rate (IDR) to depreciate more than 200 percent against the United States dollar (USD). As a result, many domestic companies went out of business or were forced to reduce their production volumes for various reasons, such as the high cost of foreign debt (payment of debt plus interest) in rupiah; high domestic inflation; high interest rates on the domestic money market which, together with many domestic banks experiencing financial difficulties due to bad loans and losses in USD trading, made it difficult for businesses to obtain credit; and high prices for imported raw materials and other production inputs in rupiah.

This crisis caused the national economy to experience the largest recession in Indonesian history since independence in 1945 (or even during the Dutch colonial period), with a negative GDP growth rate of 13 percent. At that time, the number of MSMEs had dropped to around 36.8 million units or had declined by 7.42 percent. Menegkop & UKM estimated that almost 3 million MSEs have stopped doing business, and the number of medium and large businesses that have closed their businesses was estimated to be around 14.2 and 12.7 percent of the total units from each of these groups (Tambunan, 2019). However, in 1999 when the national economy began to recover, the number of MSMEs began to grow again to 37.9 million units, or an increase of 2.98 percent, and from there it continued to grow

As shown in Table 3, in 2016 the number of MSMEs was recorded at almost 61.7 million companies or around 99 percent of the total business units in Indonesia that year. In 2018, the number increased to more than 64 million. Of this number, MSEs dominate, reaching almost 99 percent, while medium-sized enterprises are less than 0.1 percent. So, when someone talks about Indonesian MSMEs, he or she actually means MSMEs.

Table 3. Number of MSMEs and Their Workers by Sub-category in Indonesia, 2016-2018

Description	unit of measure	2016		2018	
		Total	Share (%)	Total	Share (%)
MSMEs LEs	Unit	61,651,177 5,370	99.99 0.01	64,194,057 5,550	99.99 0.01
Total companies		61,656,547	100.00	64,199,607	100,00
MSMEs LEs	People	112,828,610 3,444,746	97.04 2.96	116,978,631 3.619,507	97.00 3.00
Total workers		116,273,356	100.00	120,598.138	100.00

Source: Menegkop & UKM (http://www.depkop.go.id/)

In general, the role of MSMEs in the formation of GDP is always smaller than their role as creators of job opportunities: more than 90 percent of the total workforce absorbed in the economy works in MSMEs, but their contribution of output to GDP is far below 90 percent. As can be seen in Figure 2, MSMEs contributed more than 50 percent of Indonesia's GDP, which is larger than the GDP share of LEs. However, considering that the number of MSMEs is always far more than the number of LEs, the real contribution of MSMEs to the country's GDP is in fact much smaller than LEs. Within the MSME group, there are differences: the total contribution of MSEs to GDP is smaller than that of medium enterprises, and the contribution of this last sub-group to GDP is smaller than that of LEs.

Figure 2. Share of GDP by Business Size in Indonesia, 2016-2018 (constant 2000 prices; %)
Source: Menegkop & UKM and BPS

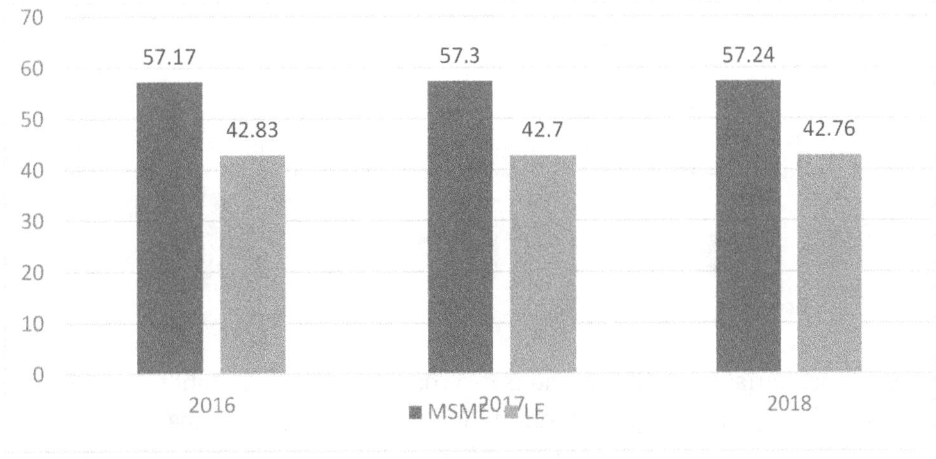

As also evident in many other countries, especially in the developing world, the development and growth of MSMEs in Indonesia, particularly MSEs, are hindered by many obstacles. These constraints (and their intensity) may differ by region within the country or between rural and urban areas, or between sectors, or even between companies in the same sector. However, there are some problems that are common to all MSMEs in any country, especially in the developing countries group. These general barriers include limited working capital and investment; difficulties in marketing, distribution and procurement of raw materials and other inputs; limited access to information about market opportunities and others; limited skilled manpower (low quality human resources) and technological capabilities; high transportation and energy costs; lack of networks; high costs due to complicated administrative and bureaucratic procedures, especially in obtaining business licenses; and uncertainty due to unclear or uncertain economic regulations and policies.

Data from the 2017 National Survey of MSEs in manufacturing Industry shows that the main problems faced by most of them were limited capital and marketing difficulties (Figure 3). Although at that time there were many special credit schemes for small entrepreneurs (many schemes still exist today), the majority of respondents, especially those in rural areas, said that they had never received credit from banks or other financial institutions. So, to finance their business activities, they depend entirely on their own money/savings, financial assistance from relatives or loans from informal moneylenders. There were many reasons given by respondents who have never dealt with a bank for loan. For example, some of them said they had never heard of or knew of any special credit schemes that they could actually take advantage of; some tried to apply but were rejected because their business was deemed unfit for funding; some withdrew because of complicated administrative procedures or simply because they could not meet the requirements including the provision of guarantees such as house or land certificates. However, there are also many respondents who do not want to borrow from formal financial institutions because they feel uncomfortable or afraid that one day they will not be able to repay their debts (BPS, 2018).

Figure 3. Types of MSEs Constraints in the Manufacturing Industry, 2017
Source: BPS (2018)

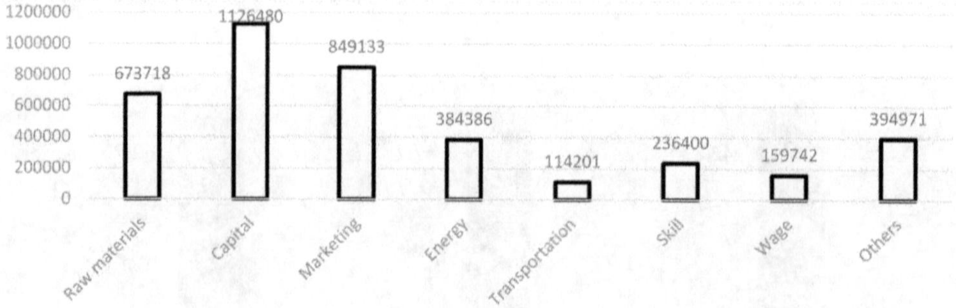

However, there are variations between industry groups as shown in Table 4 due to many causes, either directly or indirectly, including the level of difficulty/complexity in the production process; the nature, extent and/or structure of the market served; availability or price of raw materials and energy; infrastructure; and the availability of workers with the required skills; all of which are closely related to the type of goods made.

Table 4 Number of MSEs in the Manufacturing Industry by Type of Constraint and Industry Group in Indonesia, 2017

Industry*	Number of enterprises	Facing constraints	Constraints**							
			1	2	3	4	5	6	7	Others
10	1538117	979931	232395	374542	271462	131385	47665	50556	42205	138741
11	134266	83499	14544	17919	39011	8252	6330	4359	2833	10022
12	185494	126521	8731	50295	17096	12268	1896	11493	15866	60196
13	283266	174014	40498	82281	45449	28924	4807	16767	10324	10270
14	554003	338549	45517	157767	83935	34207	4628	41198	22465	42399
15	76273	53856	5946	26715	15485	5449	481	4551	2995	4143
16	608342	401956	148467	120042	130065	54594	11244	37853	20157	43453
17	6642	3510	1140	640	1049	237	26	413	365	571
18	44872	31542	3052	12428	12764	3740	796	2788	1010	3327
20	38801	33000	14363	12427	5045	2437	5352	5471	6690	6696
21	16044	12314	3008	1782	5271	1079	2125	2383	53	1900
22	30066	19845	3768	8276	5783	1474	731	1795	473	3099
23	325233	250092	52635	102612	77904	41821	12715	10202	11220	39094
24	9375	8049	6094	1121	2072	805	1014	791	140	568
25	184455	140266	21145	64903	42787	18178	5824	13800	8816	11224
26	1305	954	-	324	518	92	2	56	6	81
27	1331	1121	287	382	486	139	-	7	3	18
28	2266	1201	321	402	361	113	4	163	3	5
29	2081	1475	115	770	481	202	-	70	25	125
30	10969	9059	1830	4633	2442	2994	243	338	259	930
31	180565	147860	32701	58606	56219	25752	6415	14703	10155	9273
32	224226	108510	35697	26319	31204	9966	1234	15832	3300	8458
33	6736	4870	1464	1294	2244	278	669	811	379	378
Total	4464688	2931994	673718	1126480	849133	384386	114201	236400	159742	394971

Notes: * industry group: 10: food, 11: beverages, 12: tobacco processing, 13: textiles, 14: apparel, 15: leather, leather goods and footwear, 16: wood, wood products and cork (excluding furniture), woven articles from rattan, bamboo and the like, 17: paper and paper articles, 18: printing and reproduction of recorded media, 20: chemicals and articles of chemical substances, 21: pharmaceuticals, chemical medicinal products and traditional medicine, 22: rubber, articles of rubber and plastics, 23: non-metal minerals, 24: base metals, 25: non-machined metal goods and their equipment, 26: computers, electronic and optical goods, 27: electrical equipment, 28: YTDL machinery and equipment (excluding others), 29: motor vehicles, trailers and semi-trailers, 30: other means of transportation, 31: furniture; 32: other processing; 33: repair and installation of machinery and equipment.

** types of constraints: 1 = raw material; 2 = marketing; 3 = capital; 4 = energy; 5 transportation; 6 = skill; 7 = labor wages; 8 = others.

Source: BPS (2018)

MSME access to formal financial institutions can be a good indicator of financial inclusion because they are often excluded from formal financial sources. Figure 3 shows that in Indonesia most MSMEs, especially MSEs, do not have access to banks and other financial institutions for several reasons such as no collateral, MSE owners do not have knowledge of bank procedures, procedures are too complicated, high interest rates, or the application was rejected (Tambunan, 2011).

Indeed, a review of the literature on MSMEs in Indonesia and many other developing countries shows two things: (i) among MSMEs, MSEs are more likely to face credit constraints from formal sources than medium-sized enterprises. From the banking side, the important factors that influence their decision to lend money to these companies are competitiveness, legal framework, credit policies and the lack of information about MSE borrowers, characteristics and size of the company. From the side of MSE borrowers, they do not have financial records and valuable assets for collateral, their proposals are rejected, their type of business is considered unpromising, and they run their business in a traditional way, not well organized, and bad managed. Therefore, MSEs rely more on their savings or credit from informal sources; and (ii) most MSEs financial constraints are the main barriers to growth or even to sustain (e.g. Rahaman, 2011; ADB, 2015; Ayyagari et al., 2016; Jinjarak and Wignaraja, 2016; Kumar, 2017; Tambunan, 2009, 2018; IFC, 2017; Nguyen, 2017; Esho and Verhoef, 2018; and Choudhury and Goswami, 2019).

Based on the latest data from Bank Indonesia, as of April 2021, the total outstanding MSME loans was 1,023.0 trillion Rupiah (IDN) or only about 18.8 percent of the total credit for business (investment and working capital) and consumption credit recorded at 5,447.5 trillion rupiah. Looking at previous years, lending to MSMEs in Indonesia has indeed increased every year, although the level of credit received by companies and the rate of credit growth varied by sector. The largest number of MSME loans was found in the trade sector and the manufacturing industry, because these two are key sectors for MSMEs. However, in terms of the percentage of total credit, the average rate was below 30 percent per annum and much lower than the percentage of credits received by LEs.

In the MSME sector, MSEs are the smallest credit recipients from formal financial institutions compared to their larger counterparts, medium enterprises (Figure 4). Therefore, MSEs are the main target of government policies related to MSME funding. The government also really hope that the presence of FinTech, especially peer-to-peer (P2P) lenders, can be an alternative financing not only for MSEs but also for the middle class because many of these last two groups. also have difficulty getting credit from ban

Figure 4. Outstanding Credits of MSMEs by Subgroup, April 2021 (IDR trillion)
Notes: MIEs = microenterprises; SEs = small enterprises; MEs = medium enterprises
Source: Bank Indonesia (https://www.bi.go.id/id/statistik/ekonomi-keuangan/seki/Default.aspx)

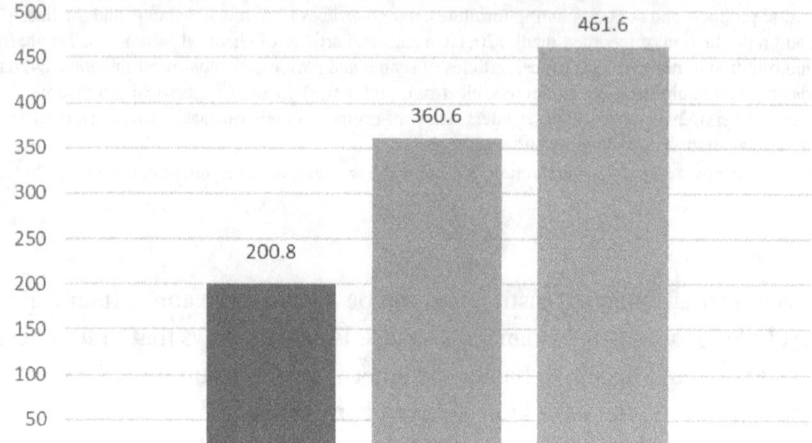

So far, the above evidence may indicate that more serious efforts are still needed for Indonesia to achieve 100 percent financial inclusion. According to a 2019 survey by the Financial Services Authority (OJK), Indonesia's financial inclusion rate stood at 76.1 percent, marking an increase of about 40 million unbanked adults from 2017, when the figure was nearly 50 percent. To address these challenges, during a survey 45 percent of FinTech companies in Indonesia said that they cooperate with traditional financial institutions such as banks and 23 percent take part in government strategic partnerships (The Jakarta Post, 2020). Indeed, the Indonesian government hopes that this strategic partnership will increase collaboration between FinTech companies and banks and other formal financial institutions which will ultimately lead to full financial inclusion.

Financial Technology: P2P Lending

The Role

As seen earlier, the portion of bank credit received by MSMEs is still small. Therefore, the existence of FinTech companies that are growing rapidly in Indonesia since the last few years is highly expected, because this new way of financing through online is considered to be a good alternative source of funding for MSMEs, especially MSEs. FinTech is an innovation in the financial services industry that utilizes technology. Among many FinTech-based products, P2P lending is the most important for MSEs. It provides an online marketplace suitable for investors, which can be individuals, multi-finance companies or even banks, who wish to invest and MSEs who wish to borrow. Thus, given the failure of many banks to provide adequate loans to MSMEs, the emergence of P2P lending offers significant opportunities (Tambunan et al, 2021).

The rapid growth of FinTech in many countries has led to many journal articles, seminar papers and reports on this new phenomenon, including, to mention some, Bruton et al. (2015), Government Office for Science (2015), Lin and Viswanathan (2015), Haddad and Hornuf (2016), BIS and FSB (2017), Yakoboski et al. (2018), Morgan and Trinh. (2019), and Oh and Rosenkran (2020). Overall, the literature reviewed shows that the development of fintech has accelerated in recent years in many countries, including Indonesia. Although it has not been proven yet worldwide, as a theoretical proposition, P2P lending companies offer a great opportunity for MSMEs to have better access to funding. This theoretical proposition is based on two assumptions. First, without discounting other factors, MSMEs' access to P2P loans should be a strong determinant of their growth. Second, the flow of funds from investors to P2P lending companies should be uninterrupted. and MSMEs have access to the internet or Wi-fi.

In Indonesia, information or empirical evidence on the actual impact of the growth of P2P lending on MSMEs and how these companies operate is still very limited. The studies available in Indonesia so far include field survey-based research conducted by Pranata (2019). It focuses on the role of digital payments (not specifically P2P loans) in accelerating the development of MSMEs in Indonesia by using evidence from some villages in two provinces, i.e. Nusa Tenggara Barat (NTB) and Bali. The paper concludes that fintech can be inclusive and beneficial to MSMEs. Based on their observations in 62 countries, including Indonesia, Oh and

Rosenkranz (2020) also concluded that P2P lending has the potential not only to promote financial inclusion in general but also to benefit MSMEs in particular by providing them better access to credit. But they also do not have data on P2P loans to MSMEs in their observed countries. The most recent is from Tambunan et al. (2021) and their findings based on exploratory research show that with the presence of

P2P lending companies, the number of MSMEs, especially MSEs in Indonesia, including those in rural areas (of course, villages with internet or Wi-fi access) to obtain funds from formal sources will increase.

Development of P2P Lending in Indonesia

In Indonesia, the existence of FinTech companies is regulated by the government or Financial Services Authority (OJK) through two regulations, namely Regulation No. 77, 2016 Concerning Loan Service to Loan Money Based on Information Technology, and Regulation No. 13, 2018 Concerning Digital Financial Innovations in the Financial Services Sector. All fintech companies must be registered and licensed by OJK. Unregistered FinTech companies are considered illegal (Tambunan et al., 2021).

Based on the most recent data as on 31th August 2020, there are 157 registered P2P lending companies, which consist of 146 conventional and 11 Syariah (OJK, 2020). Of this total, 148 companies are located in the great Jakarta, and the rest in other cities in Java; only three companies are in outside Java, i.e. 1 Lampung (West Sumatera), 1 Makassar (South Sulawesi), and 1 Badung (Bali). Regarding status, 102 companies are local and 55 are with foreign capital. Many of them have borrowers from outside Java. From this total, only 33 companies have been licensed while the rest are only registered. Even though they do not have permission yet, as long as they are already registered, they are allowed by the OJK to operate. But after operating for a year, they must apply for permission.

Based on its main activity, there are three (3) types of FinTech companies in Indonesia, namely P2P lending, credit scoring, and aggregator, and among these, P2P lending is the most popular one. P2P lending companies can be a legal entity or cooperative that have a system to implement the mechanism of lending and borrowing transactions online, either through applications or web pages. So, they act as intermediaries who bring together lenders and borrowers. Lenders and the loan recipients must first register and fill in personal data required before they can apply for a loan or loan application. P2P lending companies in Indonesia have various types of financing, which include invoice financing, supply chain financing, merchant financing, micro-financing, property financing, house renovation financing, and bailouts for rent. Financing targets of FinTech lending companies also vary from financing MSMEs, financial inclusion, village development/improvement, and women empowerment (Tambunan et al., 2021).

With the emergence of FinTech, particularly P2P lending, Indonesia's MSME funding ecosystem has changed. As illustrated by Figure 5, the financial service providers in the country can be grouped into two categories, namely banks and non-banks. The bank category can be divided further into two sub-categories, namely rural banks (i.e. BPR) and commercial banks. Then, each sub-category can be distinguished between Islamic or Syariah banks and conventional banks. A Syariah bank is a banking system based on the principles of Islamic or Syariah law and guided by Islamic economics. On the other hand, non-banks include microfinance institutions, venture capital companies, saving and loan cooperatives, pawnshop, and now also P2P lending companies.

Next, the development of FinTech lending in a country or in this case Indonesia can be illustrated by the growth in the following four indicators, namely the number of P2P companies, P2P loan outstanding or distribution, the number of P2P borrowers, and the number of P2P lenders. From Table 5, it reveals that per August 2020 total accumulation of national lending of P2P lending companies since their establishment recorded at IDR 121.87 trillion or increased 122.74 per cent on *year-on-year* (*yoy*) based; accumulation of national borrowers reached 27,379,996 entities or up 113.37 per cent *yoy*; and accumulation of all (national and foreign) lenders amounted to 669,580 or increased 26.24 per cent *yoy*. Between December 2019 and August 2020 total loan outstanding amounted to 12.13 IDR trillion or up almost 25.3 per cent *yoy*, total national new loan disbursement was 40.37 IDR trillion or an increase of 25.97 per cent *yoy*, and total active borrowers increased around 72.4 per cent *yoy* to 9.53 million entities.

Figure 5. The MSME Funding Ecosystem in Indonesia

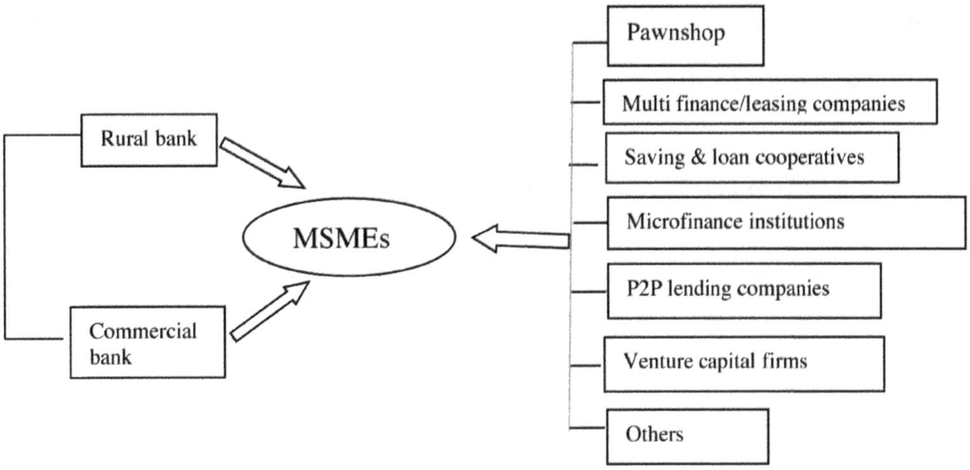

Table 5 Development of FinTech Lending in Indonesia, 2018-2020

Description	Dec.2018	Dec.2019	Aug.2020
Accumulation of lending (IDR trillion):* Java Outside Java	19.62 (707.56% *yoy*) 3.05 (705.82% *yoy*)	69.82 (255.93% *yoy*) 11.67 (282.93% *yoy*)	104.53 (122.55% *yoy*) 17.34 (123.87% *yoy*)
Borrower account accumulation (entity):* Java Outside Java	3,664,645 (1,444.19% *yoy*) 694,803 (3,011.47% *yoy*)	15,397,251 (320.16% *yoy*) 3,171.872 (356.51% *yoy*)	22,391,924 (110.42% *yoy*) 4,988,072 (127.70% *yoy*)
Lender account accumulation (entity):* Java Outside Java Outside Indonesia	155,230 (104.87% *yoy*) 50,281 (109.26% *yoy*) 1,996 (74.63% *yoy*)	500,030 (222.12% *yoy*) 102,149 (103.16% *yoy*) 3,756 (88.18% *yoy*)	549.088 (24.37% *yoy*) 116,594 (36.32% *yoy*) 3,898 (16.39% *yoy*)
Loan outstanding (IDR trillion): Java Outside Java		11.31 1.85	10.22 (22.11% *yoy*) 1.91 (45/41% *yoy*)
Loan distribution (IDR trillion): ** Java Outside Java		50.21 (188.01% yoy) 8.63 (223.01% yoy)	34.71 (26.90% yoy) 5.66 (20.59% yoy)

Notes: * total accumulation of all fintech lending companies since their establishment; ** total accumulation of all fintech lending companies since the beginning of the year period up to the last reporting month period (i.e. August 2020).

Source: OJK (2020)

Further, Table 6 shows that per 31 August 2020 there were more borrowers than loans providers or lenders which may suggest that the P2P lending market in Indonesia was experiencing excess demand, at least in that particular period. This may give a sign that the prospect for FinTech lending development in Indonesia in the near future is very bright. The majority of P2P loans borrowers (i.e. 82.10%) are in Java, i.e. the most densely populated island in the country. This distribution of active borrowers by region is also consistent with the fact that Java is the center of economic activities in Indonesia and, compared to other regions, Java has the largest contribution to the country's GDP. The majority of MSMEs in Indonesia are also found in Java.

Table 6. P2P Borrowers and Lenders in Indonesia, 31 August 2020

Description	Borrower	Lender
Account (people)	27,379,996	669,580
Male (%)	50.58	62.79
Female (%)	49.28	36.88
Business entity (%)	0.14	0.33

Source: OJK (2020)

By gender, slightly above 50 per cent of total borrowers were male, and in the lender side the percentage was much larger. Among other possible explanation factors, this gender division may reflect the fact that in general women in Indonesia still face a number of constraints (e.g. culture, traditions, wife's position in the household, and courage) in conducting financial transactions, both as borrowers and lenders, independently.

From total borrowers, only a very small percentage of them were business entities, and in the lender side the ratio was more than double. This means that from the borrower side, the existence of P2P lending companies is used more by households or individuals than by companies. Meanwhile from the lender side, the role of companies and banks as lenders or investors in P2P lending companies is still very minimal.

Finally, Table 7 shows the importance of P2P lending by province in Indonesia. As can be seen, loan outstanding, lending accumulation, new loans and number of borrower and lender accounts and the growth rate (*yoy*) of each vary by province. To certain extent, this may reflect differences in the level of economic development, local market size, and the presence of information and communication technology (e.g. internet, Wi-Fi) between the provinces. One interesting fact from this Table 7 is that although P2P lending activities are concentrated in Java with the largest amount of loan outstanding and by itself also the largest amount of national lending accumulation, new loan distribution as well as number of borrower and lender accounts are recorded in DKI Jakarta and the province of West Java, many regions outside Java such as West Sulawesi, Southeast Sulawesi, West Nusa Tenggara, and Lampung have higher growth rates than in Java.

Table 7. Loan Outstanding, National Lending Accumulation by Province

Province	LO		ANL		NNL		ANBA		ANLE	
	IDR bill,	▲%	IDR bill.	▲%	IDR bill	▲%	Entities	▲%	Entities	▲%
Aceh	49.33	60.89	390.02	145.82	140.40	32.02	132,149	137.76	4,190	31.14
North Sumatera	283.40	36.16	2,585.70	135.24	899.02	22.74	769,557	126.72	20,946	33.49
West Sumatera	99.53	55.08	795.70	120.62	260.77	2.16	263,361	88.57	4,598	41.22
Riau	110.55	70.12	1,011.18	131.69	342.49	26.,43	281,630	136.50	7,013	37.92
Jambi	44.27	2.71	557.03	80.29	143.13	9.33	147,673	127.37	3,446	34.66
South Sumatera	178.71	55.68	1,587.46	131.85	566.66	54.78	478,883	129.92	9,082	36.33
Bengkulu	21.26	35.19	237.56	91.55	64.81	-15.81	67,447	134.86	1,473	32.46
Lampung	153.50	120.79	1,115.06	126.98	396.02	47.49	360,503	158.65	6,297	49.54
Bangka Belitung	21.38	16.11	179.57	153.91	67.49	60.88	52,143	167.18	1,995	31.08
Kep. Riau	48.63	1.78	661.78	130.38	207.20	14.98	185,410	131.28	5,108	36.83
DKI Jakarta	3,678.70	21.18	37,334.85	112.08	12,249.96	28.83	6,186,226	98.79	294,973	17.55
West Java	3,051.41	25.83	33,209.80	132.55	11,157.67	27.57	8,000,718	114.91	108,576	33.15
Central Java	875.80	30.50	8,228.08	139.21	2,933.42	35.41	2,261,371	139.62	42,672	33.15
DI Yogyakarta	108.60	-65.09	1,300.35	109.72	390.94	21.77	351,791	121.86	11,440	24.85
East Java	1,353.69	25.17	13,141.22	118.62	4,521.63	15.52	3,182.096	108.76	53,883	33.87
Banten	1,152.38	36.36	11,320.62	124.68	3,727.78	27.18	2,409,722	104.16	37,544	36.21
Bali	114.80	15.78	1,548.45	89.69	403.19	1.90	318,074	113.27	8,620	35.08
West Nusa Tenggara	85.11	94.82	566.69	146.06	200.70	24.76	107,175	132.62	2,776	27.87
East Nusa Tenggara	16.64	17.69	162.03	150.14	56.36	28.45	53,799	170.93	1,897	28.52
West Kalimantan	48.06	29.57	489.84	131.42	160.92	12.40	156,999	136.23	5,137	36.73
Central Kalimantan	42.70	71.22	296.17	150.83	99.41	20.74	91,173	152.25	2,386	31.90
South Kalimantan	53.07	1.72	592.87	122.03	181.68	2.35	188,528	132.21	4,238	40.38
East Kalimantan	92.91	16.28	1,107.08	106.37	326.29	0.77	298,876	122.82	6,430	40.03
North Kalimantan	4.81	-30.52	84.59	117.69	23.94	-2.09	26,084	115.89	647	26.86
North Sulawesi	74.77	23.49	862.65	94.90	207.22	-23.62	273,066	67.97	3,318	31.20
Central Sulawesi	47.99	273.50	228.98	254.32	113.72	157.10	74,537	238.64	1,456	37.49
South Sulawesi	203.45	64.44	1,454.11	134.72	496.68	29.05	405,251	140.65	8,072	33.29
Southeast Sulawesi	45.55	190.65	223.17	224.25	96.26	96.07	68,317	200.84	1,560	29.25
Gorontalo	24.29	52.73	160.24	121.25	48.66	-3.68	54,622	124.87	870	28.32
West Sulawesi	17.11	123.48	79.07	258.33	42.39	182.00	25,752	248.47	640	22.37
Maluku	8.70	-59.69	100.87	148.93	32.83	21.15	30,973	160.72	806	25.55
North Maluku	3.99	-48.59	55.63	145.43	17.98	19.77	17,827	147.32	715	16.67
West Papua	8.36	19.18	72.66	149.35	25.99	23.06	22,244	164.75	1,392	176.19
Papua	9.69	33.23	129.98	131.11	39.99	11.86	36,019	125.47	1,486	33.51

Notes: LO = loan outstanding; ANL= accumulation of national lending; NNL= national new loan; ANBA = accumulated number of borrower account; ANLE = accumulated number of lender account

Source: OJK (2020).

Case Study

In exploring the role of P2P lending in financing MSMEs, the key question was: how important is FinTech -based P2P lending for the enterprises? To find out, the Center for Industry, SME and Business Competition Studies Universitas Trisakti in Jakarta, with the financial support from the Indonesia Financial Services Authority (OJK) has carried out an exploration research with a small survey in 2019 by using a semi-structured questionnaire (Tambunan et al., 2021). The survey has two groups of respondents, namely owners of MSEs who (ever) received P2P loans, and managers/heads of registered P2P lending companies. In the sample, there were 30 P2P lending companies randomly selected from the list of registered P2P lending companies from the OJK. Unfortunately, most of these surveyed 30 companies were reluctant to give information about their MSME customers for various reasons. So, for the survey, it only managed to get 50 MSEs from some companies. Of these 50 MSEs only 30 filled out the questionnaire, but only 10 of them were deemed usable. The majority of the surveyed MSEs were not very open in providing information. Especially regarding their financial figures such as income or revenue and the amount of P2P credit received.

These 10 MSEs are from different types of businesses such as small shop owners who sell various kinds of cell phones, cat food, toys for children, and camping equipment, producers who make shoes and furniture; and laundry business owners. In terms of sources of capital, although they also use their own money or borrow money from their suppliers or other informal sources, they also rely on loans from formal sources including fintech-based P2P lending. What is interesting from this sample is that some of them have also previously received loans from microfinance institutions (MFI) or a government specially designed credit scheme with very low interest rates for MSEs, called People Business Credit (or KUR). Most of them have never borrowed from the bank because they do not have collateral assets.

Concerning the 30 fintech-based P2P lending companies surveyed, they are all located in Jakarta. But some of them also have customers in many areas outside Jakarta, some even fund MSEs in West Nusa Tenggara and South Sulawesi. As shown in Table 4, types of financing of the sampled companies vary from invoice financing, supply chain financing, merchant financing, micro-financing, to seller financing. The main financing target of most respondents is MSEs with legal status. Some of them also provide loans for women empowerment, education, individual customers, and multifunction. Many of the surveyed companies have more than one type of financing, whereas some others focus only on financing MSMEs.

The above question, "is the presence of P2P lending benefit MSEs", should be answered from two different perspectives, namely from the perspective of MSE owners who have received P2P loans, and the perspective of P2P lending companies themselves. From the MSEs' perspective, findings from indepth-interviews with the ten respondents show that although they received loans from P2P lending, and some others also (ever) received from other sources such as KUR and MFI, their own money still plays an important role in financing their businesses. They all considered loans from P2P lending only as an additional fund when their own money, or loans from MFI are not enough to cover their expenditures. Based on interviews with them, Table 8 describes the comparison between the traditional loan financing market and the P2P lending market.

Table 8. The Traditional Loan Financing Market vs Lending Market

Major Aspect	Traditional Loan Provider	P2P Lending
Interest Rate	Low-Medium	Medium-High
Amount of loan	High	Low
Collateral	Yes	No
Party Involved	Borrower & Bank	Borrower, Lender & Platform
Regulation/Supervision	Strict	Loose
Process	Complex & Long	Simple & Fast
Transaction Cost	High	Low

Source: adopted from Table 5 in Tambunan et al. (2021).

Interestingly, only five of them said that borrowing from P2P lending was beneficial for their business, while the other five said there was no significant change in their business. For the first five people, two respondents said that their business size grew from being very small without employees to a larger one with several employees after borrowing. The other four said that their turnover had increased. However, because they do not have a good financial record (and this is indeed one of the characteristics of MSEs), it is difficult to find evidence to support their claims. At least in theory, the increase in turnover or production that they experienced could be due to fresh funds from P2P lending, although it might not be the only driver, but it could also be because, for example, their selling price became more expensive. competitive due to reduced electricity tariffs or the use of raw materials. cheaper or something. Because the performance of MSMEs is influenced by many factors at once, not only access to funding.

From the perspective of P2P lending companies, some of them only focus on MSE funding, while others also provide loans to individuals for consumption, education, property, women's empowerment, and others. For funds, everything is completely dependent on external investors such as banks, individual investors, multi-finance companies, venture capital companies, state-owned enterprises, and other institutions. However, for most of them, banks have become their main investors, often called 'super lenders', and most work with more than one bank. In fact, for some people, the bank is their only financier.

While in the distribution of funds, there were some companies that went directly to MSEs, and there were also those that channeled their funds through intermediary institutions such as cooperatives, distributors, suppliers, finance companies, and others. As they said, their main reason to use intermediaries was because it was easier or more efficient to reach many potential borrowers. In addition, there was certainty that the loan would be repaid plus interest according to the agreement. In other words, the intermediary agency acts as a guarantor.

Return to the question "how important is fintech-based P2P lending for MSMEs", the findings of this survey of course cannot provide a good answer but only provide an initial picture of the role of P2P lending because the sample is very small, only 10 MSEs. Everyone considered P2P lending very useful. There was, however, no statement from them that said explicitly that they would always borrow from P2P in the future. This means that for them P2P lending may only act as a last resort if they face difficulties in obtaining credit from other formal sources, or if they need funds quickly, or if for example a loan from a bank is not sufficient.

In addition, the 30 P2P lending companies in the sample do not have a record of business performance from the MSMEs they fund. Therefore, future research with a larger sample of P2P funding MSEs across sectors and regions is needed. Critical questions that need to be answered are: are P2P loans more beneficial for MSEs than other sources of credit they have received (if any); in the future when their business grows well and they have assets to use as collateral or when they are already bankable from a bank perspective, do they still consider P2P lending important, and do they use P2P loans for working capital or investment?

CONCLUSION

This chapter is about three related issues, i.e. financial inclusion, development of MSMEs and their access to formal financing, and the importance of FinTech-based P2P lending. With respect to the first issue, by using three indicators to measure the level of financial inclusion, namely access to bank account, credits for households, and credits for MSMEs, it can be concluded that Indonesia still has a long way to go to achieve 100 percent financial inclusion.

Regarding the second issue, considering that they are dominant and have the biggest share in creating job opportunities in the country, MSMEs are indeed very important. However, these enterprises, especially MSEs, face many obstacles, including the lack of access to funding from formal sources, especially commercial banks. Although all banks are required by the government to provide access to credit to MSMEs, as shown in this chapter, the percentage of total loans from banks to this business group, especially MSEs, is still very small. To be successful in implementing financial inclusion, all obstacles for MSEs to obtain credit must be removed, and this should be reflected by the share of MSMEs in total outstanding credit or credit distribution above 50 percent.

Regarding the role of P2P lending companies as an alternative source of funding for MSMEs, this chapter suggests that at least in theory, with the presence of P2P lending, the number of MSMEs, especially MSEs, in Indonesia, including those located in rural areas (of course, villages that have access to the Internet or Wi-fi) to obtain funds from formal sources will increase. Even though aggregate data are not available, the interviews with the ten MSEs may suggest some benefits of P2P loans.

If the finding from the interviews (although only with ten MSEs that received P2P loans) does illustrate the truth that the existence or rapid growth of FinTech or P2P lending in Indonesia in the last decade has benefited MSEs, most of which have limited access. to funding from the bank, it is then clear that the increasing role of P2P lending as an alternative source of finding for MSEs will help the Indonesian government's effort to create financial inclusion, which also means inclusive economic development in Indonesia.

REFERENCES

ADB. (2015). *Asia SME Finance Monitor 2014*. Asian Development Bank.

Ali, I., & Son, H. H. (2007). Measuring inclusive growth. *Asian Development Review*, *24*(1), 11–31.

Ali, I., & Zhuang, J. (2007). *Inclusive Growth Toward a Prosperous Asia: Policy Implications*. Economics and Research Department Working Paper No. 97. Asian Development Bank.

ASEAN. (2015). *Asean Economic Community (AEC)*. Jakarta: ASEAN Secretariat. Available at Error! Hyperlink reference not valid.

Ayyagari, M., Juarros, P., Peria, M., & Singh, S. (2016). *Access to Finance and Job Growth: Firm-Level Evidence across Developing Countries*. World Bank Policy Research Working Paper 7604.

Babajide, A. A., Adegboye, F. B., & Omankhanlen, A. E. (2015). Financial Inclusion and Economic Growth in Nigeria. *International Journal of Economics and Financial Issues*, *5*(3), 629–637. http: www.econjournals.com

BIS & FSB. (2017). *FinTech Credit: Market Structure, Business Models and Financial Stability Implications*. Report prepared by a Working Group established by the Committee on the Global Financial System (Bank for International Settlements) and the Financial Stability Board.

Booth, A., & McCawley, P. (Eds.). (1981). *The Indonesian Economy during the Soeharto Era*. Oxford University Press.

BPS. (2018). *Profil Industri Mikro dan Kecil 2017*. Badan Pusat Statistik.

Bruton, Garry, & Khavul, Siegel, & Write. (2015). New Financial Alternatives. In Seeding Entrepreneurship: Microfinance, Crowdfunding, and Peer To Peer Innovations. *Entrepreneurship Theory and Practice*, *39*(1), 9–26.

Choudhury, M., & Goswami, C. (2019). MSME Financing Gaps – Review of Literature for the Period 2005 To 2016. *Journal of Small Business and Entrepreneurship Development*, *7*(2), 50–60. doi:10.15640/jsbed.v7n2a5

Demirgüç-Kunt, A., Klapper, L., Singer, D., Ansar, S., & Hess, J. (2018), The Global Findex Database 2017. International Bank for Reconstruction and Development.

Esho, E., & Verhoef, G. (2018). *The Funding Gap and the Financing of Small and Medium Businesses: An Integrated Literature Review and an Agenda*. MPRA Paper No. 90153. University of Johannesburg. Available at: https://mpra.ub.uni muenchen.de/90153/MPRAPaperNo.90153

Government Office for Science. (2015). *Fintech futures: the UK as a world leader in financial technologies*. https://www.gov.uk/government/uploads/system/uploads/attachment_data/ file/413095/gs-15-3-fintech-futures

Hadad, M. D. (2010). *Developing a Financial Inclusion Strategy: The Case of Indonesia*. Presentation for the *2010 AFI Global Policy Forum*, Bali.

Haddad, C., & Hornuf, L. (2016). *The Emergence of the Global Fintech Market: Economic and Technological Determinants*. Available at: https://www.researchgate.net/publication/307957382

Hill, H. (Ed.). (1994). *Indonesia's New Order: The Dynamics of Socio-economic Transformation*. Allen & Unwin.

IFC. (2017). *MSME Finance Gap*. International Finance Corporation. Available at: https://www.smefinanceforum.org/sites/default/files/Data%20Sites%20downloads/MSME%20Report.pdf

Jinjarak, Y., & Wignaraja, G. (2016). An Empirical Assessment of the Export—Financial Constraint Relationship: How Different are Small and Medium Enterprises? *World Development*, *79*, 152–163. doi:10.1016/j.worlddev.2015.11.012

Joseph, S. (2019). *The Opportunity for Fintech in Indonesia's SME Financing Gap*. Technology. Available at https://www.brinknews.com/19646/

Krugman, P. (1994). The Myth of Asia's Miracle. *Foreign Affairs*, *73*(November-December), 62–78. doi:10.2307/20046929

Kumar, R. (2017). *Targeted SME Financing and Employment Effects: What Do We Know and What Can We Do Differently?* Jobs Working Paper No.3. Washington, DC: World Bank.

Lin, M., & Viswanathan, S. (2015). Home bias in online investments: An empirical study of an online crowdfunding market. *Management Science*, *62*(5), 1393–1414. doi:10.1287/mnsc.2015.2206

Morgan, P. J., & Trinh, L. Q. (2019). *Fintech and Financial Literacy in the LAO PDR*. ADBI Working Paper Series No.933. Asian Development Bank Institute.

Nguyen, T. A. N. (2017). Financing Constraints on SMEs in Emerging Markets: Does Financial Literacy Matter? *Review of Socio-Economic Perspectives*, *2*(2), 53–65.

Nurohman, Y. A., Kusuma, M., & Narulitasari, D. (2021). Fintech, Financial Inclusion, and Sustainability: A Quantitative Approach of Muslims SMEs. *International Journal of Islamic Business Ethics*, *6*(1), 54–67. doi:10.30659/ijibe.6.1.54-67

OECD. (2010). *The G-20 Toronto Summit Declaration June 26 – 27, 2010*. Toronto: G20.

Oh, E. Y., & Rosenkranz, P. (2020). *Determinants of Peer-to-Peer Lending Expansion: The Roles of Financial Development and Financial Literacy*. ADB Economics Working Paper Series, No.613. Manila: Asian Development Bank.

OJK. (2020). *Perkembangan Fintech Lending [Development of fintech lending]. Department Pengawasan IKNB 2A*. Otoritas Jasa Keuangan.

Pranata, N. (2019). The Role of Digital Payments Fintech in Accelerating the Development of MSMEs in Indonesia. In N. Nemoto & N. Yoshino (Eds.), *Fintech for Asian SMEs*. Asian Development Bank Institute.

Pukuh, N., & Widyasthika, H. F. (2017). When Growth is Inclusive in Indonesia? *Jurnal Perencanaan Pembangunan: The Indonesian Journal of Development Planning*, *1*(3), 195–209. doi:10.36574/jpp.v1i3.19

Rahaman, M. M. (2011). Access to Financing and Firm Growth. *Journal of Banking & Finance*, *35*(3), 709–723. doi:10.1016/j.jbankfin.2010.09.005

Rauniyar, G., & Kanbur, R. (2010). Inclusive growth and inclusive development: A review and synthesis of Asian Development Bank literature. *Journal of the Asia Pacific Economy*, *15*(4), 455–469. doi:10.1080/13547860.2010.517680

Sachs, I. (2004). *Inclusive Development Strategy in an Era of Globalization*. Working Paper No. 35, Policy Integration Department, World Commission on the Social Dimension of Globalization. Geneva: International Labour Office.

Sen, A. (1999). *Development as Freedom*. Knopf.

Shofawati, A. (2019). The Role of Digital Finance to Strengthen Financial Inclusion and the Growth of SME in Indonesia. *The 2nd International Conference on Islamic Economics, Business, and Philanthropy (ICIEBP)*, 389–407. Available at https://www.researchgate.net/publication/332196655_The_Role_of_Digital_Finance_to_Strengthen_Financial_Inclusion_and_the_Growth_of_SME_in_Indonesia

Tambunan, T. T. H. (2009). *SME in Asian Developing Countries*. Palgrave Macmillan Publisher. doi:10.1057/9780230250949

Tambunan, T. T. H. (2011). *Overview of Financial Framework for Supporting MSMEs in Indonesia*. Presentation for The Third Country Training Programme on Micro Finance for African Region: Managing Micro Finance Institution, the Non-Aligned Movement Centre for South-South Technical Cooperation (NAM CSSTC) and the Japan International Cooperation Agency (JICA). Jakarta: NAM Centre Building.

Tambunan, T. T. H. (2015). Financial Inclusion, Financial Education, and Financial Regulation: A Story from Indonesia. *ADBI Working Paper 535*. Asian Development Bank Institute. doi:10.2139srn.2641734

Tambunan, T. T. H. (2018). MSMEs and Access to Financing in a Developing Economy: The Indonesian Experience. In A. Woldie & B. Thomas (Eds.), *Financial Entrepreneurship for Economic Growth in Emerging Nations*. IGI Global. doi:10.4018/978-1-5225-2700-8.ch008

Tambunan, T. T. H. (2019). The impact of the economic crisis on micro, small, and medium enterprises and their crisis mitigation measures in Southeast Asia with reference to Indonesia. *Asia & the Pacific Policy Studies*, *6*(1), 1–21. doi:10.1002/app5.264

Tambunan, T. T. H., Santoso, W., Busneti, I., & Batunanggar, S. (2021). The Development of MSMEs and the Growth of Peer-to-Peer (P2P) Lending in Indonesia. *International Journal of Innovation, Creativity and Change, 15*(2), 585–611.

The Jakarta Post. (2020). *Fintech's role in financial inclusion rises but infrastructure, literacy challenges loom*. Business. Available at: https://www.thejakartapost.com/news/2020/09/24/fintechs-role-in-financial-inclusion-rises-but-infrastructure-literacy-challenges-loom.html

Wardhani, N. K. (2020). *How fintech can help Indonesia's small and medium enterprises survive the COVID-19 pandemic*. The University of Queensland. Available at https://research.uq.edu.au/article/2020/11/how-fintech-can-help-indonesia%E2%80%99s-small-and-medium-enterprises-survive-covid-19-pandemic

World Bank. (1993). *The East Asian Miracle: Economic Growth and Public Policy, Summary*. Oxford University Press.

Yakoboski, Hasler, & Lusardi. (2018). *Millennial Financial Literacy and Fin-tech*. Academic Press.

Chapter 6
An Overview of FinTech in Bangladesh:
Problems and Prospects

Sheikh Abu Taher
Jahangirnagar University, Bangladesh

Masatsugu Tsuji
Kobe International University, Japan

ABSTRACT

How the future financial industry is going to be reshaped by technological innovations is now a concern. Financial technology (FinTech), a much-discussed topic around the globe, is changing the overall financial system. The trend is not an exception in developing countries like Bangladesh. In this chapter, the authors aim to explore the current state of FinTech in Bangladesh in light with the possible challenges for growth, opportunities, and future prospects. The growth of FinTech helps a large percentage of people to become banked or has given possible access to formal finance. For having access to finance, high rate of mobile phone penetration, smooth mobile internet access, and high cost of access to formal finance are some factors that have enhanced FinTech penetration in Bangladesh for the past few years. In line with the given prospects, there are problems too. Therefore, using an in-depth study, this research addresses those issues, provides recommendations, and looks for possible solutions for the smooth operation of FinTech in Bangladesh.

INTRODUCTION

The rapid growth of Information and Communication Technology (ICT) has made enormous changes in the business eco system which is now called Industry 4.0. The changes are visible in all sphere of our daily life to solve complex issues. People's financial behavior are rapidly changing because of massive adoption of FinTech (Anshari, Almunawar & Masri, 2020). Machine learning (ML), Internet of Things (IoT), and Big Data that are all to step industry into next level (Clark, 2019). The rapid changes are

DOI: 10.4018/978-1-7998-8447-7.ch006

apparent in the financial sector too. The use of technology in financial sector is not new which started through the invention of the first automated teller machine (ATM) in June, 1967 (Reuters, 2017) and has long history of innovation ((Bátiz-Lazo & Wood, 2002). FinTech is one of the essential parts of these financial innovations to explore information technology (IT), the Internet, gadgets and devices to facilitate cutting edge financial services to all. Technology companies marked FinTech to disseminate formal financial services through online and mobile channels (Arner et al., 2015) and thereby increasing financial inclusion and financial stability in developing countries. This is an umbrella term to explain innovative technology-enabled financial services business models to deliver potential financial benefits to interacting parties (Schueffel, 2016; Zavolokina et al., 2016). FinTech is a technology enabled financial innovation that generates new products and services and ultimate material effect on financial markets and institutions and to the provision of financial services (FSB, 2020). The interaction between finance and technology which explores novel business models (Maier, 2016), or the digitalization of traditional transaction channels (Ferrari, 2016) and customization of financial services through the use of technology (Sia et al., 2016) are evolved as FinTech. It has enabled customers to execute quick payments, investments or to pay insurance premium. The after-hour transactions, or the evolution of peer to peer (P2P) lending through lending club or virtual lending platform are all these functionalities are possible with this.

FinTech firms are often found to be more agile, innovate faster, and radical in their approach to innovation due to the flexibility of legal infrastructure and comparatively low level of organization complexity (Brandl & Hornuf, 2020). While, on the other hand, in traditional system it is difficult for the financial institutions (FIs) to adapt some of the new technology due to immense regulatory requirements. The emergency of FinTech is visible in today's financial sector. The interest in this sector has been rising which is transforming the overall financial system. People can customize financial services and therefore traditional FIs are shifting their role from now to the future finance which revolutionize how customers encounter financial services (Mackenzie, 2015). The growth of FinTech is remarkable and uprising in which it outreached from 16% adoption in 2015 to 33% in 2017 and confirmed to 64% in 2019 and the global consumer awareness reported that at least one money transfer and payment through FinTech reached to 96% (Global FinTech Adoption Index, 2019). The possible reasons for this high growth are recognized as enhanced capabilities, convenient to operate and reduced prices or fees. IMF (2019) classified traditional financial services into five broad segments; such as; payments, savings, borrowings, managing risks and getting financial advice. These services are limited with speed, costs, transparency, access and security and the gaps are filled out through the invention of FinTech. Technological innovations, such as Artificial Intelligence (AI), Machine Learning (ML), cloud computing, Distributed Ledger Technology (DLT), Cryptocurrency and smart phones, intend to solve the gaps of these traditional financial services and transform to digital financial services (Gomber et al., 2017). Therefore, this becomes a promising topic around the globe to be considered for discussions ((Bofondi & Gobbi, 2017; Carney, 2017).

Bangladesh, one of the fastest growing economy in South Asia, has profound and fastest growing financial system in the world. The financial landscape is classified into formal, semi-formal and informal and are legalized by government and automated regulators. During the global financial crisis of 2007-2008, Bangladesh has found significant growth in the financial sector too. While financial crisis was a noticeable for the financial system but rapid changes in the ICT made extensive FinTech growth in the world as well as in Bangladesh. Many financial firms are started new technology to cope with these changes while some are adopting to do that to survive (Taher & Uddin, 2018). Venture Scanner data showed that $165.5 billion invested into FinTech firms in the world over the period from 2010 to

2019 which is considered as the "FinTech Revolution" (Imerman & Fabozzi, 2020). The rising trend of investment in Bangladesh FinTech sector is also apparent. Since the inception of off-branch/bank-led Mobile Financial Services (MFS) model in 2011, the banked population became 21% in 2017 from 3% in 2011 (Demirguc-Kunt et al., 2017). In order to Tracxn data, there are 100 FinTech startups available in Bangladesh until July, 2019 in which bKash lead the market (approax. 70% market share). Among these startups, only few are known to the general people and capable of attracting more customers. The significance of these firms has role to shift payments from cash to digital with cheap, easy accessibility and short-time that has effect on economic opportunity. Vision 2021, inaugurated in 2010, is the key development agenda by Bangladesh government, has pivotal focus on ICT infrastructure development. Therefore, people can easily access to digital technology such as mobile phones which is essential for MFS adoption. As more financial inclusion may be possible through FinTech, it is necessary for the researcher to conduct research in this field.

The current study aims to explore an overview of FinTech in Bangladesh with possible focus on prospects and challenges remain in the sector. As FinTech has grown as a challenge for traditional financial system, such as infrastructure, services and regulation, an in-depth study gives proper understanding of the overall situation. The research is designed as; the next section explains briefly the financial system of Bangladesh, the section three describes the current state of ICT which is essential for FinTech development, section four demonstrates overview of FinTech in Bangladesh, section six explores prospects while section seven explains challenges for FinTech development and the last section ends with conclusion and recommendation.

FINANCIAL SYSTEM

With an aim to develop a more vibrant financial sector, regulators can play significant role. Still, the financial sector of Bangladesh is underdeveloped in comparison with global competition. The sector is mainly categorized into three; such as formal, semi-formal and informal sector, respectively. This classification is done in order to their degree of regulation. The formal sector consists of 59 scheduled and 5 non – scheduled banks, 34 non-bank financial institutions (NBFIs), 62 insurance companies, and 599 micro finance institutions (MFIs) and are regulated by the Bangladesh Bank (BB), Insurance Development & Regulatory Authority, Bangladesh Security and Exchange Commission (BSEC), and Microcredit Regulatory Authority. In comparison with the capital/equity market segment, banking sector is relatively developed and the use of technology is higher (Nguyen, Ali & Islam, 2011). To make the financial sector vibrant requires fair financial services and diversified financial product which is possible through the adequate use of technology, efficient management and proper reforms. Although banking sector lead the overall financial sector, the equity market is relatively small and is still far from efficiency (Bashar, Hassan & Islam, 2007). The use of limited technology, good governance and safety and security are to blame for lower participation of potential investors in stock market in comparison with peer countries. Among 250 brokers of Dhaka Stock Exchange (DSE), only a few offers online trading facilities to investors while 90% of trading orders are completed through traditional way (e.g., in writing or phone call) (The Daily Star, 2020).

ICT SECTOR

In 2010, the national development agenda is inaugurated to achieve key development goals for Bangladesh by the year 2021 which is driven by the Vision 2021. In order to attain these goals, the government has paid notable efforts to develop ICT sector, through the framework of "Digital Bangladesh" comprised with four pillars, such as, 1) digital government for improving public services delivery 2) ICT in business for having good access to ICT for every private business 3) increasing connectivity for every citizen, and, 4) efficient human resource development (UNCTAD, 2019).

ICT plays significant role in developing education, health, business and even welfare of people in emerging countries in South Asia (Abu and Tsuji, 2011) while it has significant role in promoting FinTech too since the various patterns of financial services are delivered via Internet, computers and mobile phones. The use of ICT in banking industry is emerging rapidly to offer efficient and effective services to customers, enhance business process, managerial decision making, workgroup collaborations that help to survive in the heavily competitive industry (The Financial Express, 2016).

In Bangladesh, although the fixed-telephone per 100 population is less than 1%, the mobile phone services have reached to more than 100% level while Grameen Phone Ltd. led the market with 77.59 million subscribers of total of more than 167 million subscribers ((BTRC, 2020 & World Bank, 2019). High speed mobile phone network, such as; third generation (3G) mobile phone is introduced in October, 2012 by the state owned Teletalk. In line with this, three other mobile phone operators launched the 3G services and the country covered with this service to all 64 districts by 2014. This is a milestone for ICT sector in Bangladesh while people now afford to fair communication system for their daily lives from anywhere in the country. Besides, the Internet subscribers reached to more than 111 million mainly because of the mobile Internet alone has 102.48 million subscribers. This helps the marginal people to get access to and to connect with the latest technology and thereby increasing the financial inclusion through mobile financial services (Demirguc-Kunt et al., 2017).

Table 1. Current state of ICT in Bangladesh

Key Indicators	2000	2005	2010	2015	2019
Percentage of Fixed-telephone subscriptions	0.22	0.77	0.87	0.55	0.89
Percentage of population covered by mobile-cellular network		80.00	96.00	99.40	99.60
Percentage of Mobile-telephone subscriptions	0.22	6.47	46.03	84.08	101.55
Fixed broadband subscriptions ('000s)	no data	no data	414.57	4892.94	8085.50
Percentage of mobile-broadband subscriptions	no data	no data	0.03	16.12	52.79

Source: International Telecommunication Union, 2020

FINTECH AT A GLANCE

Financial services in all over the world have gone through a radical change due to the invention of ICT. Technological advancement and customer demand for financial services both evolve as a key factor for FinTech development so that services can be met up to the last mile. The term FinTech, therefore, can be defined as the use of technology in financial eco-system to boost the financial services to meet all customer needs. The use of technology in finance is not new and is categorized into three notable dimensions, such as; FinTech 1.0 (1866 – 1967), FinTech 2.0 (1967 – 2008), and FinTech 3.0 (2008 – present) (Arner, D., 2016). The significant development in the first phase is seen through first transatlantic cable development in 1866, Fedwire in 1918, Diner's Club in 1950, and telex in 1966. In the second phase, however, has many developments too. Among them, the development of first ATM by Barclays and handheld calculator by Texas Instruments in 1967, SWIFT in 1973, mobile phone in 1983 and online banking in 1985 are some pivotal developments in FinTech. In the third stage, launch of smartphones or iPhone in 2007, has sparked FinTech development into the shape now. The growth of smartphone technologies facilitates the MFS which is an extension of digital finance (Lee, I., & Shin, Y. J., 2018). Due to the rising demand for FinTech, a significant number of startup firms come into the market. Few startup firms started their operation during 1999 - 2000 but many of them came into the daylight after 2014. These FinTech startups are classified into 16 categories (Chemmanur et al., 2020) which are demonstrated in table 2. The growth of FinTech startups is skyrocketing too (Graph 1) while in all three region the number of startups has already become doubled in February, 2021 than the year 2018.

Table 2. Startup subcategory

Startup subcategory	
• Banking infrastructure	• Financial transaction security
• Business lending	• Institutional investing
• Consumer and commercial banking	• International money transfer
• Consumer lending	• Payment backend and infrastructure
• Consumer payments	• Personal finance
• Crowdfunding	• Point of sale payments
• Equity financing	• Retail investing
• Financial research and data	• Small and medium business tools

Source: Chemmanur et al., 2020

Figure 1. Number of FinTech startups worldwide
Source: (Statista, 2021)

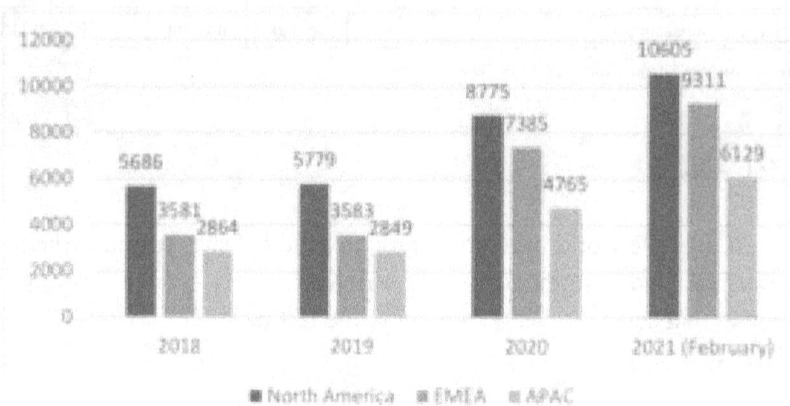

FinTech in Bangladesh

Bangladesh has seen to be one of the fastest growing economies in the world which has achieved developing country status from Least Developed Country (LDC) after 45 years in 2021. With regard to other development agenda, Bangladesh put emphasizes to capacity building of domestic financial institutions and to encourage formal financial access for all through the Vision 2021 agenda (BFIU, 2019). These initiatives led by Bangladesh government and supported by private sector innovations and therefore the country has seen remarkable growth in MFS and digital payment solutions (Country Diagnostic, 2016). The online banking services has seen a rapid growth too while 9,623 (90.81%) bank branches became fully online among 10,597 branches in total in June, 2020 (Table 3).

Table 3. Number of bank branches in Bangladesh offer online services

	Fully online	%	Partially online	%	Offline	%	Total
December'18	8471	82.39%	1189	11.57%	621	6.04%	10281
March'19	8590	83.50%	1125	10.94%	581	5.65%	10288
June'19	8676	84.18%	1050	10.19%	581	5.64%	10307
September'19	8954	86.47%	919	8.87%	482	4.65%	10355
December'19	9337	88.35%	748	7.08%	483	4.57%	10568
March'20	9580	90.45%	530	5.00%	482	4.55%	10592
June'20	9623	90.81%	591	5.58%	383	3.61%	10597

Source: Bangladesh Bank, 2020

Although many banks adopted online services, but opening a bank account remains drawbacks for the marginal population. To solve this issue, FinTech startups companies like bKash, Nagad, SurCash, Rocket, Nexus pay, iPay and other take the surge. These companies help financial solution for all with limited hassle and documental procedures. The services of these companies target to sending and receiving money, payment bills, fares, tuitions, salary disbursements, add money from formal banks or credit cards, donations, purchase tickets or even pay on POS.

Table 4. Current state of Digital Financial Services in Bangladesh

Digital Financial Services	2018	2019	2020
ATM	10280	10924	11206
POS	48228	58527	66297
CDM	1324	1407	1481
CRM	126	254	380
Debit cards	15069435	18231093	19994649
Credit cards	1372222	1537202	1619359
Prepaid cards	243432	413582	593825
Internet Banking Customers	1971984	2472151	2920933

Source: Bangladesh Bank, 2020

Digital financial services, on the other hand, is poor in comparison with global standard. In 2020, there were 11,206 ATM booths, 66,297 POS, 1,481 CDM, 380 CRM, 19,994,649 Debit cards, 1,619,359 Credit cards, 593,825 Prepaid cards, and 2,920,933 Internet banking customers, respectively (Table 4). To exploit these services, bank account is prerequisite in some context. Credit cards, however, is offered in order to the standards set by the offering banks while many banks offer debit cards when customers have an account with the bank.

ATM, CDM and CRM, some of the technology based financial services and are known to common people, offer by only few banks at the district or large cities. Therefore, customers living in village or far from city face difficulties to access these services and tend to access to MFS.

To provide financial services for all, the role of technology cannot be ignored. Specially, low-income rural population who do not have formal bank accounts, can access to MFS with their mobile phones with limited documents. In 2019, government published National Strategy for Prevention of Money Laundering and Combating Financing of Terrorism Strategy (Strategy No. 08) to promote FinTech and RegTech, financial inclusion and ensure cyber security in financial system. Also, government has set a deadline to implement Electronic Know Your Customer (e-KYC)/ Digital KYC on or before 2020 (BFIU, 2019). This policy encourages people to open an account and to connect with formal financial access without diverse documents. This is a breakthrough for promoting MFS in Bangladesh. National Identification (NID) or simply smart card provided to citizens has key role here. Through the NID, people can easily open an MFS account followed by some guided steps. Therefore, MFS account reached to 93.89 million in 2020 in comparison to 67.51 million in 2018, that is, more than 50% of the population has access to finance now. Another remarkable observation is that, among 93.89 MFS accounts, 58.63 million represent rural accounts (Table 5). This suggest that Bangladesh is the fastest-growing FinTech markets in South Asia, advancing its FinTech adoption by leveraging mobile phones.

Table 5. Current state of MFS in Bangladesh

	2018	2019	2020
MFS agent	886,471 (1.31%)	971,544 (1.22%)	1,009,423 (1.08%)
MFS male A/C	35,954,889 (53.25%)	40,314,735 (50.61%)	48,768,058 (51.94%)
MFS female A/C	31,558,910 (46.74%)	39,181,932 (49.19%)	44,917,191 (47.84%)
MFS other A/C	2,208 (0.003%)	157,081 (0.20%)	207,394 (0.22%)
MFS total A/C	67,516,007	79,653,748	93,892,643

Source: Bangladesh Bank, 2020

To leverage the new technology and the appropriate opportunity for extension of the traditional financial services, Bangladesh started its journey to adopt MFS in 2011 while the Central Bank issued 28 licenses among them 15 licenses are active so far (Bangladesh Bank, 2011, 2018). The main purpose of the regulations is to provide cost effective MFS services and to combat anti money laundering and financing of terrorism. Among the active MFS players, bKash and Nagad lead the market due to its countrywide agent network. With more than 160 million inhabitants having almost 100% mobile phone access, the country is suitable for FinTech-startups. There are more than 100 FinTech startups available in Bangladesh (Tracxn, 2021). Among them, the popular list of FinTech startups is illustrated in table 6.

Table 6. Major FinTech startups

FinTech startups	Foundation	Investment and Investors	Functions
bKash	2011	USD 11 million, Gray Ghost Ventures, Bill & Melinda Gates Foundation	MFS and payments solutions
PayWell	2012	USD 2 million, Aavishkaar Capital	Online bill payment solutions
Rocket	2012	Unknown, Dutch Bangla Bank Limited	Online payments solution
SureCash	2014	USD 7 million, DG Incubation, The Oriris Group, Beenext and Others	Prepaid reloadable mobile wallet services
SmartKompare	2015	Unknown	Online investment advisor, Online lending, personal loan, etc
Dmoney	2016	Unknown, SBK Tech Ventures	Online payments and financial solutions
iFarmer	2017	USD 74 thousands, Accelerating Asia	Crowdfunding for farming communities
Nagad	2018	Unknown, Bangladesh Post Office	Digital financial services
FundsMe	2018	Unknown, Banks and FIs in Bangladesh	Equity crowdfunding
OPORAJOY	2018	Unknown	Donation crowdfunding
SHADHIN	2018	Unknown	P2P online lending platform

Source: Author's survey; Tracxn, 2021

Particularly, FinTech startups started their journey in 2011 after the launch of bKash MFS. Government took initiatives to implement tech-based financial services, using mobile technology in particular, to all over the country. While MFS such as bKash, Nagad customers are increasing rapidly and have more than 80% market share (Bangladesh Bank, 2020), other FinTech platforms are not so popular.

FINTECH OPPORTUNITIES

FinTech revolution is mainly raised through the 2008 election agenda of Digital Bangladesh. In 2011, the MFS regulation was imposed to make more people to be connected via the formal financial network. With a growing demand for financial services and diffusion of ICT in Bangladesh, FinTech has remarkable opportunities in the financial system. World Bank Findex survey reported that from 3% formal financial access in 2011 to 21% reached in 2017. Still, there are large unbanked population, living in village in particular, are far behind from formal financial access. These groups of population may reach to the services through mobile phones.

Therefore, need for legal framework for accelerating FinTech firms is an ongoing discussion among the policy makers. As a consequence of MFS Regulations 2018, the ICT Policy 2018 and the Guidelines on eKYC, 2018 and public-private partnership, Bangladesh confirmed double digit FinTech growth since its inception. Some essential factors for FinTech promotion in Bangladesh are illustrated as follows:

- In 2011, Bangladesh Bank issued 28 licenses while 15 licenses are active to promote MFS in the country. These licenses are bank-based MFS platform in which parent company of this MFS platform are banks in particular.

- In 2015, Bangladesh Security and Exchange Commission (BSEC) reformed policy for alternative investment instruments in which venture capital funds and mutual funds or pooled investment funds may be used as alternative investment instruments by banks and NBFIs (BSEC, 2015).
- Bangladesh economy is largely depending on small and medium sized enterprises (SMEs) and one of the important reasons for SMEs growth for any economy is adequate financing. As a result of complex rules imposed by formal financial institutions, accessing finance by SMEs become difficult. While countrywide FinTech adoption reached to the expected level, these firms will be able to access the services to satisfy their needs.
- Cash in and cash out (CICO), mobile recharge are some of the essential services offered by most of the FinTech providers. These services represent more than 80% of the total transactions in 2020. Therefore, FinTech companies pay effort to innovate services based on the demand created by customers.
- Bangladesh has set a Vision 2025 to accelerate startups and Venture Capital (VC) friendly ecosystem to boost FinTech firms seven times more in comparison to now (The Financial Express, 2020). Currently, the country has USD 1.45 billion investment in total and expect to reach USD 10 billion investment with this vision and create more than 1 million jobs by this time. This Vision has direct impact on countrywide FinTech promotion in the coming days.
- The deployment of the National Payment Switch in 2012 by National Payment Switch Bangladesh (NPSB) in which all ATM transactions are routed through NPSB since 2016 (UNCTAD, 2019) and 51 licenses are already issued to this system.
- A citizen-centered approach to building an inclusive digital financial ecosystem by Digital Financial Services (DFS) Lab, a joint initiative by Bangladesh Bank and action to information (a2i), Ministry of ICT is developed to provide financial literacy and digital financial services for the last mile.
- In 2021, USD 10 million support fund announced by Startup Bangladesh, an initiative by government, to support 50 startups in 2021 (Dhaka Tribune, 2021). Many early-stage FinTech companies will get advantage from this initiative.
- Bangladesh Payment and Settlement System Regulation, 2013 allows separate private entities to act and operate their business as individual payment service providers and payment system operators. This regulation collaborates many young FinTech companies to perform their functions effectively.
- e-KYC regulation imposed by BFIU in 2019 to ease account opening with FIs so that people can access and open an account with their NID. This regulation accelerates financial inclusion at a greater space in the country.
- In Bangladesh, approximately 40% of the population lie in between the ages of 15-40 years (BBS, 2014; Statista, 2021). A large percentage of this group are unbanked or new to formal financial services. This group can expedite FinTech due to their attitude to use hassle-free tech-based financial services instead of traditional financial services.
- Cross-border cooperation like South Asian Association for Regional Cooperation (SAARC) or Bay of Bengal Initiative for Multi-Sectoral Technical and Economic Cooperation (BIMSTEC) collaboration may facilitate FinTech promotion in this region where all parties involved in the network will be benefitted.

FINTECH CHALLENGES

One of the most important limitation for FinTech promotion in Bangladesh is that regulation supported the population who have at least their identity and address but there are plenty of population who do not have either NID or their own address, still far from financial inclusion. This is one of the key challenges that divide the population into two; persons having NID or not to access to finance. Therefore, regulations must ensure to give the opportunity to be connected to financial network with proper validation and tools. Some key challenges that are listed are as follows:

- Although data shows that there are more than 80 million population have access to this service but there are many who have more than one account that represent overlapping the numbers and needs to be adjusted.
- If assume 100 million population are more than 15+ age, therefore, still 20 million are underserved through this financial revolution. Thus, 20% are not inclusive and that creates an ultimate problem in the overall development agenda.
- Customer acquisition is critically important for FinTech promotion. Need to provide more product for further development and to get acquaintance the services for all.
- Although government has paid much effort to strengthen FinTech promotion, there are certain laws inevitably contribute to slow down the FinTech companies to start their business. Collection of necessary documents to start business is one of the key barriers for FinTech entrants.
- A large percentage of inhabitants are backward with technology and financial literacy. New innovation and campaign can solve these problems.
- Although many commercial banks adopted FinTech services but those services are not user friendly or even complex to understand for the general people. Besides, uninterrupted service provision is yet to be realized by many banks in Bangladesh.
- Facilitating SME lending or SME financing is a key challenge for Bangladesh economy while many of the SMEs are not authorized under the formal financial system. Here, FinTech firms can deliver digital financial services to these SMEs and take initiatives to reduce the gaps.
- Standard regulation is a key factor for smooth banking operation. While poor or backdated regulation hinders FinTech adoption, there should impose an appropriate guideline to promote tech-based financial services by the regulators.
- Still, many people largely depend on cash instead of electronic money for daily transactions. Informal sector sellers, such as road-side temporary seller or daily commuter services, they only accept cash while this sector posits a large percentage of transaction in the country.
- Cyberthreats always a key challenge for FinTech expansion. Customers disclose massive financial data in which risk of cybersecurity increases. Strict regulation and routine monitoring are the possible factors that will lessen the level of risk.
- Capital accumulation is a key challenge for FinTech startups while government support and public-private partnership can facilitate capital formulation for this type of firm.
- Use of MFS and card-based payment are still low in e-commerce industry since cash transactions are encouraged by most of them instead of electronic transactions.
- Low interoperability among payment players is another challenge while all MFS except Nagad established their business in a bank-led model, interoperability between MFS and bank accounts are yet to be achieved (Mujeri & Azam, 2018).

CONCLUSION

The aim of the paper is to demonstrate FinTech in Bangladesh with respect to the prospects and challenges for overall expansion. In general, the financial sector in Bangladesh is underway drastic changes from traditional cash-based to cashless society. The mainstream in this regard may be the FinTech companies which may confirm to reach the country to cashless while positive contribution to the economy can be attained. The solution to the IT related problem may be handled with experience team with accurate operational software so that unwanted risk may be captured at a greater extent. FinTech firms have set their business with bundles of services to the doorsteps for the customers but less attention has given to P2P lending or crowdfunding. Thus, service diversification is necessary for the existing firms and for the entrants.

Governments, through several regulation and initiatives, intend to expand FinTech for increasing financial inclusion and financial literacy. But the regulation is not sufficient with current states since large percentage of population live in villages. This population are vulnerable since adequate frauds or uncertainties may occur with the financial transaction. Banking act should be revised and set up to the standard mark so that country-wide or ubiquitous service may be possible through the same network.

The FinTech firms' prospect is definitely good while more than 60 million population are far from formal financial access. Besides, informal businesses, such as micro and small enterprises, are apart from digital financial services while these businesses extensively depend on traditional financial system. If proper regulation and system can be developed for this group, FinTech firms may see a sharp rise in Bangladesh.

To complete this research, we face problems of collecting data since the exercise of FinTech in Bangladesh is new. Scatter information from websites, monograms, reports and statistics are collected to complete the research. New evidence, in some extent, is difficult to include. Therefore, the research poses further avenue to conduct research on FinTech promotion in Bangladesh.

REFERENCES

Abu, S. T., & Tsuji, M. (2011). The Development of ICT for Envisioning Cloud Computing and Innovation in South Asia. *International Journal of Innovation in the Digital Economy*, *2*(1), 61–72. doi:10.4018/jide.2011010105

Anshari, M., Almunawar, M. N., & Masri, M. (2020). An overview of financial technology in Indonesia. In M. Anshari, M. N. Almunawar, & M. Masri (Eds.), *Financial technology and disruptive innovation in ASEAN* (pp. 216–224). Information Science Publishing. doi:10.4018/978-1-5225-9183-2.ch012

Arner, D. (2016). *FinTech: Evolution and regulation*. Retrieved from: https://law.unimelb.edu.au/__data/assets/pdf_file/0011/1978256/D-Arner-FinTech-Evolution-Melbourne-June-2016.pdf

Arner, D. W., Barberis, J., & Buckley, R. P. (2015). The evolution of FinTech: A new post-crisis paradigm. *Georgetown Journal of International Law*, *47*, 1271. doi:10.2139srn.2676553

Bangladesh Bank. (2019a). *Bangladesh Financial Intelligence Unit (BFIU) report 2019*. Retrieved from https://www.bb.org.bd/bfiu/bfiu_lawguidelist.php

Bangladesh Bank. (2019b). *Bangladesh Mobile Financial (MFS) Regulations.* Retrieved from https://www.bb.org.bd/bfiu/bfiu_lawguidelist.php

Bangladesh Bank. (2021a). *Mobile financial services statistics.* Retrieved from https://www.bb.org.bd/en/index.php/econdata/index

Bangladesh Bank. (2021b). *Overview of financial system of Bangladesh.* Retrieved from https://www.bb.org.bd/fnansys/index.php

Bangladesh Bureau of Statistics. (2014). *Bangladesh: Demographic and health survey 2014.* Retrieved from https://www.dhsprogram.com/pubs/pdf/FR311/FR311.pdf

Bangladesh Security and Exchange Commission. (2015). *Alternative investment rules, 2015.* Retrieved from https://www.sec.gov.bd/slaws/BSEC(Alternative_Investment)_Rules,_2015_22.06.2015.pdf

Bangladesh Telecommunication Regulatory Commission. (2020). *Licenses and Statistics.* Retrieved from http://btrc.gov.bd/license-statistics

Basher, S. A., Hassan, M. K., & Islam, A. M. (2007). Time-varying volatility and equity returns in Bangladesh stock market. *Applied Financial Economics, 17*(17), 1393–1407. doi:10.1080/09603100600771034

Bátiz-Lazo, B., & Wood, D. (2002). An historical appraisal of information technology in commercial banking. *Electronic Markets, 12*(3), 192–205. doi:10.1080/101967802320245965

Bofondi, M., & Gobbi, G. (2017). The big promise of FinTech. *European Economy*, (2), 107-119.

Brandl, B., & Hornuf, L. (2020). Where did FinTechs come from, and where do they go? The transformation of the financial industry in Germany after digitalization. *Frontiers in Artificial Intelligence, 3*(1), 1–12. doi:10.3389/frai.2020.00008 PMID:33733128

Carney, M. (2017). The promise of FinTech–something new under the sun. In *Speech at Deutsche Bundesbank G20 Conference, by Bank of England Governor Mark Carney.* Retrieved from https://www.fsb.org/wp-content/uploads/The-Promise-of-FinTech-%E2%80%93-Something-New-Under-the-Sun.pdf

Chemmanur, T. J., Imerman, M. B., Rajaiya, H., & Yu, Q. (2020). Recent Developments in the FinTech Industry. *Journal of Financial Management. Markets and Institutions, 8*(01), 2040002. doi:10.1142/S2282717X20400022

Demirguc-Kunt, A., Klapper, L., Singer, D., & Van Oudheusden, P. (2017). *The global findex database.* Retrieved from http://documents. worldbank. org/curated/en/187761468179367706/pdf/WPS7255. pdf

Dhaka Tribune. (2021). *State-owned venture capital firm Startup Bangladesh sets sail.* Retrieved from https://www.dhakatribune.com/business/economy/2021/04/01/2021

Diagnostic, C. (2016). *Building Digital Bangladesh: The Way Forward for Digitizing Payments.* Retrieved from https://btca-prod. s3. amazonaws. com/documents/278/english_attachments/BTC-Bangladesh-Diagnostic Web. pdf, 1480177392.

EY Global FinTech Index. (2019). *Global FinTech adoption index.* Retrieved from https://www.ey.com/en_gl/ey-global-FinTech-adoption-indexbal

Ferrari, R. (2016). FinTech impact on retail banking–from a universal banking model to banking verticalization. In S. Chishti & J. Barberis (Eds.), *The FinTech book: The financial technology handbook for investors, entrepreneurs and visionaries* (pp. 248–252). John Wiley & Sons. doi:10.1002/9781119218906.ch65

Gomber, P., Koch, J. A., & Siering, M. (2017). Digital Finance and FinTech: Current research and future research directions. *Journal of Business Economics, 87*(5), 537–580. doi:10.100711573-017-0852-x

Hornuf, L., Klus, M. F., Lohwasser, T. S., & Schwienbacher, A. (2020). How do banks interact with FinTech startups? *Small Business Economics*, 1–22.

Imerman, M. B., & Fabozzi, F. J. (2020). Cashing in on innovation: A taxonomy of FinTech. *Journal of Asset Management, 21*(3), 167–177. doi:10.105741260-020-00163-4

IMF Policy Paper. (2019). *FinTech the experience so far*. Retrieved from https://www.imf.org/en/Publications/Policy-Papers/Issues/2019/06/27/FinTech-The-Experience-So-Far-47056

Lee, I., & Shin, Y. J. (2018). FinTech: Ecosystem, business models, investment decisions, and challenges. *Business Horizons, 61*(1), 35–46. doi:10.1016/j.bushor.2017.09.003

Lee, S. H., & Lee, D. W. (2015). FinTech-conversions of finance industry based on ICT. *Journal of the Korea Convergence Society, 6*(3), 97–102. doi:10.15207/JKCS.2015.6.3.097

Mackenzie, A. (2015). The FinTech revolution. *London Business School Review, 26*(3), 50–53. doi:10.1111/2057-1615.12059

Maier, E. (2016). Supply and demand on crowdlending platforms: Connecting small and medium-sized enterprise borrowers and consumer investors. *Journal of Retailing and Consumer Services, 33*, 143–153. doi:10.1016/j.jretconser.2016.08.004

Mujeri, M. K., & Azam, S. E. (2018). *Interoperability of Digital Finance in Bangladesh: Challenges and Taking-Off Options*. Retrieved from http://inm.org.bd/wp-content/uploads/2018/06/Working-Paper-54.pdf

Nguyen, C. V., Ali, M. M., & Islam, A. M. (2011). *The current state of the financial sector of Bangladesh: An analysis*. AIUB Bus Working Paper Series, No 2011-03. Retrieved from https://core.ac.uk/download/pdf/6323449.pdf

Reuters. (2017). *World's first ATM machine turns to gold on 50th birthday*. Retrieved from https://www.reuters.com/article/us-atm-anniversary-idUSKBN19I166

Schueffel, P. (2016). Taming the beast: A scientific definition of FinTech. *Journal of Innovation Management, 4*(4), 32–54. doi:10.24840/2183-0606_004.004_0004

Sia, S. K., Soh, C., & Weill, P. (2016). How DBS Bank Pursued a Digital Business Strategy. *MIS Quarterly Executive, 15*(2).

Statista. (2021). *Bangladesh: Age structure from 2009 to 2019*. Retrieved from https://www.statista.com/statistics/438190/age-structure-in-bangladesh/

Statista. (2021). *Number of fintech startups worldwide from 2018 to 2021, by region*. Retrieved from https://www.statista.com/statistics/893954/number-fintech-startups-by-region/

Taher, S. A., & Uddin, M. K. (2018). *Use of big data in financial sector of Bangladesh – A review.* Retrieved from https://www.econstor.eu/bitstream/10419/190348/1/A6_3_Taher-and-Uddin.pdf

The Daily Star. (2020). *FinTech to boost stocks.* Retrieved from https://www.thedailystar.net/business/news/FinTech-boost-stocks-1825978

The Financial Express. (2016). *ICT in Banking Industry.* Retrieved from https://thefinancialexpress.com.bd/views/ict-in-banking-industry

The Financial Express. (2020). *Vision 2025 launched to create startup and VC-friendly ecosystem in BD.* Retrieved from https://thefinancialexpress.com.bd/trade/vision-2025-launched-to-create-startup-and-vc-friendly-ecosystem-in-bd

The US Financial Stability Board. (2020). *Financial innovation and structural change.* Retrieved from https://www.fsb.org/work-of-the-fsb/financial-innovation-and-structural-change/fintech/

Towers-Clark, C. (2019). *Big Data, AI & IoT Part Two: Driving industry 4.0 one step at a time.* Retrieved from https://www.forbes.com/sites/charlestowersclark/2019/02/20/big-data-ai-iot-part-two-driving-industry-4-0-one-step-at-a-time/#597a782f23a0

Tracxn. (2021). *FinTech startups in Bangladesh.* Retrieved from https://tracxn.com/explore/FinTech-Startups-in-Bangladesh

UNCTAD. (2019). *Bangladesh rapid eTrade reediness assessment.* Retrieved from https://unctad.org/system/files/official-document/dtlstict2019d6_en.pdf

Zavolokina, L., Dolata, M., & Schwabe, G. (2016). The FinTech phenomenon: Antecedents of financial innovation perceived by the popular press. *Financial Innovation, 2*(1), 1–16. doi:10.118640854-016-0036-7

Chapter 7
Digital Financial Knowledge and Behavior of Generation Z in Indonesia:
A Survey of Islamic FinTech Literacy Toward Digital Financial Inclusion

Khairunnisa Musari
https://orcid.org/0000-0003-0525-9903
Kiai Haji Achmad Siddiq State Islamic University, Indonesia

Sutan Emir Hidayat
Gunadarma University, Indonesia & National Committee for Islamic Economy and Finance, Indonesia

ABSTRACT

The Indonesian Population Census 2020 reported that the majority of Indonesia's population is in the productive age group and dominated by Generation Z (27.94%). As the generation that currently dominates the population, Generation Z's characteristics are important to learn. They are the future. Generation Z has the potency to accelerate Indonesia's financial inclusion through digitalization because they are adaptable to technology. Responding to the survey results which put Generation Z in Indonesia in the first rank for the levels of happiness and religious awareness, a survey was conducted for Islamic financial technology literacy to find out how they face challenges as well as opportunities in digital era to be in line with religious values and may accelerate financial inclusion. The great potential of Generation Z for technology as well as religious awareness in turn will support financial inclusion towards inclusive development in Indonesia. Hence, this chapter will describe the survey results of digital financial knowledge and behavior of Generation Z in Indonesia.

DOI: 10.4018/978-1-7998-8447-7.ch007

BACKGROUND

Referring to the Indonesian Population Census 2020 (SP2020), Statistics Indonesia agency [BPS] (2021a, 2021b), Cabinet Secretariat of the Republic of Indonesia [Setkab] (2021), Junida (2021), Idris (2021), Sulaeman (2021), Priyanka (2021) reported that Indonesia's population in September 2020 was 270.20 million people. Since Indonesia held its first SP1961, the population has continued to increase. In the last ten years, SP2020 reported an increase in the population of 32.56 million people or an average of 3.26 million every year with the growth rate was 1.25% per year. Based on age groups, the majority of Indonesia's population is in the productive age group and most dominated by Generation Z with the proportions of 27.94% or equivalent to 74.93 million people.

Referring to Zemke, Raines, and Filipczak (2000), Oblinger and Oblinger (Eds.) (2005), Martin and Tulgan (2006), Lancaster and Stillman (2009), Broadbent, Gougoulis, Lui, Pota, and Simons (2017), Fry and Parker (2018), Francis and Hoefel (2018), McCrindle and Fell (2019), Karashchuk, Mayorova, Nikishin, and Kornilova (2020), Catalyst (2021), and Musari (2021), there are several versions in determining the name of generation and the age range. Likewise, for Generation Z, some people call it Net Generation, Post Millenial Generation, Gen Zers, Digital Generation, iGeneration, Homeland Generation or Homelanders. Regarding the age range, McCrindle Research Center addresses Generation Z was born in 1995-2009. McKinsey & Company and The Varkey Foundation remark who was born in 1995-2010. Statistics Canada (2012) denoted that Generation Z was born in 1993-2011. In line with Catalyst, Pew Research Center (Dimock, 2019) believe 1996 is a meaningful cutoff between Millennials and Generation Z for a number of reasons, including key political, economic and social factors that define the Millennial generation's formative years. BPS (2021a, 2021b) also introduced Generation Z as those were born in 1997-2012.

As the generation that currently dominates the Indonesian population, Generation Z's characters are important to be learned. They are the future of Indonesia although not all of them currently at the productive ages. In the next six years, all Generation Z will become the productive age population. At least in the next five to ten years, they will be the leaders in their respected communities. BPS (2021a) also ensured that this is an opportunity as well as a challenge for Indonesia, because this generation will determine Indonesia's future development. Dealing with the demographic changes, McCrindle and Fell (2019) warned that Generation Z has become one of the biggest issues facing employers today, specifically on how to recruit, retain and manage them.

No doubt, the number of Generation Z in Indonesia has the potential to accelerate Indonesia's financial inclusion through digitalization. Generation Z is known very adaptable to technology. The Washington Post (2016) and McKinsey & Company (Francis and Hoefel, 2018) mentioned that Generation Z as the 'true digital natives'. They have never known a world without smartphones, tablets, and social media. Thus, for this reason, it is important to ensure that Generation Z has an adequate level of digital financial literacy so that their future financial decisions become productive decisions and help accelerate the resolving of financial inclusion problems in the society.

Furthermore, Broadbent et al (2017) reported the survey results in 20 countries by Varkey Foundation that Generation Z in Indonesia reaches the highest levels of happiness with a net score of 90% and believed that commitment to religion as playing a bigger role in contributing to their overall happiness until 93%. Responding to the survey results which put Generation Z in Indonesia in the first rank for the highest levels of happiness and religious awareness, this chapter did a survey for Islamic financial technology (fintech) literacy toward digital financial inclusion of Generation Z in Indonesia. In order to assure the Generation Z in the future will face the challenges as well as opportunities to be in line with religious values and useful for accelerating financial inclusion, this chapter will describe the survey results for digital financial knowledge and behavior of Generation Z in Indonesia.

This survey worked in two phases. The first phase was conducted in February 2021 and the second phase in July 2021. In the first phase, a survey was conducted on undergraduate students at UIN Kiai Haji Achmad Siddiq, Jember, by using a questionnaire that was distributed to 322 students at the Faculty of Islamic Economics and Business. The first phase was oriented to find variants of answers to the tendency of their age group representing Generation Z towards fintech. The variants from the first phase answers of the survey were later developed for a larger scope, namely the national level. In the second phase, this research uses a questionnaire distributed through various social media channels, professional association, and student organization networks for 10 days with data received as many as 245 respondents from various regions in Indonesia.

The analytical tool used in this study is descriptive statistics because the purpose of this study is only to describe the Generation Z's knowledge about fintech services, particularly about digital payment, peer to peer (P2P) lending, and the usage intention, then about their behavior for saving, investing, and donating or doing *zakat, infaq, sadaqa, waqf* (ZISWAF) through fintech. By describing the knowledge and behavior of Generation Z, it is expected that policymakers and other stakeholders can create a digital financial literacy roadmap for the next five to ten years to improve and direct Generation Z to be in line with religious values and help accelerate digital financial inclusion. This chapter believes the great potential of Generation Z in Indonesia for technology and religious awareness will in turn support financial inclusive development in Indonesia.

GENERATION Z IN INDONESIA

Fact and Figures

The large number of productive age cohort in population structure becomes the social capital of development. SP2020 (BPS, 2021a, 2021b) recorded the majority of the Indonesian population was dominated by Generation Z and Y. The proportion of Generation Z was 27.94% and Generation Y was 25.87% of the total population. These two generations are included in the productive age which can be an opportunity to accelerate economic growth. In demographic side, all Generation X and Y in 2020 are in the productive age group. While Generation Z consists of productive and not yet productive people. In about six years, all Generation Z will be in the productive age population group. The composition of the Indonesian population in each generation as of September 2020 based on SP2020 is shown in Figure 1.

BPS (2021a, 2021b), Setkab (2021), Junida (2021), Idris (2021), Sulaeman (2021), Priyanka (2021) informed that the source of classification for generations in SP2020 is according to William H. Frey in Analysis of Census Bureau Population Estimates. However, referring to the Demographic Evolution of the American Electorate 1974–2060 in which Frey was involved with Teixeira and Griffin (2015), the classification was divided into nine generations during 1883 to 2060 as shown in Table 1.

Figure 1. Composition of the generations in Indonesia based on SP2020 per September 2020
Source: BPS (2021a), Processed

Classification of Generation	Age Range (Year)	The Number (Million People)
Pre-Boomers	<1945	5.03
Baby Boomers	1946-1964	31.01
Generation X	1965-1980	58.65
Generation Y	1981-1996	69.38
Generation Z	1997-2012	74.93
Generation Alpha	>2013	29.17

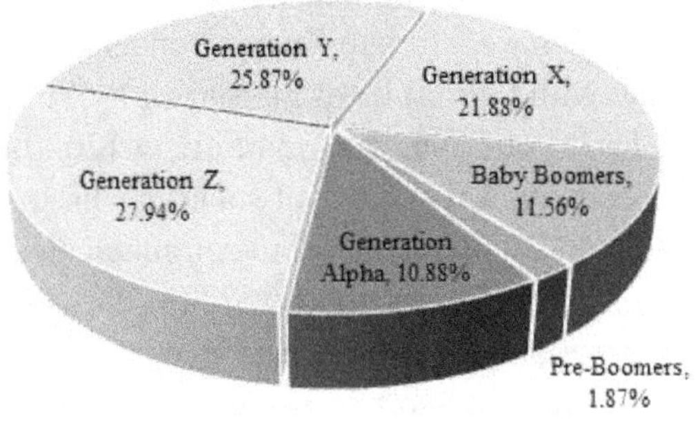

Table 1. Classification of Generation

Classification of Generation	Age Range (Year)
Lost	1883-1900
Greatest	1901-1927
Silent	1928-1945
Baby Boomer	1946-1964
Generation X	1965-1980
Millennial	1981-2000
Post-Millennial 1	2001-2020
Post-Millennial 2	2021-2040
Post-Millennial 3	2041-2060

Source: Teixeira, Frey, and Griffin (2015)

Referring to BPS (2021b), the proportion of persons aged 0-14 years decreased from 44.12% in 1971 to 23.33% in 2020. The working age group (15-64 years) increased from 53.39% to 70.72%. The proportion of person aged 65 years and above increased from 2.49% to 5.95%. This shows that Indonesia is still in the era of the demographic bonus. The difference between the percentages of the productive and non-productive age population (0–14 years and 65 years and above) looks sharper in 2020.

Furthermore, study by Dwidienawati and Gandasari (2018) taking 89 samples of Generation Z in Indonesia confirmed that Generation Z in Indonesia is realistic and needs security and stability. Money is an important motivation so that they are willing to work hard and being relocated for a good job opportunity. They prefer face-to-face communication with their boss. They are also global citizens who are socially responsible.

Then, through deep interview to 23 respondents, Simangunsong (2018) found that Generation Z in Indonesia has a strong tendency to shop online. Generation Z shows distinctive behaviours particularly when shopping for clothes, food, and beverage. While Asyifa (2020) found Generation Z in Indonesia through 235 respondents prefer to read digital text through their mobile phone than printed text. Although they are well literate and understand how to use the technology and read the digital text, it was found that they still have a lack to find and understand the meaning of text.

In line with the results of the survey by Supratman (2018) on 225 informants and Suwana, Pramiyanti, Mayangsari, Nuraeni, and Firdaus (2020) on 326 respondents which showed that Generation Z in Indonesia are active users of social media in their daily lives for various purposes, this survey also found that all 245 respondents to communicate using Whatsapp (100%), Instagram (64.9%), Telegram (44.1%), Line (31%), Facebook (27.3%), Messenger (11.4%), and Signal (3.3%). Quite surprising, there are still Generation Z in Indonesia who use text messaging services. Respondents of this survey showed that 23.7% still use Short Message Service (SMS).

Distribution of Respondents

Generation Z who became respondents in this study were dominated by 72.2% women and 27.8% men. As much as 96.32% were Muslim, 1.22% were Christian, and the rest were Catholic, Hindu, and Buddhist with each of the 0.82%. For job status, the majority of respondents were students of higher education institution/college/university as much as 84.1%, followed by high school students as much as 6.1%, and employees of private companies 4.1%. The rest were teachers, entrepreneurs/MSME owners, freelancers, employees of banking institutions, employees of state institutions/government agencies, employees of SMEs, health care workers, fresh graduates, and jobless.

Based on a year of birth, respondents of Generation Z were born in 2000 dominates in this survey as much as 24.5%. Then, they are followed by respondents with the year of birth 2001, 1999, 1998, and 1997 with each magnitude 20%, 15.1%, 13.9%, and 11.8%. Overall, the distribution of the year of birth of the respondents in this survey is shown in Figure 2.

Figure 2. Distribution of respondents by year of birth

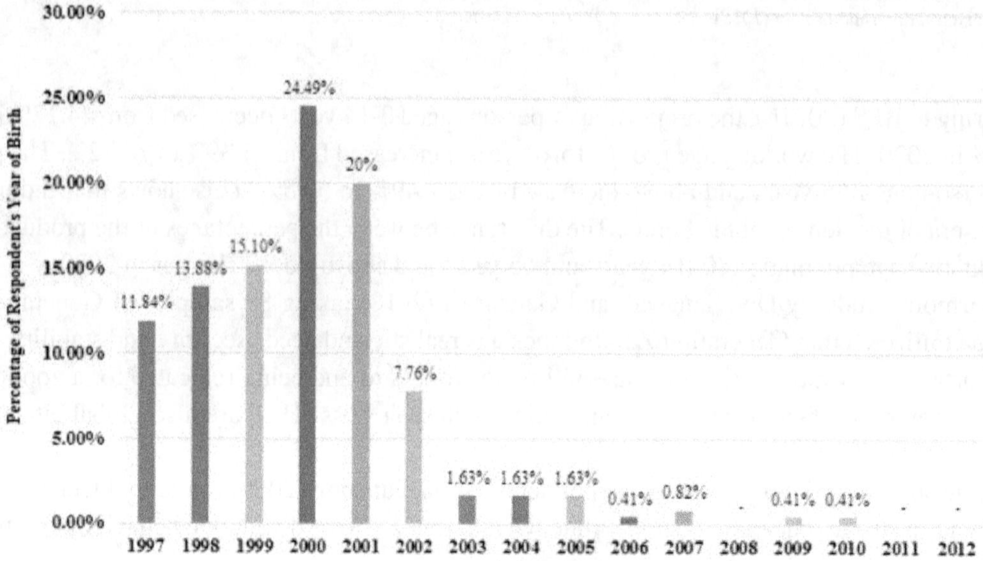

Further, the respondents are spread across three countries, namely Indonesia, Malaysia, and Australia. In Indonesia, from 34 provinces, there are 17 provinces that have respondent representation or about 50% of all provinces in Indonesia. Based on the number of districts/cities, the widest distribution of respondents in Province of Jawa Timur and Jawa Barat. In Jawa Timur, respondents were spread over 19 districts/cities out of a total of 38 regencies/cities or about 50% representation of all regencies/cities in this province. In Jawa Barat, the respondents were spread over 12 districts/cities out of a total of 27 districts/cities in this province or about 44.2% representation of all regencies/cities. The distribution of respondents by province and district/city in this study can be seen in Figure 3.

Figure 3. Distribution of respondents by province and district/city

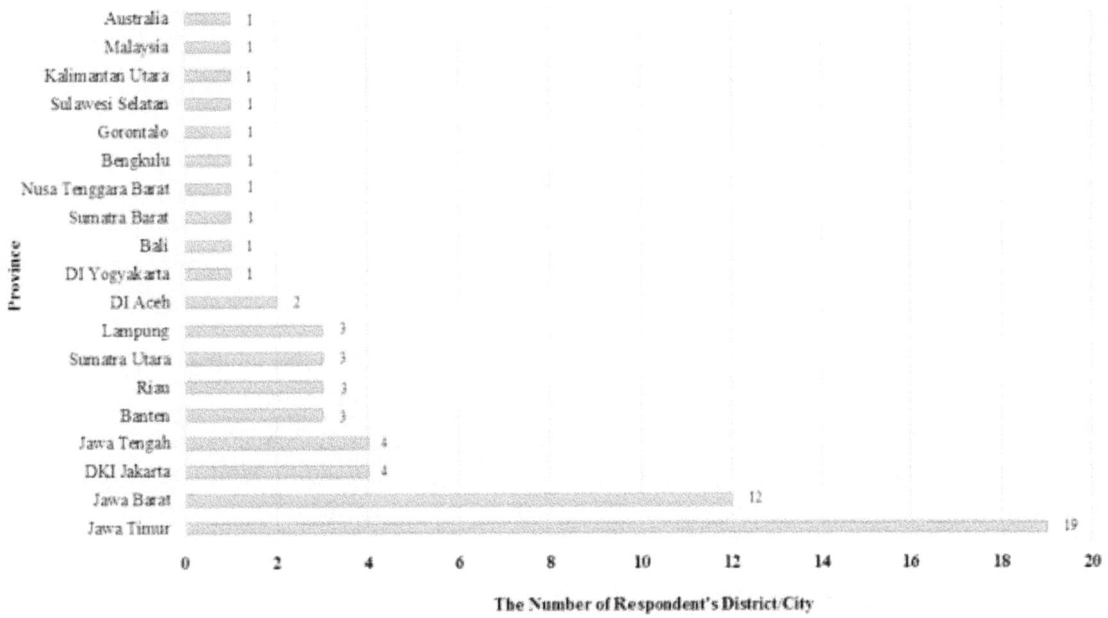

The composition of the geographic distribution of respondents in this survey is in line with the demographics of the Indonesian population by island, which is still concentrated in Jawa (Java). Referring to SP2020, BPS (2021a, 2021b) and Setkab (2021) denoted the Jawa (Java) with an area of about 7% of the total areas of Indonesia is inhabited by 151.6 million people or 56.10% of Indonesian population, followed by Sumatra (21.68%), Sulawesi (7.36%), Kalimantan (6.15%), Bali-Nusa Tenggara (5.54%), and Maluku-Papua (3.17%). The most populated province in Indonesia is Jawa Barat with 48,27 million people, then followed by Jawa Timur with 40.67 million and Jawa Tengah with 36.52 million people.

Of the 245 generation Z respondents, as many as 44.9% have their own income or money from their parents per month in the range of <IDR500,000, 28.2% in the range IDR500,001-1,000,000, and 16.3% in the range IDR1,000,001-2,500,000. Then, average consumption or personal expenses per month that are borne by themselves, as much as 58.8% are in the range of <IDR500,000, 26.5% in the range IDR500,001-1,000,000, and 9% in the range IDR1,000,001-2,500,000. The composition of own income

or money from parents per month and average consumption or personal expenses per month by respondents in this study is shown in Table 2.

Table 2. Distribution of income or money from parents and average consumption or personal expenses of respondents per month

Range	Respondents with	
	Own income or money from parents per month	Average consumption or personal expenses per month
<IDR500.000	44.9%	58.8%
IDR501.000- 1.000.000	28.2%	26.5%
IDR1.000.001- 2.500.000	16.3%	9%
IDR2.500.001- 5.000.000	6.5%	4.1%
IDR5.000.001- 7.500.000	1.2%	0.8%
IDR7.500.001- 10.000.000	1.2%	-
IDR10.000.001- 15.000.000	0.8%	0.4%
IDR15.000.001- 20.000.000	0.4%	-
>IDR 20.000.000	0.4%	0.4%

Regarding the survey of Islamic fintech literacy toward digital financial inclusion, Figure 4 shows the response of respondents when asked how to know about the Islamic economics. As many as 58.4% of the respondents have studied/currently are studying Islamic Economics/Sharia Banking/Sharia Accounting/Sharia Business Management/ Management of *Waqf Zakat*/and its kind, 29% of respondents admitted that they know little about Islamic economics, have read or heard.

Figure 4. How to know about Islamic economics

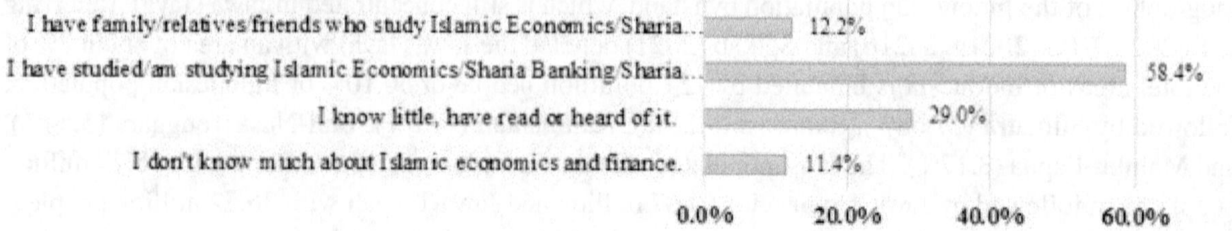

Then, 12.2% of respondents claimed to have family/relatives/friends who studied Islamic Economics/ Sharia Banking/Sharia Accounting/Sharia Business Management/Management of *Waqf Zakat*/and its kind. As many as 11.4% admitted that they did not know much about Islamic economics and finance. As many as 4.5% knew about Islamic economics because they work in organizations/institutions/ agencies/colleges in which pursue Islamic Economics/Sharia Banking/ Sharia Accounting/Sharia Business Management/Management of *Waqf Zakat*/and its kind. The remaining 0.8% claimed to have heard from lecturers and religious teacher *(ustaz)* on Islamic economics.

KNOWLEDGE OF GENERATION Z

Fintech Services

Regarding the knowledge of fintech, the understanding of respondents is quite good. This is reflected in 67.8% of them that respond 'Innovation in the financial services industry that utilizes the use of technology to carry out specific financial transaction mechanisms to accelerate and facilitate aspects of the financial services provided' and 53.5% of them also respond 'Digital technology in the financial services industry'. However, it should not be ignored that there are respondents who consider fintech as a banking service such as SMS banking, internet banking, mobile banking, etc. (31%), digital technology in the industry in general (11.8%), new technology in the digital era industry (11.8%), and marketplaces such as Tokopedia, Shopee, Lazada, Bukalapak, etc (11.4%). Table 3 summarizes various responses related to knowledge about fintech.

Table 3. Knowledge about fintech

Knowledge about fintech	Response
Innovation in the financial services industry that utilizes the use of technology to carry out specific financial transaction mechanisms to accelerate and facilitate aspects of the financial services provided.	67.8%
Digital technology in the financial services industry.	53.5%
Banking services such as SMS banking, internet banking, mobile banking, etc.	31%
Online loan service *(pinjol)*	15.9%
Digital technology in industry in general.	11.8%
New technology in the digital age.	11.8%
Marketplaces such as Tokopedia, Shopee, Lazada, Bukalapak, etc.	11.4%
Do not know	0.8%

Regarding the knowledge about the types of fintech services, the majority 87.3% of respondents recognize them in form of digital payments and 59.6% in digital loans. Some respondents also understand the types of fintech services as business financing (33.9%), crowdfunding (29%), financial planning (29.4%), investment risk management (19.6%), and e-aggregator (13.1%). Interestingly, there are 25 respondents or the equivalent of 10.2% who really know that clearing and settlement are also types of fintech. This is reflected in the number of respondents who chose clearing and also chose settlement. Generally, clearing and settlement services are indeed an integrated unit. Figure 5 presents various responses related to knowledges about the types of fintech services.

Figure 5. Knowledges about the types of fintech services

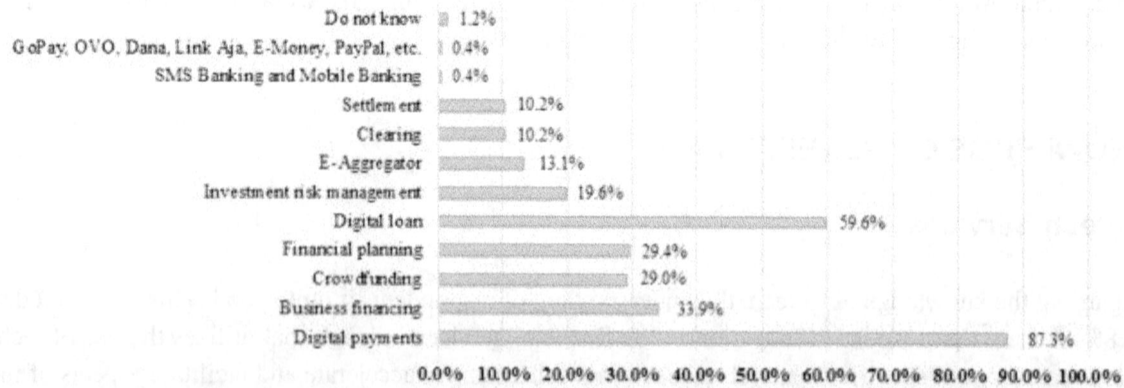

Based on respondents' basic knowledge about fintech, it can be concluded that this term is embedded in the minds of respondents as the use of technology in the financial system that results in new products, services, technology, and/or business models. From various types of fintech-based services, responses of respondents show that fintech is identified with two things, namely digital payments and digital loan *(pinjol)*. These two types of services are indeed the most widespread in Indonesia.

Digital Payment

Regarding the knowledge about the authority of digital payment system, 92.7% of respondents chose the Financial Services Authority (OJK). This indicates that the majority of respondents do not know or do not understand that there is a different authority between the digital payment system and digital loans *(pinjol)*. The number of victims of illegal digital loans has raised the name of OJK as the authority for P2P lending. This is what should be suspected as the cause of the respondent's understanding that the authority for the digital payment system also lies with the OJK.

Referring to the Act of the Republic of Indonesia Number 23 Year 1999 concerning Bank Indonesia, Chapter III Article 7 and 8 are stated that the objective of Bank Indonesia is to achieve and maintain the stability of the rupiah. One way to achieve this goal, Bank Indonesia has the task of regulating and maintaining the smooth running of the payment system. Then, in Chapter 1, terminology of payment system is "*... a system that includes a set of rules, institutions and mechanisms, which are used to conduct the transfer of funds to fulfill an obligation arising from an economic activity*".

Therefore, it is clear that the authority of digital payment system in Indonesia is Bank Indonesia as Central Bank of the Republic of Indonesia. Overall, the choice of respondents regarding the knowledge about the authority of digital payment system is shown in Figure 6. A number of respondents also not only chose OJK as the payment system authority, but there are also those who think that the Ministry of Finance (MoF), Ministry of Communications and Informatics (MoCI), even the Indonesian National Police (POLRI) also become the authority of digital payments system.

Figure 6. Knowledge about the authority of digital payment system

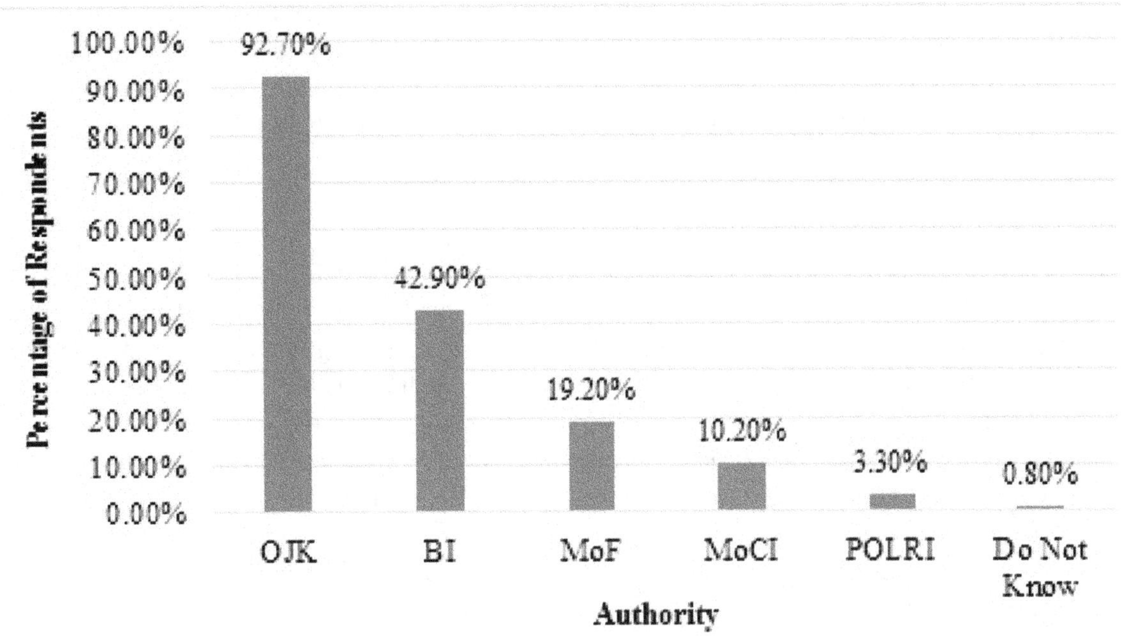

Furthermore, there is 13.5% of respondents or equivalent with 33 respondents who do not use digital payment application. The majority respondents have used application such as GoPay (58.8%), OVO (53.9%), Shopee Pay (35.9%), Quick Response Code Indonesian Standard (QRIS) of mobile banking (16.3%), and Link AJA (14.3%). Likewise with sharia applications, there are 20% of respondents who have used the form of Link AJA Syariah (7.8%) and QRIS of mobile banking of Islamic Bank (12.2%). Overall, this data shows that Generation Z uses more than one platform of digital payment system application. This result is also in line with the survey of Pradiatiningtyas, Dewa, Safitri, and Kiswati (2020) in Yogyakarta Special Region Province that Generation Z intensely uses digital payment in daily life and the brand of digital payment platform that is commonly used are OVO and GoPay. Then, most respondents use both at the same time (61%) rather than just using OVO (20%) or just using GoPay (19%).

Figure 7. Reasons not to use digital payments application

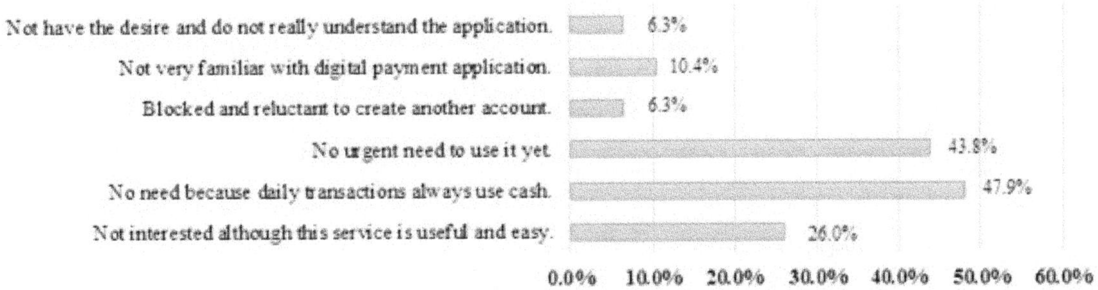

Then, for respondents who do not use digital payment application, Figure 7 shows the reasons are: they do not need because daily transactions always use cash (47.9%), there is no urgent need to use it (43.8%), not yet interested even though this service is useful and easy (26%), not very familiar with digital payment system applications (10.4%), blocked and lazy to create another account (6.3%), and do not have the desire and do not really understand about this applications (6.3%).

P2P Lending

Of the 245 respondents, 95.9% never use this P2P lending service and 4.1% have used this service. When asked about 'What do you know about P2P lending?', more than half of the respondents answered as digital loans. As many as 22.4% respondent also knew that P2P lending facilitates investor for doing investment. Interestingly, 23.7% of respondents believe P2P lending has low interest rates. In fact, the criticism that has surfaced against P2P lending services from the OJK is the high interest rates.

Sukmana (2019) wrote that the existence of fintech that was not registered with the OJK was like a loan shark who transformed along with the development of digital technology. However, Ananta and Hastuti (2019) explained that the Indonesian Joint Funding Fintech Association (AFPI) sets a maximum loan interest of 0.8% per day. AFPI was appointed by the Financial Services Authority (OJK) as the official association of information technology based lending and borrowing service providers in Indonesia. If the interest rate per day is converted per month, then the rate is a maximum of 24% and can touch 292% per year. Obviously, this rate far exceeds bank loan interest.

Moreover, this survey found a misunderstanding about P2P lending. Although the percentage is small, it should not be ignored. There are 6.1% of respondents think that P2P lending services to Electricity payment/buying tokens, buying credit, paying for telephones, buying tickets, etc. And 5.7% think P2P lending can help pay bills for electricity, telephone, leasing, insurance, etc. This further strengthens that Generation Z, who are mostly students of higher education institution/college/university, is still unable to distinguish the existence of P2P lending and digital payments. Table 4 below summarizes the complete answers of respondents regarding P2P lending.

Table 4. Knowledge about P2P lending

Knowledge about P2P lending	Response
Digital loans *(pinjol)*	58%
MSMEs Financing	31%
Fast loans, without collateral, just an ID card, and low interest rates	23.7%
Fast loans, without collateral, just an ID card, and profit sharing.	18%
Electricity payment services/buying tokens, buying credit, paying for telephones, buying tickets, etc	6.1%
Can be used for investment by becoming an investor for MSMEs	22.4%
Can help pay bills for electricity, telephone, leasing, insurance, etc	5.7%
Do not know	6.4%
A means for companies and capital owners to transact	0.4%

This survey found P2P lending service companies which have accessed by respondents are Amarta, Dana Mas, Investree, KoinWorks, Uang Teman, Modalku, Kredit Pintar, EasyCash, and Shopee Pay Later. A number of respondents who have accessed P2P lending services, the majority use sharia platforms. Most use Dana Syariah, the rest evenly use Berkah, Ammana, Alami Sharia, Qazwa, and Duha Syariah. This is understandable considering that 84.1% of respondents were student of higher education institution/college/university and 58.4% of the respondents have studied/currently study Islamic Economics/ Sharia Banking/Sharia Accounting/Sharia Business Management/Management of *Zakat Waqf.*

Then, for respondents who never accessed P2P lending services, Figure 8 shows the following reasons: They are not interested yet (45.3%), they do not understand about this service (32.9%), they are afraid because there are many slanted stories about this service (14.1%), there is no need yet (35.3%), they avoid borrowing money from financial institutions or anything similar because they do not want to be in debt. (26.5%), and they prefer to find a loan at the bank because it is more credible (4.1%).

Figure 8. The reasons never accessed P2P lending services

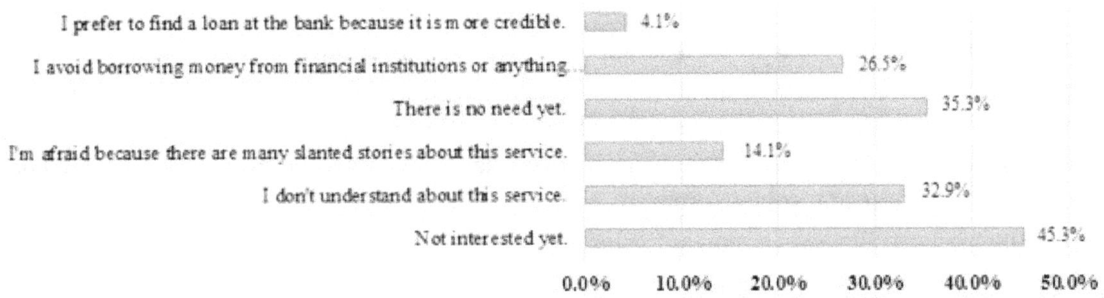

Usage Intention

For respondents who use digital payment application, the reasons for deciding to use this application is shown in Figure 9 below. Most respondents find it helpful because this application helps facilitate online transactions (79.7%), save money and time, no need to go out to the bank or payment outlet/office or purchase location (61.8%), Helps make it easier to pay monthly bills, such as telephone, electricity, water, leasing, insurance, etc (45.2%), many promos, discounts, and cash back (42.9%), and help make it easier to find transportation, buy food, deliver goods, etc (35.9%).

Furthermore, the result of this survey is more detailed in expressing the usage intention of respondents. If grouped in categorization, refer to Aseng (2020) and Tri and Panggabean (2021), these intentions can be spread into a number of determinant factors of Generation Z to use mobile payment services, ie culture, social influence, trust, effort expectancy, performance expectancy, perceived security, facilitating conditions, and perceived enjoyment.

For respondents who have ever used or are currently using P2P lending services, the reasons for deciding to use this service is shown in Table 5 below. Most respondents find this service helpful because get a loan quickly, just wait 1-2 days (29.6%), just need small funds so that they do not need to borrow from the bank, just through P2P lending (14.8%), can be a means of investment by participating in MSME financing (13.0%), get a loan at a very low interest rate (11.1%), get a loan without collateral, the requirements are easy, just an ID card and fill out the data form (11.1%), they have extra funds that are not being used, so they want to channel them to help MSMEs or those in need (5.6%). Surprisingly, there are respondents who are already investors (1.9%).

Figure 9. Reason for using digital payment application

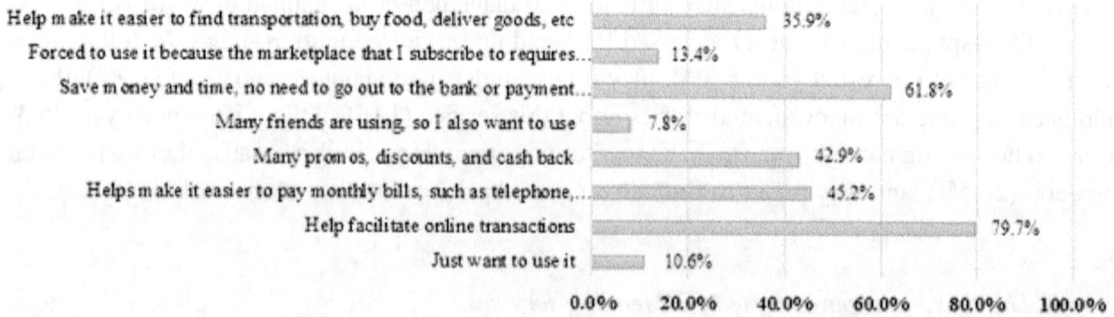

Moreover, the low usage intention Generation Z to P2P lending as an investment vehicle by participating in MSME financing also occurs in the millennial generation. A study by Lestari (2019) revealed that millennials are not interested in investing as lenders in P2P lending because the level of investment risk is considered to be greater than other types of investments. The types of investments that are chosen are stocks, savings, deposits, gold, to property.

Tabel 5. Reason for using P2P lending services

Reason for using P2P lending services	Response
Get a loan quickly, just wait 1-2 days	29.6%
Get a loan at a very low interest rate	11.1%
Get a loan without collateral, the requirements are easy, just an ID card and fill out the data form	11.1%
I need small funds so that I don't need to borrow from the bank, just through P2P lending	14.8%
Can be a means of investment by participating in MSME financing.	13.0%
I have extra funds that are not being used, so I want to channel them to help MSMEs or those in need	5.6%
I didn't have enough money to buy something I really wanted, so I looked for extras from P2P lending.	1.9%
My money is not enough to pay for very urgent and emergency needs, so I tried a digital loan application	3.7%
I am embarrassed to borrow from relatives or neighbors, so I try to borrow through this application	1.9%
Become a P2P lending investor	1.9%

In this section, there is another misunderstanding about P2P lending so it invites interest respondent to submit the loan. Although the percentage is small, it should not be ignored. There are 11.1% of respondents think that digital loan *(pinjol)* has a very low interest rate. In line with the previous studies such as Sandy (2020), Intan (2021), Rafie (2021), Laucereno (2021), Yovanda (2021), and Isnaini (2021) also reminded that high-interest P2P lending is an illegal fintech company. There are seven characteristics of P2P lending companies that the customers should be aware of, ie does not have legality because it is not registered or does not have official permit from OJK; imposes very high interest, fines, and fees; unethical collect process; requests excessive access to personal data; complaints are not handled; office location is unclear or unknown; offers via spam SMS.

BEHAVIOR OF GENERATION Z

Saving, Investment, and Donate/ZISWAF

Generation Z in Indonesia is quite understanding and accustomed to saving activities. There is 46.9% said 'I always do saving every month just in case there is a sudden need in the future', 41.2% said 'I try to save even though I can't always do it consistently because there is always a need so it's often used up', and 31.8% said 'I will save when there is something I want to buy or do'. Just 3.7% of respondents who usually save the change when shopping, 2.9% of respondents who never do saving, and 9% who rarely save because the money is always used up. Figure 10 below shows the responses to the saving habits.

Figure 10. Habits for savings

Figure 11. Investment initiatives

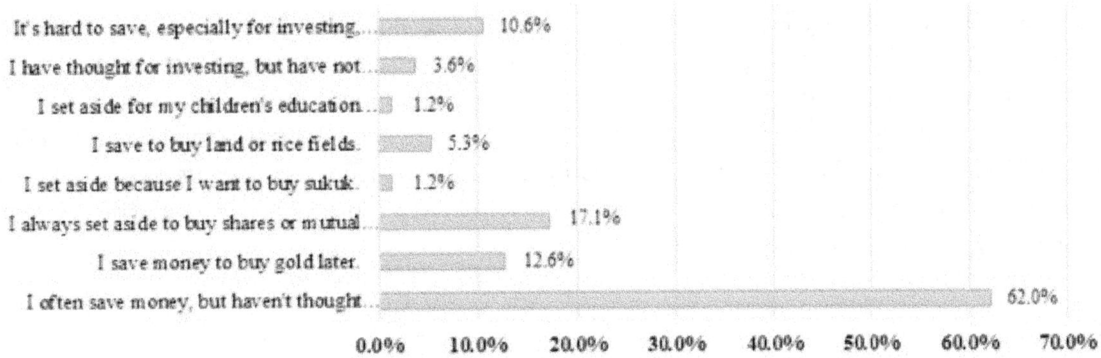

Regarding investment initiatives, Figure 11 shows 62% of respondents admitted that they often save, but have not thought about investing; 17.1% regularly set aside funds to buy shares or mutual funds or anything similar; 12.6% save money to buy gold later; 5.3% save to buy land or rice fields; 1.2% save to buy sukuk; and 1.2% save to invest in insurance for children's education. The remaining 3.6% admitted that they have thought for investing, but have not taken action for it due to various reasons, such as still have no income or prioritize for saving activities. However, as many as 10.6% of respondents admitted that they hard to save, especially for investing, it is hard to do for them.

Regarding the question 'Have you ever been in debt?', Figure 12 presents the three biggest responses by 245 respondents of Generation Z in Indonesia, ie, they do not want to be in debt, they avoid debt as much as possible, either to friends, relatives or banks or other financial institutions (56.7%); once owed a friend because forgot to bring money (49.4%); never been in debt because there is no need that requires debt and may go into debt if there is a terrific need (9%). Another responses showed that they have ever been in debt with borrow money from friends or relatives for the daily needs (1.6%); credit to bank/cooperative, but look for sharia one (0.4%); credit to bank for working capital (1.2%); borrow to digital loan *(pinjol)* (1.2%); borrow to loan shark or moneylenders (1.2%); using credit cards only for urgent needs (0.4%); and borrow to parents (0.4%).

Figure 12. Have you ever been in debt?

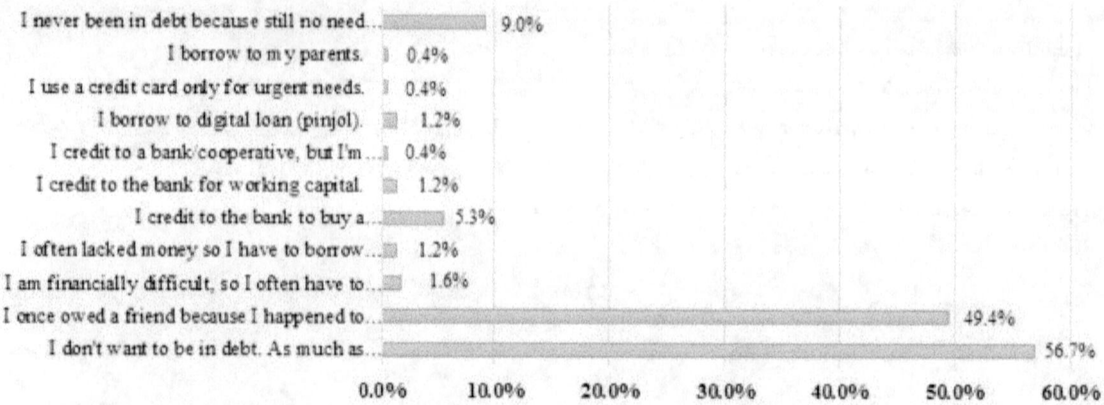

Additionally, the interesting thing found in this survey is the initiative by Generation Z to donate or doing ZISWAF. Although 41% of respondents do not feel obligated to set aside for ZISWAF, but actually they do donate. This can be guessed from 34.7% of respondents who donate and help others, but never intend or do not consider it as ZISWAF. Then, 13.9% of respondents usually set aside for donating/ZISWAF regularly, but since the pandemic, it's become rare and 13.9% still routinely set aside for donating/ZISWAF, even during the pandemic. Only 2% of 236 Muslim respondents or equivalent to 5 respondents who admitted never set aside for donating/ZISWAF. Table 6 below summarizes the habits for donating/ZISWAF of the respondents.

Table 6. Habits for donating/ZISWAF

Habits for donating/ZISWAF	Response
I'm still funded by my parents, haven't worked, so I don't feel obligated to set aside for ZISWAF.	41.2%
I often donate, often help others, but I never intended to be a ZISWAF.	34.7%
I usually set aside for donating/ZISWAF regularly, but since the pandemic, it's become rare because my income has decreased.	13.9%
I routinely set aside for donating/ZISWAF, even during the pandemic I still save as usual.	13.9%
I rarely donate/ZISWAF because I also really need it.	5.3%
I already have a subscription to amil institution that regularly receives ZISWAF from me.	2%
I never set aside for donating/ZISWAF.	2%
I immediately cut the zakat every time I get a salary.	1.6%

Related to fintech, 35.7% of respondents often or always donate/ZISWAF in cash directly to the person they give, 35.2% of respondents in donating/ZISWAF already use digital payment applications, 27.6% of respondents use digital payment application as well as cash directly to those in needs or through institutions. Figure 13 shows the responses of respondents. There is 6.0% of respondents usually ask a friend or acquaintance who has the application and they then change with cash and 4% usually transfer through a teller at the bank. Then, 3.5% of 231 Muslim respondents who never donate/ZISWAF by using digital payment application or equivalent to eight respondents and only 0.4% of them donate/ZISWAF via mobile banking.

Figure 13. Donate/ZISWAF with fintech

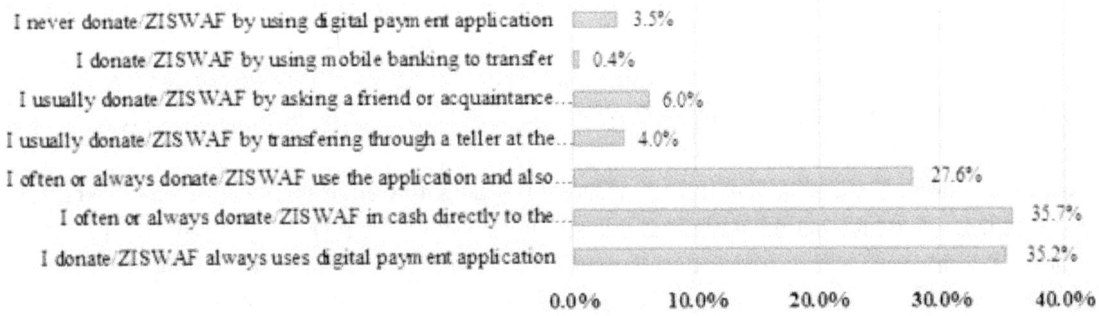

Furthermore, related to the survey of Islamic Fintech as part of Islamic Economics and Finance, it is found that Generation Z views intention as not a requirement for doing charity. Whereas intention becomes something important in Islam. Referring to Rosidi (2017), the intention is the key to whether or not an act of worship of a person is accepted by Allah. What will someone get is the fruit of what he intended.

Regarding sharia fintech literacy towards digital financial inclusion, this survey shows Generation Z in Indonesia has sufficient knowledge about fintech and the behavior that follows it according to their level of knowledge. Although it is still not optimal, the results of this survey indicate that Generation Z in Indonesia likes to do charity, they avoid debt as much as possible, they like to save and start thinking about investing. This explains why the majority of Generation Z access digital payment applications, and much less of them access digital loan *(pinjol)* services.

Lyman and Lauer (2015) found that in order to accelerate digital access of the excluded and underserved populations, there are three key components of digital financial inclusion namely a digital transactional platform, retail agents, and the use by customers and agents of a device to transact through the platform. Today, all the three key components can be accessed by the Generation Z.

Absolutely, digital financial inclusion manifests huge potential to give the ability to save to the previously 'excluded and underserved people', make payments, access financing, and insurance. Digital financial inclusion provides opportunities to allow them to manage an irregular income stream, plan for the future, protect them financially from natural disasters and economic shocks as well as find new pathways to survive and obtain a living.

Endeavors to help the 'excluded and underserved people' cannot solely promote access to digital financial services. They must have sufficient financial and digital literacy if we want to improve the welfare of the 'excluded and underserved people'. Referring to Hidayat and Rafiki (2021), financial literacy and awareness are very much related to financial inclusion. Thus, it is at this level that religious values will help encourage, maintain, direct, and guide them in utilizing technology as an effort to optimize themselves and manage various resources well. The results of this survey offer hope as well as confidence for Generation Z in Indonesia to utilize technology and have religious awareness which in turn will support inclusive development in Indonesia.

CONCLUSION

As the generation that currently dominates Indonesian population, Generation Z's characters are important to be learned since they are the future of this nation. Generation Z has the potential to accelerate Indonesian financial inclusion through digitalization because they are adaptable to technology. The great potential of Generation Z for technology as well as religious awareness in turn will support financial inclusion towards inclusive development in Indonesia. With the distribution of respondents reaching 50% of the total 34 provinces in Indonesia plus 2 other countries, this survey is expected to truly represent Generation Z in Indonesia.

This survey shows Generation Z in Indonesia has sufficient knowledge about fintech and the behaviour in line to their level of knowledge. Although it is still not optimal, the results of this survey indicate that Generation Z in Indonesia likes to do charity, they avoid debt as much as possible, they like to save and start thinking about investing. This explains why the majority of Generation Z access digital payment applications, but minimum access to digital loan *(pinjol)* services. Overall, the results of this survey offer hope as well as confidence for Generation Z in Indonesia to utilize technology and have religious awareness which in turn will support inclusive development in Indonesia.

REFERENCES

Abyan, M. A. (2018). *Konsep Penggunaan Financial Technology dalam Membantu Masyarakat Sub Urban di Indonesia dalam Melakukan Transaksi Finansial*. Research Gate. Retrieved from https://www.researchgate.net/publication/324386435_Konsep_Penggunaan_Financial_Technology_dalam_Membantu_Masyarakat_Sub_Urban_di_Indonesia_dalam_Melakukan_Transaksi_Finansial doi:10.13140/RG.2.2.36402.30404

Adam, A. (2017, April 28). Selamat tinggal generasi milenial, selamat datang generasi Z. *Tirto*. Retrieved from https://tirto.id/selamat-tinggal-generasi-milenial-selamat-datang-generasi-z-cnzX

Ananta, Y., & Hastuti, R. K. (2019, July 17). Tak percaya bunga fintech setinggi langit? Ini buktinya! *CNBC Indonesia*. Retrieved from https://www.cnbcindonesia.com/tech/20190716204353-37-85447/tak-percaya-bunga-fintech-setinggi-langit-ini-buktinya

Aseng, A. C. (2020). Factors influencing generation z intention in using fintech digital payment services. *Cogito Smart Journal*, *6*(2), 155–166. doi:10.31154/cogito.v6i2.260.155-166

Asyifa, D. I. (2020). Exploring Indonesian gen z digital reading issues. In *Conference Proceeding UHAMKA International Conference on English Language Teaching (ELT) and Computer Assisted Language Learning (CALL) (UICELL)*. Jakarta: Universitas Muhammadiyah Prof. Dr. HAMKA.

Bassiouni, D., & Hackley, C. (2014). Generation z children's adaptation to digital consumer culture: A critical literature review. *Journal of Customer Behaviour*, *13*(2), 113–133. doi:10.1362/147539214X14024779483591

BPS - Statistics Indonesia. (2021a, January 21). *Berita resmi statistik no. 7/01/Th.XXIV concerning hasil sensus penduduk 2020.* Jakarta: Statistics Indonesia (BPS).

BPS - Statistics Indonesia. (2021b). *The Indonesian population census 2020 highlights.* A material presentation for United Nations Expert Group Meeting.

Broadbent, E., Gougoulis, J., Lui, N., Pota, V., & Simons, J. (2017). *Generation Z: Global citizenship survey*. The Varkey Foundation.

Catalyst. (2021, March 2). Generations: Demographic trends in population and workforce (Quick take). *Catalyst.* Retrieved from https://www.catalyst.org/research/generations-demographic-trends-in-population-and-workforce/

Dimock, M. (2019, January 17). *Defining generations: Where millennials end and generation Z begins.* Pew Research Center. Retrieved from https://www.pewresearch.org/fact-tank/2019/01/17/where-millennials-end-and-generation-z-begins/

Dwidienawati, D., & Gandasari, D. (2018). Understanding Indonesia's generation Z. *International Journal of Engineering & Technology*, *7*(3.25), 245-252.

Evans, K. (2021, February 4). *Indonesia's 2020 census: A first glimpse.* The Australia-Indonesia Centre (AIC). Retrieved from https://australiaindonesia.com/aic/commentary/ indonesias-2020-census-a-first-glimpse/

Francis, T., & Hoefel, F. (2018, November 12). *'True Gen': Generation Z and its implications for companies*. Academic Press.

Fry, R., & Parker, K. (2018, November 15). *Early Benchmarks Show 'Post-Millennials' on Track to Be Most Diverse, Best-Educated Generation Yet*. Pew Research Center. Retrieved from https://www.pewresearch.org/social-trends/2018/11/15/early-benchmarks-show-post-millennials-on-track-to-be-most-diverse-best-educated-generation-yet/

Hidayat, S. E., & Rafiki, A. (2021). Comparative analysis of customers' awareness toward CSR practices of Islamic banks: Bahrain vs Saudi Arabia. Social Responsibility Journal. doi:10.1108/SRJ-05-2020-0174

Idris, M. (2021, January 22). Generasi Z dan Milenial Dominasi Jumlah Penduduk Indonesia. *Kompas*. Retrieved from https://money.kompas.com/read/2021/01/22/145001126/generasi-z-dan-milenial-dominasi-jumlah-penduduk-indonesia?page=all

Intan, N. (2021, June 25). OJK ungkap tujuh ciri pinjol ilegal dan rentenir online. *Republika*. Retrieved from https://www.republika.co.id/berita/qv8klw423/ojk-ungkap-tujuh-ciri-pinjol-ilegal-dan-rentenir-emonlineem

Isnaini, I. H. (2021, June 24). Awas! Rentenir online gentayangan, kenali 7 ciri-cirinya. *SindoNews*. Retrieved from https://ekbis.sindonews.com/read/464934/178/awas-rentenir-online-gentayangan-kenali-7-ciri-cirinya-1624503982

Junida, A. I. (2021, January 21). BPS: Penduduk Indonesia didominasi generasi Z dan milenial. *Antaranews*. Retrieved from https://www.antaranews.com/berita/1960808/bps-penduduk-indonesia-didominasi-generasi-z-dan-milenial

Karashchuk, O. S., Mayorova, E. A., Nikishin, A. F., & Kornilova, O. V. (2020). The method for determining time-generation range. *SAGE Open*, *10*(October-December), 1–8. doi:10.1177/2158244020968082

Lancaster, L. C., & Stillman, D. (2009). *When generations collide: Who they are. Why they clash. How to solve the generational puzzle at work*. HarperCollins.

Laucereno, S. F. (2021, June 29). Awas terjebak! Catat nih ciri-ciri rentenir online. *Detik*. Retrieved from https://finance.detik.com/fintech/d-5623866/awas-terjebak-catat-nih-ciri-ciri-rentenir-online

Lestari, N. P. M. (2019). Pemahaman generasi milenial berinvestasi di peer to peer lending. *Jurnal Manajemen Bisnis*, *16*(3), 17–30. doi:10.38043/jmb.v16i3.2229

Lyman, T., & Lauer, K. (2015, March 10). *What is digital financial inclusion and why does it matter?* Consultative Group to Assist the Poor (CGAP). Retrieved from https://www.cgap.org/blog/what-digital-financial-inclusion-and-why-does-it-matter

Martin, C. A., & Tulgan, B. (2006). *Managing the generation mix: From urgency to opportunity*. HRD Press.

McCrindle, M., & Fell, A. (2019). *Understanding generation Z: Recruiting, training and leading the next generation*. McCrindle Research Pty Ltd.

Musari, K. (2021, June 23). Ketika ekonom rabani 'generasi z' Jawa Timur menyambut era digital. *Kempalan.* Retrieved from https://kempalan.com/2021/06/23/ketika-ekonom-rabani-generasi-z-jawa-timur-menyambut-era-digital/

Nur, T., & Panggabean, R. R. (2021). Factors influencing the adoption of mobile payment method among generation z: The extended utaut approach. *Journal of Accounting Research, Organization, and Economics*, *4*(1), 14–28.

Oblinger, D., Oblinger, J. L., & Lippincott, J. K. (2005). *Educating the net generation.* Brockport Bookshelf. Retrieved from https://digitalcommons.brockport.edu/bookshelf/272

Oblinger, D. G., & Oblinger, J. L. (Eds.). (2005). *Educating the net generation.* Educause.

Parker, K., & Igielnik, R. (2020, May 14). *On the cusp of adulthood and facing an uncertain future: what we know about gen Z so far.* Pew Research Center. Retrieved from https://www.pewresearch.org/social-trends/2020/05/14/on-the-cusp-of-adulthood-and-facing-an -uncertain-future-what-we-know-about-gen-z-so-far-2/

Pradiatiningtyas, D., Dewa, C. B., Safitri, L. A., & Kiswati, S. (2020). The effect of satisfaction and loyalty towards digital payment system users among generation Z in Yogyakarta special region. *Journal of Physics: Conference Series*, *1641*(012110), 1–6. doi:10.1088/1742-6596/1641/1/012110

Pryanka, A. (2021, January 21). BPS: Gen Z dan Milenial Dominasi Penduduk Indonesia. *Republika.* Retrieved from https://www.republika.co.id/berita/qna4mf457/bps-gen-z-dan-milenial-dominasi-penduduk-indonesia

Putra, Y. S. (2016). Theoritical review: Teori perbedaan generasi. *Among Makarti, 9*(2), 123-134.

Putri, A. S. (2020, January 8). Jumlah Kabupaten dan Provinsi di Indonesia. *Kompas.* Retrieved from https://www.kompas.com/skola/read/2020/01/08/150000469/jumlah-kabupaten-dan-provinsi-di-indonesia?page=2

Rafie, B. T. (2021, June 25). Simak ciri pinjol ilegal: Penawaran lewat SMS, bunga mencekik. *Kontan.* Retrieved from https://keuangan.kontan.co.id/news/simak-ciri-pinjol-ilegal-penawaran-lewat-sms-bunga-mencekik

Rosidi, A. (2017). Niat menurut hadis dan implikasinya terhadap proses pembelajaran. *Jurnal Inspirasi, 1*(1), 39–50.

Sandy, K. F. (2020, December 4). 7 ciri-ciri fintech ilegal, bunga tinggi dan petugas penagih tidak beretika. *iNews.* Retrieved from https://www.inews.id/finance/bisnis/7-ciri-ciri-fintech-ilegal-bunga-tinggi-dan-petugas-penagih-tidak-beretika

Saputra, R., Kartawinata, B. R., Wijayangka, C., & Moeliono, N. N. K. (2019). Analisis faktor investasi pada mahasiswa generasi Z. *Jurnal Ilmu Keuangan dan Perbankan (JIKA), 9*(1), 42-58.

Setkab - Cabinet Secretariat of the Republic of Indonesia. (2021, January 23). *Statistics Indonesia releases 2020 census results.* Office of Assistant to Deputy Cabinet Secretary for State Documents & Translation. Retrieved from https://setkab.go.id/en/statistics-indonesia-releases-2020-census-results/

Simangunsong, E. (2018, June). Generation-Z buying behaviour in Indonesia: Opportunities for retail businesses. *MIX: Jurnal Ilmiah Manajemen, 8*(2), 243–253. doi:10.22441/mix.2018.v8i2.004

Statistics Canada (2012). *Catalogue No. 98-311-X2011003 Census in Brief, Generations in Canada: Age and sex, 2011 Census*. Ottawa: Authority of the Minister responsible for Statistics Canada, Minister of Industry.

Sukmana, Y. (2019, February 28). Ketua OJK: Sekarang rentenir sudah online. *Kompas*. Retrieved from https://ekonomi.kompas.com/read/2019/02/28/155407326/ketua-ojk-sekarang-rentenir-sudah-online

Sulaeman. (2021, January 21). Per 2020, Penduduk RI Didominasi Generasi Z. *Merdeka*. Retrieved from https://www.merdeka.com/uang/per-2020-penduduk-ri-didominasi-generasi-z.html

Supratman, L. P. (2018). Penggunaan media sosial oleh digital native. *Jurnal Ilmu Komunikasi, 15*(1), 47–60. doi:10.24002/jik.v15i1.1243

Suwana, F., Pramiyanti, A., Mayangsari, I., Nuraeni, R., & Firdaus, Y. (2020). Digital media use of gen z during covid-19 pandemic. *Jurnal Sosioteknologi, 19*(3), 327–340. doi:10.5614ostek.itbj.2020.19.3.2

Teixeira, R., Frey, W. H., & Griffin, R. (2015). *States of change: The demographic evolution of the American electorate*. Academic Press.

The Washington Post. (2016). *Generation Z: What it's like to grow up in the age of likes, LOLs, and longing*. New York: Diversion Books.

Yovanda, Y. R. (2021, June 24). 7 ciri rentenir online yang harus dihindari agar tidak terjebak bayar bunga gila-gilaan. *Tribunnews*. Retrieved from https://www.tribunnews.com/bisnis/2021/06/24/7-ciri-rentenir-online-yang-harus-dihindari-agar-tidak-terjebak-bayar-bunga-gila-gilaan

Zemke, R., Raines, C., & Filipczak, B. (2000). *Generations at work: Managing the clash of boomers, gen xers, and gen yers in the workplace*. Amacom.

ADDITIONAL READING

Amuda, Y. J., & Embi, N. A. C. (2013). Alleviation of poverty among oic countries through sadaqat, cash waqf and public funding. *International Journal of Trade. Economics and Finance, 4*(6), 403–408.

Aziz, F., Mahmud, M., & ul Karim, E. (2008). The nature of infaq and its effects on distribution of wealth. *KASBIT Business Journal, 1*(1), 44-48.

Çizakça, M. (1998). Awqaf in history and its implications for modern Islamic economies. *Islamic Economic Studies, 6*(1), 43–70.

Iqbal, M. (1985). Zakah, moderation and aggregate consumption in an Islamic economy. *Journal of Research in Islamic Economics, 3*(1), 45–61.

Marshall, V. W. (1983). Generations, age groups and cohorts: Conceptual distinctions. *Canadian Journal on Aging/La Revue Canadienne Du Vieillissement, 2*(2), 51–62. doi:10.1017/S0714980800015701

KEY TERMS AND DEFINITIONS

Digital Financial Inclusion: Digital access to and use of formal financial services which should be suited to excluded and underserved populations' needs, and delivered responsibly, at a cost both affordable to customers and sustainable for providers.

Infaq: Sunnah charity; non-obligatory charity; a type of charity in Islam that is given without any expectation of reward or return; pious spending in the way of Allah; monetary expenditure by a Muslim, both high and low income, both in the open heart and narrow, that may be given to anyone.

Sadaqa: Charity given voluntarily in order to please Allah; the term used to describe an act of kindness that is given to someone without the expectation of anything in return; voluntary charity without a set amount; the act of charity given purely out of compassion, love, friendship, religious duty or generosity.

Waqf: Islamic endowment; a special type of philanthropic activity in perpetuity; a voluntary and irrevocable endowment of sharia with compliant assets for sharia with compliant purposes; assets or cash that are purchased, bequeathed or donated for being held in perpetual trust for specific or general charitable causes that are socially beneficial; detention of a property so that its produce or income may always be available for religious, social or charitable purposes.

Zakat: A compulsory act of worship that requires a Muslim who owns wealth equal to or above the nishab (pre-defined threshold) to donate 2.5% of their wealth to eligible recipients; a religious obligation, ordering all Muslims who meet the necessary criteria to donate a certain portion of wealth each year to charitable causes; 2.5% of wealth that has been in one's possession for a lunar year; one of the five pillars of Islam and an act of worship.

Chapter 8
The Challenges of FinTech Inclusion and Digitization of SMEs in Indonesia

Syafrizal Helmi Situmorang
https://orcid.org/0000-0002-3988-5622
Universitas Sumatera Utara, Indonesia

ABSTRACT

The COVID-19 pandemic has changed people's digital behavior and caused giant leaps in various digital businesses. SMEs face various challenging factors in the transformation of their business into a digital ecosystem. Currently, Indonesia is the country with the fastest-growing digital economy and FinTech in ASEAN. Fintech plays a vital role in the digital economy, especially helping SMEs go digital and accelerate their business performance, such as venture capital financing, digital payment services, and financial arrangements. However, the role of fintech has not been maximized in increasing financial inclusion. There are still various obstacles and challenges such as technology adoption, financial literacy, digital literacy, financial inclusion, and fintech inclusion, and various program efforts from all stakeholders to bring SMEs into the digital ecosystem. Without cooperation, increasing financial literacy and financial inclusion and fintech inclusion will be challenging to achieve.

INTRODUCTION

Industrial revolution 4.0. has provided challenges and opportunities for economic development such as digitalization, automation, and artificial intelligence in various financial and business activities. The industrial revolution 4.0 has changed the rules of business competition to face a volatile environment (Volatile, Uncertain, Complex, Ambiguous). Not finished adapting to changes and advances in digital technology, the COVID-19 pandemic has hit us. This situation gave rise to panic, socio-economic pressures, governance crises and policies for handling pandemics in various countries. Social and physical distancing policies are carried out to reduce the interaction and spread of COVID-19, which has led to an economic slowdown around the world. The transportation, tourism, food, accommodation, retail,

DOI: 10.4018/978-1-7998-8447-7.ch008

services and manufacturing sectors are most affected by COVID-19. Research from the Central Statistics Agency (2020) states that around 82% of businesses experienced a decline in income, and 35.6% of companies reduced the number of employees working. As a result, many workers were laid off, the unemployment rate increased, and people's purchasing power decreased. Several research results also show that many SMEs are experiencing a liquidity crisis (Gourinchas & Kalemli-Özcan, 2020), supply chain disruptions (McCann & Myers, 2020), and are forced to reduce the number of employees and temporarily close. (Bartik et al., 2020).

This crisis spreads to the financial sector, namely non-performing loan risk, decreased investment flows, business performance, and people's purchasing power. The IMF has projected a decline in the global growth 4.9% in 2020, or 1.9 percentage points below the World Economic Outlook forecast (April 2020). Even though a year has passed since the pandemic, the prospects for global recovery are still marked by uncertainty. The OECD's Economic Outlook (2020) has projected a 6% decline in global GDP and a 7.6% decline in the event of a second pandemic wave. The ILO (2020) estimates that the impact of COVID-19 will increase global unemployment by between 5.3 million ("low scenario") and 24.7 million (the "high" scenario). This condition indicates that maintaining business operations will be very difficult for SMEs. The research results of Buffington et al. (2020) showed that nearly 90% of small businesses experienced a substantial (51%) or moderate (38%) negative impact from the pandemic; 45% of enterprises experience supply chain disruptions, and 25% of businesses have cash reserves of less than 1-2 months. The COVID-19 pandemic has caused an economic recession. The SME sector, which has proven to withstand every crisis, has also been hit hard by the pandemic. The SME sector is the backbone of the Indonesian economy, where 99% of business actors in Indonesia. MSMEs, absorb up to 116 million workers or 97% of the total workforce and contribute 61% of national GDP and 14% of total non-oil and gas exports, and 60% of total investment.

SMEs experienced a decline in sales, difficulties with capital and supply of raw materials due to decreased purchasing power and the COVID-19 social distancing policy. The Bank Indonesia survey (2020) noted that only 12.5% of SMEs could survive because they had adapted to the implementation of digitalization. Unfortunately, this digitalization opportunity has not been fully utilized by SMEs in Indonesia. Overall, the digitization of SMEs in Indonesia is still very low; only less than 15% have ever used digital platforms. The Indonesian Ministry of Cooperatives and SMEs noted that until May 2021, the number of SMEs players already onboarding is only reached 13,7 million or only 21% of the total 64 million SMEs in Indonesia. The low level of digital engagement is due to Baby Boomers and Generation X still dominating SME ownership. They lack knowledge of technology and are used to traditionally doing business. This situation causes the low adoption of technology by SMEs.

Social and physical distancing policies have accelerated the growth of FinTech, such as investment, digital payments, remittances, insurance, and loans. Changes in digital behaviour are causing giant leaps in various digital industry businesses. There has been a shift in people's transaction behaviour from the physical economy to the virtual economy. The SEA 2020 economic report states that more than 30% of consumers have been forced to start using digital services due to the pandemic. They are beginning to take advantage of digital services such as online education, buying basic daily necessities, finance, entertainment, and more for the first time. During the COVID-19 pandemic, digital wallets have become the most widely used FinTech product by the public (DS Research, 2020). Bona et al. (2020) explained that there had been a change in shopping patterns and consumer preferences during the pandemic. They prefer to buy products or services through digital channels. 9 out of 10 consumers intend to continue using digital services (Google, Temasek, and Bain e-Conomy SEA 2020).

One way for SMEs to survive, develop, and even win in the face of market competition amid this crisis is by transforming into a digital ecosystem such as digitizing business management, integration with logistics services, and digital payment systems. The Deloitte Report (2015) states that encouraging digital engagement in MSMEs will increase economic growth by 2%. Digital transformation will impact increasing financial capacity that supports investment, job creation, business development, income, and people's purchasing power. e-Conomy SEA report (2019) show that Indonesia's digital economy is the largest and fastest-growing ASEAN. FinTech plays a vital role in the digital economy. Along with the development of the digital economy, the FinTech industry is also increasing. The effectiveness of the financial infrastructure will depend heavily on digital payment channels, the presence of digital identification systems, and data. Building a solid digital financial infrastructure today has the potential for economic returns 20% greater than before the pandemic (White et al., 2018).

Variation business model, unique ecosystem, and regulatory approach make FinTech Indonesia is the fastest growing country among ASEAN countries. Based on the MSC Indonesia study (2020), FinTech is the most dominant startup category in Indonesia. It is hoped that FinTech can accelerate the digital transformation of the SME business. Gabor & Brooks (2016) emphasize the importance of digital-based financial inclusion to generate a digital ecosystem that maps, expands, and monetizes the digital footprint. Various studies in Indonesia show that FinTech contributes to the development of SMEs such as venture capital financing, digital payment services and financial arrangements (Muzdalifa et al. 2018). Unfortunately, the role of FinTech has not been maximized in increasing Financial Inclusion (Rudinasari, 2018; Sari & Rinofah, 2019; Dewi, 2020). However, several subsequent research results show that FinTech-based financial services positively influence financial literacy and financial inclusion (Mulasari & Julialevi, 2020; Marini et al., 2020). This implication shows the progress and development of FinTech in Indonesia.

FINTECH DEVELOPMENT

FinTech describes a type of startup that uses technology to create financial products or services. Arslanian & Fischer (2019) stated that the FinTech revolution occurred due to the rapid changes in the business environment driven by macroeconomic changes, government regulations, the technological revolution, and shifting customer expectations. According to Gupta and Mandhy (2018), FinTech as a discipline relies on three basic concepts: data retrieval, data analysis, intelligence, and implementation. These concepts, if applied, will produce new business models in financial service institutions such as Compliance and Transaction Processing, Insurance Calculations, Investment Solutions, Financing Solutions, Investment Decisions, and Risk Management. Furthermore, the pandemic has also forced FinTech to adapt, re-project market risk, human resource readiness, and technology readiness. As a result, the FinTech industry in Indonesia continues to experience an increase in users.

At the beginning of FinTech development in 2016, the available FinTech service solutions focused only on digital payments and online loans (peer-to-peer lending). Today, the context of financial services and technology is changing rapidly and dynamically. We are witnessing various new business model innovations, the entry of new competitors, and new technologies in the financial services business. FinTech startup activities are practically divided into two, namely (1) providing technology-based financial services so that business operations are more efficient and scale faster. Usually, this FinTech startup model works with financial institutions to replace existing processes and systems. (2) Providing new solutions for certain financial service activities using technology. This model is highly developed and dominates the FinTech ecosystem. Now, millions of FinTech startups are emerging worldwide, with various business models to meet customer needs. The learning and transformation carried out by millions of FinTech startups will disrupt financial management and create new categorizations of digital financial services in the future (Arjunwadkar, 2018).

The digital economy and finance development continue to increase with public acceptance and preference for cashless transactions and online shopping. Reflected this growth was in the value of Electronic Money transactions in the first quarter of 2021, amounting to Rp 61.35 trillion, increasing 42.46% (YoY). IDC (2020) states that despite the global pandemic, direct digital transformation investment from 2020 to 2023 is growing at a compound annual growth rate (CAGR) of 15.5% and is expected to continue to increase as companies invest in digital enterprises in the future. The increasing number of FinTech in Indonesia has made the Government issues regulations to prevent consumer fraud. In addition, the Government has also formed an association called the Indonesian Joint Funding FinTech Association (https://afpi.or.id/about).

Financial services authority (OJK) divides FinTech into four categories according to its working principle (1) funding such as aggregators, funding agents, and financial planners. (2) financing such as blockchain-based, ECF, project financing, financial agents, property investment management, and P2P lending. (3) Insurance such as InsurTech and Insurance Broker Marketplace. (4) enablers include claim service handling, credit scoring, RegTech, transaction authentication, E-KYC, and online distress solutions. Practically, FinTech business models in Indonesia are very diverse such as Investment (IndoGold, Tanamduit, Pegadaian, Bareksa, Bibit), Equity Crowdfunding (Modalku, Koinwork, Investree), P2P Lending (Investree, Amartha, Danamas), E-money Digital Wallet (GoPay, OVO, Danaku, Link Aja) Digital Financial Innovation, Insurtech: insurance services, insurance company applications, bancassurance, aggregator sites, and enabler technology) and Remittance. Remittance service allows for foreign exchange financial transactions (cross-border money transfers). The remittance service market segment is Indonesian migrant workers on various continents, from Asia, Australia, America, Africa, and Europe. Remittance services help migrant workers to send money to families in Indonesia.

The Indonesian Joint Funding FinTech Association (2020) stated that the P2P Lending FinTech business continues to experience significant growth. The growth can be seen from the level of credit quality that it is getting better (95.78%). FinTech lending in Indonesia reaches Rp. 181.67 trillion (March 2021). This value has increased by 16.53% since the end of 2020 to date (year-to-date). /YTD) with details of the number of borrowers reaching 55.34 million entities, lenders as many as 612.84 thousand entities. In Indonesia, investment interest in the FinTech sector is quite considerable. As much as 22% of loans to MSMEs are provided by non-bank financial institutions such as finance companies, micro-credit institutions, and other financial institutions. Investors see the lucrative market potential of the FinTech industry. The synergy between FinTech and SMEs will benefit both parties. FinTech anticipates low risk, and SMEs will get loans at lower interest rates than banks. SMEs are one of the most significant users of FinTech lending services. Based on the Financial Services Authority (April 2021), 541 active lender accounts came from abroad. 24.1% of the total loans came from abroad.

The startup business in technology-based financial services (FinTech) has enormous market potential and will continue to grow in Indonesia. The synergy of actions to accelerate access to financing and FinTech will help SMEs develop and expand. FinTech technology solutions also help SMEs conduct digital transactions and facilitate fast-track transactions globally. For example, recently, BukuWarung (bukuwarung.com) received Series A funding of US$60 million and BukuKas (bukukas.co.id), which also received Series B funding of US$50 million. These two FinTech are free business finance applications that millions of SMEs in Indonesia have used their apps. This funding shows bright prospects for accounting FinTech startups. They have successfully transformed traditional bookkeeping into digital finance that is more comprehensive and easily accessible to millions of SMEs throughout Indonesia. The technology implemented by FinTech improves the bookkeeping process by helping merchants save all types of transactions, including debt, expenses, and sales, and provides the ability to monitor cash flow through business reports. Thanks to the automatic debit reminder feature provided by the app, merchants receive debt payments 3x faster than they should, so they enjoy the faster cash flow.

FinTech has threatened the financial services industry in three ways. First, unlike traditional funding methods, online platforms allow financial service providers to offer various innovative services that remove intermediaries and administrative layers, making transactions more efficient and error-free. Second, network financial services allow faster access to various transactions, including checking financial status, making payments, interesting and transferring funds. Third, the operation behind financial organizations is equally changed (Fenwick et al., 2017). FinTech refers to various technologies that have a broad impact on payment methods, funding, loans, investment, financial services, and currencies such as Digital payments, crowdfunding, and cryptocurrency. The activity of crowdfunding is merely one of many components of FinTech. (Ma&Liu, 2017). Crowdfunding is part of the Fintech Revolution that conducts financial disintermediating through technology to offer capital to SMEs and the company's early stages in the economy (Chapman, 2019).

CROWDFUNDING MODEL FOR SME

Crowdfunding is part of fintech lenders that have challenged traditional business models by reducing finance risks and creating market efficiency (Fenwick et al., 2017) and financial innovation (Stefani et al., 2020). Crowdfunding is a fast-developing practice in which entrepreneurs seek finance for their business ventures from a potentially large number of people (Short et al., 2017). Crowdfunding allows any founder of a non-profit, cultural, or social project to raise funds from multiple people, often in exchange for a future product or equity (Mollick, 2014). The crowdfunding model is a new phenomenon that allows people to finance projects or business ideas that interest them using online platforms (Bottiglia and Pichler, 2016). Crowdfunding is a relatively new funding practice in which people provide small amounts of funds to projects that interest them. Bellefamme et al. (2014) explained that crowdfunding is financing projects or companies through the Internet. Financial resources come from many people, who can provide money in donations or exchange for monetary or non-monetary rewards.

Crowdfunding has fundamentally changed the way SMEs or startup entrepreneurs access alternative funding outside of conventional banking. Tomczak and Brem (2013) pointed out that Crowdfunding consists of components determined by fundraisers, platforms, and regulators. The fundraiser decides the type of Crowdfunding and the return of funds provided to investors, and the platform chooses the kind of investment that can make. Haas et al. (2014) explained the fundraising model's uniqueness for capital seekers and investors through crowdfunding intermediaries (platforms). The function of the crowdfunding intermediary as a market maker has united capital and funding agents. Thus, Crowdfunding as a digital financial model shows the potential for disruption in the financial intermediation business. Fintech development in Indonesia tends to be very massive, especially in the field of loan money. This can not be separated from the many conveniences for users in loaning money for making business and limited access to banking. Eldridge, Nisar, and Torchia (2019) show crowdfunding have a positive impact on the chances of growth of small companies; unfortunately, Crowdfunding has not had a significant influence on innovation in small companies

Blakstad & Allen (2018) explain that Crowdfunding as an alternative financial provider has reshaped the financial services ecosystem by filling the gap of services that traditional banks cannot serve, especially in underserved populations. The phrase "crowdfunding" is a catch-all term encompassing a wide range of level fundraising models, such as investments or non-investment finance. (Shneor et al., 2020). In addition, crowdfunding can categorize as 'share-based (investors become shareholders and receive dividends) or 'reward-based (investors will receive products or prizes from their investments. Pietro (2019) divides into two Crowdfunding business models, namely the Investment model (Lending and ECF) and non-Investment models (Reward and Donation-based).

P2P lending. Financial Service Authority (OJK) has regulated the FinTech Peer-to-Peer (P2P) Lending model through OJK Regulation No.77/OJK.01/2016. The regulation explains that the FinTech Peer-to-Peer Lending model can provide loans of up to 2 billion Rupiahs. P2P lending is a suitable means to get a fast, easy, unsecured loan without collateral and offers a more competitive interest rate under banking. This advantage is made possible by technological innovations in credit scoring systems, semi-automated risk assessment methods, and maximizing other supporting data. The P2P lending industry will attract much attention from local and global investors because of the potential for attractive returns and the high success rate of loan repayments. FinTech startups minimize risk by diversifying their portfolios and providing varied rates of return and a more comprehensive range of products, resulting in higher lender trust.

The disadvantage of P2P Lending for Borrowers is that the interest rates on P2P Lending loans will spike when creditworthiness is due, especially if the borrower is late in paying or defaulting on the loan. The downside is that Bills will continue to increase significantly. This situation creates adverse excesses for the development of FinTech. Thus, for SMEs, the peer-to-peer lending model is only suitable for short-term loans and is not ideal for investment financing. Indonesian consumer institutions have received thousands of complaints about financial services, and 33% of them were cases of illegal online loans. The Financial Services Authority and the Investment Alert Task Force have closed no less than 1,200 illicit loans. This situation occurs due to a lack of knowledge about financial literacy. To avoid this unwanted incident, SME business players must increase their financial literacy and financial inclusion knowledge and avoid borrowing from illegal FinTech. In addition, loans should be allocated to productive debt that will create future returns.

Crowdfunding Security (SCF). The concept of Crowdfunding equity (ECF) has opened up opportunities for SMEs to offer their shares through a fundraising platform. ECF is an alternative funding source for start-up companies and unbankable SMEs to develop their businesses. FinTech ECF is a stock issuance service. Through Financial Services Authority Regulation Number 37/POJK.04/2018 concerning Crowdfunding Services Through Information Technology-Based Share Offerings. SMEs are allowed to raise funds through the capital market. ECF can increase the number of SME investors from the capital market. SMEs can work with FinTech to raise funds from capital market investors. In Indonesia, the term equity crowdfunding (ECF) has changed to Securities Crowdfunding (SCF). This change is an extension of the previous regulation from equity only to equity and debt. SCF is a method of raising funds with a joint venture scheme carried out by business actors to start or expand their business. Investors can purchase and acquire shares, proof of debt ownership (bonds), or joint ownership certificates (Sukuk). A claim of the company is received according to a percentage of the value of the contribution amount. SCF can gather SME funding needs quickly through the capital market. Investors will get profits in dividends or profit-sharing from business profits that are distributed regularly.

Rewards-based. Reward-based non-investment model is an attractive fundraising option for SMEs because donors do not expect monetary gains but unique services, gifts, or buying new products in advance (pre-sale) at attractive prices in return for investment. Rockethub, Kickstarter, Quirky, Invested. In, Somolend and IndieGoGo are some examples of these platforms. This model will effective if SMEs have a product or service idea validated better than the incumbent, have promising business prospects, and meet future market needs. Usually, new SMEs have early adopters, minimum viable products, or beta versions of products and require continued funding to finance the development of their business products. Leboeuf and Schwienbacher (2017) state Supporters of this crowdfunding model can help entrepreneurs support business plans, consume (buy) product of SMEs, philanthropy, or gain recognition by becoming members of a group. On the other hand, professional investors should benefit from their investment activities, especially if they manage funds for their clients, even if they may pursue other objectives, such as promoting socially responsible investing and economic development. However, the final aim is usually the second. Overall, reward-based crowdfunding is considered one of the most popular alternative types of crowdfunding because it is safe and minimal risk. Through its resources, the reward-based Crowdfunding business model can educate and help SMEs take advantage of digital technology so that SME businesses can grow, develop and reduce the risk of failure.

Donation-Based. Leboeuf and Schwienbacher (2017) state it is essential to distinguish between donations or rewards. In reward-based crowdfunding, supporters may be eligible for bonuses, depending on the entrepreneur's commitment and the amount promised during the event. In donation-based crowdfunding, supporters will not get any tips for their contributions. Crowdfunding Donation is a fundraising campaign for humanitarian causes, such as educational aid, victims of natural disasters, medical expenses, and charities. This model does not provide refunds that have been donated. In Indonesia, crowdfunding platforms for donation types such as kitabisa.com, rumahyatim.org, ruanginsanberbagi.org, sharinghappiness.org are increasing. The emergence of the COVID-19 pandemic has increased social solidarity and cohesion. The spirit of good people's power makes social crowdfunding platforms grow. The World Giving Index (2021) was issued by the charity Charities Aid Foundation (CAF). Indonesia has been named the most generous country in the world. Indonesia has the highest overall index score, with 69, taller than 59 (2018). In 2020, eight out of ten Indonesians donated, and the service fee for volunteers in the country is much higher than average. The phenomenon of digital donations is increasing due to the ease of donating through digital payment platforms such as OVO, Gopay, Dana, LinkAja, Tokopedia, and Shopee, which allow donations with very affordable nominal.

COMPARISON OF P2P LENDING AND CROWDFUNDING MODEL

The difference between P2P Lending and Crowdfunding is (1) The compensation system. In P2P Lending, compensation is in the form of interest for both the borrower and the lender. While Crowdfunding, the payment can be in the form of shares or prizes. (2) Debt payment obligations. In P2P Lending, SMEs are bound by a written agreement regarding the number of funds lent and the obligation to pay bills every month until they are paid off. While in Crowdfunding, there is no agreement on bill payments because the funds collected are voluntary. (3) Details of business information. In P2P Lending, SMEs must provide detailed business information. Crowdfunding is more about explaining a unique business idea (4). Business interference. In P2P Lending, investors will not interfere with business development if the loan is repaid on time. While Crowdfunding, where investors want reports on business developments. Not infrequently, investors are directly involved in business operations. It aims to reduce the risk of business failure. (5) P2P lending only distributes funds; equity crowdfunding (ECF) can buy shares, Sukuk, or bonds. For SMEs, the crowdfunding model is preferred. For investors, the crowdfunding system is safer and less risky.

FINTECH: AN ALTERNATIVE FINANCING FOR SMES

Small and medium enterprises are the backbone of economies worldwide. For banks, SMEs offer enormous potential, but often SMEs are not bankable and meet licensing loan requirements. Most banks lack information regarding SMEs' accurate assessment and creditworthiness, which results in an increased cost of bank risk for the SME segment compared to the corporate segment. Bank financing schemes tend to mitigate risk by asking for more excellent guarantees than SME financing. The biggest problem in financial inclusion in SMEs is Access to financial service because it consists of cash flow problems, bookkeeping, information asymmetry about business quality (DSResearch, 2020), lack of business experience, operating history, or track record (Stemler, 2013). All of this leads to stricter SME loan requirements due to provisions related to bank risk management and the prudential principle of banks. According to the International Finance Corporation (2017), the unmet financing needs of SMEs reach **$5.2 trillion per year**. This financing gap is likely to widen significantly after the COVID-19 pandemic. In countries that lack sufficient seed and startup capital, FinTech can help fill the funding gap by allowing the unskilled to invest in innovative startups (Hornuf and Schwienbach 2017).

The COVID-19 pandemic has caused many SMEs to need financing from banks to survive and restart their businesses. The results of the Central Research Agency Indonesia Survey (2020) show that 7 out of every 10 MSE business actors need business capital assistance as the most needed during the pandemic. Unfortunately, many financial institutions are tightening their belts on access to finance because they are concerned that it could disrupt financial liquidity. Based on the Ministry of SME Cooperatives (2020) data, the proportion of SME loans to total bank loans has only reached 19.97%. To anticipate this, Bank Indonesia (BI) injected liquidity worth Rp 792 trillion (May 2021), reducing interest rates to 3.5%. Bank Indonesia (BI) stated that the interest rate was the lowest in history, but the SME sector was still seen as a high-risk business. In Indonesia, it is estimated that 67% of SMEs have not received financing. Most SME players are categorized as unbankable or underserved, making it difficult to get fast access to funding from banks. This situation makes them have to be creative in finding alternative funding sources such as personal funds, family, or close friends (Agrawal, Catalini, & Goldfar, 2014; Belleflamme, Lambert, & Schwienbacher, 2014). In Indonesia, SMEs often get loans from cooperatives, savings and loan cooperatives, BMTs, village funds, or moneylenders.

Based on DSInnovate's research (2021), 70% of SMEs said that the main challenge in running their business was obtaining capital financing. Capital requirement and adequacy are challenges faced by SME business actors in improving their business performance. The Financial Service Authority (OJK) reports that only 18.3% of SMEs have been approved for loans by conventional financial institutions due to the inability of SMEs to provide adequate financial reports. This gap is exploited by FinTech. In 2020, as much as 74 trillion Rupiah was disbursed by FinTech to SMEs in Indonesia (up 27% compared to the previous year). The Indonesian Joint Funding FinTech Association (AFPI) noted that FinTech borrowers came from online and offline SME players. FinTech industry funding plays an essential role for the national economy and is an alternative answer to digital financing during a pandemic. DSInnovate's (2020) FinTech has played a role in increasing financial inclusion and encouraging community involvement through easy access to finance from FinTech funding. To further enhance the role of FinTech for SMEs, the Financial Services Authority has provided space for a small company with a capital of less than **IDR 30 billion** to raise funds from the public outside the capital market to open up more opportunities for SMEs to develop their business, by utilizing the crowdfunding FinTech platform.

FinTech makes it easier for consumers, including SME players, to use various financial services such as payments, loans, investments, and insurance. Via smartphones. FinTech inclusion aims to ensure access, business operations, and digital financial services for SMEs such as ordering systems, inventory, sales, payments to customer feedback. The Financial Services Authority (OJK) targets at least 75% of the adult population in Indonesia to access the services of financial institutions. FinTech and digital platforms offer alternative business models and solutions that can expand the reach of providing adequate financial services, especially SMEs. The FinTech platform is also expected to be able to improve and accelerate banking through collaboration and partnerships. The role of banks in the financial services sector is less than optimal, and there are still many people who do not have access to banking. According to DS research and AFPI (2020) studies, most FinTech lending businesses currently target the product segment. Provide capital loans to help SMEs. In addition, through digital transactions, FinTech will help suppress the spread of covid because direct interaction between producers of consumer funds can be done virtually.

The development of SMEs is hampered due to the limited conservative banking principles, and there are still many people who have not accessed banking. It is estimated that around 53% of SMEs are still in the informal sector. This condition is a challenge for the government to encourage SMEs to upgrade from casual to formal businesses. One of the ways the government enables SMEs to enter the digital ecosystem is to collaborate with FinTech. The FinTech platform is expected to be able to increase financial literacy and inclusion through collaboration and partnerships. The government also strives to increase FinTech inclusion among SMEs by encouraging SMEs to enter the digital sector. To facilitate the potential of local economic actors in Indonesia. SMEs get various facilities such as broader market access, business networks, financing/capital, assistance in improving product quality, opportunities to participate more in the supply of State Own Enterprises (SOEs) needs. Digital Market Platform SMEs are also given the convenience to become business suppliers of SOEs to protect fair business competition. Digital Market Platform is collaborating with nine government SOEs to prepare the SME Digital Market.

CHALLENGES OF SME DIGITIZATION AND FINANCIAL INCLUSION

Technology has three significant impacts on business and industry (1) Process automation, where machines or algorithms replace manual work done by humans. (2) Lowering the cost of obtaining information (3) more efficient manufacturing and distribution processes (Kark et al., 2019; Tilley, 2017). Digital Technology, like digital finance, comprises many new financial products and financial services (Gomber, Koch, and Siering, 2017). Digital technology enables all types of transactions to access financial services more quickly over the Internet. It permits people to access finance from distant places and at any time, including checking financial status, making payments, withdrawing, and transferring funds. (Manyika et al., 2016). Digital finance is a new method for expanding financial inclusion by including disadvantaged groups in mainstream economic activities (Gabor & Brooks, 2016). Financial inclusion means serve unbanked businesses and offering financial services at a meager cost and fill a gap that banks have never tackled with well thought through and low-cost service offerings (Lacasse et al. 2016). Trough, Digital finance, with its unique features, has played an essential role in the process of inclusive growth of the country by expanding opportunities for all people to participate in economic activities (Siddik and Kabiraj, 2020)

Digital technology is key to capturing growth opportunities in new markets. Digitization helps SMEs improve customer experience, be more efficient, improve security, develop new services, and create new business models. Griffith (2020) states that FinTechs help reduces operational costs, provide more personalized services through data, and respond to customer behavior changes. The development of various digital markets allows for creative collaboration between e-commerce players and SMEs. The use of technology for business will increase the involvement of SMEs in the digital market. This engagement will increase digital literacy, financial literacy, and digital financial inclusion. For e-commerce players, the increase in SMEs connected to their market platforms will increase the number of transactions and increase the valuation of their business marketplace. So, the empowerment of digitalization and FinTech Inclusion for SMEs is a mutual need that is mutually beneficial to strengthen the digital market ecosystem. The focus of FinTech in empowering SMEs is vital because of its enormous contribution to the national economy. Manyika et al. (2016) state that the wide-ranging usage of digital finance could increase the annual gross domestic product (GDP). In 2020 digital economies in Indonesia grew by 11 percent compared to 2019 and contributed to the US $ 44 billion. SEA Economic Report (2020) Predict the Indonesian Digital Economy will contribute to the US $ 124 billion economies in 2025. A research report Digital Trade in Indonesia estimated contribution of e-commerce to Indonesian GDP is projected to penetrate Rp. 2,305 trillion or grew 18 times in 2030 (Hinrich & Alphabeta, 2019)

Several things challenge SMEs to enter the digital ecosystem: (1) the lack of knowledge and skills in utilizing digital platforms. SME business people are not used to using digital technology in their business operations. Assistance and training are needed so that they adapt to enter the digital ecosystem. (2) uneven access to digital infrastructure in many rural and remote areas. ICT Infrastructure is the primary capital for economic growth. An increase in internet access is correlated with economic growth and GDP. Indonesia's geographical condition as an archipelagic country makes it challenging to distribute digital infrastructure evenly throughout Indonesia. The Indonesian government has prepared a national fiber-optic network development project called the palapa ring to accelerate Indonesia's digital transformation. East Venture Study (2021) results that the government's efforts to encourage the development of digital infrastructure have proven to be successful. This result can be seen from the increase in Indonesia's digital competitiveness index. In the face of the COVID-19 pandemic, Indonesia's digital adoption has accelerated, and the Internet penetration rate in Indonesia's 34 provinces and 25 major cities has reached 73%. (3) This geographical location also makes inter-island logistics costs high in Indonesia. Fortunately, this challenge is usually overcome by free shipping programs from marketplace or e-commerce providers (4) the lack of information and education about the use of services provided by FinTech. The variety of existing FinTech platforms makes SMEs confused about making the right choice in using digital media.

Despite smartphone ownership, high internet penetration, and adequate digital infrastructure, SMEs' digital literacy and inclusion are still unsatisfactory. For example, the National Financial Literacy and Inclusion Survey (2019) showed that the financial literacy index only reached 38.03% (an increase of 8.33% from 2016), and the financial inclusion index was 76.19% (a rise of 8.39% from 2016). In general, the financial inclusion index in Indonesia only reached 76%, lower than Singapore's 86%, Malaysia's 85%, and Thailand's 82%. OJK estimates that 51% of the adult population does not have an account with a financial institution. FinTech must take advantage of this opportunity because financial inclusion has not yet reached remote parts of Indonesia. The FinTech industry has made a positive contribution to the economy by disbursing loans of Rp128.7 trillion, or an increase of 113% per year. It is hoped that FinTech can develop its function as a financial planner and expand the access of SMEs in E-commerce marketing. Until now, there are still many SMEs who have difficulty marketing their products through E-commerce. This is due to several factors such as knowledge, skills, telecommunications infrastructure, and funding. FinTech is expected to function as an aggregator, innovative credit scoring, equity crowdfunding, and project financing services.

The OJK-BCG Joint Research (2020) results stated that SMEs expect the most desired financial assistance: operational subsidies, technology solution provider services, incentives for using digital platforms, and subsidies for digital devices to support their business operations. The government was initiated Various programs to increase the involvement of SMEs. FinTech collaborations with multiple parties, including financial institutions such as banks, BPR, and BPD, are encouraged to expand the reach of financing. FinTech funding actors must also update technology, especially in credit scoring analysis, to speed up time and minimize credit decisions for SMEs. Technology plays an essential role in business success to increase revenue growth, increase employee productivity and gain more customers. The challenge is how to determine the right mix of technology investments such as Chatbots, Machine Learning, Artificial Intelligence (AI), Digital payment systems, Customer Relationship Management (CRM) in Business Processes, and Movement to the Cloud). Strategic assistance and digital solutions are needed for SMEs in identifying business opportunities from existing technology.

Other challenges faced by SMEs are the low access to market information, financing, high transaction costs, negotiations, contracts, and digitalization for business operations. The synergy between stakeholders is needed to ensure uniformity and continuity of activities to improve financial literacy, digital literacy, and FinTech inclusion for SME business actors. Development of human resource capacity (HR), increasing production capacity and product quality and building an excellent brand to the market. The government has targeted 30 million MSMEs to go digital by 2023. The growth of FinTech is expected to be in line with the development of SMEs in Indonesia. Synergy and collaboration between stakeholders are needed to facilitate and encourage SMEs to be integrated into the digital ecosystem. The digitization of SMEs is limited to the onboarding stage to the e-commerce platform and how to make these business actors survive, compete, and develop their market. The SME Empowerment Report (2020) shows that SMEs recognize increased business competition due to digital technology. To increase market trust and credibility, OJK continues to improve regulations so that the FinTech industry is healthier and more stable from the threat of a crisis. Increased public confidence in FinTech has an impact on increasing financial inclusion.

The next challenge is to accelerate digital transformation and digital financial integration. Digital transformation can encourage changes in the business model, increasing opportunities that produce added value and a digital business mindset for SMEs. The Acceleration of Digital Transformation and Digital Finance is one of the keys to restoring the national economy. Through a digital nation Indonesian Framework, the Indonesian government continues to accelerate digital transformation in three key areas: government, economy, and community. The government also focuses on expanding the broadband infrastructure network and use of digital technology, and preparation for 5G network implementation. Meanwhile, infrastructure development targets facilitation and acceleration in national priority sectors with application-based digital solutions. The benefit of digital infrastructure is expected to strengthen and utilize the digital economy, especially economic and financial inclusion, including SMEs. For example, Bank Indonesia has prepared the use of QR Indonesia Standard (QRIS) to realize the digital transformation of the financial sector, especially payment systems that can encourage an increase in economic transactions, especially FinTech inclusion of SMEs. Bank Indonesia noted, until July 2021, more than 8 million merchants have been integrated with the Indonesian Quick Response Code Indonesian Standard (QRIS).

The emergence of various facilities in obtaining funding from FinTech has harmful excesses such as leakage of customer data, loss of investment funds, exorbitant interest rates, or other legal aspects caused by failure to repay loans. The public needs to be given education and literacy regarding the advantages and disadvantages of FinTech, such as (1) prospective borrowers must also understand the risks of this kind of lending model, interest, fees, and fines. (2) prospective borrowers must ensure that the FinTech company is registered with the Financial Services Authority (3) prospective borrowers need to measure their financial ability according to the penalty for paying bills. Do not take a new loan to pay off an old loan. Several problems arise from complaints related to online loans. Illegal online loan platforms often take advantage of customers' data to intimidate customers if they are late or do not pay their loans. However, many of these problems remain unresolved. This is due to weak regulations and sanctions for rogue online lenders. It is resulting in a lack of legal protection for online loan consumers. It takes a concerted effort from all stakeholders to maintain public trust in FinTech so that this industry can grow healthy and sustained.

CONCLUSION

FinTech has disrupted the financial services sector. Online platforms allow FinTech to offer various new services that eliminate intermediaries and administrative layers (decentralized, flat, efficient). Transactions are more effective, fast, low cost, more reliable, and valid. SMEs are an essential part of the future FinTech business. FinTech must assist SMEs in developing product standards, facilitating the digitization of their business processes, and creating an integrated digital ecosystem. The integration of FinTech services will accelerate the transformation of SMEs to enter the digital financial services ecosystem. Financial problems arise due to a lack of access to capital.

Collaboration P2P lending, Credit scoring startups, accounting, and banking are needed to accelerate SME funding decisions. Verification of potential borrowers, SME financial audits, SME creditworthiness assessments for loans can be calculated and analyzed using digital platforms. FinTech integrates various business processes such as inventory, transaction recording, payments, and back-end processing so that SMEs can receive payments, manage tables, take orders, invoices, and even payroll and tax applications. The results will provide more insight for SME business people to make decisions for their business development. Increasing the competitiveness of SMEs will create new opportunities, reduce barriers to market entry, improve business processes, reach broader markets, and attract new customers.

Banking and FinTech collaborations such as Expenditure Management, Asset Financing, Billing Management, Service Offerings (Payroll, Tax Administration, Complex Administration) are still needed to provide economic benefits for MSME actors. FinTech will get lending channels, and banks will implement new technologies. In addition, SMEs need assistance and training related to FinTech Inclusion to monitor financial performance, prepare cash flow reports, asset-liability balances, and profit and loss. Thus, MSMEs can save time and make it easier to design their business books. FinTech is also challenged to elaborate and innovate in training and assist SMEs to understand the use of transaction data. With the help of FinTech, SMEs can find out the shopping habits of consumers to recommend products that are more in line with consumer needs and estimate the level of inventory needed at a particular time.

SMEs also need to learn about digital risks such as (1) security systems against hacking payment systems (2) protection of consumer transaction data. Consumers' data for privacy must protect sMEs. (3) QR Code protection from being confused with other parties because there is a possibility that an irresponsible party replaces the QR Code to channel consumer payments to their balance. (4) risk of loss of accounting data. Because accounting services use online features, there is a risk of data loss if the service provider's application is in trouble or no longer operating. Therefore, MSMEs are advised to back up bookkeeping data in a separate database and understand accounting principles. Finally, improving digital financial services and FinTech inclusion for SMEs requires synergy between stakeholders. The digital ecosystem will grow well if there is synergy between SMEs, FinTech startups, marketplaces, digital banking, regulators, and other digital financial innovators. without cooperation, the target to increase financial literacy and financial inclusion and FinTech inclusion will be challenging to achieve.

REFERENCES

Agrawal, A., Catalini, C., & Goldfarb, A. (2014). The simple economics of crowdfunding, innovation policy and the economy. *Innovation Policy and the Economy*, *14*(1), 63–97. doi:10.1086/674021

Arjunwadkar, P. Y (2018). *FinTech: The Technology Driving Disruption in the Financial Services*. CRC Press, Taylor & Francis Group Industry.

Arslanian, H., & Fischer, F. (2019). *The Future of Finance: The Impact of FinTech*. AI, and Crypto on Financial Services, Palgrave Macmillan. doi:10.1007/978-3-030-14533-0

Bank Indonesia. (2021). *Archipelago Report*. https://www.bi.go.id/id/publikasi/laporan/Documents/Laporan_Nusantara_April_2021.pdf

Bartik, A. (2020). *How Are Small Businesses Adjusting To Covid-19? Early Evidence From A Survey*. Nber Working Paper Series, No. 26989. Nber. https://www.nber.org/papers/w26989

Belleflamme, P., Lambert, T., & Schwienbacher, A. (2013). Individual crowdfunding practices. *Venture Capital*, *15*(4), 313–333. doi:10.1080/13691066.2013.785151

Belleflamme, P., Lambert, T., & Schwienbacher, A. (2014). Crowdfunding: Tapping the right crowd. *Journal of Business Venturing*, *29*(5), 585–609. doi:10.1016/j.jbusvent.2013.07.003

Blakstad, S., & Allen, R. (2018). *FinTech Revolution: Universal Inclusion in the New Financial Ecosystem*. Palgrave Macmillan. doi:10.1007/978-3-319-76014-8

Bona, C., Koslow, L., Frantz, R., Nadres, B., & Ratajczak, D. (2020). *How Marketers Can Win with Gen Z and Millennials Post-COVID-19*. https://www.bcg.com/publications/2020/how-marketers-can-win-with-gen-z-millennials-post-covid

Bottiglia, R., & Pichler, F. (2016). *Crowdfunding for SMEs: A European Perspective*. Palgrave Macmillan Studies in Banking and Financial Institutions, Springer Nature. doi:10.1057/978-1-137-56021-6

Buffington, C. (2020). *Measuring the Effect of COVID-19 on US Small Businesss: The Small Business Pulse Survey*. No. CES-20-16, US Census Bureau. https://www.census.gov/library/working-papers/2020/adrm/CES-WP-20-16.html

CAF. (2021). *World Giving Index 2021*. https://www.cafonline.org/about-us/publications/2021-publications/caf-world-giving-index-2021

Central Research Agency Indonesia. (2020). *Analysis of the Results of the Covid-19 Impact Survey on Business Actors*. https://www.bps.go.id/publication.html?Publikasi%5BtahunJudul%5D=&Publikasi%5BkataKunci%5D=dampak+covid&Publikasi%5BcekJudul%5D=0&yt0=Tampilkan

ChapmanP. (2019). *Crowfunding*. https://www.elgaronline.com/view/edcoll/9781788979016/14_chapter3.xhtml doi:10.4337/9781788979023.00015

Chappell, G., Harreis, H., Havas, A., Nuzzo, A., Pepanides, T., & Rowshankish, K. (2018). *The lending revolution: How digital credit is changing banks from the inside*. https://www.mckinsey.com/business-functions/risk/our-insights/the-lending-revolution-how-digital-credit-is-changing-banks-from-the-inside

Deloitte, A. E. R. (2015). *SMEs Powering Indonesia's success*. https://www2.deloitte.com/id/en/pages/financial-advisory/articles/smes-powering-indonesia-success-report.html

Dewi, M. A. (2020). The Impact of FinTech on the Development of Financial Inclusion in MSMEs in East Java. *Gorontalo Accounting Journal*, *3*(2), 68–83. doi:10.32662/gaj.v3i2.973

Di Pietro, F. (2019). Deciphering Crowdfunding. In *Disrupting Finance FinTech and Strategy in the 21st Century*. Palgrave Studies in Digital Business & Enabling Technologies.

DS Research & AFPI. (2020). Evolving Landscape of FinTech Lending in Indonesia. https://dailysocial.id/research/evolving-landscape-of-FinTech-lending-in-indonesia-2020

DSInnovate. (2021). *Spectrums The Power of E-commerce Spectrums*. https://dailysocial.id/research/the-power-of-e-commerce-spectrums

DSResearch. (2020). *Evolving Landscape of FinTech Lending in Indonesia 2020*. https://dailysocial.id/research/evolving-landscape-of-FinTech-lending-in-indonesia-2020

DSResearch & Bank CIMB Niaga. (2020). *FinTech Report 2020: Maintaining Growth during Pandemic*. https://dailysocial.id/research/FinTech-report-2020

DSResearch & Mandiri Capital Indonesia. (2020). *SME Empowerment*. https://dailysocial.id/research/sme-empowerment-report-2020

Eldridge, D., Nisar, T. M., & Torchia, M. (2019). What impact does equity crowdfunding have on SME innovation and growth? An empirical study. *Small Bus Econ, 56*, 105–120. https://link.springer.com/article/10.1007%2Fs11187-019-00210-4

Fenwick, M., McCahery, J. A., & Vermeulen, E. P. M. (2017) *Fintech and the Financing of Entrepreneurs: From Crowdfunding to Marketplace Lending*. TILEC Discussion Paper No. 2017-25, ECGI - Law Working Paper No. 369/2017, Lex Research Topics in Corporate Law & Economics Working Paper No. 2017-3. Available at https://ssrn.com/abstract=2967891 doi:10.2139/ssrn.2967891

Financial Service Authority. (2019). *National Financial Literacy and Inclusion Survey*. https://www.ojk.go.id/id/berita-dan-activities/publikasi/Pages/Survei-Nasional-Literasi-dan-Inclusion-Keuangan-2019.aspx

Financial Service Authority. (2021). *Statistics FinTech Lending*. https://www.ojk.go.id/id/kanal/iknb/data-dan-statistik/FinTech/Pages/Statistik-FinTech-Lending-Periode-April-2021-.aspx#

Financial Service Authority –Boston Consulting Group. (2020). *How MSMEs & Banking Can Succeed in the Era of Disruption, Economy & Digital, Joint Research*. https://www.ojk.go.id/id/data-dan-statistik/research/prosiding/Documents/Kajian%20Bagaimana%20UMKM%20dan%20Perbankan%20Dapat%20Sukses%20di%20Era%20Disrupsi%20Ekonomi%20dan%20Digital.pdf

Gabor, D., & Brooks, S. (2016). The digital revolution in financial inclusion: International development in the FinTech era. *New Political Economy*, *22*(4), 423–436. doi:10.1080/13563467.2017.1259298

Gomber, P., Koch, J. A., & Siering, M. (2017). Digital Finance and FinTech: Current research and future research directions. *Journal of Business Economics*, *87*(5), 537–580. doi:10.100711573-017-0852-x

Google, Temasek, & Bain. (2019). *e-Conomy SEA report 2019: Swipe up and to the right: Southeast Asia's $100 billion Internet economy*. https://www.thinkwithgoogle.com/intl/en-apac/consumer-insights/consumer-journey/e-conomy-sea-2020-resilient-and-racing-ahead-what-marketers-need-to-know-about-this-years-digital-shifts

Google, Temasek, & Bain. (2020). *e-Conomy SEA report 2020, Resilient and racing ahead — What marketers need to know about this year's digital shifts*. https://www.thinkwithgoogle.com/intl/en-apac/consumer-insights/consumer-journey/e-conomy-sea-2020-resilient-and-racing-ahead-what-marketers-need-to-know-about-this-years-digital-shifts/

Gourinchas, P., & Kalemli-Özcan, S. (2020). *COVID-19 and business failures*. UC Berkeley. doi:10.3386/w27877

Griffiths, P. (2020). *The FinTech Industry: Crowdfunding in Context*. Advances in Crowdfunding. doi:10.1007/978-3-030-46309-0_11

Gupta, P., & Mandhy Tham, T. (2018). *FinTech: The New DNA of Financial Services*. Walter de Gruyter Inc. doi:10.1515/9781547400904

Haas, P., Blohm, I., & Leimeister, J. M. (2014). *An empirical taxonomy of crowdfunding intermediaries*. International conference on information systems, Auckland, New Zealand.

Hornuf, L., & Schwienbacher, A. (2017). Should Securities Regulation Promote Equity Crowdfunding? *Small Business Economics*, *49*(3), 579–593. doi:10.100711187-017-9839-9

ILO. (2020). *ILO Monitor: COVID-19 and the world of work*. https://gisanddata.maps.arcgis.com/apps/opsdashboard/index.html#/bda7594740fd40299423467b48e9ecf6

International Data Corporation. (2020). *DC FutureScape: Worldwide Digital Transformation 2021 Predictions*. https://www.idc.com/getdoc.jsp?containerId=US46880818

International Finance Corporation. (2017). *Assessment Of The Shortfalls And Opportunities In Financing Micro, Small And Medium Enterprises In Emerging Markets.* https://www.ifc.org/wps/wcm/connect/03522e90-a13d-4a02-87cd-9ee9a297b311/121264-WP-PUBLIC- MSMEReportFINAL.pdf?MOD=AJPERES&CVID=m5SwAQA

International Monetary Fund. (2021). *World Economic Outlook Reports April 2021.* https://www.imf.org/en/publications/weo

Kark, K., Briggs, B., & Terzioglu, A. (2019). The future of work in technology. *Deloitte Insight.* https://www2.deloitte.com/us/en/insights/focus/technology-and-the-future-of-work/tech-leaders-reimagining-work-workforce-workplace.html

Kata Data. (2021). *Only 12.5% of MSMEs in Indonesia are Immune from the Covid-19 Pandemic.* https://katadata.co.id/agustiyanti/finansial/605d9f635fdf7/hanya-12-5-umkm-di-indonesia-yang-kebal-dari-pandemi-covid-19

Kontan. (2021). *Bank Indonesia urges banks to lower loan interest rates and extend MSE credit.* https://keuangan.kontan.co.id/news/bank-indonesia-imbau-perbankan-terurunkan-bunga-kredit-dan-salurkan-kredit-umkm

Lacasse, R. M., Lambert, B. A., Osmani, E., Couture, C., Roy, N., Sylvain, J., & Nadeau, F. (2016). A Digital Tsunami: Fintech and Crowdfunding. *Proceedings of International Scientific Conference on Digital Intelligence.*

Leboeuf, G., & Schwienbacher, A. (2017). *Crowdfunding as a New Financing Tool in The Economics of Crowdfunding Startups, Portals, and Investor Behavior.* Springer Nature.

Ma, Y., & Liu, D. (2017). Introduction to the special issue on Crowdfunding and FinTech. *Financial Innovation, 3*(1), 8. doi:10.118640854-017-0058-9

Manyika, J., Lund, S., Singer, M., White, O., & Berry, C. (2016). *Digital finance for all: Powering inclusive growth in emerging economies.* McKinsey Global Institute.

Marini, Linawati, & Putra. (2020). The Role of FinTech on Financial Inclusion in South Tangerang MSMEs. *Sustainability: Journal of Management and Journal of Accounting, 5*(2), 91-104. doi:10.32493/keberlanjutan.v5i2.y2020.p91-104

McCann, F., & Myers, S. (2020). *COVID-19 and the transmission of shocks through domestic supply chains. Financial Stability Notes, No. 3.* Central Bank of Ireland.

Mollick, E. R. (2014). The Dynamics of Crowdfunding: An Exploratory Study. *Journal of Business Venturing, 29*(1), 1–16. doi:10.1016/j.jbusvent.2013.06.005

Mulasiwi, M. C., & Julialevi, O. K. (2020). Optimization of Financial Technology (FinTech) on Increasing Financial Literacy and Inclusion of Purwokerto Medium Enterprises. *Performance, 27*(1), 12–20. doi:10.20884/1.jp.2020.27.1.2284

Muzdalifa, I., Rahma, I. A., & Novalia, B. G. (2018). The Role of FinTech in Improving Financial Inclusion in MSMEs in Indonesia (Islamic Finance Approach). *Home, 3*(1). Advance online publication. doi:10.30651/jms.v3i1.1618

OECD. (2020). OECD Economic Outlook. OECD Publishing. doi:10.1787/0d1d1e2e-en

Report, M. S. C. (2020). *Impact of COVID-19 on FinTechs: Indonesia*. https://www.microsave.net/wp-content/uploads/2020/09/Impact-of-COVID-19-on-FinTechs.pdf

Rusdianasari, F. (2018). The Role of Financial Inclusion through FinTech Integration in Indonesia's Financial System Stability. *Journal of Applied Quantitative Economics*, 244-253. . doi:10.24843/JEKT.2018.v11.i02.p10

Sari, P., & Rinofah, R. (2019). The Influence Of Financial Technology On Financial Satisfaction With Financial Achievements As A Mediation Variable. *Business Studies Widya Wiwaha College of Economics*, *27*(2), 134–146. doi:10.32477/jkb.v27i2.56

Shneor, R., Zhao, L., & Flåten, T.B. (2020). *Advances in Crowdfunding: Research and Practice*. Palgrave Macmillan. doi:10.1007/978-3-030-46309-0

Short, J. C., Ketchen, D. J. Jr, McKenny, A. F., Allison, T. H., & Ireland, R. D. (2017). Research on crowdfunding: Reviewing the (very recent) past and celebrating the present. *Entrepreneurship Theory and Practice*, *41*(2), 149–160. doi:10.1111/etap.12270

Siddik, N. A., & Kabiraj, S. (2020). Digital Finance for Financial Inclusion and Inclusive Growth. In Digital Transformation in Business and Society. Palgrave Macmillan. doi:10.1007/978-3-030-08277-2_10

Stefani, U., Schiavone, F., Laperche, B., & Burger-Helmchen, T. (2020). New tools and practices for financing novelty: A research agenda. *European Journal of Innovation Management*, *23*(2), 314–328. doi:10.1108/EJIM-08-2019-0228

Stemler, A. (2013). The jobs act and crowdfunding: Harnessing the power and money of the masses. *Business Horizons*, *56*(3), 271–275. doi:10.1016/j.bushor.2013.01.007

The Hinrich Foundation & AlphaBeta. (2019). *The digital Komodo Dragon: How Indonesia can capture the digital trade opportunity at home and abroad*. https://alphabeta.com/our-research/the-digital-komodo-dragon-how-indonesia-can-capture-the-digital-trade-opportunity-at-home-and-abroad/

Tilley, J. (2017). *Automation, robotics, and the factory of the future*. https://www.mckinsey.com/business-functions/operations/our-insights/automation-robotics-and-the-factory-of-the-future

Tomczak, A., & Brem, A. (2013). A conceptualized investment model of crowdfunding. *Venture Capital*, *15*(4), 335–359. doi:10.1080/13691066.2013.847614

Venture, E. (2021). *Digital Competitiveness Index 2021: Momentum Of Acceleration Of Digital Economic Transformation, Mapping of Digital Competitiveness in 34 Provinces and 25 Cities in Indonesia*. https://east.vc/dci/#form

White, O., Madgavkar, A., Sibanda, T., Townsend, Z., & Ramírez, M. J. (2021). *COVID-19: Making the case for robust digital financial infrastructure*. McKinsey Global Institute.

Chapter 9
How the Development of FinTech Can Bolster Financial Inclusion Under an Era of Disruptive Innovation?
Case Study on China

Poshan Yu
https://orcid.org/0000-0003-1069-3675
Soochow University, China

Chenghai Li
Independent Researcher, China

Michael Sampat
Independent Researcher, Canada

Zuozhang Chen
Soochow University, China

ABSTRACT

FinTech provides more inclusive financial services for individual users and companies. China, with the highest penetration rate of online payment around the world, enables individual users to enjoy in-depth inclusive lending services. This chapter will portray and assess FinTech's adoption, challenges, and its potentials to China. Based on previous literature, the characteristics of FinTech in China and the roles of government in promoting FinTech to Chinese business will be discussed. This chapter will also select cases from Hangzhou and the Greater Bay Area in order to analyze the opportunities and challenges for Chinese companies integrating FinTech into its business operations.

DOI: 10.4018/978-1-7998-8447-7.ch009

INTRODUCTION

Definition of FinTech

As a combination of technology and finance, FinTech has become the main form of financial innovation in this century. According to the Financial Stability Board's (FSB) definition (FSB, 2017), lots of technology-enabled financial innovations, such as Peer to Peer (P2P) lending, electronic payment, crowdfunding, cryptocurrencies, are included in the FinTech industry. FSB defines FinTech as technology-enabled innovation in financial services that can result in new business models, applications, processes or products with an associated material effect on the provision of financial services. This definition has been adopted by the People's Bank of China (PBOC) in its FinTech Development Plan (2019–2021). Before this, FinTech was often referred to as internet finance in China.

FSB also notes that FinTech is low cost and high efficiency as it not only promotes the availability of financial resources and improves the symmetry of transaction information, but also enhances the disintermediation of resource allocation (FSB, 2016).

LITERATURE REVIEW

The development of FinTech and its relationship with financial inclusion have been widely studied. In a study conducted by Croutzet and Dabbous (2021), the impact of FinTech on renewable energy use is examined. FinTech can incentivize the use of renewable energy and helps fund its development. Patwardhan et al. (2018) conducted interview-based studies with FinTech providers and regulators to provide more insight into the potential impact of FinTech development on enhancing financial inclusion outcomes. Hill (2018) discussed the development of FinTech in a global setting, especially in some European countries and in Asia. They reflect on the differences of the FinTech development among countries in terms of banking structure, regulations, institutions, maturation, consumer preferences, and cultural traditions. Hill points out that Chinese FinTech may have the greatest number of FinTech companies and users.

Hill (2018) also indicated that many Asian countries have active FinTech ecosystems. Besides that, various studies have been conducted to examine the FinTech advancement in developing countries. For instance, Lyons, Kass-Hanna and Fava (2021) did a comparative study on FinTech in emerging economies. They also discussed the linkages between FinTech development and financial inclusion. Muthukannan et al. (2021) studied the Indonesian FinTech Ecosystem. Abbasi et al. (2021) utilized firm-level data from OECD countries and examined the association between FinTech and Small and Medium Enterprise (SME) efficiency.

The development of FinTech in China has been widely discussed. Lee, Li, Yu and Zhao (2021) examined whether the development of the FinTech industry affects cost efficiency and the technology adopted for China's banking industry. Shim and Shin (2016) explored the interaction between FinTech and its yet unfolding social and political context.

Meanwhile, some researchers considered that the development of the FinTech industry also results in new risks (FSB, 2017; Ng & Kwok, 2017; Lee & Shin, 2018; Gai, Qiu & Sun, 2018). Furthermore, with the emerging technology's significantly accelerated speed and volume of financial transactions, greater volatility and instability of the entire financial market might occur (IMF, 2017). Therefore, measuring the risk level of China's FinTech industry is important for financial stability (Yao, Li & Sun, 2021).

OVERVIEW OF THIS CHAPTER

In recent years, the FinTech market has been growing rapidly around the world. In the Asia-Pacific region, particularly, it is growing at a significant rate. Chinese FinTech companies are among the top companies in the Asia-Pacific region and worldwide. The emerging FinTech industry in China leads the world in market size and total users (McKinsey, 2016; KPMG, 2019).

This chapter analyzes FinTech investment in China, studying different FinTech sectors including online payment, P2P lending, insurance, and crowdfunding.

China's online payment is well-developed. The progress of P2P lending is facing many challenges, however, this is in line with the development of P2P lending around the world. Insurtech was largely developed by traditional insurance companies. At the same time, crowdfunding platforms are also booming and showing a good trend. Hangzhou, Zhejiang Province and the Greater Bay Area are prominent in China's FinTech industry and have become the objects of our study.

The government has played a very important role in the development of FinTech in China. This chapter summarizes Chinese government policy on FinTech in recent years, focusing on relevant policies of Zhejiang Province and the Greater Bay Area.

A case study is undertaken, the research subject being Ant Financial in Hangzhou and Kingdee Financial in Shenzhen. Ant group focuses on technical services, especially small and micro customers. Kingdee financial has advantages in SaaS Cloud services and efficient credit. These are all strengths that can be learned from.

There are also some failed cases of FinTech companies in China. Zhongdai.com and Shuyin are chosen as examples in this chapter. This chapter analyzes opportunities and challenges for Chinese companies integrating FinTech into their business operations.

BACKGROUND

Global Development of FinTech

Global investment in FinTech has tripled from 920 million dollars in 2008 to 2.97 billion dollars in 2013 (Hwang, 2014). The total value of investments into FinTech companies worldwide increased dramatically between 2010 and 2019, fueled by high confidence in FinTech it reached 168 billion USD. In 2020, however, FinTech companies saw investments drop by more than a third to 105.3 billion USD (Figure 1). The effects of COVID-19 triggered a temporary decrease in deals (Deloitte, 2020).

Because of the increasing intensity of investment, the number of FinTech companies has also been growing in recent years. Figure 2 shows the number of FinTech startups worldwide from 2018 to February 2021, in the Asia -Pacific regions (APAC), Americas and Europe, the Middle East and Africa (EMEA) respectively.

Although the Asia-Pacific region had the lowest number of FinTech companies of these three regions, it is growing at a rapid rate, surpassing EMEA and becoming the highest in February 2021 (Figure 3).

Global FinTech revenues in 2018 were about \$109 billion and are expected to grow to more than \$222 billion in 2024, which is a pre-COVID-19 forecast (Figure 4).

The FinTech markets in the APAC and Americas regions are currently the largest, with each having around 40% of the global market share. The EMEA region is significantly smaller, with around 20% of

Figure 1. Total investments into FinTech companies globall 2010-2020
Data Source(s): KPMG; PitchBook

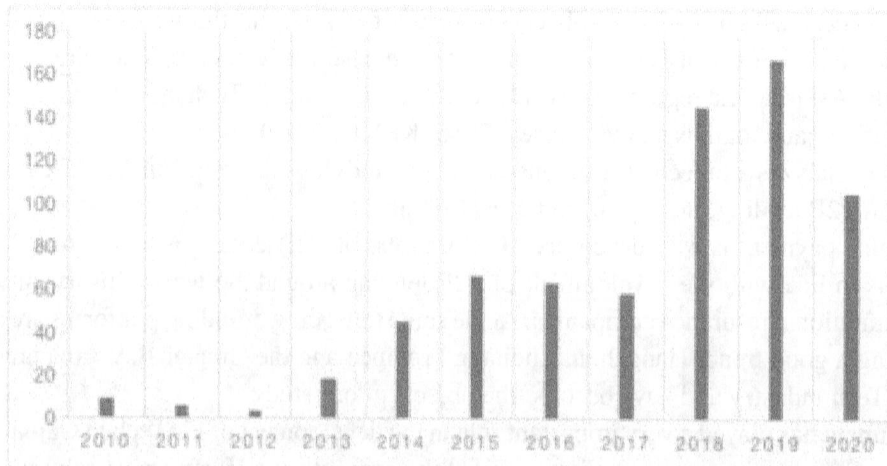

Figure 2. Number of FinTech startups worldwide from 2018 to February 2021, by region
Data Source(s): BCG

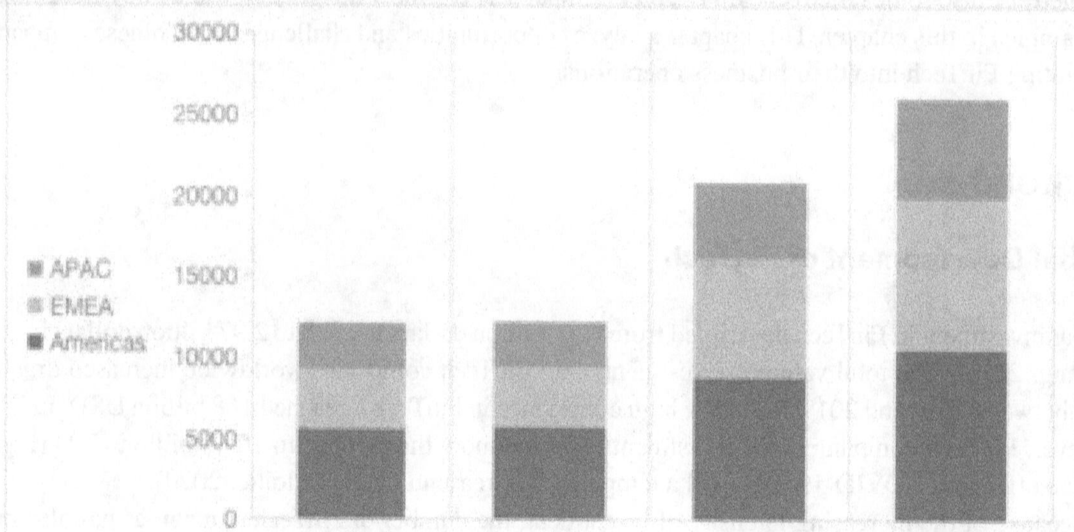

the total market share. The FinTech market in the APAC region is projected to be the fastest-growing (Deloitte, 2020).

Figure 3. The Growing Rate of the Number of FinTech startups worldwide from 2019 to February 2021
Data Source(s): BCG

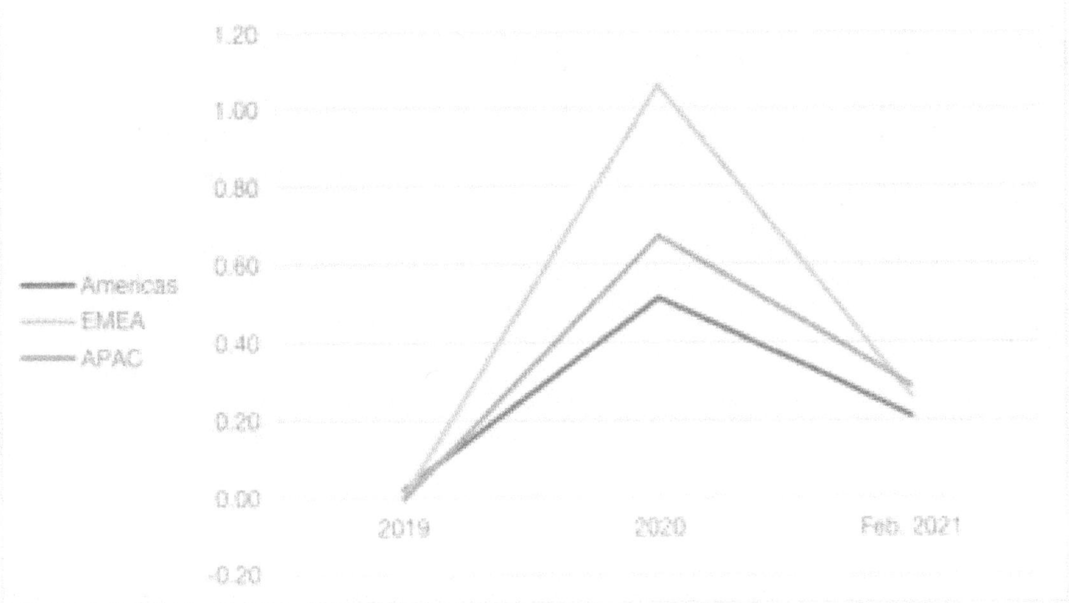

Figure 4. Global FinTech revenue from 2017 to February 2024, in billion USD
Data Source(s): Mordor Intelligence; Deloitte

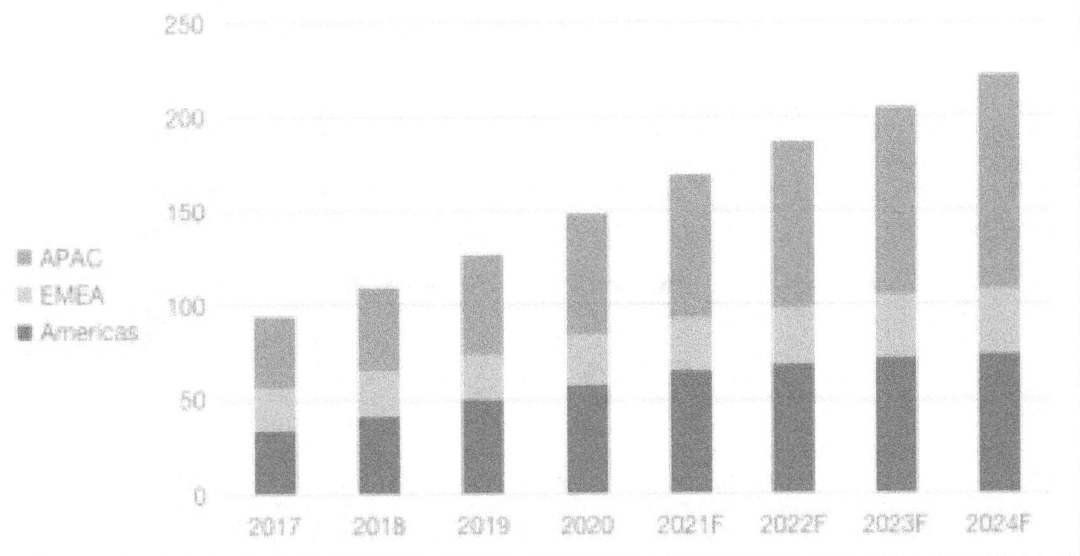

According to Deloitte (2020), the digital payments market is the largest segment within the FinTech spectrum and accounts for more than 80% of global FinTech revenues. Although COVID-19 causes uncertainty in the FinTech market, it creates opportunities for the FinTech market as well. The adaptability and innovation of FinTechs make the sector well positioned to realize its growth path.

FinTech Development in the APAC Region

Now we move from global to APAC region. As is mentioned above, the FinTech market in the APAC region is forecasted to have the fastest growth. Figure 5 illustrates the situation of FinTech investment in the APAC region in recent years.

Figure 5. FinTech investments value in APAC 2016-2020, in billion USD
Data Source(s): KPMG; PitchBook

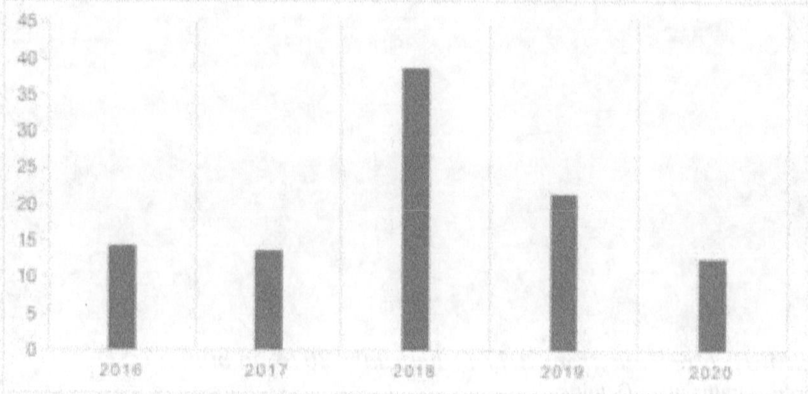

Figure 6. Major FinTech companies APAC 2021, by total funding amount
Data Source(s): CrunchBase

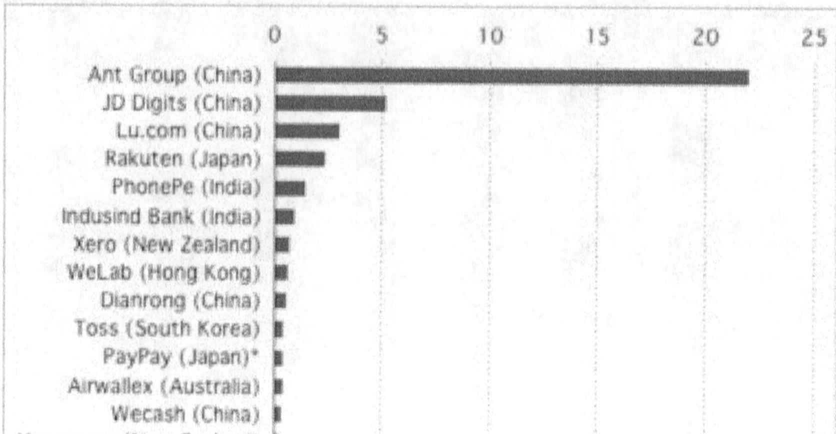

Figure 6 illustrates the major FinTech companies in the Asia-Pacific in 2021, which are ranked from most to least in total funding amount (in billion USD). Chinese companies hold the top three spot and account for a third of the top-ranked FinTech companies in APAC.

China's FinTech Development

The emerging FinTech industry in China leads the world when it comes to the market size and total users (McKinsey, 2016; KPMG, 2019). Next, we will take a look at its outstanding performance in investment, revenue and other aspects.

Figure 7. Investment in technology by Chinese financial institutions 2019-2023, in billion USD
Data Source(s): iResearch. Note: actual figures up until 2020. These numbers are originally denominated in CNY and were converted to USD by the May 2021 CNY/USD FX rate of 0.155.

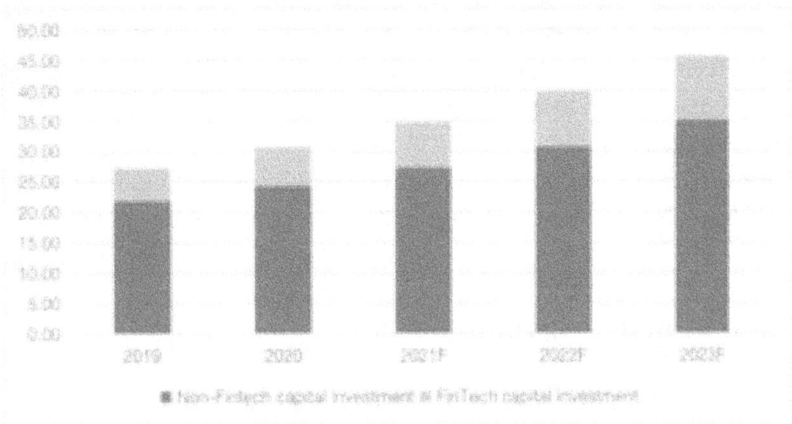

Figure 8. Total revenue of FinTech market in China from 2013 to 2020
Data Resource(s): 2018-2019 China FinTech Whitepaper. Note: actual figures up until 2019. These numbers are originally denominated in CNY and were converted to USD by the May 2021 CNY/USD FX rate of 0.155.

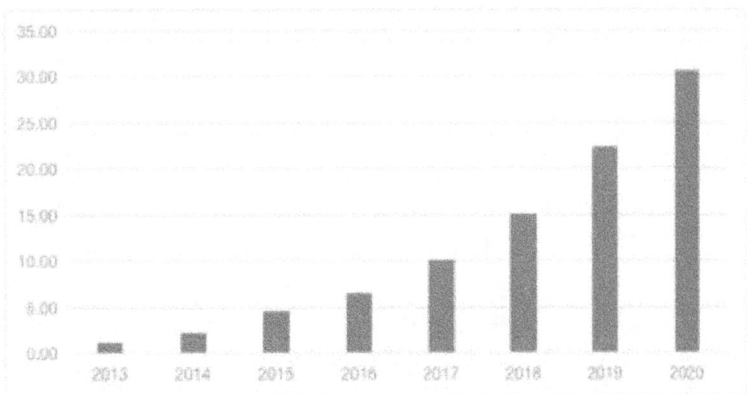

As is shown above (Figure 8 & Figure 4), China's FinTech market accounts for 20.5% of the global market and 57.5% of the APAC market.

The deep integration of technology and finance plays an important role in China's economic development, which can promote economic structural transformation, facilitate the development of innovation and entrepreneurship, and accelerate the marketization process of the financial industry. Meanwhile, it is conducive to micro and small enterprises (MSEs) and farmers' loans, which can improve transaction efficiency and reduce transaction costs.

CHARACTERISTICS OF FINTECH IN CHINA

In the introduction section, we have discussed the market size of China's FinTech industry and its proportion in the global and APAC region, which reflects China's leadership position in FinTech development. According to the World Economic Forum (WEF, 2021), more than a billion consumers are enjoying the benefits of FinTech today in areas such as mobile payments, banking, insurance, investment and consumer lending. FinTech has also helped more than 30 million MSEs access loans. Businesses in the supply chain can now benefit from more inclusive and affordable financial services thanks to the application of technologies such as big data and blockchain.

In this section, we will discuss the characteristics of China's FinTech industry. This section will analyze the structure of FinTech investment in China and discuss FinTech development in various sectors. In the end, this section will discuss the distribution and development of FinTech companies in China.

Analysis of China's FinTech Investment

In 2019, the overall investment in technology in China's banking sector reached 121.48 billion yuan, and the investment in FinTech reached 23.08 billion yuan. The overall technology investment in China's insurance industry reached 31.95 billion yuan, with 12.46 billion yuan for financial technology. The overall investment in technology in China's securities industry reached 21.67 billion yuan, and the investment in financial technology reached 640 million yuan. In 2019, the overall technology investment in China's fund industry is 1.98 billion yuan, and the financial technology investment is 90 million yuan. (iResearch, 2020).

Figure 9. Structure of Technology Capital Investment of Chinese Financial Institutions
Data Source(s): iResearch

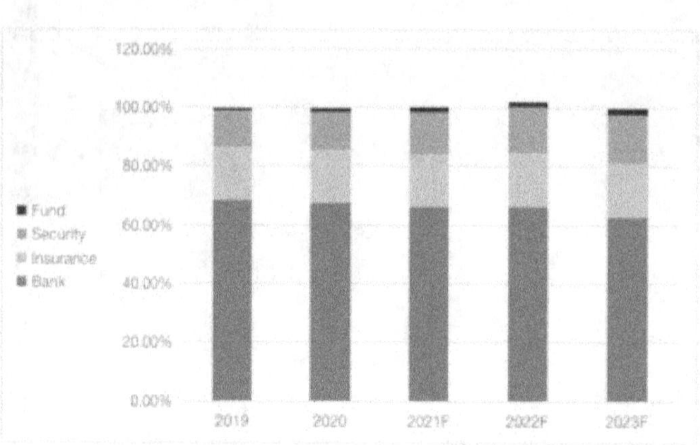

As mentioned in the introduction, Chinese FinTech companies rank first in financing in the Asia-Pacific region, but also rank among the top three in the world (iResearch, 2020). The next section will discuss the development of FinTech in various sectors and the advancement of FinTech companies in China.

FinTech Development of Different Sectors in China

Online Payment

Payments have continued to migrate away from cash and become less visible to the customer as consumers shift purchases to online and mobile channels (WEF, 2017). The global online shopping market is growing quickly at the expense of in-person shopping. In China, online sales of physical goods grew rapidly. From January to October 2020, China's online retail sales of physical goods increased by 16.0% year on year, significantly higher than the total retail sales of consumer goods in the same period (NBS, 2020).

Online payment has a large number of users in China. This statistic shows the number of mobile payment users in China from 2013 to December 2020 (Figure 10). As of December 2020, around 852.5 million people used mobile payment transactions in China, up from around 765 million users in March 2020.

Figure 10. Mobile payment users in China 2013-2020
Data Source(s): CNNIC

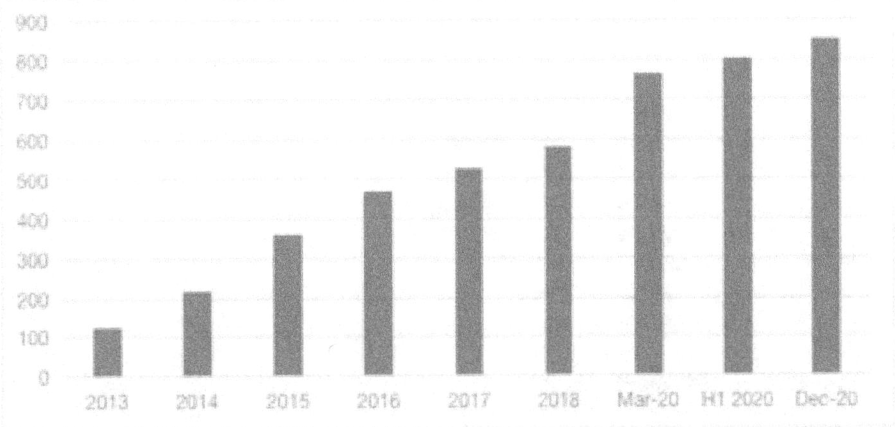

As is shown below (Figure 11), the penetration of online payment in China reached 86.4% in December 2020. China's mobile payment usage penetration rate ranks No. 1 in the world according to statistics in 2019 (Figure 12).

Figure 11. Penetration rate of online payment in China 2008-2020
Data Source(s): CNNIC

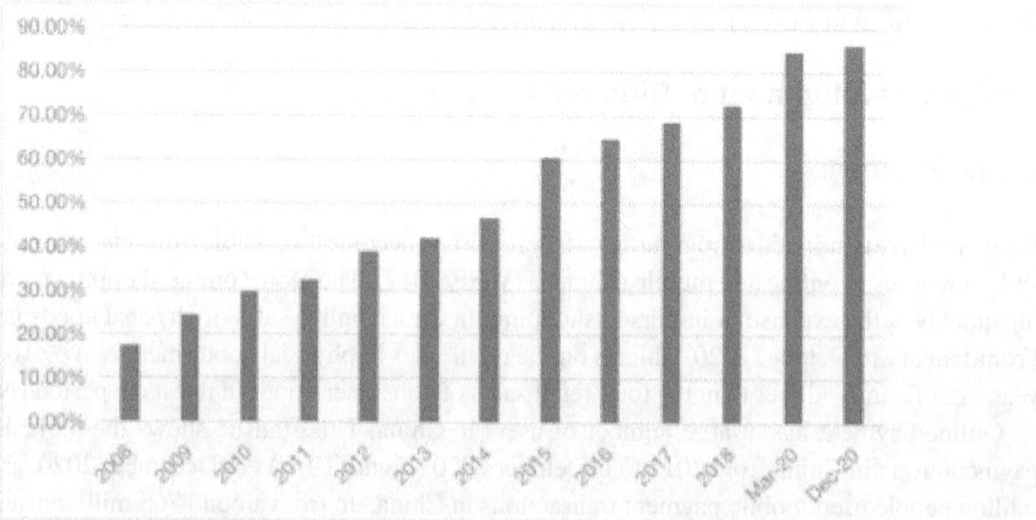

Figure 12. Global proximity mobile payment usage penetration 2019, by country
Data Source(s): eMarketer

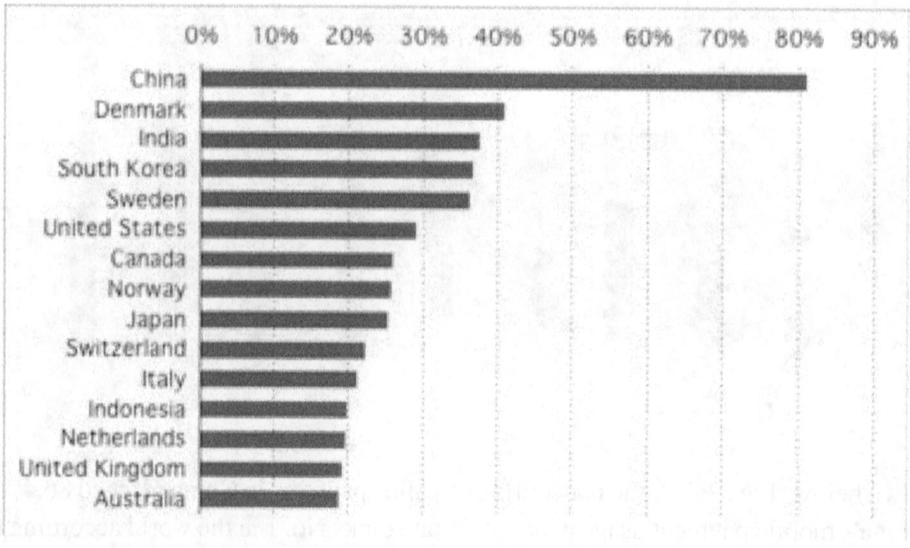

When it comes to the breakdown of online payment transactions, Internet finance accounts for the largest portion, following with personal business and online consumption (Figure 13).

Figure 13. Breakdown of online payment transactions in China 2019, by type
Data Source(s): iResearch

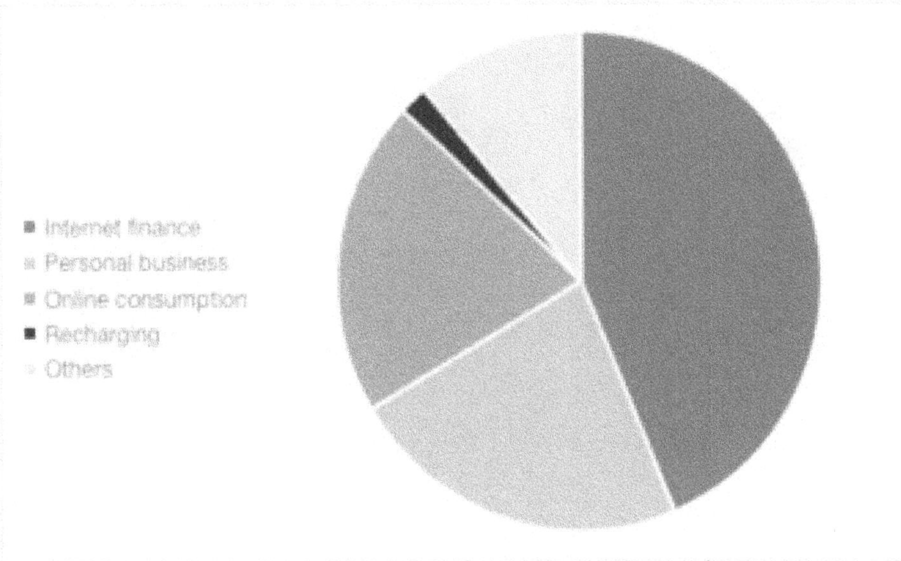

Alipay is the leading third-party payment provider in China. In 2016, Alipay had 450 million users, which was about 40 times as much as Apple Pay users. In 2019, it accounts for 54.4% of third-party payment providers (iResearch, 2020).

Now, FinTech companies are expanding their business scope beyond online payment systems into advanced financial services, from money market funds (MMFs) to lending services, online funds, and Internet-based private banking services (Shim and Shin, 2016). The development of P2P lending in China will be discussed in the next part.

P2P Lending

Peer-to-peer lending, also known as P2P lending, is an innovative Internet-based lending model that enables individuals to lend and borrow money without the intervention of conventional financial institutions (Serrano-Cinca, Gutiérrez-Nieto & López-Palacios, 2015).

Figure 14 shows the alternative lending transaction value in countries worldwide in 2019. China has the highest alternative lending transaction value in the world.

P2P services were growing quickly, reaching a significant number of customers across the globe. Individual and small-business borrowers expect their lenders to deliver the seamless digital origination and rapid adjudication pioneered by leading FinTechs.

The number of P2P lending platforms in China peaked in 2015, which is more than double the number in 2014. However, it continued to decline in the following years, down to 343 in 2019 (Figure 15). Meanwhile, the number of lenders on online P2P lending platforms in China peaked in 2017, experiencing a decline since then (Figure 16).

Figure 14. Alternative Lending transaction value in countries worldwide 2019, in billion USD
Data Source(s): Statista

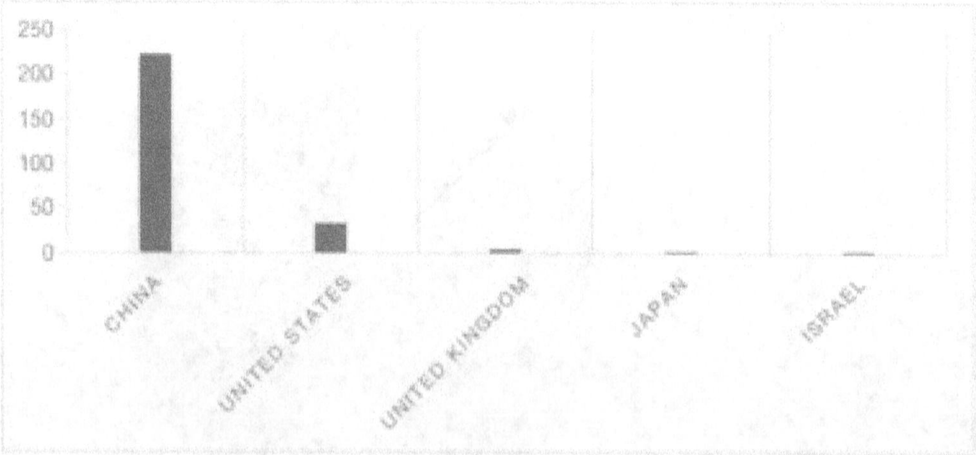

Figure 15. Number of online P2P lending platforms in China 2010-2019
Data Source(s): Website (wdzj.com)

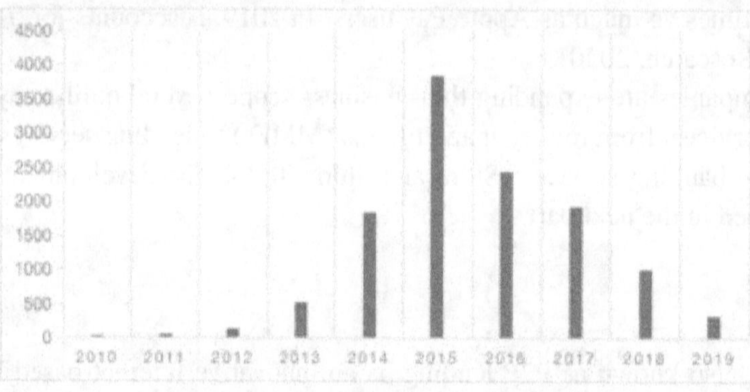

The number of platforms and users has declined for good reason. As is shown below, the number of problematic P2P platforms in China was increasing year by year (Figure 17) and the cumulative number was 2923 in 2019.

Figure 18 shows the share of problematic P2P lending platform issues in China in 2019. Absconding platform operator accounts formed the largest portion of P2P lending platform issues, followed by fund withdraw issues and financial crime.

However, the average length of loans on online P2P lending platforms in China generally shows an upward tendency from 2012 to 2019 (Figure 19).

Offering faster loans and leveraging nontraditional underwriting methods, P2P lending platforms shift customer expectations on what to expect from the loan experience. P2P lending posed little systemic risk; it was always a small sector. At its peak, outstanding loans barely reached RMB 2 trillion and hovered just below RMB 1 trillion for most of the industry's existence (Qiancheng Research Institute, 2019).

Figure 16. Number of lenders on online P2P lending platforms in China 2010-2019, in thousand
Data Source(s): Website (wdzj.com)

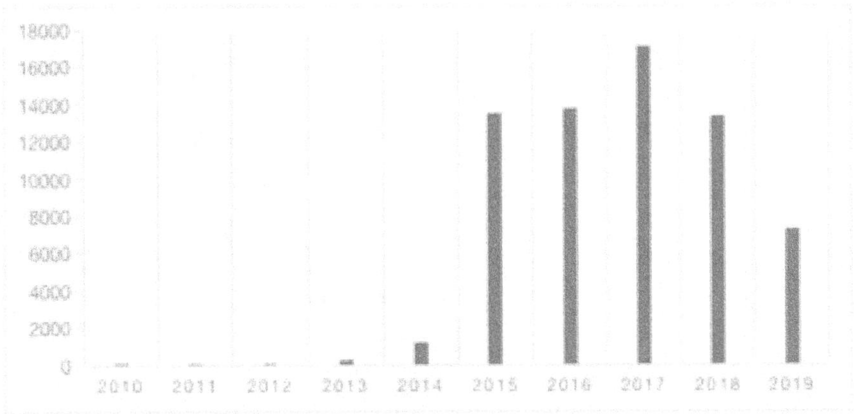

Figure 17. Total number of problematic P2P credit platforms in China 2015-2019
Data Source(s): Wangdaizhijia

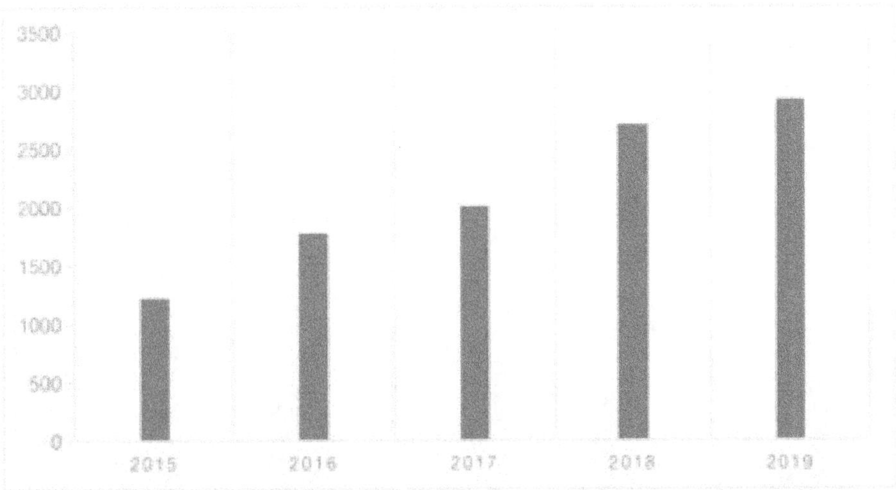

The main challenge the P2P sector presented was that each platform involved numerous investors, often to the order of tens of thousands or even millions. Therefore, bad loans led to social problems as investors took to the streets demanding their money back, and regulatory agencies decided they had to intervene. After several rounds of back and forth, P2P lending was finally banned at the end of 2020, 13 years after its launch. The ban in 2020 presented a lose-lose situation: lenders suffered financial losses, entrepreneurs were dealt severe blows and some even faced legal consequences despite their initial good intentions, and the private lending sector's experimental online efforts ground to a halt. (WEF, 2021).

Figure 18. Share of problematic P2P lending platform issues in China 2019, by type
Data Source(s): Wangdaizhijia

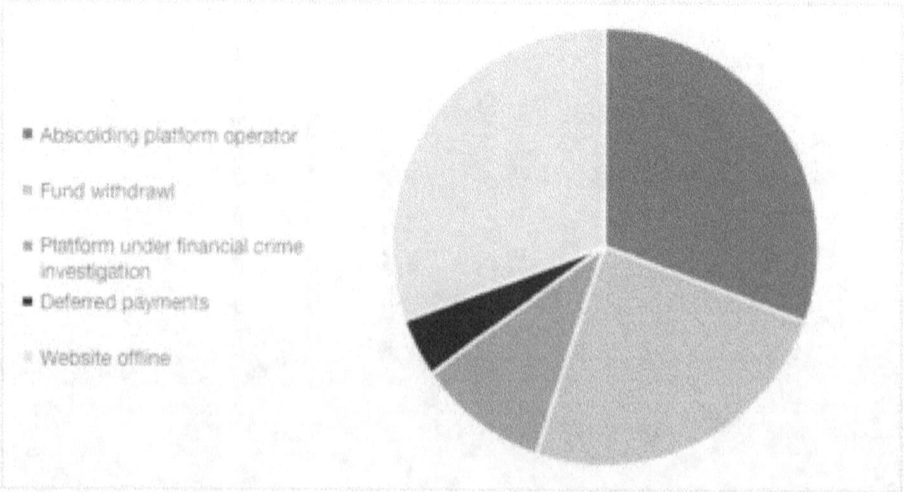

Figure 19. Average length of loans on online P2P lending platforms in China 2012-2019
Data Source(s): Website (wdzj.com)

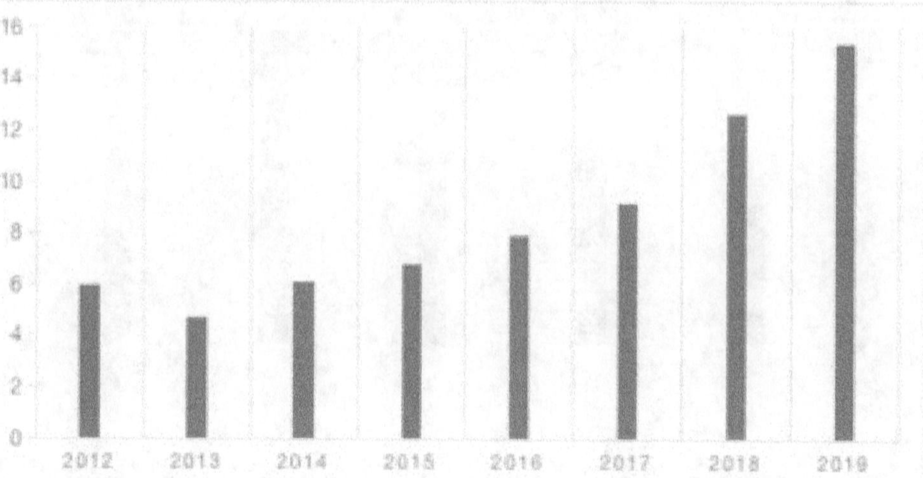

Insurance

Since 2011, the booming development of InsurTech has had a huge impact on the financial and insurance industries (Wang, 2021). Figure 20 shows the sales volume of online insurance policies in China.

Life insurers face pressure to reinvent their product strategies to meet the needs of their next generation of customers. Figures 21 and 22 show the value of the online life insurance premium income in China and the leading online life insurance platforms respectively.

Figure 20. Sales volume of online insurance policies in China 2016-2019, in billion units
Data Source(s): iResearch; IAC

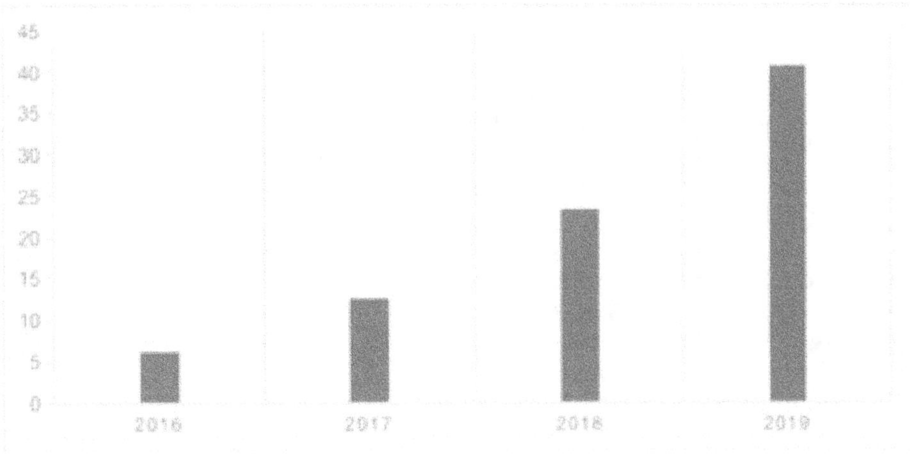

Figure 21. Value of the online life insurance premium income in China 2014-2020, in billion USD
Data Source(s): IAC. Note: actual figures up until 2018. These numbers are originally denominated in CNY and were converted to USD by the May 2021 CNY/USD FX rate of 0.155.

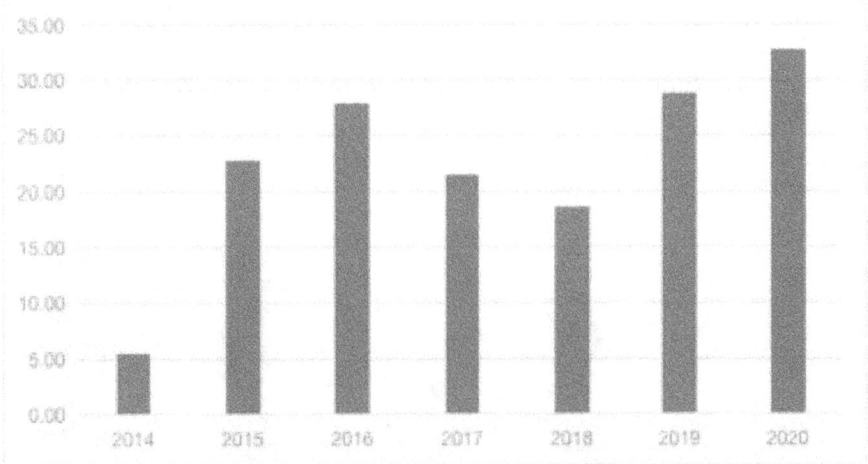

Insurers are challenged by the rise of "insurtechs" and a structural transformation of their customer base, forcing them to adopt new technologies more quickly (WEF, 2017). For example, the leading online life insurance platforms in China are all originally traditional insurance companies.

Figure 22. Leading online life insurance platforms in China 2020, based on premium income
Data Source(s): IAC

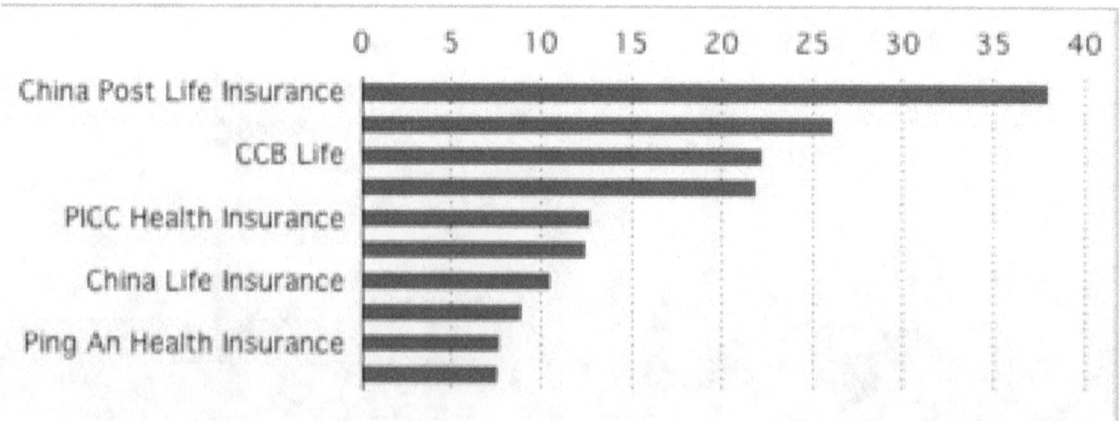

Crowdfunding

Crowdfunding is the process of funding a project by raising small monetary contributions from large numbers of individuals (Safouane, John & Gergely, 2021). Crowdfunding platforms in China have grown rapidly, driven by strong demand from both investors and entrepreneurs. Figure 23 and Figure 24 show the number and the value of successful crowdfunding campaigns in China respectively.

Figure 23. Number of successful crowdfunding campaigns in China H1 2016-H1 2018
Data Source(s): Forward Intelligence (Qianzhan); Zhongchoujia

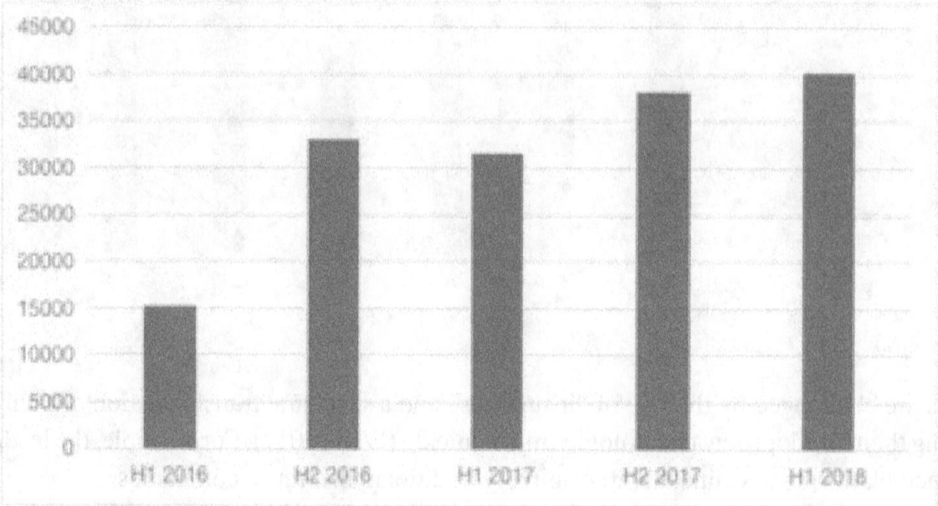

Figure 24. Value of successful crowdfunding campaigns in China H1 2016-H1 2018
Data Source(s): Forward Intelligence (Qianzhan); Zhongchoujia

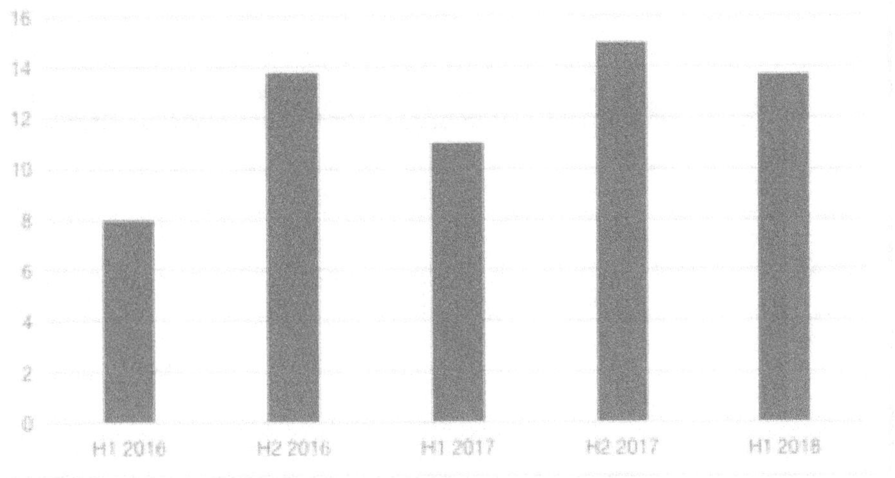

The number of successful crowdfunding campaigns (Figure 23) and value of them (Figure 24) both experienced fluctuation from 2016-2018. There was a drop in both in 2017.

Figure 25. Share of crowdfunding platforms in China 2019, by type
Data Source(s): Forward Intelligence (Qianzhan); Zhongchoujia

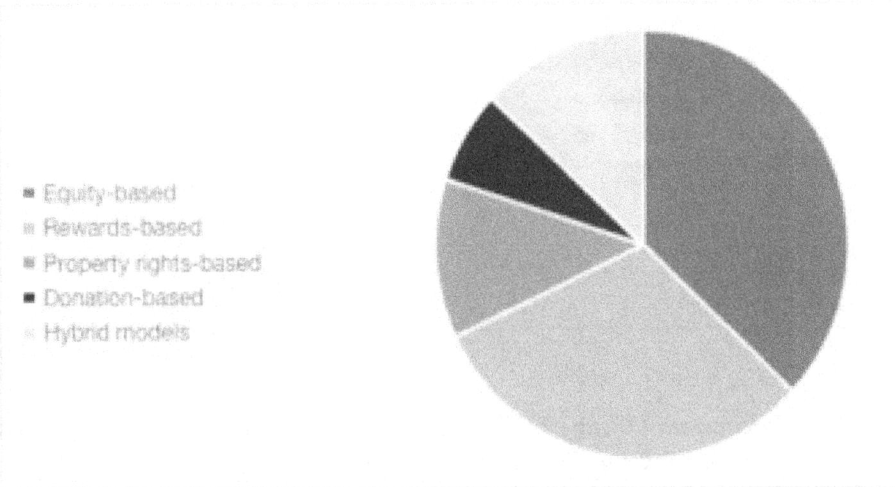

The figure above compares the share of crowdfunding platforms in China in 2019 by type. Equity-based crowdfunding platforms account for the largest portion, followed by rewards-based platforms (Figure 25). The leading platforms of equity-based and reward-based crowdfunding platforms are shown below (Figure 26 & Figure 27).

Figure 26. Leading equity-based crowdfunding platforms in China 2019, based on funds raised
Data Source(s): Forward Intelligence (Qianzhan); Zhongchoujia

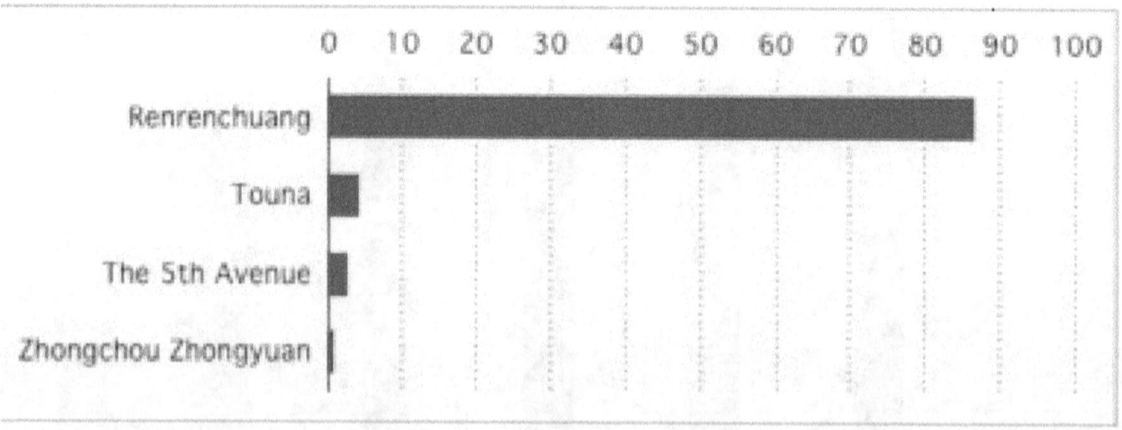

Figure 27. Leading reward-based crowdfunding platforms in China 2019, based on funds raised
Data Source(s): Forward Intelligence (Qianzhan); Zhongchoujia

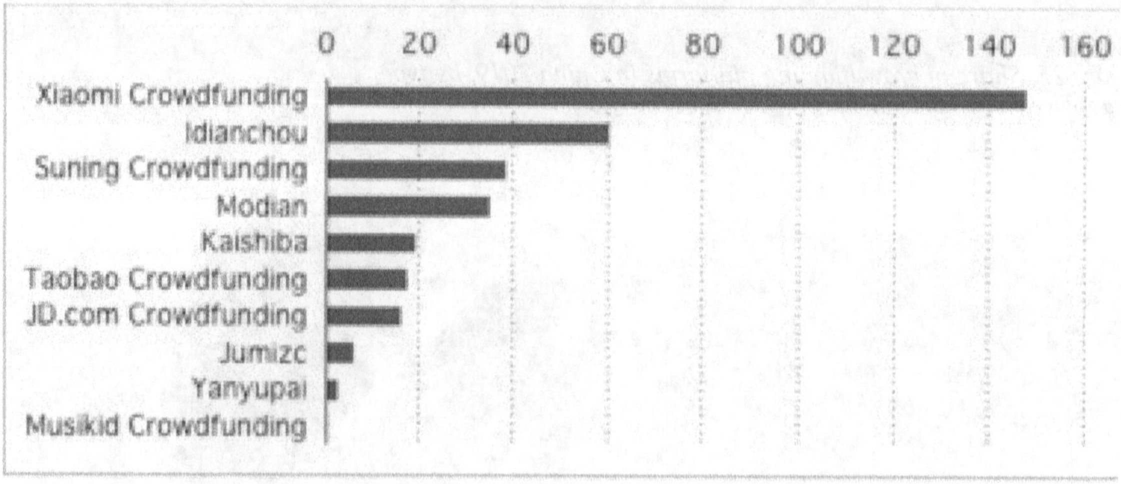

However, the World Economic Forum (2017) pointed out that equity crowdfunding remains disconnected from the broader financial system, limiting its long-term scalability. In general, the crowdfunding platforms in China show a good trend but need further development.

Conclusion on the Characteristics of FinTech Development in China

In the analysis of the different sectors above, China's online payment is well developed. The development of P2P lending is facing many challenges, which is in line with the development of P2P lending in the world. Insurtech was largely developed by traditional insurance companies. At the same time, crowdfunding platforms are also booming and showing a good trend.

China is playing an increasingly important role in the booming FinTech sector. This can be seen from the 1261 Chinese start-up financial technology enterprises included in CYZone (2018) Venture Capital Database for portrait analysis, enterprise types involved in credit, consumer finance, third-party payment, and so on. The enterprise geographical layout tends to the first-tier and quasi-first-tier developed cities. The financing rounds ranged from seed round to E round, mainly early-stage start-up projects, of which the A/A+ round took up the largest proportion, accounting for more than 1/3 of the total. Most of the companies have not been established for a long time, with start-ups of less than five years accounting for nearly 80% of them.

THE ROLES OF GOVERNMENT IN PROMOTING FINTECH TO CHINESE BUSINESSES

The Institution Theory

This chapter refers to the Institution Theory from the book Institutions and Economic Growth: An Historical Introduction (North, 1989). In this essay, the interdependence of political and economic institutions is examined against premises in neoclassical theories of economies. This essay examines the assumptions around whether institutions matter in the development of economies. According to North (1989), institutions are rules, enforcement characteristics of rules, and norms of behavior that structure repeated human interaction. Hence, they limit and define the choice set of neoclassical theory. North analyses the initial historical conditions in England and Spain, English development, Spanish development, and finally the consequences for the New World, pointing out the relationship between institutions and economic growth. In the following section, we discuss China's FinTech policies and the role of the government in promoting FinTech to Chinese businesses.

FinTech Policy in China

In the global FinTech race, the Chinese government has taken an active policy lead. From 2014 to 2018, the State Council has written Internet finance into government work reports to provide policy guidance. From "promoting the healthy development of Internet finance" proposed in the Government Work Report of the State Council in 2014 to "standardizing the development of Internet finance" in 2016 and launching the special rectification work of Internet finance nationwide, the policy guidance of the central government on China's FinTech innovation has gone through a process from encouragement to standardization (Chen & Chen, 2021).

In 2017, the People's Bank of China (PBOC) set up a FinTech committee to strengthen research planning and coordination of FinTech work. As a technology-driven financial innovation, FinTech has injected new vitality into financial development but also brings new challenges to financial security. The PBOC will strengthen the application of regulatory technology (Regtech), actively use big data, artificial intelligence, cloud computing, and other technologies to enrich financial regulatory means and improve the ability to identify, prevent, and resolve cross-industry and cross-market financial risks (PBOC, 2017).

On August 22, 2019, the PBOC (2019) announced that it had issued the Financial Technology (FinTech) Development Plan (2019-2021), and proposed to establish and improve the "four beams and eight pillars" of China's FinTech development by 2021. The plan defines the guiding ideology, basic principles, development goals, key tasks and safeguard measures for FinTech work in the next three years. The plan proposes that by 2021, China's FinTech development will be at the leading level in the world, and the application of FinTech will be advanced and controllable, the capabilities of financial services will be steadily enhanced, the level of financial risk control will be significantly improved, the efficiency of financial supervision will continue to improve, the support for FinTech will continue to improve, and the FinTech industry will flourish.

While encouraging the development of FinTech, China also attaches importance to the regulation of FinTech innovation. The PBOC (2019) has actively established a system of basic rules for the regulation of FinTech, exploring flexible management methods such as information disclosure, product publicity and social supervision. Efforts should be made to build inclusive and prudent regulatory tools for FinTech innovation, to make financial regulation more professional, unified, and penetrating.

The Fifth Plenary Session of the 19th CPC Central Committee (2020) deliberated and adopted the Proposal of the CPC Central Committee on Formulating the Fourteenth Five-Year Plan for National Economic and Social Development and the Vision Goals for the Year 2035. It stated that "we should build the system and mechanism for the financial sector to effectively support the real economy, improve the level of financial technology, and enhance financial inclusion." This shows that as the two core elements of economic growth, the deep integration of science, technology, and finance is the driving force for China's high-quality development in the new era. Meanwhile, it also shows the importance the Chinese government attaches to the development of FinTech.

FinTech Policy in Zhejiang and Greater Bay Area

Policy in Zhejiang Province

This year, Xi Jinping visited Zhejiang Province. In a historic move, he endowed Zhejiang with a new goal and new positioning, "striving to become an important window for comprehensively displaying the superiority of the socialist system with Chinese characteristics in the new era". The People's Bank of China Hangzhou Central Sub-branch actively implements the FinTech Development Plan (2019-2021). It takes the FinTech Application Pilot Project as the starting point to promote the high-quality development of FinTech in the province.

Hangzhou, along with Beijing, San Francisco, New York, London, Shanghai, Shenzhen and Chicago, ranks among the world's eight FinTech hub cities, according to the "Global FinTech Hub Report 2020" (Zhejiang University, 2020) released by Zhejiang University. As a pioneer city and active region of FinTech in China, Hangzhou has always been at the forefront of the global FinTech development wave, with a solid development foundation, obvious development advantages, and huge development potential.

As early as the Qiantang River Forum in 2017, Hangzhou set the goal of building itself into an international FinTech center. In May 2019, Zhejiang Digital Economy Development Leading Group (2019) issued "the Action Plan for the Construction of Zhejiang Emerging Financial Center", which proposed to take FinTech as an important driving force and strive to form a healthy and orderly FinTech good ecology. At the same time, at the promotion conference of building Hangzhou International FinTech Center, the "Special Plan for the Construction of Hangzhou International FinTech Center" (Zhejiang

Development and Reform Commission, 2019) was officially released, which clearly defined the target positioning, main tasks, spatial layout and policy support. Over the next three years, Hangzhou will be committed to building itself into "China's Leading FinTech City" and "Global FinTech Application and Innovation Center".

Policy in Greater Bay Area

The Guangdong-Hong Kong-Macao Greater Bay Area is the emerging bay area following the San Francisco Bay Area, New York Bay Area, and Tokyo Bay Area, with high market vitality, open and international characteristics. From the gulf of international advanced experience, the developed financial industry is the common feature of each big bay area. On the tide of FinTech, "smart finance" and "inclusive finance" will become important trends in the future development of the financial industry. The Greater Bay Area has a good foundation for the technology industry, and Hong Kong's status as an international financial center makes it suitable to take FinTech as the starting point and promote the development of finance and technology through FinTech.

The "Opinions on Financial Support for the Development of the Greater Bay Area" (PBOC, 2020) points out that we should vigorously develop financial technology, deepen financial technology cooperation in the Greater Bay Area, and strengthen the construction of financial technology carriers. We will support mainland research on blockchain, big data, artificial intelligence and other innovative technologies in the Greater Bay Area. In the future, FinTech will be an important starting point for the Greater Bay Area to build a modern financial system and improve the level of financial service innovation.

"Support Shenzhen construction of socialism with Chinese characteristics the opinions of the demonstration zone" (CPC Central Committee & The State Council, 2019), put forward the idea to carry out the market access mechanism reform pilot and regulatory system, the positive development of intellectual economy, use digital innovation and economic development experimental zones, and support the research on digital currency in Shenzhen and other innovative applications in mobile payment.

In October 2020, "the Implementation Plan for the Pilot Comprehensive Reform of Shenzhen Pilot Demonstration Zone for Building Socialism with Chinese Characteristics (2020-2025)" (Office of the CPC Central Committee & The State Council, 2019) emphasizes the establishment of a FinTech innovation platform based on the Shenzhen branch of the Digital Currency Institute of the People's Bank of China.

DISCUSSION OF CHINESE CASES

Ant Financial

Introduction of Ant Financial

Ant Group is the parent company of mobile payment platform Alipay and the world's leading open FinTech platform (the official website of Ant Group, n.d.). Ant Financial got its start with Alipay, which was established in 2004 in Zhejiang province. In March 2013, Ant Group announced that it would build the Small and Micro Financial Service Group, referred to as "Small and Micro Financial". Small and Micro Financial became the predecessor of Ant Financial. In October 2014, Ant Financial was officially established. Its businesses include Alipay, Yu'ebao, and E-commerce Bank, etc. After more than ten years of development, Ant Group has become more than just a simple payment tool. It has more than ten business segments covering a variety of FinTech models, such as Zhima Credit, insurance, wealth management, and crowdfunding, etc., taking a leading position in the FinTech industry (Dong, 2020).

According to the information from the official website of Ant Group (n.d.), Ant Financial uses technology to enable ordinary people and MSEs to enjoy equal financial and life services. It provides dozens of solutions for companies using the latest technology in financial intelligence, financial security, massive financial trading, new-generation interactive tech, and blockchain application (iResearch, 2020).

The Current Situation of Ant Financial

Ant Financial has successfully helped numerous financial institutions to achieve FinTech transformation. This covers banking, insurance, securities, and non-financial sectors, for such firms as Huaxia Bank, Guangfa Bank, Tianhong Fund, Bank of Xi'an, Bank of Nanjing, Paytm, Netbank, and HLNDSLN Hengsheng Electronics. Ant Financial also has many partners around the world, including Paytm in India, Turemoney in Thailand, Kakao Pay in South Korea, and TouchNGo in Malaysia.

In terms of products, many are involved in the fields of financial intelligence, financial security, financial distributed architecture, mobile development, blockchain, financial distributed database and so on. In terms of technology, it has digital forms of banking, insurance, securities, supervision in the digital financial technology overall solution.

Here are some statistics on Alipay, the most important platform of Ant Financial. The annual active users of the Alipay App are over 1 billion and Alipay APP has 711 million monthly active users. The monthly active merchants of the Alipay App are more than 80 million and the annual active users of Alipay APP digital finance reached 729 million (iResearch, 2020).

Yu'ebao is Ant Financial's balance value and fund management service product, launched in June 2013. Yu'e refers to the remaining sum. Yu'ebao is easy to operate and features low thresholds and zero commission. The money in it can be used at will. In addition to financial management functions, Yu'ebao can also be directly used for shopping, transfer, payment and repayment, etc. It is a cash management tool in the era of mobile Internet. Yu'e Bao remains China's largest money fund (Ant Group official website, n.d.)

According to its official website, Ant financial shares technology with partners around the world to jointly provide users with mobile payment and digital inclusive financial services.

The Advantages of Ant Group

After years of development, Alibaba, the affiliate company of Ant Financial, has accumulated technological advantages in areas such as big data and cloud computing, putting Ant Financial in the leading position in technology. Secondly, it has long been a problem for MSEs to get loans. Under the policy of inclusive finance vigorously advocated by the government, Ant Financial has successfully explored ways to provide investment, financing, and financial services to MSEs and long-tail customers with years of practice (Chen, 2020). As a result of this experience, their competitive advantage is obvious.

1. **Focusing on technical services**

At the Bo'ao Forum for Asia in 2018, Chen Shengqiang, CEO of Internet giant JD Finance, and Zhu Guang, CEO of Baidu Finance, simultaneously declared that they would no longer seek to be financial products in the future. Instead, they would return to technological positioning and strive to become FinTech suppliers.

Ant Financial has long had the strategic intention of building FinTech capabilities, shifting its strategic focus from financial product-oriented to FinTech service-oriented. Since 2014, Ant Financial has been making strategic investments in Hundsun Electronics (the largest IT solution provider for the financial industry), Paytm, Chaoyang Continuance, Runhe Software, Weida Jinke, and other financial technology enterprises, laying out financial infrastructure, focusing on the construction of professional platforms for financial institutions. According to the data of Alibaba Group in the 2018 fiscal year, the revenue of Alibaba Cloud in 2018 was 13.39 billion yuan, ranking among the "3A" giants in the international cloud computing market and becoming a cloud computing enterprise on a par with Amazon AWS and Microsoft Azure. In June 2017, Ant Financial announced the opening of its financial technology services to fund companies, banks and other financial institutions, gradually opening up its financial links, user portraits, precision marketing, risk management, financial cloud computing, artificial intelligence, and other FinTech applications accumulated over the years. On the one hand, it enables traditional finance, and on the other hand, it establishes the Internet finance ecology.

2. Focusing on small and micro customers

Traditional commercial banks have abundant capital, national credit and high capital security which is incomparable to any Internet platform enterprise. However, traditional finance has disadvantages such as high threshold, cumbersome procedures, complex procedures, and low efficiency. They also require land, real estate, plant and equipment, and other collateral to control risks. Their target customers are mostly customers with strong assets and large funds.

Internet finance has the advantages of low threshold, high participation, simple processes, efficient operation and low intermediate cost. Ant Financial serves a large number of customers with small funds, which are so-called "ants". Unlike traditional finance, Internet finance has no threshold, no guarantee, no mortgage, few procedures, easy loans, and so on. With the technical support of the most efficient big data analysis system, Ant Financial's quick and simplified lending process, flexible lending standards, and the cost advantage of intelligent network operation make the marginal customers that are not recognized by large commercial banks become the new financial blue ocean of Ant Financial. It has made a great contribution to financial inclusion in China and the world.

Kingdee Financial

Introduction of Kingdee Financial

Kingdee Financial is a financial services provider. It belongs to Kingdee International Software Group (Kingdee for short), founded in 1993 and headquartered in Shenzhen. According to information on the official website of Kingdee (n.d.), they started as a financial software company, and through three historical transformations, it has continuously carried out self-innovation and breakthrough.

Based on massive user scenarios and authorized data, Kingdee financial develops financial technologies, provides efficient financial value-added services for Kingdee's unique data, and helps enterprises to establish reliable asset credit data and obtain more efficient financing.

In 2015, Kingdee Group established Kingdee Financial, which belongs to the FinTech sector of Kingdee Group. Kingdee Financial owns Kingdee Credit and enterprise credit service platform Kingdee Xiaodai.

In September 2019, Kingdee China, a wholly-owned subsidiary of Kingdee Group, CITIC Company and CITIC Trust set up CITIC Consumer Finance. Kingdee China invested 90 million RMB, accounting for 30% of the registered capital.

The Current Situation of Kingdee

Today, Kingdee has become the choice of enterprise in the new era of the digital economy. Half of the Fortune 100 enterprises in China choose Kingdee, the total Kingdee users have exceeded 260 million.

According to data from international research agency IDC (2020), "Proportion of China's Enterprise Application SaaS Manufacturers' Revenue in 2020H1" shows that Kingdee ranked first. Kingdee is the ERP supplier with the highest market share for domestic growth enterprises. It provides perfect management services for enterprises and has cooperated with nearly 6.8 million firms including Minsheng Bank, Ping'an Bank, Bank of Communications, NetBank, WeBank, Jingdong Finance and so on. The coverage rate of Kingdee Xiaodai in third-tier cities and below reaches 95% nationwide. They have provided borrowing services to 60,000 borrowers, mainly MSEs, individual industrial and commercial households, and the average loan amount of each household reaches 180,000.

Kingdee Financial is ranked among the top 50 leading FinTech companies in China by KPMG and IDC. Kingdee Financial won Second Prize at the Shenzhen Financial Innovation Award by the Shenzhen Local Financial Supervision Administration.

The Advantages of Kingdee

1. **Advantages in SaaS Cloud Services**

Kingdee Financial employs digital technologies, including artificial intelligence, BlockChain, Cloud Computing, IoT, and Big Data. The most prominent of these is its Cloud Computing services. In 2011, the State Council (2011) made clear the strategic positioning of deepening the commercial application of Cloud Computing in China. Kingdee actively promotes Cloud management and is committed to becoming the world's leading Cloud management service provider. It has specific Cloud services for MSEs, growing businesses and large businesses respectively.

Kingdee Cloud Star focuses on the online operation and digital management of small enterprise, empowering firms with "new finance and taxation, new marketing, and new platform". It provides SaaS services such as financial cloud, tax cloud, purchase, sale and storage cloud, order mall, and supports small enterprises to expand open-source, intelligent management, and real-time decision-making.

Kingdee Cloud Starry Sky focuses on growing enterprises and provides an open ERP cloud platform for enterprises in the era of the digital economy with characteristics of "openness, standard and social interaction". Its services include finance, supply chain, intelligent manufacturing, amoeba management, Omni-channel marketing, e-commerce, HR, enterprise Internet services, helping enterprises to realize the new digital marketing ecology and management restructuring, all to improve the digital capabilities of firms.

The Kingdee Cloud Constellation is a SaaS Cloud service for the digital transformation of large enterprises and central state-owned enterprises, formerly known as Kingdee Cloud Cangqiong SAS service. It is based on Kingdee Cloud Cangqiong PaaS platform, embedded with low code development family, technology middle platform, business middle platform, data middle platform, etc. It provides financial Cloud and employee service Cloud. There are more than 200 standard applications such as human Cloud, collaborative Cloud, project Cloud, supply chain Cloud and procurement Cloud, and more than 500 ecological applications with rich content and superior functions. It has been deeply applied by Huawei, Hisense, China Tobacco Yunnan, SF Express, State Power Investment Group, Hebei Iron and Steel Group, Wen's Group and other large enterprises. Official website of Kingdee (n.d.).

Specializing in Cloud technology and providing different cloud services for enterprises of different sizes is one of Kingdee's biggest strengths.

2. **Efficient Credit**

As a platform of Kingdee Financial, Kingdee Credit combines the application process of cooperative financial institutions with Kingdee's data structure to build a credit system driven by financial invoice data and realize an online and automatic solution. Customers only need to complete enterprise certification, data authorization, and credit investigation authorization at Kingdee Benefit to enter the bank for examination and approval, to avoid customers' supplementary information being repeated. Through customer application, the application process is constantly optimized, and enterprise loans are easier with technology.

On its official website of Kingdee Xiaodai (n.d.), it is said that the maximum loan amount is 3 million, the fastest loan is 7 minutes and the lowest interest rate is 5.4% annualized. Being able to provide convenient and efficient loans is the advantage of Kingdee Financial. It is also the embodiment of financial inclusiveness.

Failed Cases of FinTech Companies in China

P2P Online Lending Company Zhongdai.com Announced Its Collapse A Month After Its Launch

On April 2, 2013, only one month after its launch, Zhongdai.com declared bankruptcy, becoming the shortest-lived P2P online loan company in history. In its "letter to investors", the company said that the lack of experience of the entire management team had caused operational risks and that all investments had resulted in irretrievable financial losses. The statement also said that investors' losses have been advanced to investors with their own funds following a certain percentage of the advance money transferred to investors through online banking. Data show that Zhongdai.com, with a registered capital of 10 million yuan, belongs to Hainan Zhongdai.com Investment Consulting, headquartered in Haikou, positioning itself as a financing platform for MSEs. It also claims to be a "P2P online financial service platform," providing a variety of loan intermediary services. According to the statistics of the third-party online lending platform, the financing transactions of Zhongdai.com totalled nearly 4 million during its operation. The investment model of Zhongdai.com is the same as that of most P2P companies: investors transfer the investment funds to Zhongdai.com through the third-party payment service GuoPay or banks. After the bidding is completed, the money will be transferred to the borrower by Zhongdai.com. As for the specific reasons for the company's collapse, Lu Ruhua, the legal representative of the company, once told the media that the bankruptcy of Zhongdai.com was caused by a project. Due to the lack of experience in the industry, the audit work was not properly done. Zhongdai.com failed to find in a timely manner that the mortgaged property of a 3 million yuan financing project had been mortgaged to several people at the same time. In the case of difficult to recover funds, the loan network can only go bankrupt (Lyu, 2014).

Shuyin is on the Verge of Bankruptcy

Shuyin, referred to as "digital bank," was once famous for its endorsement by Hangzhou Municipal Party Committee and Zhejiang Provincial Party Committee. It is also the first Internet financial enterprise to obtain the license issued by the China Banking Regulatory Commission and the only Internet financial enterprise to introduce the personal identity authentication system of the central bank in China. Shuyin is like the supermarket of financial products. It integrates the credit products of banks and enables customers to compare and apply for loans through its platform. Shuyin's main customers include natural persons and small businesses. The funds are provided by formal financial institutions, and the process of loan approval and issuance is completed by banks. More than a dozen commercial banks, including China Construction Bank and Agricultural Bank of China, have cooperative relationships with Shuyin. Shuyin had previously said it made money by charging banks commissions of 1‰ to 3‰.

In 2010, Shuyin obtained the first round of 50-million-yuan investment, the introduction of Zhejiang Bank Capital accounted for 10% of the shares, the company's overall valuation reached 500 million yuan. Forbes magazine also rated it as one of the 50 most promising small businesses in China in the next three years. At the same time, digital bank online also plans to prepare a housing area of one hundred thousand square meters of digital bank science-and-technology park.

But Shuyin was unable to obtain the ability of sustainable development. For the big banks, the borrowers offered by Shuyin are not large enough. Banks think it is not necessary to pay commissions, and Shuyin does not bear the risk of bad loans, so the initiative was in the hands of banks. On the other hand, in order to attract quality customers, Shuyin had chosen not to charge this commission, thus it can charge neither banks nor consumers anything online. Its profit model is not clear. However, the annual cost of Shuyin which includes the cost of advertising, venue rent, and labor salary, was more than 50 million yuan, which put intense pressure on major shareholders to continue to invest. After the Spring Festival in 2013, Zhejiang Bank Capital, the major shareholder, suddenly announced its withdrawal, resulting in a sudden rupture of the capital chain and the enterprise was in trouble. Although company officials deny that the company is closing, the fact that it is operating abnormally is undeniable. Shuyin is on the verge of bankruptcy (Lyu, 2014).

OPPORTUNITIES AND CHALLENGES FOR CHINESE COMPANIES INTEGRATING FINTECH INTO ITS BUSINESS OPERATIONS

Developments in FinTech have prompted companies to take action. On the one hand, traditional banks have joined hands with Internet giants to develop financial technology to cope with the new competition pattern. On the other hand, Internet companies trace their roots back to science and technology to promote the transformation and upgrading of the traditional financial industry (Yao, 2020). As the boundary of traditional finance is constantly broken, information technology and finance begin to integrate more deeply. Against the background of preventing financial risks, strengthening financial supervision and promoting financial services for the development of the real economy are placed in a more important position. With the rapid development of financial technology, various development modes have been derived, but many risks have been accumulated behind its rapid development.

Opportunities and Challenges for Traditional Financial Industry

A wide range of traditional banking products, from payments to investment advice, is being challenged by innovative FinTech products (Shin & Lee, 2018).

Traditional banking services can only master some relatively static and fragmented information, but lack a dynamic grasp of customers' overall business behavior, fund dynamics, upstream and downstream related enterprises, market share, and other information. As a result, FinTech has had a big impact on the traditional banking sector. In fact, FinTech has had a great impact on the whole traditional financial industry.

However, as shown under "Characteristics of FinTech in China" in this chapter, the leading online life insurance platforms in China are all original traditional insurance companies. The traditional insurance industry has made good use of FinTech, which is often known as Insurtech.

The challenges of FinTech to the traditional banking industry can also be turned into opportunities. At present, the banking industry's performance in FinTech development is not stellar, but in fact, banks have an innate advantage in the application of FinTech. In China, the credibility of banks depends to a large extent on the credibility of the government. The government of China has high credibility, so banks can make full use of their own credibility to promote the application of FinTech (Ouyang, 2021). Ky et al. (2019) found that the successful implementation of FinTech products in banks increases bank profitability and efficiency and enhances customer interactions and develops new customer segments. Wang et al. (2020) concluded that FinTech products play a vital role in facilitating a bank's risk-taking behavior to achieve its main corporate objectives, acquiring and maintaining customers by providing quality and timely service, as well as reducing customer costs and increasing bank profitability.

Opportunities and Challenges for Emerging FinTech Companies

The development of FinTech promotes the progress of the financial industry and the development of inclusive finance. The application of FinTech has improved the efficiency of operating transactions, innovated the development model of the financial industry, and become an important driving force in the development of the modern financial industry. It has given rise to many new business models, but a lot of models without the experience of market baptism will produce a large number of bankrupt enterprises after the market gradually stabilizes, which causes a lot of instability in financial markets. These problems also bring challenges to regulatory authorities. We will focus on the challenges for emerging FinTech companies in the discussion below.

Among the traditional financial-related enterprises, the risks they face include credit risk, market risk, operational risk, legal risk, liquidity risk, interest rate risk and so on. Facing these problems, enterprises have already had more complete solutions (Lai, Sun & Sun, 2021). But as FinTech permeates the economy, it will also create new risks, which contain both challenges and opportunities.

Credit Risk

Credit risk is the main risk faced by financial activities, which is affected by many factors. Ant Group innovates big data risk control technology and carries out credit rating based on users' consumption data, which is mainly reflected in the business development of Huabei and Jiebei. While innovating the financial transaction mode and improving the efficiency of financial services, the risks and hidden dangers of Huabei and Jiebei businesses cannot be ignored. The personal credit investigation model they developed focuses on the long-tail customer group, but it relies on the ABS model for financing and leverage, which further amplifies the potential default risk and can quickly lead to the hidden systemic risk in the financial market (Yin & Chen, 2021).

Technical Risk

The effective business development of financial technology companies cannot be separated from solid technical support. However, in the application of specific business scenarios, FinTech still faces the problem of technical failure caused by the imperfect underlying algorithm (Ouyang, 2021). Ant group's pay treasure, for example, meant to pay by superposition of high-frequency scenario accumulated flow, making business for pure online, once the system is abnormal, will not be able to support the payment of rails and other financial services to carry out the science and technology. This makes it is necessary to develop the vast amounts of online business with a high degree of dependence on network infrastructure. In the process of complex data processing, the defects and loopholes of the information system can easily cause unexpected losses (Yin & Chen, 2021).

Customer Management Risk

As competition is high for customer acquisition and retention, customer management is crucial. Many customers use multiple services from different FinTech firms for different needs (Ouyang, 2021). Some easily copied technology will have a great threat of substitutes. However, advanced technology and accurate customer positioning can help increase customer engagement. As discussed above, Kingdee Financial is committed to becoming the world's leading Cloud management service provider. It has specific Cloud services for MSEs, growing businesses and large businesses respectively.

Lack of Legal Supervision

The incomplete supervision law makes it difficult to identify the risk object, which increases the potential risk, especially in the process of network financing business. As discussed in the case of Zhongdai.com, it failed to timely find that the mortgaged property of a 3 million yuan financing project had been mortgaged to several people at the same time. In the case of difficult to recover funds, the loan network can only go bankrupt.

CONCLUSION AND RECOMMENDATIONS

FinTech has always been associated with the terms“advanced” and “competitive” in the financial industry (Acar and Çıtak, 2019; Gai et al., 2018; Wojcik and Ioannou, 2020).

Based on abundant literature and data, this chapter analyzes the development situation, investment distribution and market distribution of China's FinTech, studying the characteristics of China's FinTech development. At the same time, this chapter studies the policies related to FinTech and the role of the government in the development of FinTech in China, referring to institution theory. This chapter focuses on the overall development of domestic FinTech companies and their geographical distribution, selecting successful and unsuccessful cases, and analyzing the opportunities and challenges of China's FinTech development.

Traditional financial institutions should join hands with financial technology to provide differentiated, targeted and preferential financial services by using high-tech finance such as big data, cloud computing, 5G, and artificial intelligence, so as to reduce financing costs for enterprises and individuals while defusing related credit risks. Financial institutions should make full use of the advantages of FinTech and their own advantages in mining data information to establish their own linkage platforms for data analysis, risk early-warning, and customer information, allowing them to form targeted contingency plans.

FinTech companies should make use of emerging technologies to tap long-tail customers, expand the boundaries of financial services, reduce the cost of customer acquisition, and meet the diversified and personalized needs of customers. It can meanwhile solve the financing problems of MSEs and develop inclusive finance. In terms of risk management, the development of financial technology promotes intelligent risk management, but also puts forward higher requirements for technical risk management.

FinTech is an unstoppable trend. How enterprises find their place in the wave of FinTech development, and how the Chinese government should encourage and regulate FinTech innovation, are and will continue to be questions worth thinking about.

REFERENCES

Abbasi, K., Alam, A., Du, M. A., & Huynh, T. L. D. (2021). FinTech, SME efficiency and national culture: Evidence from OECD countries. *Technological Forecasting and Social Change*, *163*, 120454. Advance online publication. doi:10.1016/j.techfore.2020.120454

Acar, O., & Çıtak, Y. E. (2019). FinTech integration process suggestion for banks. *Procedia Computer Science*, *15892019*, 971–978. doi:10.1016/j.procs.2019.09.138

Chen, W., & Chen, X.H. (2021). Enabling Government and Efficient Market in FinTech Innovation-Evidence from China's net loan industry. *International Financial Research*, 27-36. doi:10.16475/j.cnki.1006-1029.2021.03.003

Chen, Y. C. (2020). Look at the comparative advantage of Internet finance from Ant Financial. *Modern Marketing*, *1*, 35-36. doi:10.19932/j.cnki.22-1256/f.2020.01.020

CPC Central Committee. (2020). *Proposal of the CPC Central Committee on Formulating the Fourteenth Five-Year Plan for National Economic and Social Development and the Long-Term Goals for the year 2035*. http://www.gov.cn/zhengce/2020-11/03/content_5556991.htm

CPC Central Committee & The State Council. (2019). *Support Shenzhen construction of socialism with Chinese characteristics the opinions of the demonstration zone.* http://www.gov.cn/zhengce/2019-08/18/content_5422183.htm

Croutzet, A., & Dabbous, A. (2021). Do FinTech trigger renewable energy use? Evidence from OECD countries. *Renewable Energy, 179*, 1608–1617. doi:10.1016/j.renene.2021.07.144

CYZone. (2018). *2018-2019 China FinTech Whitepaper.* https://oss.cyzone.cn/2019/0402/1382923a6a7e1b6c875f323f1c3a7b80.pdf

Deloitte. (2020). *FinTech | On the brink of further disruption.* https://www2.deloitte.com/content/dam/Deloitte/nl/Documents/financial-services/deloitte-nl-fsi-FinTech-report-1.pdf

Dong, J. X. (2020). Analysis of Competitive Advantage of Internet Financial Platform Enterprises Based on Porter's Five Forces Model -- Taking Ant Financial as an Example. *Commercial Economy, 10,* 175-176. doi:10.19905/j.cnki.syjj1982.2020.10.072

EY. (2019). *Global FinTech adoption index 2019.* https://www.ey.com/en_gl/ey-global-FinTech-adoption-index

Financial Stability Board. (2016). *Financial Stability Board agrees 2017 work plan.* https://www.fsb.org/wp-content/uploads/Financial-Stability-Board-agrees-2017-workplan.pdf

Financial Stability Board. (2017). *Financial stability implications from FinTech.* https://www.fsb.org/2017/06/financial-stability-implications-fromFinTech/

Financial Stability Board. (2017). *FinTech credit: Market structure, business models and financial stability implications.* https://www.bis.org/publ/cgfs_fs b1.pdf

Gai, K., Qiu, M., & Sun, X. (2018). A survey on FinTech. *Journal of Network and Computer Applications, 103*, 262–273. doi:10.1016/j.jnca.2017.10.011

Hill, J. (2018). FinTech in a Global Setting. In J. Hill (Ed.), *FinTech and the Remaking of Financial Institutions* (pp. 269–283). Academic Press. doi:10.1016/B978-0-12-813497-9.00014-7

Huang, Y. M. (2020). Evaluation on the effect of strategic transformation of Kingdee under the background of cloud era. *Modern Business, 28*, 135–137.

Hwang, S.-S. (2014). *What We Need in the FinTech Craze.* http://www.lgcnsblog.com/technology/what-we-need-in-the-fiFinTech-craze/

IDC. (2020). *China's enterprise application SaaS market will outpace the trend.* https://www.idc.com/url.do?url=/getdoc.jsp?containerId=prCHC47172620&position=1&transactionId=111279551&term=5Lit5Zu95LyB5Lia57qn5bqU55So77yIRUHvvIlTYWFT5biC5Zy66Lef6Liq56CU56m25oql5ZGK&page=1&perPage=25

International Monetary Fund. (2017). *FinTech and financial services: initial considerations.* https://www.imf.org/~/media/Files/Publications/SDN/2017/sdn1705.ashx

iResearch. (2020). *Dawn - 2020 China FinTech industry development research report.* http://report.iresearch.cn/report/202011/3687.shtml

KPMG. (2019). *The pulse of FinTech 2018: biannual global analysis of investment in FinTech.* https://assets.kpmg/content/dam/kpmg/xx/pdf/2019/02/the-pulse-of-FinTech-2018.pdf

Ky, S., Rugemintwari, C., & Sauviat, A. (2019). *Is FinTech good for bank performance? The Case of Mobile Money in the East African Community.* Hal-02155077.

Lai, H., Sun, S. R., & Sun, N. (2021). Enterprise risk research based on FinTech listed companies. *Science Technology and Industry, 21*(04), 145–149.

Lee, C. C., Li, X. R., Yu, C. H., & Zhao, J. S. (2021). Does FinTech innovation improve bank efficiency? Evidence from China's banking industry. *International Review of Economics & Finance, 74*, 468–483.

Lee, I., & Shin, Y. J. (2018). FinTech: ecosystem, business models, investment decisions, and challenges. *Business Horizons, 61*, 35–46. .09.003 doi:10.1016/j.bushor.2017

Lyons, A. C., Kass-Hanna, J., & Fava, A. (2021). FinTech development and savings, borrowing, and remittances: A comparative study of emerging economies. *Emerging Markets Review.* doi:10.1016/j.ememar.2021.100842

Lyu, Q. (2014). Seven unsuccessful cases of Internet finance. *China Internet Weekly, 4*, 26–29.

McKinsey. (2016). *What's next for China's booming FinTech sector?* https://www.mckinsey.com/industries/financial-services/our-insights/whats-nextfor-chinas-booming-FinTech-sector

Muthukannan, P., Tan, B., Tan, F. T. C., & Leong, C. (2021). Novel mechanisms of scalability of financial services in an emerging market context: Insights from Indonesian FinTech Ecosystem. *International Journal of Information Management, 61*. doi:10.1016/j.ijinfomgt.2021.102403

National Bureau of Statistics. (2020). *Zhang Min, a statistician from the trade and foreign economy department of the National Bureau of Statistics, interprets October's retail sales data.* http://www.stats.gov.cn/tjsj/sjjd/202011/t20201116_1803215.html

Ng, A. W., & Kwok, B. K. B. (2017). Emergence of FinTech and cybersecurity in a global financial center: strategic approach by a regulator. *Financial Regulation and Compliance, 25*(4), 422–434. doi:10.1108/JFRC-01-2017-0013

North, D. C. (1989). Institutions and Economic Growth. *World Development, 17*(9), 1319–1332.

Office of the CPC Central Committee & The State Council. (2019). *The Implementation Plan for the Pilot Comprehensive Reform of Shenzhen Pilot Demonstration Zone for Building Socialism with Chinese Characteristics (2020-2025).* http://www.gov.cn/zhengce/2020-10/11/content_5550408.htm

Ouyang, L. (2021). Opportunities and challenges of FinTech innovation. *Economic Research Guide, 464*, 53–55.

Patwardhan, A., Singleton, K., & Schmitz, K. (2018). *Financial Inclusion in the Digital Age. CreditEase.* International Finance Corporation, the Stanford Graduate School of Business. https://responsiblefinanceforum.org/wp-content/uploads/2018/03/FinancialInclusionintheDigitalAge.pdf

PBOC. (2020). *The Opinions on Financial Support for the Development of the Greater Bay Area.* http://www.pbc.gov.cn/goutongjiaoliu/113456/113469/4023428/index.html

People's Bank of China. (2017). *The People's Bank of China set up a FinTech Committee.* http://www.pbc.gov.cn/goutongjiaoliu/113456/113469/3307529/index.html

People's Bank of China. (2019). *The People's Bank of China has launched a pilot program to regulate FinTech innovation.* http://www.pbc.gov.cn/goutongjiaoliu/113456/113469/3933971/index.html

People's Bank of China. (2019). *The People's Bank of China issued the Financial Technology Development Plan (2019-2021).* http://www.pbc.gov.cn/goutongjiaoliu/113456/113469/3878634/index.html

PwC. (2017). *Summary of the 2017 global FinTech survey in China.* https://www.pwccn.com/zh/fifinancial-services/fiFinTech/global-fiFinTech-survey-china-summary-2017.pdf

Qiancheng Research Institute of Internet Finance. (2019). *2018 National Online*. Lending Bulletin.

Safouane, M. B., John, M., & Gergely, T. (2021). Current trends in and future potential of crowdfunding to finance R&D of treatments for neglected tropical diseases. *Drug Discovery Today*. doi:10.1016/j.drudis.2021.02.021

Serrano-Cinca, C., Gutiérrez-Nieto, B., & López-Palacios, L. (2015). Determinants of default in P2P lending. *PLoS One*, *10*(10), 1–22. doi:10.1371/journal.pone.0139427

Shim, Y. W., & Shin, D. H. (2016). Analyzing China's FinTech Industry from the Perspective of Actor–Network Theory. *Telecommunications Policy*, *40*, 168–181.

Shin, Y. J., & Lee, I. (2018). FinTech: Ecosystem, business models, investment decisions, and challenges. *Business Horizons*, *61*, 35–46.

State Council. (2011). *Decision on Accelerating the Cultivation and Development of Strategic Emerging Industries.* http://www.gov.cn/zwgk/2010-10/18/content_1724848.htm

Wang, Q. X. (2021). The impact of Insurtech on Chinese insurance industry. *Procedia Computer Science*, *187*, 30–35.

Wang, R., Liu, J., & Luo, H. (2021). FinTech development and bank risk taking in China. *European Journal of Finance*, *27*, 4–5, 397–418. doi:10.1080/1351847X.2020.1805782

Wojcik, D., & Ioannou, S. (2020). COVID-19 and finance: Market developments so far and potential impacts on the financial sector and centres. *Tijdschrift voor Economische en Sociale Geografie*, *111*(3), 387–400.

World Economic Forum. (2017). *Beyond FinTech: A Pragmatic Assessment of Disruptive Potential in Financial Services.* https://www3.weforum.org/docs/Beyond_FinTech_-_A_Pragmatic_Assessment_of_Disruptive_Potential_in_Financial_Services.pdf

World Economic Forum. (2020). *The Next Chapter for FinTech in China.* https://www3.weforum.org/docs/WEF_The_Next_Chapter_for_FinTech_in_China_2021.pdf

Yao, F. (2020). A Brief Analysis of Opportunities and Challenges of FinTech Based on Solow Economic Growth Model. *Journal of Contemporary Accounting*, *2021*(02), 70–72.

Yao, Y. H., Li, J. P., & Sun, X. L. (2021). Measuring the risk of Chinese FinTech industry: evidence from the stock index. *Finance Research Letters, 39*. doi:10.1016/j.frl.2020.101564

Yin, R. H., & Chen, X. Y. (2021). Risk analysis and regulatory response strategies for FinTech companies — A case study of Ant Group. *Rural Finance Research, 03*, 69–78.

Zhejiang Development and Reform Commission. (2019). *Special Plan for the Construction of Hangzhou International FinTech Center.* http://zjjcmspublic.oss-cn-hangzhou-zwynet-d01-a.internet.cloud.zj.gov.cn//jcms_files/jcms1/web149/site/attach/0/0c5407d88303477e87f691fd19e58a7d.pdf

Zhejiang Digital Economy Development Leading Group. (2019). *The Action Plan for the Construction of Zhejiang Emerging Financial Center.* http://zjjcmspublic.oss-cn-hangzhou-zwynet-d01-a.internet.cloud.zj.gov.cn//jcms_files/jcms1/web2701/site/attach/0/4ac81a8c611f489fae4b609bf87b55ad.pdf

Zhejiang University. (2020). *Global FinTech Hub Report 2020.* http://upload.xinhua08.com/2020/0911/1599789773612.pdf

Chapter 10
Securing Financial Inclusiveness Adoption of Blockchain FinTech Compliance

Heru Susanto
https://orcid.org/0000-0002-1823-357X
University of Technology Brunei, Brunei & National Research and Innovation Agency, Indonesia & Tunghai University, Taiwan

Fahmi Ibrahim
https://orcid.org/0000-0001-5016-7755
University of Technology Brunei, Brunei

Rodiah
Department of Informatics, Gunadarma University, Indonesia

Didi Rosiyadi
National Research and Innovation Agency, Indonesia

Desi Setiana
University of Brunei Darussalam, Brunei & Ministry of Law and Human Rights, Indonesia

Alifya Kayla Shafa Susanto
Department of Information Security, School of Computing and Informatics, University of Technology Brunei, Brunei

Nicolas Kusuma
Department of Informatics, Gunadarma University, Indonesia

Iwan Setiawan
National Research and Innovation Agency, Indonesia

ABSTRACT

Financial technology (FinTech) as part of financial inlcussion changes conventional business models to be information technology minded. The presence of FinTech in the wider community makes it easy for access to financial service products and transactions and payment systems more practically, efficiently, and economically. Unfortunately, as the security risk in transacting increases, cyber security in the financial services industry and FinTech service providers is considered a major target by cybercriminals. This study proposed a security management approach through hybrid blockchain method implemented through flask framework and encryption to protect transaction data. The results are promising. Referring to accuracy, this study successfully reduces data leakage and misuse of personal data and financial data in FinTechs.

DOI: 10.4018/978-1-7998-8447-7.ch010

INTRODUCTION

Financial technology or FinTech is a merger of financial services with technology that changes conventional business models to be based on information technology. FinTech is present in the wider community because of people's lifestyles which are currently dominated by the use of information technology and the demands of a fast-paced life. With FinTech, all problems related to financial product services and buying and selling transactions are made easier because people do not need to look for goods in shopping places and transfer funds at banks or ATMs or in other words, the presence of FinTech in the wider community makes it easy for the public to access financial service products so that transactions, and payment systems can be done more practically, efficiently and economically. The presence of FinTech in the community is caused people's lifestyles which are currently dominated by the use of information technology and the demands of a fast-paced life. Here, the FinTech may lead to adoption and implementation of financial inclusion for stakeholders such as financial services, buying and selling transactions become easier, single click and 24/7 services. From the customer point of view the existence of financial inclusion provides several benefits such as; cheaper services, more choices and lower prices. In other hand, fintech service providers, take advatages through simplifies the transaction chain, reduces capital-operational costs, and protected the information flow. FinTech as a tools of financial inclusion can replace the role of formal financial institutions such as banks. In the case of payment systems, FinTech has a role in providing markets niche for business players as well as being a tool for payment, settlement and clearing. FinTech can help the implementation of more efficient investment services, minimize the risks of conventional payment systems, and help those who need to save, borrow funds and participate in capital. The ease of access to financial product services and buying and selling transactions at FinTech poses a security risk in the case of transactions. Leakage and misuse of personal data and financial data by unauthorized parties is one of the main issues.

Although FinTech is easy access of financial product services, unfortunately the security risk in transacting increases. Cyber security in the FinTech service providers is considered a major target by cybercriminals. Leakage and misuse of personal data and financial data by irresponsible parties, and the lack of public knowledge about the processes that occur within FinTech are the main problems that occur in FinTech technology. Although most ICT (Information and Communication Technology) systems are designed to have a considerable amount of strength in order to sustain and assist organisations in protecting information from security threats, they are not completely immune from the threats. Organisations pay increasing attention to information protection as the impact of information security breaches today have a more tangible effect. Information security contributes to the success of organisations, as it gives a solid foundation to increase both efficiency and productivity. Many Fintech business organisations realise that compliance with the information security will affect their business prospects. Securing information resources from unauthorised access is extremely important. Information security needs to be managed in a proper and systematic manner as information security is quite complex. One of the effective ways to manage information security is to comply with an information security through blockchain approach. G. Zyskind *et all.,* (2015) stated that decentralized platform using the blockchain to change the protocol into an automated access-control manager and did not require trust from third parties. Third parties defined by digital authored monetary financial transaction, such as; visa, mastercard, paypal, WePay. Transactions through this approach acquire pointer data ledger to construct hashing SHA-256 schema. In other hand, Kosba *et all.,* (2016) reveal decentralized smart-contract-system (SMS) that hiding and encryptics financial transactions information through blockchain. However, The

SMS emerged from decentralized cryptocurrency that allows parties unrecognized each other to make transactions safely without the involvement of a third party. The new technology on Bitcoin, known as pegged sidechains, which allows bitcoin to be transferred through many blockchain, that gives users access to new and innovative cryptocurrency systems.

This research focus on blockchain approach to securing fintech transaction. Moreover, the blockchain implemented through encrypted Flask-framework by Python programming language. In this study, the accuracy of fintech transaction determined based on the user's data to reduce data leakage and misuse of fintech transaction. The implementation of blockchain methods will actually build more trustworthy infrastructure for the fintech services, this application is the greatest transformation of public sector, thus create a more citizen-focused, more over it allow individual to own their identifies for every transaction to be verified. In other hand, fintech services is fragile since cyber security issues through unauthorized user can hack the processes. Blockchain could potentially improve cyber defense, prevent fraudulent activities through mechanisms, and detect data tempering based on its underlying characteristic of immutability.

Problem Statements and Research Objective

This study focus on how securing fintech transaction. Since several problems posibbly arised in time of fintect processes, that can be formulated as follows;

1. How to encrypt Transaction ID, Public Key, and Private Key for transactions on FinTech?
2. How to determine the accuracy parameters of user transaction data at FinTech?
3. How to do transaction data mining to add new transaction blocks to the blockchain.

Based on the problems stated, the purpose of the study includes: (1) Encrypt the Transaction ID, Public Key, and Private Key for transactions on FinTech. (2) Determine the accuracy parameters of the FinTech transaction data provided by the user. (3) Perform transaction data mining to add new transaction processes to the blockchain.

Writing Organization

The research organizing systematic academic writing, as follows; *INTRODUCTION*; This section consists of research background such as; problem formulation, research objectives, and research methods. *LITERATURE REVIEW*; The section revelas of previous research and a theoretical study that used in this study related to securing transaction data using the blockchain method. Thean *RESEARCH METHODS* section. *RESULTS AND DISCUSSION;* this descripts and argues of the result in encrypting FinTech transaction data using the blockchain method. And finally *CONCLUSIONS AND SUGGESTIONS* section.

LITERATURE REVIEW

Current Research

Zyskind *et all.*, (2015) conducted a decentralized platform using blockchain implementation to shifted the blockchain protocol into an automated access-control manager without third parties approval. There are three entities involved in this system, namely users, application service providers, and entities to maintain the data block and storage of distributed private key value. The transaction is illustrated when the user registers, then the user identity sent to the blockchain, while the user location is encrypted using an encryption key and sent to the blockchain key value using a data pointer in the ledger, where the pointer is hashed through SHA-256. Both the service and user can request data using transactions with the associated pointer (key). Next the blockchain verifies digital signature belongs to the user and service concerned. Finally, users can change the permissions granted to the service at any time by issuing transactions with a series of new permissions, including revoking access to previously stored data. Overall, this study constructs the securing of personal data that should not be entrusted to third parties that may lead to have the possibility attacked. Kosba *et all.*, (2016) revealing a decentralized smart contract system that encrypts financial transactions to the blockchain from public view. The SMS that emerged from decentralized cryptocurrency allows parties who untrust each other to make transactions safely without the involvement of a third party. Here, Kosba *et all.*, formalize the blockchain cryptographic model for independent processes for the public adoption on a decentralized blockchain.

The Blockchain first appeared and was conceptualized by Satoshi Nakamoto in 2008 which was then implemented at the core of the bitcoin where the blockchain functioned as a public ledger for all transactions that occur on the network. The use of the blockchain in bitcoin makes bitcoin the first digital currency capable of overcoming double-spending without requiring trusted authority or third parties. Moreover, Back *et all.* (2014) introduced bitcoin technologies known as pegged sidechains that allows bitcoin and other ledger assets to be transferred between many blockchain. This technology gives users access to new and innovative cryptocurrency systems that may easily operate and avoid shortages of liquidity market fluctuations related to new currencies. However, Crosby *et al.*, (2016) conducted hypotheses on Blockchain technology. Blockchain is basically a distributed database of records or public ledgers of all digital transactions or events that have been executed and shared among the participating parties. Every transaction in the public ledger is verified by consensus of the majority of participants in the system. Once approved, information can not be deleted. The summary of current blockchain emerging technology as describe in the table 1. In cryptography, the password algorithm scheme is divided into two namely block cipher and stream cipher which is decribed in following sections.

Table 1. Summary of Related Research

Year	Authors	Area
2014	A. Back, M. Corallo, L. Dashjr et al	*Enabling Blockchain Innovations With Pegged Sidechains*
2015	G. Zyskind, O. Nathan, A. Pentland	*Decentralizing Privacy: Using Blockchain to Protect Personal Data*
2016	A. Kosba, A. Miller, E. Shi et al.	*Hawk: The Blockchain Model of Cryptography and Preserving Smart Contracts*
2016	M. Crosby, P. Pattanayak, S. Verma et al.	*Blockchain Technology: Beyond Bitcoin*
2017	K. Lakhani, M. Lansity	*The Truth About Blockchain*

Block Cipher

In cryptography, block ciphers are deterministic algorithms that operate on groups of fixed length bits called by *blocks*, with unchanging transformations that determined by symmetric keys. The block cipher encrypts all blocks containing plaintext bits at the same time by using the same key. This means that the encryption of any plaintext bit in a given block depends on every other plaintext bit in the same block. In practice, most block ciphers have a block length of 128 bits (16 bytes) such as the Advanced Encryption Standard (AES) encryption algorithm, or have a block length of 64 bits (8 bytes) as in the Data Encryption Standard (DES) or triple encryption algorithm DES (3DES).Block cipher encrypts a block containing plaintext or message (m) into a block containing ciphertext (c) under the action of a secret key (k) so that it can be formulated c = ENCk (m), ENC is Encription Process. The exact form of encryption transformation will be determined by the choice of the block cipher and the value of the k key. The encryption process is reversed through a decryption process that will use the same key that has been provided by the user so that it can be formulated m = DECk (c). The illustration of the block cipher is shown in Figure 1.

Figure 1. Illustration of Block Cipher

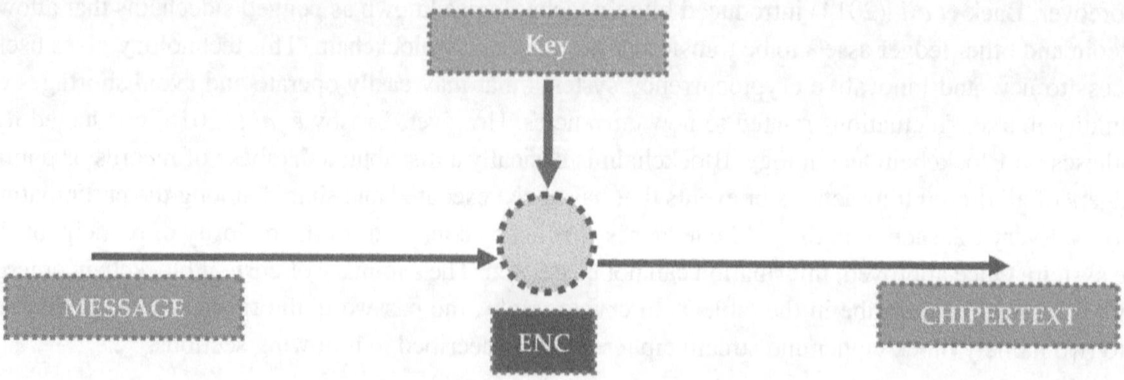

Block ciphers have two important parameters:

1. The size of the block, symbolized by the symbol b.
2. The size of the key, symbolized by the symbol k. For a given key, a b-bit block cipher maps the μ group of b-bit 2^b inputs into the same group of output 2^b (Figure 2)

m = {0…00. 0…01, 0…10, 0…11, ……, 1… 1}

Figure 2. Mapping of μ groups from 2^b b-bits into the same group from output 2^b

$$m = \{\overbrace{0\ldots00}^{b}.\ \overbrace{0\ldots01}^{b},\ \overbrace{0\ldots10}^{b},\ \overbrace{0\ldots11}^{b},\ \ldots\ldots,\ \overbrace{1\ldots\ 1}^{b}\}$$

However, each possible output appears once only. This mapping is a permutation of a group of inputs and while the secret key is varied, different permutations are obtained. This makes the block cipher a way to generate permutation groups where the group is given an index by using the secret key (k). For secure block ciphers, no information is exploited regarding leakage of the encryption process as information may contain key choices, information about encryption and decryption such as invisible input, and permutations generated using different keys.

Stream Cipher

Stream ciphers are symmetric key ciphers where plaintext digits are combined with pseudorandom digit ciphers. In a stream cipher, each plaintext digit is encrypted one by one with the appropriate keystream digit to provide the streamciphertext digit. Stream ciphers encrypt bits individually. This is achieved by adding a key stream to the plaintext bit. Stream ciphers are divided into 2 namely synchronous stream ciphers and asynchronous stream ciphers. In synchronous stream ciphers, key streams only depend on keys. Whereas in asynchronous stream cipher, key stream also depends on ciphertext. Illustration of synchronous stream cipher and asynchronous stream cipher is shown in Figure 3 where the dotted lines in the picture show asynchronous stream cipher.

Figure 3. Asynchronous stream cipher and synchronous stream cipher

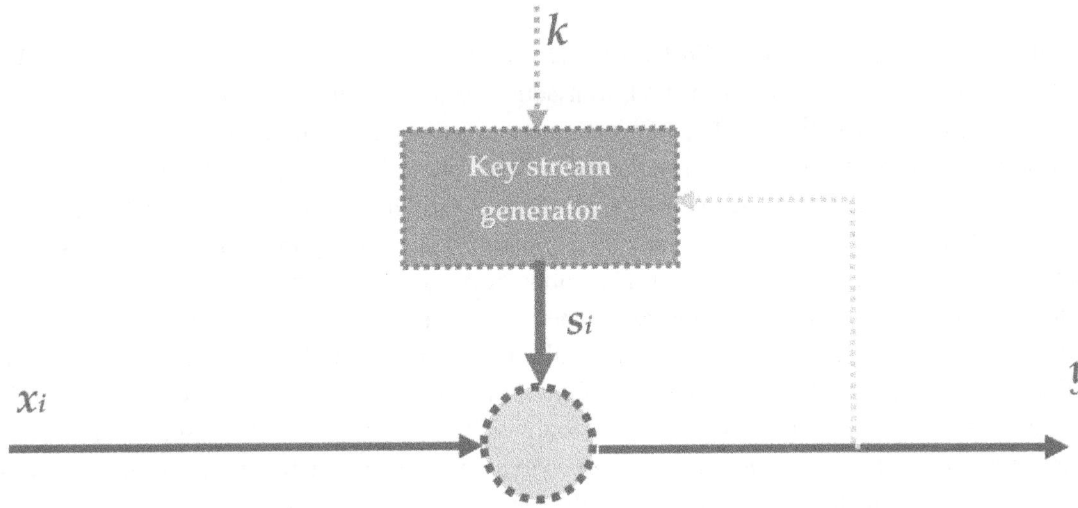

RESEARCH METHOD

The research method used in this study consists of several stages of the process as seen in Figure 4.

Figure 4. Stages of Research Methods

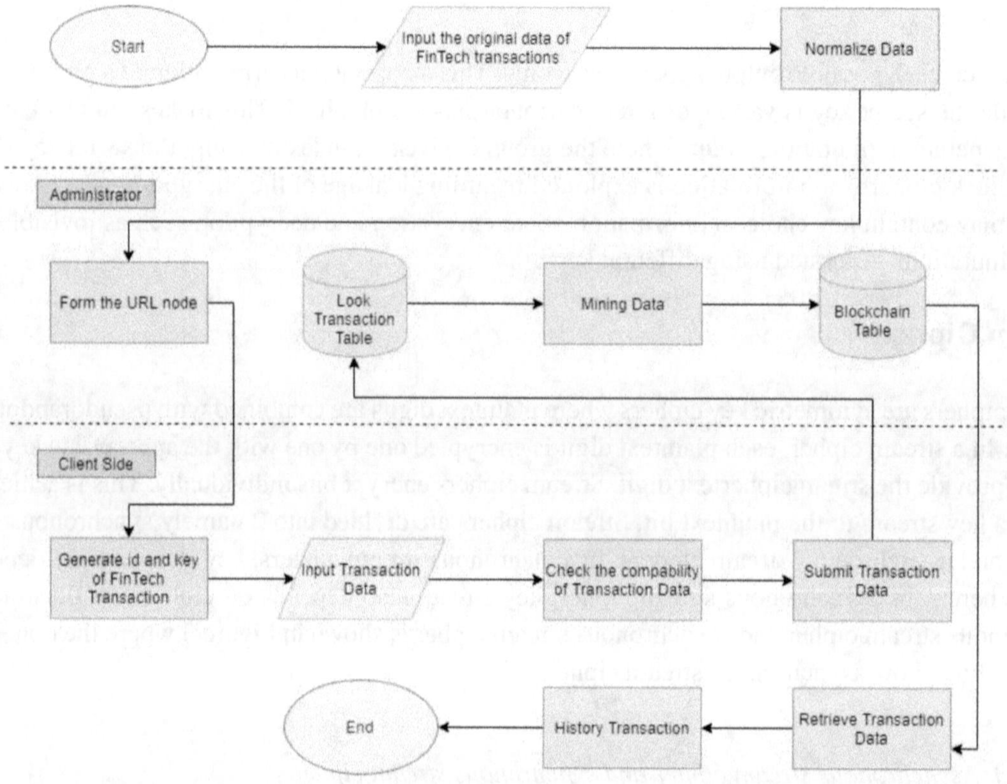

The initial phase begins with the FinTech transaction data input. Then, normalization of FinTech transaction data is performed so that FinTech transaction data which initially consists of eight parameters only becomes five parameters. The transaction process that occurs in FinTech is divided into two sides of processes, namely the administrator and the client side. The former, a URL node is formed to store transaction data entered by FinTech users. The latter, FinTech users generate transaction id, public key, and private key that will be used in making transactions at FinTech. In the next step, FinTech users input transaction data using transaction IDs, public keys, and private keys that have been obtained from the generated key. Then, it is followed by checking the suitability of transaction data to ensure that transaction data entered by FinTech users is valid transaction data. After transaction data entered by FinTech users is appropriate, FinTech users submit transaction data so that FinTech transaction data enters the transaction table. Back on the administrator side, the administrator can see any transaction data that enters the transaction table. The next step is mining a new transaction block where transaction data in the transaction table will be entered into the blockchain table containing transaction identities.

The final stage of this research method is on the client side, FinTech users can retrieve data by entering an active URL node so FinTech users can view the history of transactions that have been carried out.

Source Data

Source data used in this study deal with 8 parameters of real fintech transaction datasets in the form of a ledger skeleton consisting of; date, day, month, hour, transaction, debit, credit, balance.

Data Normalization

The data normalization process is carried out on the original simulation data before the transaction process is carried out in FinTech. This stage is carried out with the aim to reduce the number of data parameters that will be used in the transaction. At this stage, the original transaction simulation data which initially has 8 parameters is normalized into 5 parameters namely Transaction Id, Recipient Address, Sender Address, Value, Timestamp.

Administrator Side of Process

URL Node Formation

Formation of the URL node is done with the aim to accommodate, retrieve blockchain data, and update the blockchain if it is not synchronized. At this stage, the administrator configures by entering multiple URL nodes separated by commas. Next, the administrator submits the URL node so that the URL node is active and can be used by storing transaction data of FinTech users, and retrieving transaction data by FinTech users so that FinTech users can view the transaction history that has been done. The flow diagram of the formation of the URL node, as follows;

1. Enter the URL node configuration view.
2. The administrator enters the localhost URL that will be used to collect, retrieve transaction data, and update the blockchain. In this case, if the number of URLs entered by the administrator is more than 1 (2 or more), then each URL entered must be separated by a comma (,) then submit. Conversely, if the URL entered is only 1, then the administrator only needs to submit.
3. After the URL is submitted, the URL node is active and can be used to hold, retrieve data, and update the blockchain.

Transaction Table

Transaction table contains transaction data entered by FinTech users. In the transaction table, transaction data entered by FinTech users will be temporarily accommodated before mining to be entered into the blockchain table for the formation of new transaction blocks. The Transaction Table consists of 4 parameters, namely Transaction ID, Recipient Address, Sender Address, and Value.

Blockchain Table

The blockchain table contains FinTech transaction data that has been mined from the transaction table. The blockchain table contains transaction identities consisting of 5 parameters, namely Transaction Id, Recipient Address, Sender Address, Value, and Timestamp. The blockchain table scheme used.

Client Side of Process

Generate Id and Key Transactions

At this stage a transaction id, public key, and private key will be generated which will be used by FinTech users in conducting transactions. Transaction IDs and public key and private key pairs are generated through public / private key encryption techniques using the RSA encryption algorithm. FinTech users must remember or save the transaction id, as well as this public key and private key pair so that it can be used to make transactions inside FinTech. Encryption flow diagram using the RSA algorithm, as follows;

1. First, determine two prime numbers, namely p and q, where the value of p does not equal q and the value of p is greater than q.
2. Next, calculate the value of n where n = p * q and M = (p-1) * (q-1).
3. Determine the value of e where 1 <e <n-1
4. Calculate the greatest common factor (FPB) of e and m. If FPB (e, m) is equal to 1, then determine the value of d. Conversely, if FPB (e, m) is not equal to 1, then re-determine the value of e.
5. Calculate the value of ed where ed = 1 mod m. If ed = 1 mod m, then encrypt the message (plaintext) where C = Po mod n. Conversely, if ed is not the same as 1 mod m, then re-determine the value of d.
6. Encryption in the plaintext produces ciphertext. At this stage, decryption can be done to change the ciphertext into a plaintext. If the decryption stage is performed, the ciphertext is decrypted by the formula P = Cd mod n so as to produce the original message (plaintext).

Transaction Data Input

After generating transaction id, public key, and private key, the next step is entering transaction data. This stage is done construct the *transaction_id*, public key as *Sender Address*, private key as *Sender Private Key, Recipient Address*, and Value as the nominal amount of *money to be transferred*. Following is the flowchart of the flow diagram.

1. First, FinTech users generate transaction IDs and public and private key pairs.
2. After getting the transaction id, as well as the public key and private key pairs needed for the transaction, the user enters into the Make Transaction view to make transactions on FinTech.
3. Furthermore, FinTech users carry out transactions by entering the transaction data required.
4. The next step is to check the transaction data entered by the FinTech user. If the transaction data entered by FinTech users is complete and correct, then a transaction can be generated. Conversely, if transaction data entered by FinTech users is incomplete, FinTech users are asked to complete transaction data.

Transaction Data Suitability Check

At this stage, the transaction data is checked with the aim of ensuring that transaction data provided by FinTech users is valid and correct data. After the user enters the required transaction data, FinTech users confirm the transaction by checking each transaction data and checking whether the digital signature of the client is a valid and correct digital signature, as follows;

1. First, FinTech users generate transaction.
2. After generating the transaction a notification pop up will appear. This notification functions so that FinTech users can check whether the transaction data and digital signature are valid and correct.
3. Then the transaction data and digital signature will be checked. If transaction data and digital signatures are valid and correct, then FinTech users are asked to enter an active URL node to collect and retrieve transaction data. Conversely, if transaction data or digital signatures are invalid, then FinTech users are asked to correct their transaction data.
4. After the user checks the transaction data, digital signatures, and enters an active URL node, FinTech users can submit transactions where the FinTech user transaction data will be entered into the transaction table and mining will be done for later inserted into a new transaction block on the blockchain and retrieved by FinTech users.

RESULT AND DISCUSSION

Case 1: Server Side

In the first case the localhost URL 127.0.0.1.5000 is used to make transactions on FinTech and retrieve transaction data from the localhost server. The transaction process that occurs in the first case there are 8 processes. The process that occurs starts from the formation of URL nodes, generation of transaction IDs and transaction keys, transaction data input, transaction data checking and transaction submission, transaction table checking, mining and checking blockchain tables, retrive and transaction data history, and checking transaction data accuracy using parameters accuracy. Each process will be explained in the next section.

URL Node Formation

Before forming the URL node, the first step is to run the Python program file through the Ubuntu Linux terminal as shown in Figure 5 and Fugure 6.

In forming the URL node, the administrator accesses the Configuration view first, then the administrator will enter the localhost URL to form an active URL node which can then be used by FinTech users to store and retrieve transaction data (retrieve). If the URL entered by the administrator is 2 or more, then each URL is separated by a comma (,). In the first case, the administrator enters 3 localhost URL addresses, 127.0.0.1% 001, 127.0.0.1.5002 and 127.0.0.1.5003.

Figure 5. Running the Python blockchain.py Program File

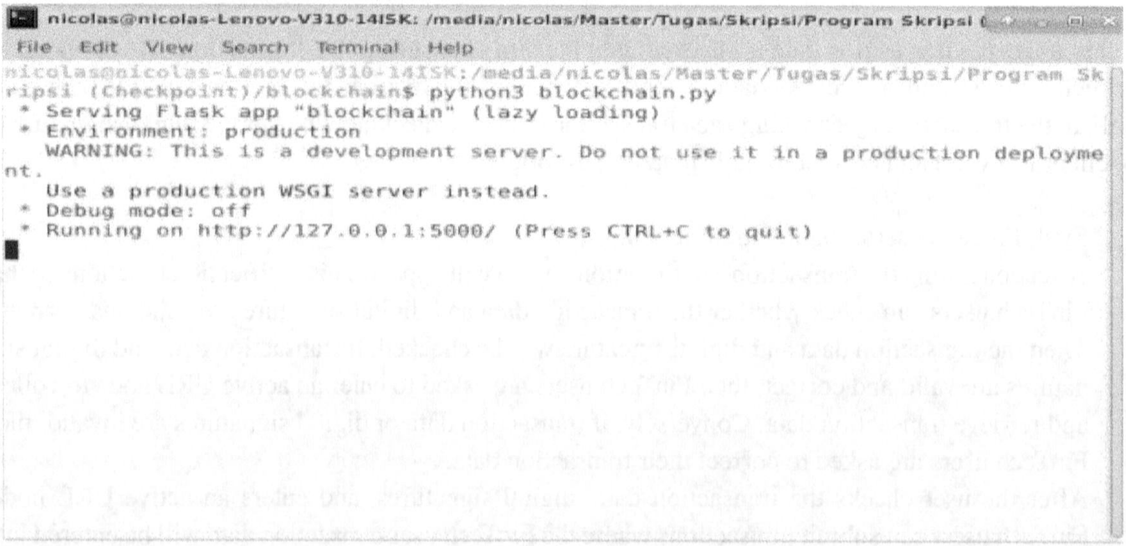

Figure 6. Running the Python Program File blockchain client.py

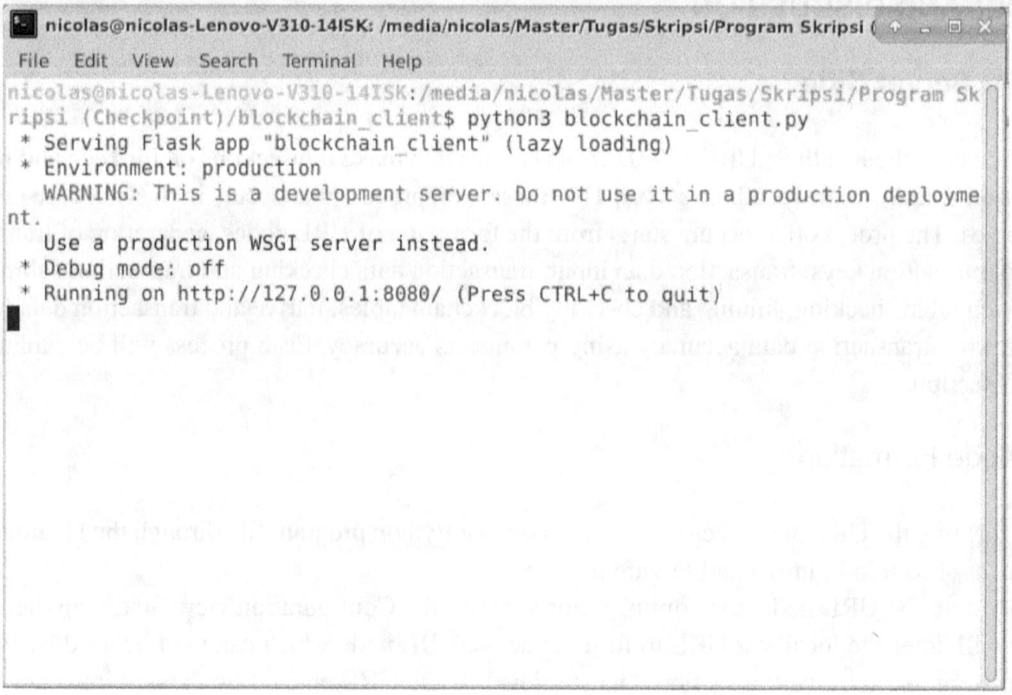

Data Accuracy Check Using Accuracy Parameters

The technique used to check the accuracy of transaction data in the blockchain table is a permutation technique so that each group of accuracy parameters has different accuracy (lowest point and highest point of accuracy is different) so that the accuracy of each transaction data is different. In the first case, the accuracy of data from a transaction will be displayed using five different groups of accuracy parameters. By using the permutation technique 2/3, 60% (3 out of 5 transaction parameters) will be determined which have the greatest influence on FinTech transactions as shown in Figure 7, Figure 8, Figure 9, Figure 10, and Figure 11.

Figure 7. Accuracy of First Case Transaction Data Using Group-A Accuracy Parameters

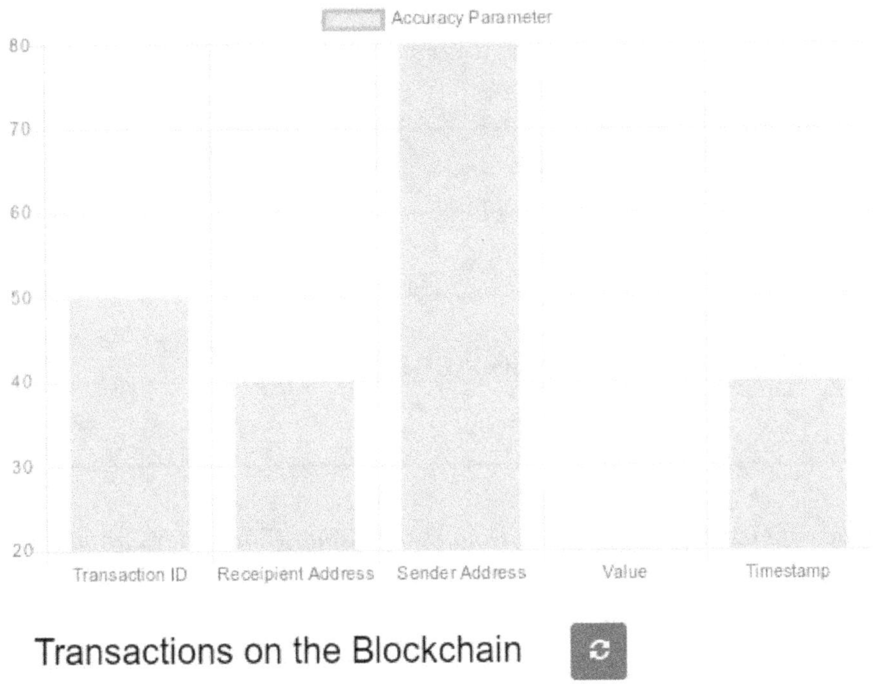

Figure 7 using the accuracy parameters of group A, each accuracy obtained from Transaction Id, Recipient Address, Sender Address, and TimeStamp are 50%, 40%, 80%, 20%, and 40%, respectively. By using the 2/3 permutation technique, it can be concluded that the Transaction ID, Sender Address, and Recipient Address have a major influence on FinTech transactions.

Figure 8, using the accuracy parameters of group B, each accuracy obtained from Transaction Id, Recipient Address, Sender Address, and TimeStamp are 40%, 20%, 80%, 50%, and 30%, respectively. By using the 2/3 permutation technique, it can be concluded that the Transaction Id, Sender Address, and Value have a great influence on FinTech transactions.

Figure 8. Accuracy of the First Case Transaction Data Using Group-B Accuracy Parameters

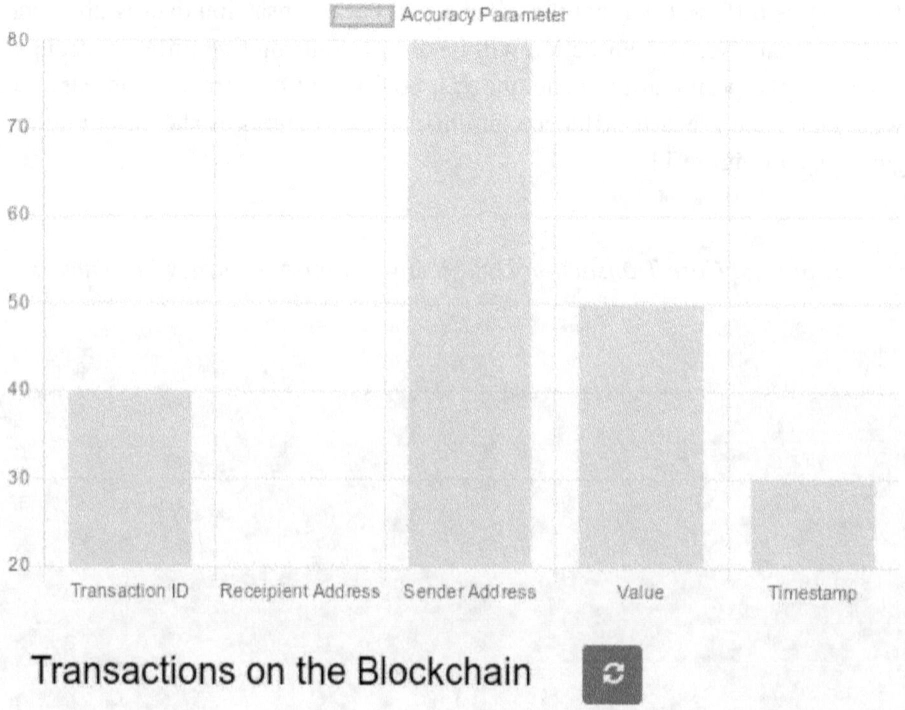

Figure 9. Accuracy of First Case Transaction Data Using Group-C Accuracy Parameters

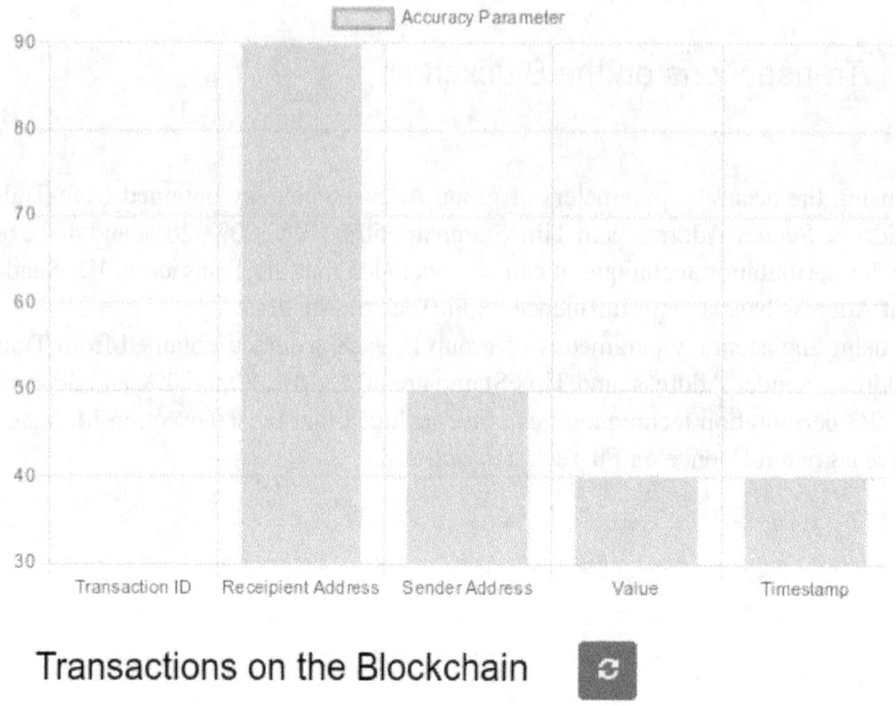

Figure 9, using the accuracy parameter C group, each accuracy obtained from Transaction Id, Recipient Address, Sender Address, and TimeStamp are 20%, 90%, 50%, 40%, and 40%, respectively. By using the permutation technique 2/3, it can be concluded that the Recipient Address, Sender Address, and Value have a great influence on FinTech transactions.

Figure 10. Accuracy of First Case Transaction Data Using Group-D Accuracy Parameters

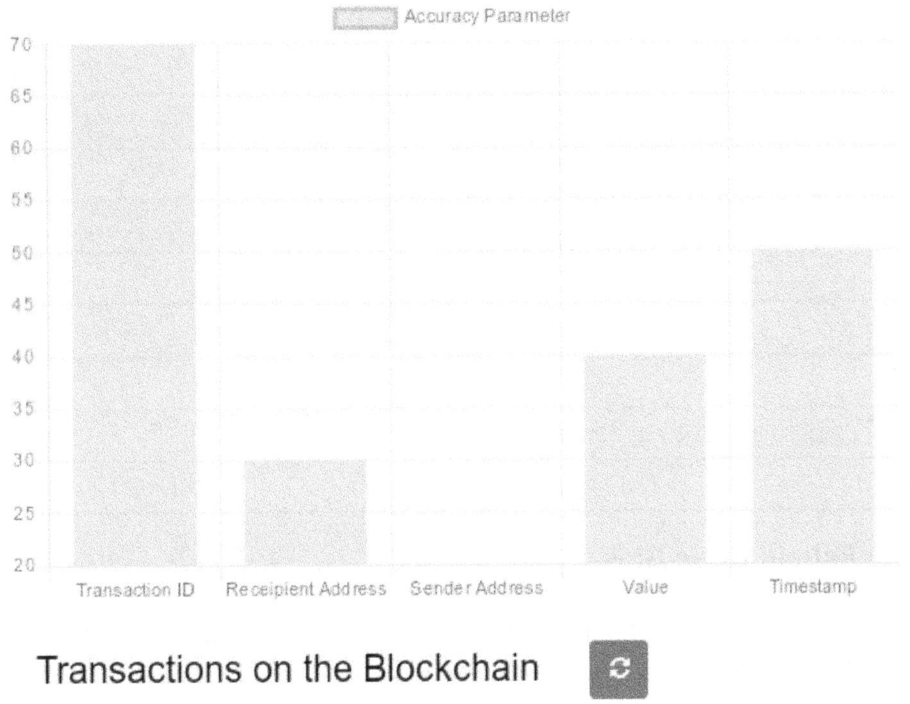

Figure 10, using the accuracy parameter D group, obtained each accuracy of the Transaction Id, Recipient Address, Sender Address, and TimeStamp respectively 70%, 30%, 20%, 40%, and 50%. By using the permutation technique 2/3, it can be concluded that the Transaction Id, Value, and Timestamp provide a large influence in FinTech transactions

Figure 11, using the accuracy parameter E group, each accuracy obtained from Transaction Id, Recipient Address, Sender Address, and TimeStamp are 60%, 40%, 20%, 50%, and 30%, respectively. By using the permutation technique 2/3, it can be concluded that the Transaction Id, Recipient Address, and Value have a great influence on FinTech transactions

Figure 11. Accuracy of First Case Transaction Data Using Group-E Accuracy Parameters

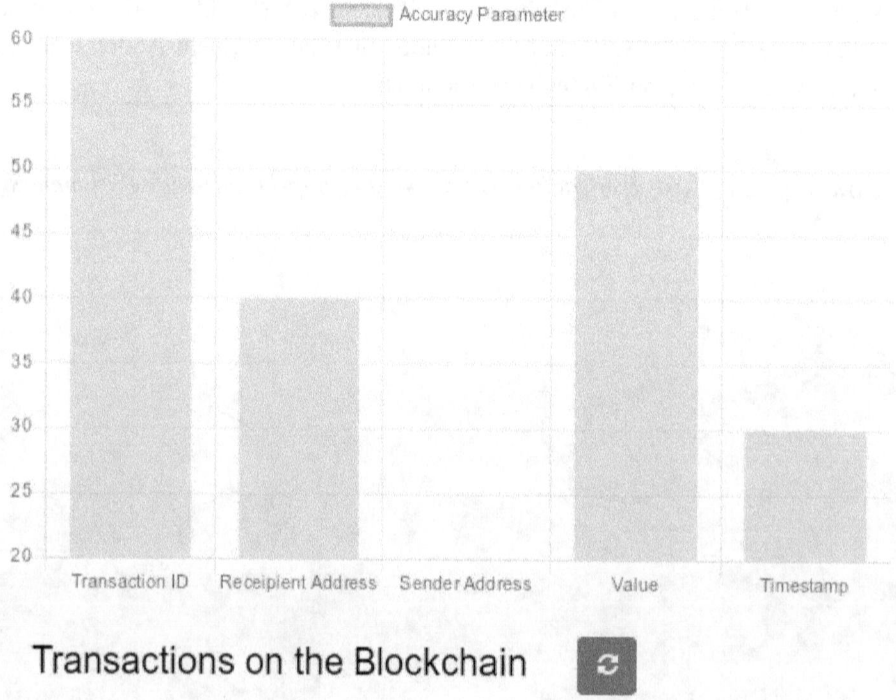

Case 2: Blockchain Node Side

In the first case, localhost URL 127.0.0.1.5000 is used to make transactions on FinTech and retrieve transaction data from the localhost server. In the second case, a different localhost URL will be used that has been configured and formed by the administrator which in this case is the blockchain node 127.0.0.1.5001. The transaction process that occurs in the second case there are 8 processes. The process that occurs starts from the formation of URL nodes, generation of transaction IDs and transaction keys, transaction data input, transaction data checking and transaction submission, transaction table checking, mining and checking blockchain tables, retrive and transaction data history, and checking transaction data accuracy using parameters accuracy. Each process will be explained in the next section.

Data Accuracy Check Using Accuracy Parameters

The technique used to check the accuracy of transaction data in the blockchain table is a permutation technique so that each group of accuracy parameters has different accuracy (lowest point and highest point of accuracy is different) so that the accuracy of each transaction data is different. In the second case, the accuracy of data from a transaction will be displayed using five different groups of accuracy parameters as shown in Figure 12, Figure 13, Figure 14, Figure 14, and Figure 16.

Figure 12, using the accuracy parameters of group A, each accuracy obtained from Transaction Id, Recipient Address, Sender Address, and TimeStamp are 30%, 60%, 20%, 50%, and 40%, respectively. By using the 2/3 permutation technique, it can be concluded that the Recipient Address, Value, and Timestamp have a major influence on FinTech transactions.

Figure 13, using the accuracy parameters of group B, each accuracy obtained from Transaction Id, Recipient Address, Sender Address, and TimeStamp are 40%, 50%, 20%, 30%, and 80%, respectively. By using the permutation technique 2/3 it can be concluded that, Transaction Id, Recipient Address, and TimeStamp provide a large influence in FinTech transactions.

Figure 14, using the accuracy parameters of group C, each accuracy obtained from Transaction Id, Recipient Address, Sender Address, and TimeStamp are 30%, 50%, 40%, 60%, and 20%, respectively. By using the 2/3 permutation technique, it can be concluded that the Recipient Address, Sender Address, and Value have a great influence on FinTech transactions.

Figure 15, using the accuracy parameter D group, each accuracy obtained from Transaction Id, Recipient Address, Sender Address, and TimeStamp are 30%, 20%, 80%, 40%, and 50%, respectively. By using the 2/3 permutation technique, it can be concluded that Sender Address, Value, and Timestamp have a great influence on FinTech transactions.

Figure 16, using the accuracy parameter D group, each accuracy obtained from Transaction Id, Recipient Address, Sender Address, and TimeStamp are 50%, 40%, 30%, 90%, and 20%, respectively. By using the permutation technique 2/3, it can be concluded that the Transaction Id, Recipient Address, and Value have a great influence on FinTech transactions.

Figure 12. Accuracy of Second Case Transaction Data Using Group-A Accuracy Parameters

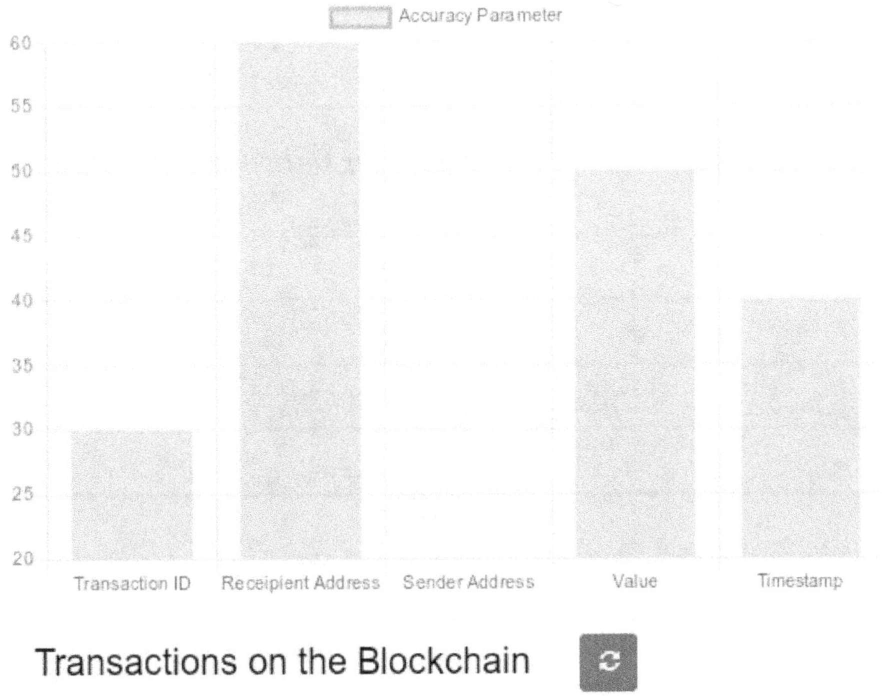

Figure 13. Accuracy of Second Case Transaction Data Using Group-B Accuracy Parameters

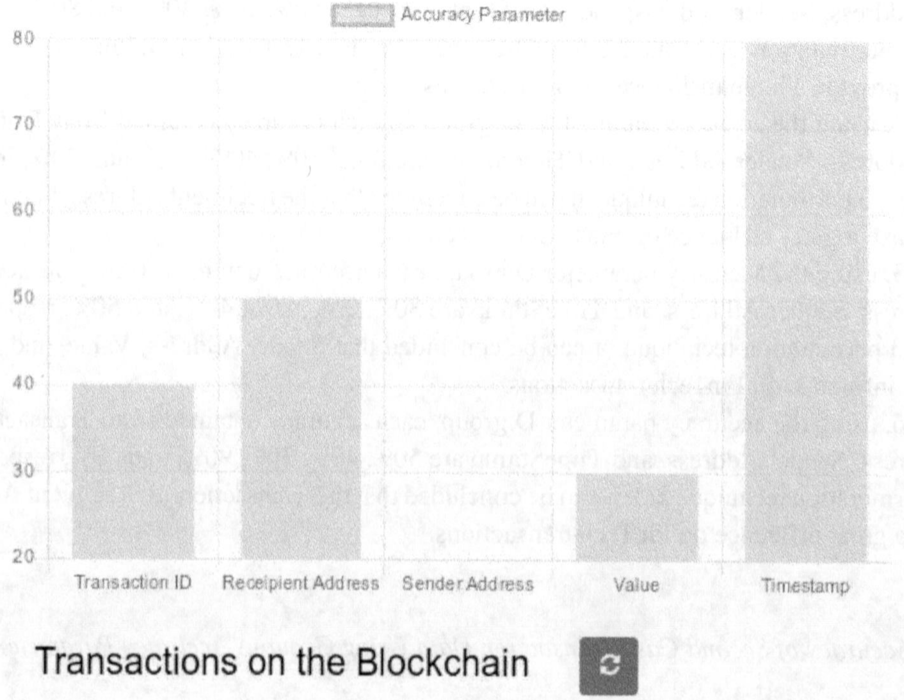

Figure 14. Accuracy of Second Case Transaction Data Using Group-C Accuracy Parameters

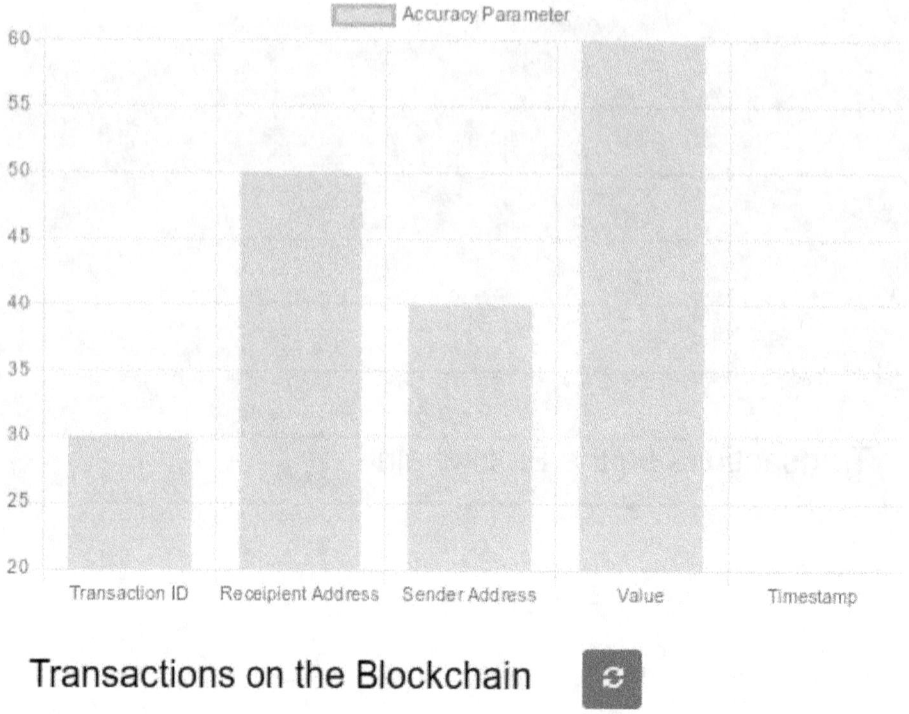

Figure 15. Accuracy of Second Transaction Data Using Cases Group-D Accuracy Parameters

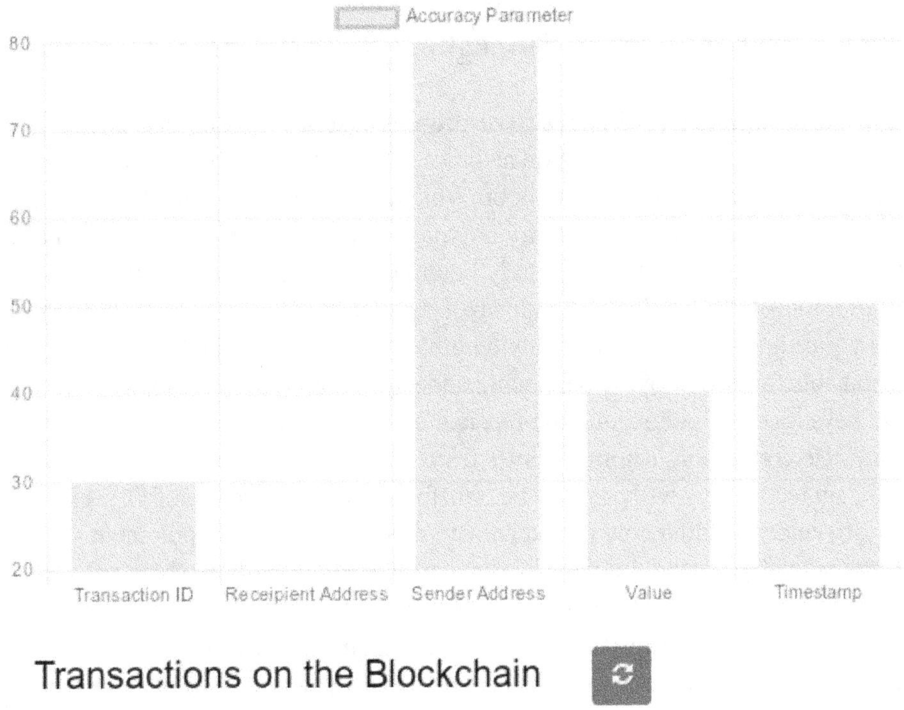

Figure 16. Check Transaction Data Accuracy Using Group-E Accuracy Parameters

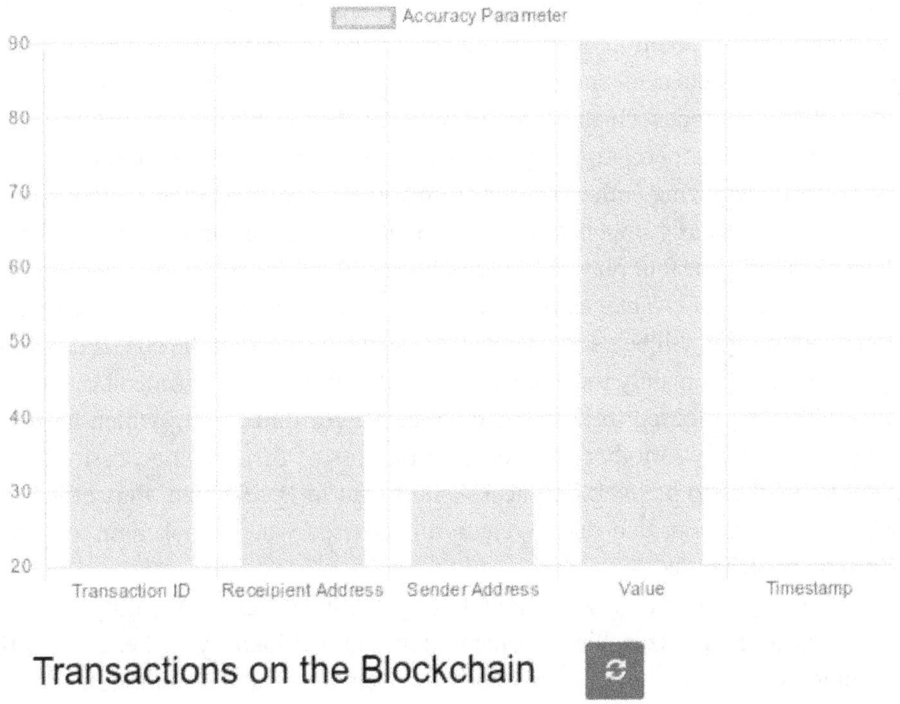

DISCUSSION

Financial Inclusiveness: Fintech Blockchain Approaches

Based of research finding mentioned in **result section**, blockchain can be defined as a shared ledger system or an established record of data not owned by a single entity and is used to record data transactions across multiple computers. Other than bitcoin which propagated the idea of Blockchain, the factors as to why the technology has gained popularity are that any digital asset or transaction can be inserted as a block of data (e.g. block) which are securely bound to each other using cryptography (e.g. chain), the industry does not matter. The block is made up of data, hash (A cryptographic fixed output through a mathematical algorithm from an input of any length) and previous hash. Every other member of the network is responsible for verifying the data being added to the Blockchain is real. This is done using a system of three keys (private, public, and the receiver's key) that allow members to check the veracity of the data while also confirming whom it comes from.

Here, blockchain technology will prove to be transformative in the realm of IT security, to the entire solution. Hence, by understanding how Blockchain could be used would supplement the overall protection of data with the existing technology for IT security. The Blockchain is able to ensure data remains private and secure by breaking a large amount of data into smaller chunks, and distributes them across the entire network of computers instead of uploading and storing everything to a cloud server or a single location. This effectively cuts out the need to engage a third party in processing a transaction so the risk of placing the trust on another party in not leaking any data to outsiders is negated. Moreover, encryption is performed at every transaction and the alteration of any data can be proven. The distributed nature of Blockchain creates a method of checking file signatures across all the ledgers on all the nodes in the network which would verify that they haven't been changed. If someone or a cybercriminal do change a record, then the signature or a new record is rendered invalid. Furthermore, cyber criminals that break into traditional networks and corrupt/steal data stored in a single location would no longer be a feasible method with the addition of Blockchain. Because the data are spread out to various nodes or computers that will cross-checked and encrypt the data. The only possibilities of hacking would be to target the majority of the nodes which is well beyond the abilities of current cybercriminals as there would be a need for enough supercomputing power and time. Finally, the Blockchain can restrict access to specific users by requiring authentication from various nodes in order to gain some privileges. Generally, Blockchain is a nearly impenetrable technology used to prevent any type of data breaches, identity thefts, cyber-attacks or foul play in transactions.

However, some key risk/disadvantages will need to be comprehended so that by keeping these limitations in mind, the technology will be used in a way that steers away from the risk and progress towards the benefits. The limitation is mainly the expensive cost that follows decentralization due to the outrageous amount of electricity needed to keep the computer algorithms going which have caused some miners to steal power illegally. Another risk could be the loss of the key in accessing the Blockchain which would cause the user to be unable to access their data in Blockchain, thus effectively freezing their assets such as Bitcoins. For that reason, caution is advised when Blockchain technology is used and it should still be implemented.

The industries ranging from banking, online retailing and healthcare to the duty of the government such as national security and citizenship documentation requires identity authentication that consists of a process complexly merged into the global commerce and culture. The situation such as databases being hacked and breached accounts have shed light on the rising issues of a technologically advanced society, without the necessary identity-based security innovations to prevent those situations from occurring. Digital identity can be uniquely authenticated in an indisputable, and safe manner with Blockchain technology, whereas current methods employ traditional password-based systems whereby the password may be accidentally shared or stowed in insecure systems. Blockchain-based authentication systems use digital signatures from the public/private key cryptography to prove the irrefutable identity of the owner even if the owner is anonymous.

This study reveal fintech transaction within financial inclussion ecosystem through mobile device users that are not taking cyber security measures seriously and continued to stay negligent towards the dangers of cyber threats occurring to mobile devices. There are discovered a number of reasons behind user's behaviour of not implementing any security measures in general such as:

- User's habit of making irrational thoughts or decisions such as clicking "I accept" without reading what they are actually agreeing to and not contemplating about the consequences of their behaviour
- User's extreme preference for convenience rather than taking the more difficult method namely security
- User's extreme priority on fulfilling user's desire rather than going for security such as downloading applications that they deem very important when there are alternatives that could be a much secure
- The financial costs of opting for security such as purchasing security software such as anti-virus is much greater than the security gains felt by the user.
- Users felt that the level of effort required to fully exercise security measures is too high such as remembering different passwords for different accounts and keeping anti-virus updated regularly.
- Users don't perceive any benefit and believes their behaviour will not affect security at all or users instead justify the cyber risk they perceived such as believing connecting themselves to an unsecure website for a short period of time is a safe action or by thinking there is no possibility of them being attacked or breached
- Users are lacking the knowledge and skills to handle any security issue such as ways and method of handling any fraudulent activities they encountered
- Users do not understand that any behaviour they have conducted will have an impact on the security risks as well as their level of vulnerability to these risks
- Users are simply forgotten to take on security measures due to various distractions encountered while surfing online

In order to increase the level of awareness amongst mobile device users, it is necessary to increase their awareness on how each of their actions and behaviour could affect the security of their mobile devices. In order to do so, a new framework which has been proposed which has been created by analysing and assessing a number of factors that influences user's cyber security behaviour (Figure 17).

Figure 17. User Behaviour of Security Awareness

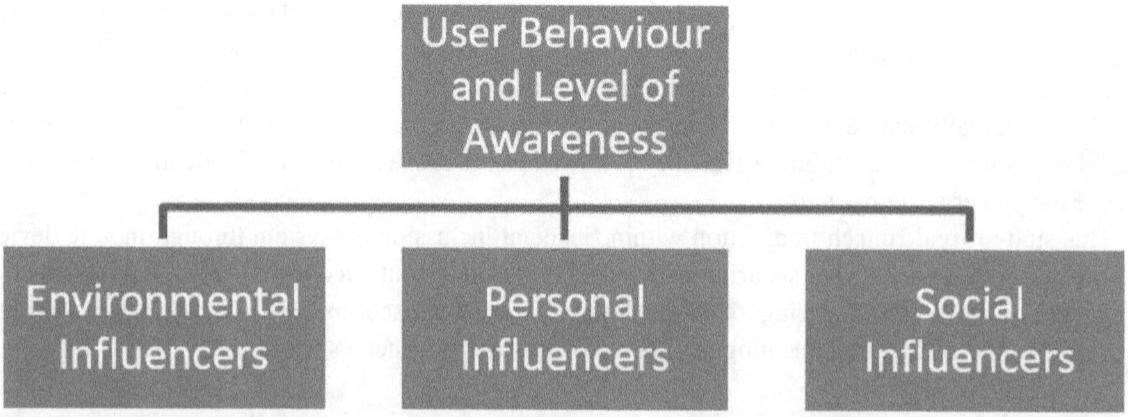

Environmental Influencers

Design Factors

To ensuring security of fintech transaction trough blockchain as discussed within result section, it has been discovered that creating a good design or interface for a security software or application has an impact on user's willingness to use such applications. The interface design is deemed as a crucial property compared to user participation in regards to security systems in computer. The rationale behind this discovery is that a good design can effectively transmit the correct information in an orderly manner to users, thus allowing users to make an accurate and precise decision in regards to the system's state, structure as well as the security aspect of it. When this is applied to the context of mobile devices, having a good design such as good visualisations and smooth interface allows the security applications to effectively communicate its users with the necessary information useful for users to assess their current security status and risk as well as making informed decisions. Additionally, it can also promote constant interactivity with users which will then eventually result in enticing user's involvement and willingness to use such security applications.

Economic Factors

When users are determining themselves on how to behave, they will usually conduct a cost benefit analysis on the situation. One of the factors that could affect the analysis and consequently their behaviour is the presence of incentives, whether they are in the form of positive incentives such as rewards or any sort of benefits bestowed to the users or the incentives could also be negative in nature such as the cost or punishment for certain conduct or behaviour. When the economic factors of performing insecure actions are seen as acceptable to users, they would perform those risky actions such as visiting insecure websites and dismissing any security risk and credentials that could endanger both the user's mobile device as well as their sensitive information. The relationship between rewards and user's probability of behaving securely and it has been revealed that punishment, rewards as well as control assurance has an impact on user's conformity. Additionally, the concept of rewards can be utilised to motivate users in practicing and implementing security measures.

Personal Influencers

Knowledge, Skills and Understanding

It is very important for users to have the knowledge, understanding as well as the skills in order to defend themselves against fraudulent or unlwaful attacks. It is necessary for users to be equipped with the essential knowledge in order to perform and promote security measures as well as actions. The lack of user's knowledge in regards best security within the security aspect could result in a security failure. But one of the challenges faced by users is that it is quite difficult for users to conform to best practices of protecting their mobile device because users wouldn't know which specific type of attack or risk they will encounter, especially during these times where by the nature of cyber attacks are always changing as attackers could find many different method to perform fraudulent actions. Due to such uncertainties, users tend to rely on their individual heuristics ability or skills that enables users to make quick and efficient judgements as well as decisions within a short period of time. However, it is also noted that even though the use of heuristics is beneficial, it may lead users to create biases. There is an assumption that knowledge is a 'thing' or an object which can be made explicit and codifiable or 'standardized data' that may result to 'information overload' where the amount of information/data is becoming unmanageable (Ibrahim and Reid, 2010) that caused it to lose its 'tacitness' (Hislop, 2013). In practice, it has frequently proven to be very difficult (or very time-consuming) for experts to provide a description of their (often tacit) knowledge divorced from the actual activity (Greiner, 2007). Removed from the context of their activity, experts have difficulty articulating the skills, knowledge, and heuristics that comprise their expertise. Drawing from KM concept, this perspective suffers from 'synoptic delusion'; the mistaken concept that it is possible to collect organisational knowledge in a single repository (Tsoukas, 2005:p.100).

On the other hand, the availability and delivery of constant and beneficial information is required in order for users to exhibit security behaviours but it is also noted that such information might not be enough to inspire or motivate users to change their behaviours into a more security oriented in nature. Users still exhibit poor security behaviours even after attending cyber awareness training and campaigns and further added that it is not recommended to refer to user's knowledge level as a determiner of good cyber security behaviours.

Perceptions, Attitudes and Beliefs

In other hand, the customer attitude toward FinTech transaction can be defined as a person's inclination to judge or assess something in a particular way. Attitude has been known to influence an individual's behaviour, whereby individuals and users each own a number of beliefs and attitudes unique to themselves that may affect their behaviour in various aspects which also include their security behaviours. But it is noted that uncomfortable tensions may occur as a result of the misalignment between attitude and behaviours and the only solution to solve it is by undergoing change to one's attitude or behaviour. Within the discussion on the matter of behaviours, it will always involve various different factors that interact together in complex ways and researchers have come up with various models to illustrate such relationships such as:

1. Rational choice based model - One of the main assumption within the rational choice model or also known as rational action model, is that it assumes that users has perfect information. What is meant by perfect information here is that users are assumed to acquire all information regarding every possible choices or alternatives and then users will act on it by behaving in a manner that will provide them with the best outcome out of all possible choices. An individual's act of processing the obtained information doesn't necessarily lead to the generation of a rational behaviour and consequently, individuals does not necessarily perform a rational choice in order to achieve the optimum result. Hence, according to this model, it can be said that every mobile device users are already equipped with the cognitive ability and motivation required to make rational decisions when faced with security incidents such as the act of applying facts in assessing cyber incidents. However, it is also noted that there is a challenge in doing so primarily due to the uncertainties of outcome or end results when dealing with anything related to cyber security.
2. Theory and model of planned behaviour - The main motive behind the use of the planned behaviour model amongst researchers is to analyse and describe the behaviours exhibited by individuals that are equipped with the ability to exercise self-control. One of the assumption that has been created within this model is that it assumes that any behaviour is planned and any individuals that plans to act or behave in a certain way will actually commit to it and behave in the way they have initially planned. A fundamental element within the planned behaviour model is behavioural intent, where the intention to behave in a certain way is subject to the attitude towards the expected outcome of the desired behaviour as well as the evaluation of cost and benefit produce by the behaviour. Thus, according to this model, it can be said that when users believes that by behaving securely and employing security measures to their mobile devices will produce positive outcome to themselves, the users will effectively perform the security behaviour that they had planned in their minds.
3. Protection motivation model - The protection motivation model was created with an intention to aid individuals in resolving and coping with their fear appeals and this model believes that the behaviour of individuals are influenced by two appraisals namely the threat appraisal and the coping appraisal. The threat appraisal refers to user's perception on the gravity of an incident and user's perception on the likelihood of an incident or vulnerability while the coping appraisal refers to user's efficacy of the suggested precautionary behaviour as well as user's perception of their own efficacy (self-efficacy).
4. Learning model - One of the assumptions made within the learning model is that it assumes that behaviour is a process that individuals need to learn and that the learning process is influenced by two different elements which are incentives in the form of punishment or rewards and the social environment surrounding the individual which includes role models.
5. Change models - Change models are known to be built by the assumption that changes in behaviour is a step-by-step process that involves many stages and it does not ever occur in a single step or occasion. Researchers have constructed various change models and some of the most frequently models that have been implemented includes Lewin's 3-stage model of change management and Kotter's 8-step theory of change management.

Social Influencers

Social Norms at Home, Workplace and Lifestyle

It is in human nature that every person are bound to be influenced by the people that surrounds them regularly which includes family members, friends, top managers, work colleagues or other various entities that could be labelled as a role model to the particular individual. In other words, the behaviour, norms or beliefs of another person could heavily influence user's behaviour towards SMD[1] security. In the context of organisational workplace, one of the main predictors of employee's behaviour towards the implementation of security policies is how employees perceived the expectation set by the managers on complying with the security measures or policies.

Additionally, the main reason of employees ignoring the instruction of the organisation to employ security practices and measures such as encrypting their email messages is primarily due to employee's not seeing the practices being exercised by fellow peers and managers. Thus, within the context of mobile device security, it is highlighted that user's chances of exhibiting security behaviours are increased exponentially when the entities or role models surrounding the user is exhibiting similar security practices or behaviours. When users feel that they are doing an activity that is similar to their role models or the neighbouring people, it could result in a sort of connection or "aligned" interest that could significantly promote the users of SMD (Smart Mobile Device) to conduct a set of security behaviour.

Generation-Z Perception Towards SMD Security

It is a widely known fact that generation Z are regarded as the generation of youths that does not remember any strand of moments or memories without the usage of smart mobile devices, and they are considered as the top targets of attackers due to their constant usage of mobile devices. This is where the youth's awareness on cyber threats as well as the best practice of security behaviour on SMD comes into the bigger picture. Generation Z was observed to express concerns on the security of their mobile devices where within the research, it was discovered that about 40% of the Generation Z youths expressed their desire to be able to know the person they are communicating with when making online shopping or retail through authentication so that they are able to trust the person they are interacting with. It further added that generation Z are also concerned on various aspects of security such as the likelihood of their mobile device being hacked and the risk associated with cyber crimes which includes fraud and identity theft.

Even though it seemed that the Generation Z are actively concerned about security issues, there were also evidence from other research which states that the Gen-Z are overconfident in their ability to tackle security issues. The Gen-Z assumed to themselves that they are very cyber secure but in reality, it was the vice versa. It is also revealed in recent studies that most of the Gen-Z youths are more open or encouraged to the idea of balancing between their desirability for a greater personalized experience and their concerns on security/privacy issues. In conclusion, it can be seen that despite the concerns for financial transaction security, some of the youths are behaving overconfidently towards their ability to protect themselves from cyber incidents while some behavioural patterns seen in youths presently are their willingness to trade their privacy just for some personalized environment or experience. One way to solve these behavioural problems is by creating or promoting security awareness on their behaviour. There could be different ways to solve them, thus this indicates that there is more work and research to be done on the topic of SMD information security and its relationship with the main users of mobile device, the Generation Z.

EFFECT OF SECURITY AWARENESS TO CUSTOMER TRUST

Various researches had been established and conducted that was looking into the relationship between awareness of security and customer trust. Users could detect that there are possibility of risk associated with their transaction such as trust as well as privacy risk when a vendor or an organisation requested users to provide information that are considered irrelevant for the transaction such as asking questions on the user's age or gender. Trust among public towards organisations or corporations had been deteriorating for the past few years and one of the main rationale behind the drop of public trust is due to the advancement of cyber crime and cyber criminals, especially within this technologically advanced era. The modus operandi of the cybercrime includes Illegal Contents, Data Forgery., Cyber Espionage, Cyber Extortion and Sabotage, unauthorized Access to Computer System and Service, Infringements of Privacy, Offense against Intellectual Property.

CONCLUSION

1. In conclusion, with the increase in SMD usability especially for financial inclusion through FinTech contributed, it is expected that more cyber attacks or incidents such as malware will be aimed towards the mobile device users.
2. The study found aimed at measuring the level of smart mobile device security and privacy awareness. A framework have been proposed in order to increase the awareness level of mobile device users which is based on the security behaviours exhibited by SMD users. Within the framework, it is highlighted that in order to increase the level of SMD security and privacy awareness, users need increase their level of awareness on security behaviours by understanding the importance and rationale behind various cyber security behaviours.
3. From the technical view, this study conclude that be drawn from making FinTech transaction encryption using the required blockchain method are:
    a. Generating a transaction id with a private key pair successfully using RSA so that it can be used to process FinTech transactions on the client side.
    b. History of transactions completed with all FinTech transactions ever done by the client in the form of a blockchain table consisting of Transaction ID parameters, Recipient Address, Sender Address, Value, Time Stamp, and placement of blocks on the blockchain through client transaction information How using cryptographic hashes using the SHA-256 algorithm.
    c. Ciphertext the results of the encryption process on the Transaction ID, Public Key, and Private Key successfully obtained through the generating process can be used by clients to make transactions.
    d. Accuracy of FinTech user transaction data is successful in the form of a histogram graph using permutation techniques. From two different cases obtained different accuracy using 5 different groups of accuracy parameters. In the first case, reach 90% for the recipient's address and get 20% in the Transaction ID, Recipient Address, Sender's Address and Value with different

parameters. At the second level, the highest level is 90% for Value and the lowest level is 20% Recipient Address, Sender Address, and Timestamp with different parameters.

e. Digital computing technology adoption was promising and varied significantly, reasons included cultural, demographic and technological, many of which were a function of economies.

RECOMMENDATION

It is recommended that further development can be carried out on FinTech data transaction encryption with a successful process occurring therein. Development can be done by adding other security features that can further tighten and facilitate transactions that occur at FinTech so that transactions on FinTech can run safely and FinTech transaction data is resistant to destruction, alteration, and hacking by unsupported people. Development can be done by increasing the number of transaction data that can be sorted into transaction data into the transaction table that collects data.

ACKNOWLEDGMENT

Heru Susanto as main contributors. Where Heru Susanto as lead author for this research publication. The remains as contributor and I wish to thank Fahmi Ibrahim, Didi Rosiyadi, Rodiah, Desi Setiana, Alifya Kayla Shafa Susanto, Nicolas Kusuma, Akbari Indra Basuki dan Iwan Setiawan helped to improve the manuscript and helping to search the literature. All authors read and approved the final manuscript.

REFERENCES

Andress, J. (2014). *The Basics of Information Security: Understanding the Fundamentals of InfoSec in Theory and Practice*. Syngress.

Beckers, K. (2015). *Pattern and Security Requirements: Engineering-Based Establishment of Security Standards*. Springer. doi:10.1007/978-3-319-16664-3

Bidgoli, H. (2006). Handbook of Information Security: Threats, Vulnerability, Prevention, Detection, and Management. John Wiley & Sons Inc.

Boritz, J. E. (2005). IS Practitioners Views on Core Concepts of Information Integrity. *International Journal of Accounting Information Systems.*

Copperwaite & Leifer. (2015). *Learning Flask Framework.* Packt Publishing Ltd.

Dam & Lin. (1996). *Cryptography's Role in Securing the Information Society.* Committee to Study National Cryptography Policy, National Research Council.

Forme, S. (2014). *CSS: Basics - Professional.* Sparks Publications.

Harris, P. (2018). *What Is HTML Code?* Power Kids Press.

Johng, Y. (2008). IBM System i Security: Protecting i5/OS Data with Encryption. IBM.

Katz, J., & Lindell, Y. (2007). *Introduction to Modern Cryptography: Priniciples and Protocols*. Chapman and Hall / CRC. doi:10.1201/9781420010756

Knudsen, L. R., & Robshaw, M. (2011). *The Block Cipher Companion*. Springer. doi:10.1007/978-3-642-17342-4

Leu, F. Y., Ko, C. Y., Lin, Y. C., Susanto, H., & Yu, H. C. (2017). Fall Detection and Motion Classification by Using Decision Tree on Mobile Phone. In Smart Sensors Networks (pp. 205-237). doi:10.1016/B978-0-12-809859-2.00013-9

Leu, F. Y., Liu, C. Y., Liu, J. C., Jiang, F. C., & Susanto, H. (2015). S-PMIPv6: An intra-LMA model for IPv6 mobility. *Journal of Network and Computer Applications*, *58*, 180–191. doi:10.1016/j.jnca.2015.08.014

Lie & Bert. (1999). *Cascading Style Sheets, designing for the Web*. Addison Wesley.

Liu, J. C., Leu, F. Y., Lin, G. L., & Susanto, H. (2018). An MFCC-based text-independent speaker identification system for access control. *Concurrency and Computation*, *30*(2), e4255.

Loukas, G., & Oke, G. (2010). Protection Against Denial of Service Attacks: A Survey. *The Computer Journal*, *53*(7), 1020–1037. doi:10.1093/comjnl/bxp078

McDougal, A. (2018). *Fun with Flowcharts*. The Rosen Publishing Group, Inc.

Mukhtar, H. (2018). *KriptografiuntukKeamanan Data*. Deepublish Publisher.

Naik, G. S. (2019). *Mastering Python Scripting for System Administrators*. Packt.

Reinhardt, A., & Dufrasne, B. (2019). *IBM DS8880 Encryption for data at rest and Transparent Cloud Tiering (DS8000 Release 8.5)*. IBM.

Sahoo, R., & Sahoo, G. (2016). Computer Science with Python. New Delhi: New Saraswati House (India) Pvt. Ltd.

Sitorus, L. (2015). *Algoritma dan Pemrograman*. CV Andi Offset.

Spinelli, R. (2017). What is Blockchain Technology, Cryptocurrency Bitcoin, Ethereum and Smart Contracts? In Blockchain for dummies. Smashwords.

Sprulock, J. (2013). *Bootstrap*. O'Reilly Media.

Susanto, H., & Almunawar, M. N. (2015). Managing Compliance with an Information Security Management Standard. In Encyclopedia of Information Science and Technology (3rd ed., pp. 1452–1463). IGI Global. doi:10.4018/978-1-4666-5888-2.ch138

Susanto, H., & Almunawar, M. N. (2016). Security and Privacy Issues in Cloud-Based E-Government. In *Cloud Computing Technologies for Connected Government* (pp. 292–321). IGI Global. doi:10.4018/978-1-4666-8629-8.ch012

Susanto, H., & Almunawar, M. N. (2018). *Information Security Management Systems: A Novel Framework and Software as a Tool for Compliance with Information Security Standard*. CRC Press.

Telles, M. A. (2008). *Python Power! The Comprehensive Guide*. Thomson Course Technology.

van der Westhuizen, P. (2016). *Bootstrap for ASP.NET MVC*. Packt Publishing Ltd.

Whitman, M. E., & Mattord, H. J. (2009). *Principles of Information Security* (3rd ed.). Course Technology.

ADDITIONAL READING

Alghamdi, I. A., Goodwin, R., & Rampersad, G. (2011). E-government readiness assessment for government organizations in developing countries. *Computer and Information Science*, *4*(3), 3. doi:10.5539/cis.v4n3p3

Grabara, J., Kolcun, M., & Kot, S. (2014). The Role of Information Systems in Transport Logistics. *International Journal of Educational Research*, *2*(2), 1–8.

Leu, F. Y., Liu, C. Y., Liu, J. C., Jiang, F. C., & Susanto, H. (2015). S-PMIPv6: An Intra-LMA Model for IPv6 Mobility. *Journal of Network and Computer Applications*, *2015*(58), 180–191. doi:10.1016/j.jnca.2015.08.014

Liu, J. C., Leu, F. Y., Lin, G. L., & Susanto, H. (2018). An MFCC-Based Text-Independent Speaker Identification System for Access Control. *Concurr. Comput. Pract. Exp.*, *30*(2), e4255. doi:10.1002/cpe.4255

Nograšek, J., & Vintar, M. (2014). E-government and organisational transformation of government: Black box revisited? *Government Information Quarterly*, *31*(1), 108–118. doi:10.1016/j.giq.2013.07.006

Olphert, W., & Damodaran, L. (2007). Citizen participation and engagement in the design of e-government services: The missing link in effective ICT design and delivery. *Journal of the Association for Information Systems*, *8*(9), 27. doi:10.17705/1jais.00137

Susanto, H. (2017). Biochemistry Apps as Enabler of Compound and DNA Computational: Next Generation Computing Technology. Applied Chemistry and Chemical Engineering. *Experimental Techniques and Methodical Developments*, *4*, 181.

KEY TERMS AND DEFINITIONS

Blockchain: Can be defined as a shared ledger system or an established record of data not owned by a single entity and is used to record data transactions across multiple computers. Other than bitcoin which propagated the idea of Blockchain, the factors as to why the technology has gained popularity are that any digital asset or transaction can be inserted as a block of data (e.g. block) which are securely bound to each other using cryptography (e.g. chain), the industry does not matter. The block is made up of data, hash (A cryptographic fixed output through a mathematical algorithm from an input of any length) and previous hash. Every other member of the network is responsible for verifying the data being added to the Blockchain is real. This is done using a system of three keys (private, public, and the receiver's key) that allow members to check the veracity of the data while also confirming whom it comes from.

Cryptography or Cryptology: (From Ancient Greek: κρυπτός, romanized: kryptós "hidden, secret"; and γράφειν graphein, "to write", or -λογία -logia, "study", respectively), is the practice and study of techniques for secure communication in the presence of third parties called adversaries. More generally, cryptography is about constructing and analyzing protocols that prevent third parties or the public from reading private messages; various aspects in information security such as data confidentiality, data integrity, authentication, and non-repudiation are central to modern cryptography. Modern cryptography exists at the intersection of the disciplines of mathematics, computer science, electrical engineering, communication science, and physics. Applications of cryptography include electronic commerce, chip-based payment cards, digital currencies, computer passwords, and military communications.

Cybercrime or Computer-Oriented Crime: Is a crime that involves a computer and a network. The computer may have been used in the commission of a crime, or it may be the target. Cybercrimes can be defined as: "Offences that are committed against individuals or groups of individuals with a criminal motive to intentionally harm the reputation of the victim or cause physical or mental harm, or loss, to the victim directly or indirectly, using modern telecommunication networks such as Internet (networks including chat rooms, emails, notice boards and groups) and mobile phones (Bluetooth/SMS/MMS)". Cybercrime may threaten a person or a nation's security and financial health. Issues surrounding these types of crimes have become high-profile, particularly those regarding hacking, copyright infringement, unwarranted mass-surveillance, sextortion, child pornography, and child grooming.

Encryption: Is the process of encoding information. This process converts the original representation of the information, known as plaintext, into an alternative form known as ciphertext. Only authorized parties can decipher a ciphertext back to plaintext and access the original information. Encryption does not itself prevent interference but denies the intelligible content to a would-be interceptor. For technical reasons, an encryption scheme usually uses a pseudo-random encryption key generated by an algorithm. It is possible to decrypt the message without possessing the key, but, for a well-designed encryption scheme, considerable computational resources and skills are required. An authorized recipient can easily decrypt the message with the key provided by the originator to recipients but not to unauthorized users. Historically, various forms of encryption have been used to aid in cryptography. Early encryption techniques were often utilized in military messaging. Since then, new techniques have emerged and become commonplace in all areas of modern computing. Modern encryption schemes utilize the concepts of public-key and symmetric-key. Modern encryption techniques ensure security because modern computers are inefficient at cracking the encryption.

ENDNOTE

1 Smart mobile devices

Chapter 11
Government Challenges Over Global Electronic Commerce Using FinTech:
Design of Consumer Payment Tax (CPT) System

Yeoul Hwangbo
Asian Study Society, South Korea

ABSTRACT

The challenge over most countries has been legislating related acts and regulations on global electronic commerce taxation, but they have not implemented the consumption tax system for global electronic commerce so far. Consumer payment tax (CPT) is based on fintech and thereby proposed so that consumers can pay the consumption taxes to related taxation office of the countries in accordance with consumer country's jurisdiction principle, considering the CPT is assessed to satisfy most of the electronic commerce taxation criteria and has the potential to be applied to electronic commerce.

INTRODUCTION

Fintech has evolved and provided huge benefits for businesses and consumers around the world in an efficient way to trade goods and services globally, especially contents transaction, while at the same time, it simultaneously poses a new set of challenges facing governments' own tax jurisdiction, with particular emphasis on consumption taxes. As the name implies, the consumption tax is levied on consumers and the country wherein a consumer lives – consumer's country- has its jurisdiction to collect the consumption tax according to an internationally agreed principle. However, there has been a gray area whether they pay the taxes to the consumer countries in accordance with the consumer country tax jurisdiction, as long as the global electronic commerce taxation is paid in such an existing way that the consumption taxes

DOI: 10.4018/978-1-7998-8447-7.ch011

used to be collected by business and conveyed to the taxation office of supplier. Moreover, distributed cryptocurrencies or virtual assets such as Bitcoin is making the taxation matters worse.

Likewise, differences in the tax systems among various countries pose another challenge to tax administration, causing to reduce in tax revenue for the consumer's countries. While the U.S. has adopted the sale tax system, most EU members have applied the Value Added Tax (VAT) system, and ASEAN member countries have various consumptions taxes including VAT, Goods, and Service Tax (GST). In accordance with the existing method, supplier used to collect consumption taxes and pay to their taxation office periodically. Furthermore, global electronic commerce suppliers, with particular emphasis on major providers, have probably been providing their good and services without paying associated consumption taxes that it can worse a financial inclusion between developed and developing countries in the level of jurisdiction, taking into consideration that most global suppliers are from developed countries, but consumers are located in developing countries. The emergence of fintech is providing a promising vehicle of tackling this phenomenon by closing the gap in the global digital economy, bringing a long-term societal transformational change, while leading to inclusive economic growth helping move towards a more just and equitable society (Roland Schwinn and Ernie G.S. Teo, 2018, pp. 481-492).

Fan Li (2017) looked at the problems generated from the new tax policy, study and analyze the related causes and rethink the insufficiency of the whole customs management model. Taxation of e-commerce is currently high on the political agenda, both in the European Union and beyond, with significant efforts being put into creating rules ensuring undistorted functioning of the internal market and effective taxation of the digital economy without creating barriers for online trade (Marta Papis-Almansa, 2019, pp. 220-221). In Indonesia, the revenue loss is potentially getting bigger in the coming years if the government still fails to collect the tax and tax policy in Indonesian e-commerce can be potentially used for the purpose of regulating the economy, such as to control excessive online import purchasing (Sigit Setiawan, 2018, pp. 7-8). There is an urgent need for a change in the tax legislation related to arising field of electronic commerce because it deprives governments of tax revenues and gives foreign-based digital businesses an advantage over their tax-paying domestic competitor (Nazarov et al, 2019). Technical recommendations are to develop current tax laws in line with the technological developments of global e-commerce laws, to raise the efficiency of income and sales tax assessors through scientific and practical courses, to increase international cooperation in the field of e-commerce and to benefit from the experiences of developed countries in this field (Rafat Salameh et al, 2021, pp.4-5).

In order to deal with this taxation dilemma caused by global electronic commerce, the Organization for Economic Cooperation and Development (OECD) officially set the fundamental taxation principle of global electronic commerce (OECD, 2001, pp. 17-48) and the European Union (E.U.) released its directive for the E.U. member countries (E.U., 2000). However, technical solutions have not yet been fully developed for the global electronic commerce taxation. the U.K defined place of supply for electronic commerce (HM Revenue & Customs, 2020), but does not seem to force overseas businesses located in other regions. Though most ASEAN member states (AMCs) have legislated the regulation and set policy to taxing global electronic commerce (J&T Express, 2020) recently, it is unlikely to levy and collect their consumption taxes in accordance with their acts and regulations. It is thought to be due to the lack of the technology protocol of global commerce taxation.

This chapter will raise the following set of questions: (i) can the advent of Fintech change existing method that suppliers used to pay consumption taxes on behalf of consumer? (ii) What are the features of methods of fintech-enabled consumption tax systems so as to fulfill the principle of consumer's jurisdiction that was internationally agreed? and (iii) How can the consumption tax system influence the financial inclusiveness?

CONTROVERSY OVER TAXING THE GLOBAL ELECTRONIC COMMERCE

Ambiguous Place of Supply and Business Presence in Global Electronic Commerce

Place of supply has been used for taxing consumption taxes, while as business presence has been applied to business taxes and income taxes. As such, place of supply and business presence is required to be precisely defined for levying consumption taxes and business taxes, but would be shacked by global electronic commerce.

Let's assume case of different countries wherein the consumer, e-shopping server, and manager, are located. As shown in Figure 1, suppose a consumer resides in country A, a shopping mall server is operated in country B, while goods and/or services are stored in country C and online shops do their business in country A, B, and C. Which country is considered to be the place of supply in the case that country A has consumer, country B is equipped with the shopping mall server, and shopping mall manager operates in country C? The traditional taxes are mainly based on physical location. In the case of consumption taxes, merchant usually collects the taxes from consumers and pay it to its taxation office to which both the merchant and consumer belong, because consumption taxes paid by merchant would be more efficient than consumer's tax payment in terms of tax administration. However, transaction of goods and services blurred physical locations in the global electronic commerce. This kind of ambiguous situation may tempt the shopping mall servers to move to a tax haven country for evading consumption tax.

Figure 1. Global Electronic Commerce among Different Countries

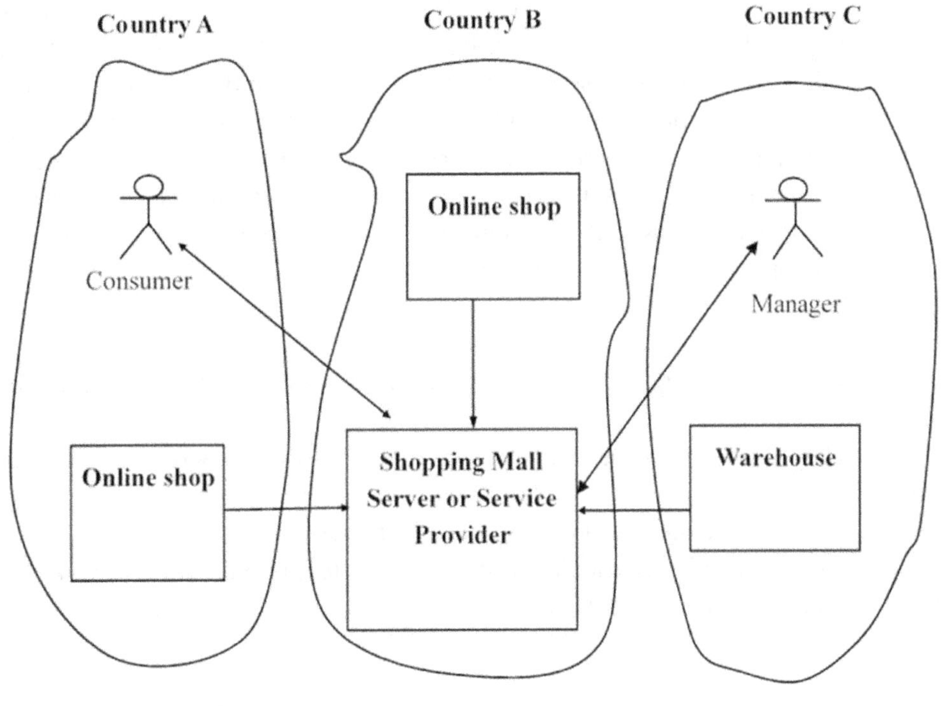

Another conflict can be raised due to the different consumption tax systems. For example, the U.S. adopts the sales tax system, while the European Union (E.U.) and most ASEAN member countries apply the Value Added Tax (VAT) system with various tax rates.

Controversy over Cross-Border Electronic Commerce

There have been many discussions over tax jurisdiction settlements, including (i) the custom and taxation issues raised by William J. Clinton, the president of the United States in July 1997, (ii) the Bonn meeting of economic, trade, and technology ministers for discussing tax issues concerning electronic commerce in 1997, and (iii) the OECD conference. Meanwhile, the European Union, where most of member states have adopted the VAT tax scheme, showed serious concerns that their tax revenues might be reduced. The electronic commerce taxation issue was raised once again at the OECD conference titled "Dismantling the Barrier to Global Electronic Commerce", which was held in Turku, Finland in November 1997. The focus of the discussion has been whether the tax jurisdiction should belong to the country where the e-mall's server located or the country where the consumer resides. To finally resolve this cyber-taxation dilemma, the OECD organised the conference held in Ottawa, Canada in October 1998 (OECD, 1998).

And, it was agreed that the consumer's country has the tax jurisdiction over cross border electronic commerce. To elaborate electronic commerce tax system, the Committee on Fiscal Affairs (CFA) of the OECD has put out the following seven criteria: (i) Equitable: taxation should be neutral and equitable. Conventional and electronic commerce should be subjected to similar tax laws; (ii) Simplicity: the tax rules should be clear and simple to understand; (iii) Effectiveness: Tax administrative costs should be minimized; (iv) Certainty: tax calculations should be accurate; (v) Avoid Economic Distortion: tax evasion, avoidance, and types of tax frauds should be minimized; (vi) Flexibility and dynamic: it should be flexible and dynamic to ensure that the tax systems keep pace with technological and other environmental changes; and (vii) Fair sharing: taxes should be distributed fairly.

In January 2001, the OECD outlined detailed methods for taxing electronic commerce (OECD, 2001). Self-assessment rule is applied to the B2B type of transaction, while registration of non-residence rule is applied to B2C transactions. According to the rule of self-assessment, recipient is required to estimate the tax amount on imported products or services and remit that tax amount to the domestic tax authority. Many countries already use this self-assessment rule to levy taxes in B2B transactions. For the B2C type of transactions, the registration of non-resident rule is applied where the supplier is required to register with the tax authority of the customer's country, which aimed to collect consumption tax from non-resident businesses within that jurisdiction for the purpose of increasing the government revenue.

The Committee on Fiscal Affairs of the Organization of Economic Cooperation and Development (OECD) set the following seven criteria to apply to a newly developed consumption tax system of global electronic commerce (OECD, 1997).

- ***Criterion 1***: The system should be equitable. Taxpayers in similar situations should be taxed in the same way.
- ***Criterion 2***: The system should be simple. This implied a low transaction and auditing cost for implementation.
- ***Criterion 3***: The rules should provide confidence for the tax payers.
- ***Criterion 4***: Any system adopted should be effective so as to minimise tax evasion and avoidance. Auditing is the cost for such a minimization.

- ***Criterion 5***: Economic distortions should be avoided. The system should not motivate seeking a tax haven.
- ***Criterion 6***: The tax base should be fairly shared between countries. This can reduce the cost for clearance between countries.
- ***Criterion 7***: Adopt the current tax arrangements to the Internet rather than introducing new forms of taxation. So, the sales tax and VAT are preferred to be implemented for the cyber trading instead of a new tax such as the bit tax.

The E.U sets out the directives for basic requirements focused on defining an appropriate electronic commerce framework wherein covers the services including online information services, online selling of products and services, online advertising, professional services and entertainment services and basic intermediary services (E.U, 2020). Though a few researches attempted to design and develop a taxation, robust taxation fintech systems have not been developed and operated so far by the above-mentioned criteria.

Development of Consumption Tax System for Global Electronic Commerce

J.K. Lee and Yeoul Hwangbo (2000) proposed new taxation method named as Consumer Delivered Sales Tax titled as CDS Tax in short. The CDS tax has the characteristic of a kind of sales tax, but it is directly delivered by the consumer without the intervention of the supplier in the electronic commerce environment. The specifically designed CDS tax, designated as the Canonical CDS tax, was defined as follows: "The Canonical CDS tax is imposed by the supplier country's taxation office consistently to the consumers in both physical and cyber-space. The tax bill is issued by the merchant's software to the consumer's system at the price billing time, and charged at the time of the consumer's price payment by transferring the tax amount to the taxation office's account in the same bank if the bank is authorized to handle tax collection." However, CDS tax delivery is contrary to traditional consumption taxes including VAT and sales tax in terms of tax collection method. In reality, the conventional tax delivery method has difficulties in adopting new taxation method and dramatically reforming the existing taxation way to collect tax from business.

Yeoul Hwangbo (2004) developed Global Electronic Tax Invoice System (GETI). This study dealt with controversial issues surrounding cyber-taxation and recommended a feasible consumption tax system architecture called Global Electronic Tax Invoice System (GETI). GETI is an electronic consumption tax architecture to provide "all-in-one" tax and e-payment services through a trusted third party (TTP). GETI was designed to streamline the overall cyber-taxation process and provided a simplified and transparent tax invoice service through an authorized TTP. To ensure information security, GETI incorporated Public Key Infrastructure (PKI) based digital certificates and other data encryption schemes (Yeoul Hwangbo, 2011, pp.73-90) when calculating, reporting, paying, and auditing tax in the electronic commerce environment. As paper-based tax invoice systems are gradually being phased out and are replaced with electronic tax invoice systems, there has been an increasing need to develop a reliable, efficient, transparent, and secured cyber-taxation architecture. To design the architecture, several desirable attributes were considered to be reliability, efficiency, transparency and security. Likewise, GETI was developed with these attributes in mind. In order for the GETI to be operational, taxation service provider was poisoned as TTP which was required to play pivotal role in conducting consumption tax services including tax calculation, tax report, tax payment, and tax auditing. In this regard, Yeoul Hwangbo developed GETI and thereby proposed ASEAN Global Electronic Commerce Taxation Hub (Yeoul Hwangbo, 2012).

TAX PAYMENT WAYS IN ACCORDANCE WITH CONSUMPTION TAX JURISDICTION

Consumption tax jurisdiction should be the consumer's country wherein consumers stay and consume goods and services. In order to comply with the principle of consumption tax jurisdiction, two tax payment ways are considered: One is a supplier payment way that has been applied so far, and the other is a consumer payment way to be designed in this chapter.

Supplier Payment Model

The supplier payment model is the same way as existing consumption tax collection procedure in global electronic commerce. This model implies that the tax goes to the country wherein the supplier provides services and goods, as depicted in Figure 2. In this case, conceptually, the consumer sends the tax and the amount of price for goods and services to the supplier, and the supplier pays the tax to the taxation office of the country to which the supplier belongs. According to this model, the consumer is regarded as the visitor to the supplier's country. In practice, the tax as well as the amount of price may be transferred from the consumer's bank account to the supplier's bank account when consumer uses the electronic funds transfer (EFT) or his or her credit card. The supplier or supplier's bank are responsible for collecting the tax from consumers and delivering it to the taxation office where consumers spend goods and services provided by supplier. Otherwise. the taxation office in supplier country should deliver the amount of consumptions taxes to the taxation office in consumer countries to fulfill the consumer country jurisdiction principle. But it does not seem to be easy to return and settle consumption taxes from the taxation offices of suppler country to that of consumer country due to additional cost. This way does not fulfill criterion 4 (any system adopted should be effective so as to minimize tax evasion and avoidance. Auditing is the cost for such a minimization) and criterion 5 (economic distortions should be avoided. the system should not motivate seeking a tax haven).

Figure 2. Supplier Payment Model

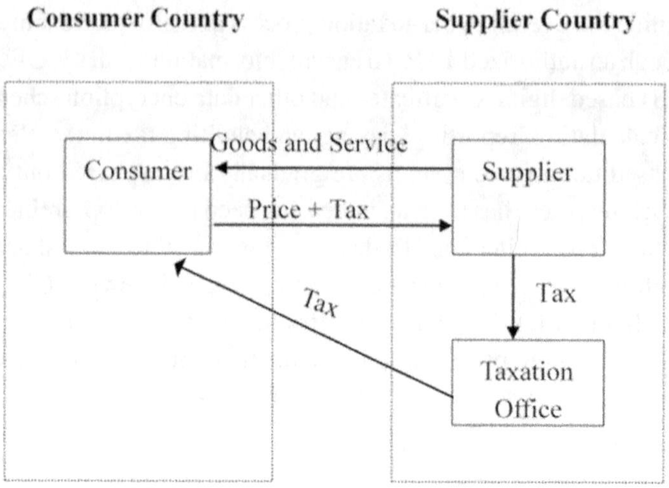

It is therefore worth of noting that the current consumption tax payment way is not suitable and should be reconsidered to apply for global electronic commerce. In other word, governments do not necessarily stick to this indirect taxation way for consumption tax payment in the era of fintech.

Consumer Payment Model

This model implies that the tax revenue belongs to the country wherein consumer resides, as shown in Figure 3. In this case, the consumer just sends the amount of price only to the supplier, while the related tax is paid to the taxation office of the consumer's own country, pursuant to the consumer country jurisdiction principle. This is meant to change consumption tax from indirect tax to direct tax that is enabled by the advent of fintech. This method can fulfill all the criteria including criterion 1 (equitable), criterion 2 (simple), criterion 3 (confidence for taxpayer), criterion 4 (minimize tax evasion), criterion 5 (prevent economic distortion), criterion 6 (reduce the cost for tax clearance), and criterion 7 (current tax arrangement).

This chapter tries to design a ***Consumer Direct Consumption Payment Tax (CPT) System*** that can be justified not only by satisfying all electronic commerce tax criteria, but also by exploiting technologies in the era of fintech that would be otherwise difficult to apply direct taxation method to pay consumption taxes. The CPT is the same as the sales tax and the VAT in terms of levying consumption itself. While the VAT and the sales tax cannot be paid without the involvement of merchant in current tax system, the CPT is designed to be operable by consumer excluding merchant, for the purpose of realising the consumer-based jurisdiction principle.

Figure 3. Consumer Payment Model

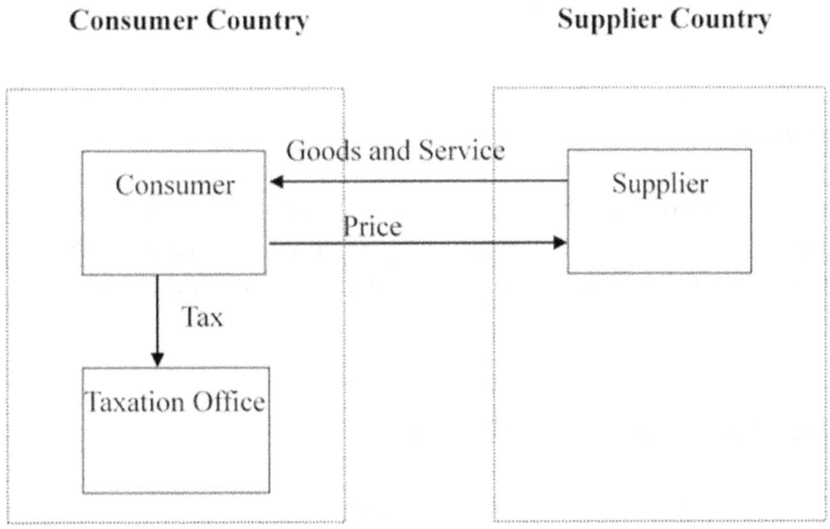

Consumer Payment Tax (CPT)

When it comes to global electronic commerce, the consumer-based jurisdiction model is likely to make it harder for sales tax and VAT to be adopted and applied from the perspective of tax administration. It is because merchant is required to have business license from the consumer jurisdiction countries and pay the consumption taxes to the taxation offices of consumer jurisdiction countries, as long as countries stick to current tax payment methods. In this background. New model is devised and named as **Consumer Payment Tax (CPT)**.

Consumer Payment Tax (CPT) is defined as the direct consumer payment method that consumer pays the consumption taxes in a consistent manner between online and offline to related taxation office of the countries in which consumption actually occurs in accordance with consumer country jurisdiction principle, using relevant technology components and models of fintech.

Canonical CPT system is based on bank transaction (depicted in Figure 4). The tax bill is issued by the merchant's fintech tax solution to the consumer at the invoice billing time, and charged at the time of consumer's price payment by transferring the tax amount to the taxation office's account in the consumer's country. Detailed tax payment procedures can vary depending upon the methods of electronic payment (this issue will be dealt with later).

The variables of the CPT system are ***Tax Payer, Tax Deliverer, Consumer's Location, Tax Billing Agent, Tax Billing Time, Tax Collection Time, Tax Stages, and Tax Rate Determinant.***
For instance, the Canonical CPT tax system can be represented as follows:

Canonical CPT (Tax Payer = consumer,
Tax Deliverer = consumer's bank,
Consumer's Location = consumption place,
Tax Billing Agent = software to be shared by merchant,
Tax Billing Time *= billing time,*
Tax Collection Time = payment time of goods and services,
Tax Stages = single,
Tax Rate Determinant = consumer's country)

Though actual consumption place is fitted with the principle of consumer's location, it is needed to simplify the consumer's location (e.g., consumer's country or residence address) through the agreement between/among countries that might otherwise cause excessive cost for identifying the consumption place exactly.

CPT SYSTEMS USING FINTECH SOLUTION

To put the CPT system into practice, it should be applicable to the typical electronic payment systems, such as Electronic Fund Transfer (EFT), electronic credit card, and electronic cash systems. Fintech is the application of technologies that are not new one, but represent a paradigm shift. This chapters identified meaningful fintech methods (EFT, Credit Card, Electronic Cash, CBDC and so on) to be exploited for global electronic commerce, which can contribute to the financial and fiscal inclusiveness in a way to settle a jurisdiction dilemma between supplier's and consumer's countries, considering global dominant electronic commerce suppliers have been in developed countries rather than developing countries.

When the protocol of the Canonical CPT tax system was designed, it was assumed that the EFT was the default payment method. So, the protocol compatible with EFT is basically the same as the procedure in Figure 4. This CPT system can be operable using credit card and electronic cash to be discussed as follow.

Electronic Funds Transfer (EFT)

Figure 4. Process of CPT System using Electronic Funds Transfer (EFT)

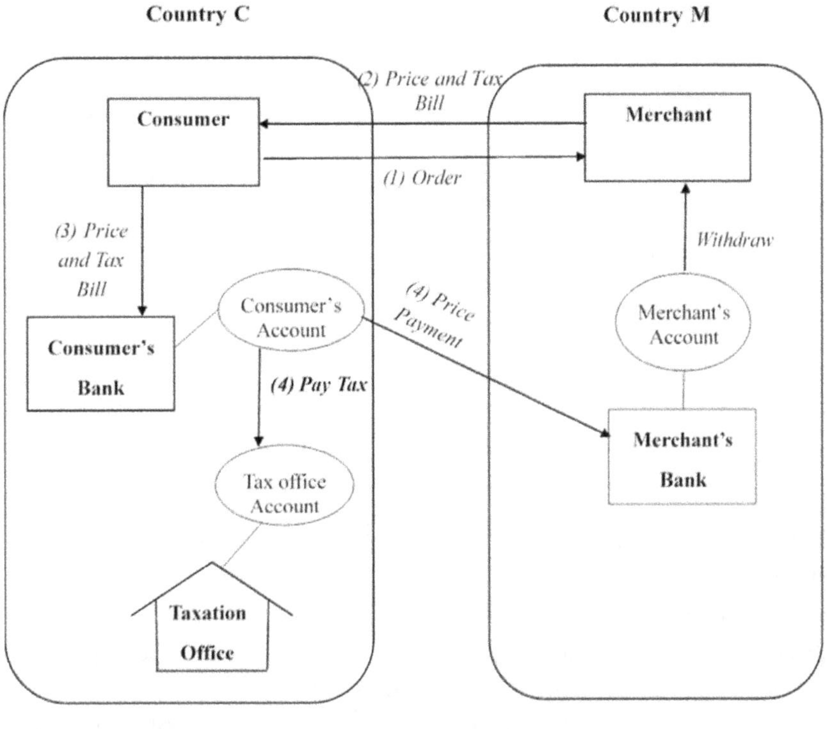

Electronic Credit Card

The electronic credit card assumes that the credit card is used on the Internet. The tax delivery method using the credit card system is similar to that using the EFT, except for the fact that the payment time and settlement time are not the same (see Figure 5).

The processes 1, 2 and 3 in Figure 5 are the same as those with EFT in Figure 4.

Figure 5. Process of CPT System using Credit Card

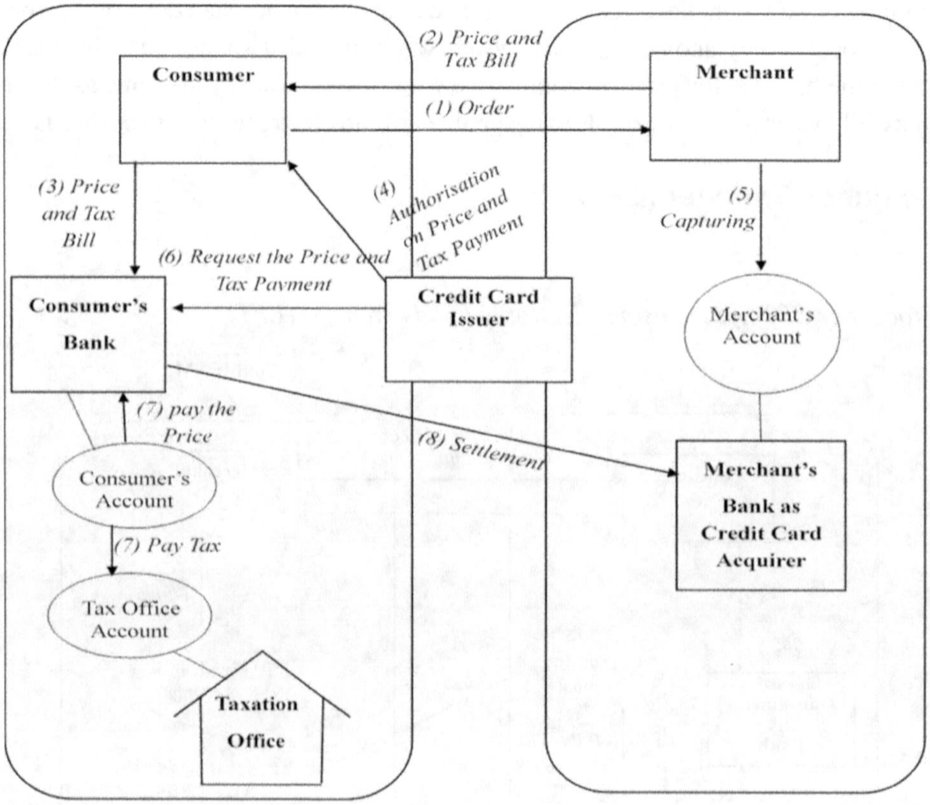

(Process 4) Unlike the case of EFT, the credit card issuer provides consumer with authorization needed for payment of price and tax.

(Process 5) The price payment to the merchant will be initiated when the merchant requests payment to the acquirer bank which may be the merchant's bank. This step is called the capturing process. The acquirer bank requests settlement to the credit card issuer.

(Process 6) The credit card issuer requests that the price be paid from the consumer's bank to merchant's bank on a predetermined day of the month.

(Process 7) The consumer simultaneously pays the prices for electronic commerce and related tax to the taxation office to be fitted with the jurisdiction.

(Process 8) Prices of electronic commerce are settled between the consumer bank and the merchant bank.

Credit card can be one of the most popular payment methods for global electronic commerce and key credit card issuers have global networks. the CPT taxation protocol must be implementable on the credit card payment mechanism without difficulties.

Electronic Cash: Virtual Asset and Central Bank Digital Cash (CBDC)

Blockchain is considered as an innovative technology to swiftly transfer value around the world. The fast-evolving blockchain and distributed ledger technologies have the potential to radically change the financial landscape. But, their speed, global reach and above all - anonymity - also attract those who want to escape authorities' scrutiny. Virtual assets have become widely available and have started to be used as payment products. However, without established regulation and oversight, the sector is often still referred to as the wild west of the finance industry (FATF, 2020, pp. 6-11).

Satoshi Nakamoto (2008) was the initiator of the block chain technology and proposed the electronic cash system named as Bit Coin. The bit coin operation is based on public-key infrastructure (PKI). The bit coin is transferred or paid to the next person by digitally signing a hash result of the previous transaction using the private key with the public key and the same procedures are completed till the end of block shown in Figure 6. A proof of-work system was invented to solve the problem of determining representation in majority decision making. The majority decision is represented by the longest chain, which has the greatest proof-of-work effort invested in it (Satoshi Nakamoto, 2008)

Figure 6. Block Chain Transaction
Source: Satoshi Nakamoto, p. 2

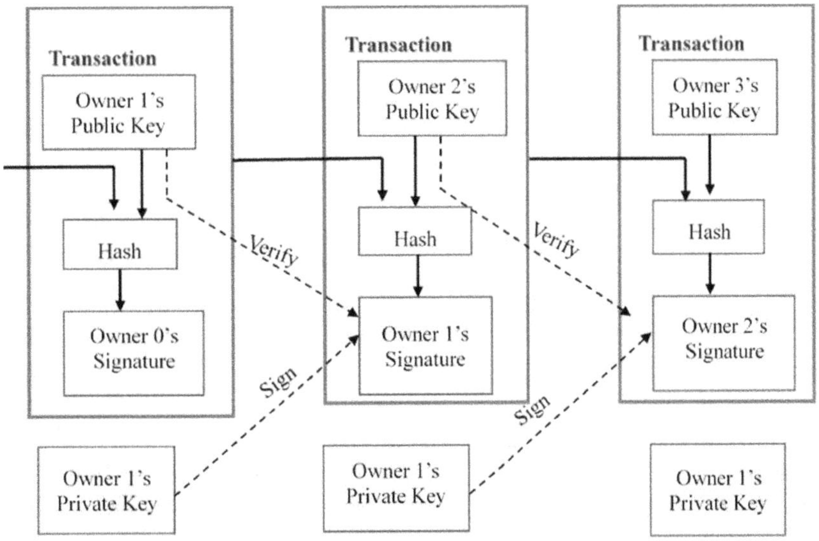

There have currently been traded various cryptocurrencies only between person to person, but through virtual asset service provider. The cryptocurrencies have high risks due to the facts of (i) volatile value, (ii) unregulated, (iii) vulnerable hacking in virtual asset trade provider, (iv) untested and not-verified system, (v) insecure private key management, and so on. The critical risks of cryptocurrencies have possibly been used for the purposes of illegal trading, crimes, and tax evasion. From the perspective of taxation, the challenges that are posed by block chain are the identification of tax payers, certification of documents, tax point detection, and prevention of more readily accessible tax havens and monitoring money laundry. Likewise, cryptocurrencies have become highly volatile investment asset creating big winners and big Characteristics of losers rather than a now form of currency. For the skeptics, the crypto market is nothing more than a digital gambling too volatile to be trusted. Virtual asset's properties and challenges to tax administration are shown in Figure 7. Added to this, cryptocurrencies would be a threat to the legal tender of national authority. For these reasons, cryptocurrencies have not been acknowledged as an official money and are currently positioned as an asset which is named as the virtual asset by most governments.

Figure 7. Taxation Office Challenges posed by Virtual Asset

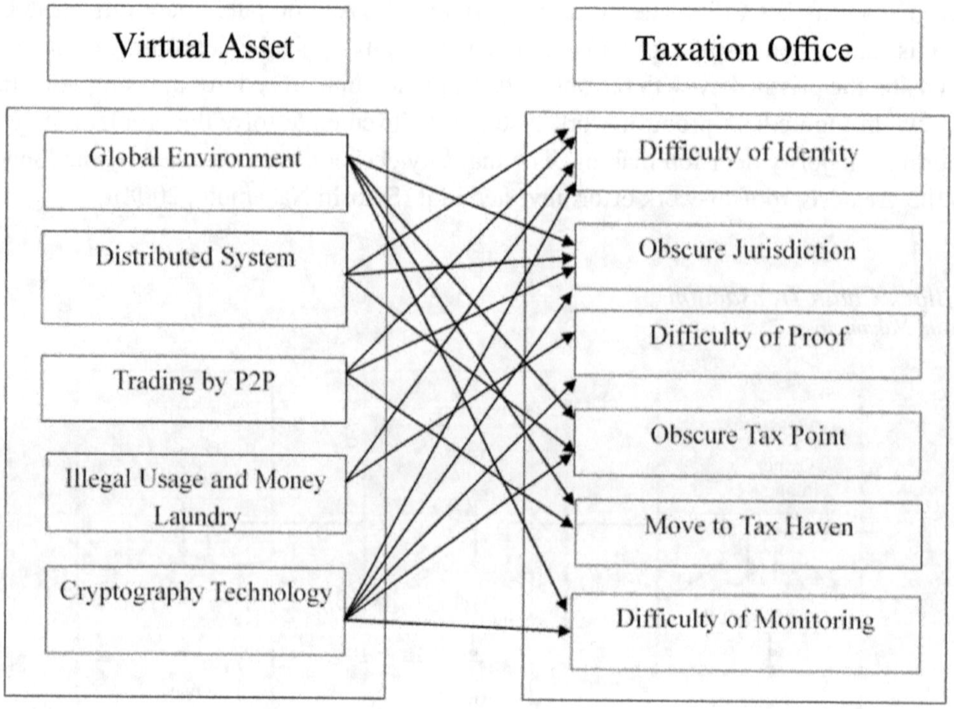

Meanwhile, Central Bank Digital Cash (CBDC) has been planned as legal tender, which is distinct from virtual currency issued by the private sector. The same exchange rate as that of real money is applied, there is no risk of change in value, and the public confidence of money is guaranteed because it is issued by the central bank. Block chain and distributed ledger does not seem to be mandatory in CBDC. Likewise, the CBDC has been planned to be issued by governments. Particularly, China is likely to be keen and take progressive steps to implement CBDC. Since 2014, China's central bank has been conducting the project called Digital Currency Electronic Payment (DCEP), which is referred to as the "digital yuan". the People's Bank of China has initiated and tested the DCEP system since 2020 (Christopher A. McNally. 2020).

Table 1 showed the contrast between virtual asset and CBDC: CBDC as electronic cash, has the features of central bank issuance, national credit, purpose of micro payment for transaction and commerce, citizenship, and government control, whileas virtual asset has no particular issuance, credit creation by mining, not limited particular purposes such as store of value, transaction, investment, smart contract and cannot be controlled by governments.

Table 1. Comparison between Virtual Asset and CBDC

Classification	Virtual Asset	Central Bank Digital Cash (CBDC)
Issuance	· No Constraint	· Central Bank
Start Time	· 2008 (Bit Coin)	· 2020 (People's Bank of China)
Credit Creation	· Mining	· National Credit
Purpose	· Not limited to particular purpose · Currently for the various purposes such as (i) Store of Value, (ii) Transaction, (iii) Investment, (iv) Smart Contract and so on	· Micro Payment for Transaction and Commerce
Users	· Global users	· Intended for the person with particular nationality
Management and Control	· Decentralised	· Government

The CBDC may make tax avoidance and tax evasion much more difficult, but it does not seem to fully deal with the taxation of cross border electronic commerce due to a restricted individual country. As such, CBDC may possibly pose the risks of consumption taxes when it comes to global transaction.

Electronic cash has various types including block chain-based cryptocurrencies, CBDC, gift card, mileages and other types of micro-payment value. The values of various digital cashes can be stored in the digital wallet that has typically two types of hardware wallet and software wallet. Since most of electronic cashes can be used without real-time intervention of banks for every transaction, it does not seem to be easy to pay tax at the time of use. Particularly in the case that electronic cash is paid off-line, it is impossible to deliver the tax to the taxation office.

The possible ways are to (i) design two separate sections of price section and tax section in a digital wallet; and (ii) transfer the collected tax to the tax section in the digital wallet at the same time of price payment.

The question is raised on when and how to deliver the collected tax in the tax section of the digital wallet to the taxation office. There can be two potential answers: one is a real-time tax payment by developing and using a taxation module software in the digital wallet, and the other tax payment can be completed in a batch way to transfer taxes to the taxation office at the time of refilling electronic cash value into the digital wallet, in the case of off-line payments using transportation card and other service card. As long as the tax collected in the digital wallet cannot be used for other purposes, there would be no temptation for the consumers not to deliver the tax to the taxation office.

Figure 8 shows the tax payment in electronic cash of which process 1, 2 and 3 are the same as those of the EFT in Figure 5

(Process 4) There are two options of the tax payment using the electronic cash in the digital wallet

(Step 4-1: Realtime) The tax is paid to the wallet of taxation office at the same time of paying the prices

(Step 4-2: Batch) The tax is delivered in a batch way when refilling the value of electronic cash or paying the tax spontaneously.

(Process 5) The accumulated taxes are stored in the digital wallet of the taxation office and transfer the taxes to the bank account of the taxation office.

Figure 8. Process of CPT System using Electronic Cash

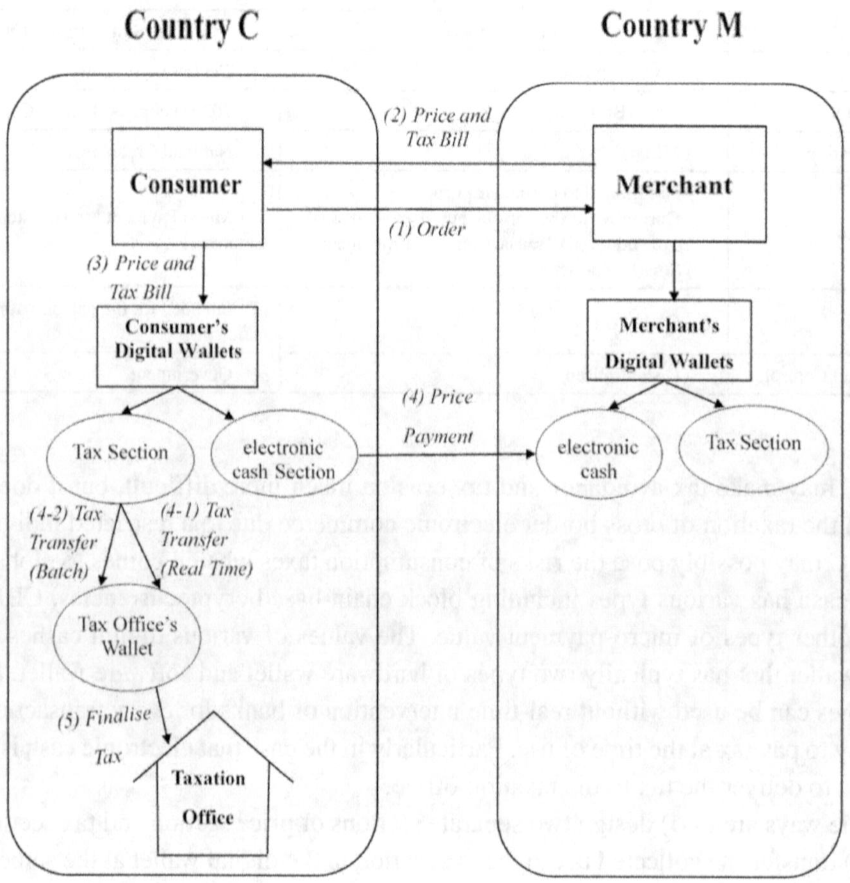

THRUSTED THIRD PARTY (TTP) MODEL FOR THE CPT SYSTEM

Yeoul Hwangbo (op. cit., 2004) proposed the trusted third party (TTP) model that were named as Global Electronic Commerce Tax Invoice (GETI) system in 2004 and Global Electronic Commerce Tax Hub (GetH) system (op. cit., 2012) in 2012. In the early discussions of taxing cross border, OECD released a global registration body proposal (OECD, 2021, pp.15-16), which laid the foundation on the above GETI and GetH system. GETI and GetH are ultimately regarded as CPT system.

This TTP architecture was designed to deal with cross border transactions in compliance with the non-resident registration, which means that overseas merchants are required to register their business presence to the consumer's country, before doing any B2C business in the country. GETI and GetH systems adopted the TTP model to play the role of the global registration body and carry out e-tax services associated with the cross border electronic commerce taxation such as (i) business registration, (ii) tax database management, (iii) tax invoices issuance, (iv) tax calculation and reporting, and (iv) tax payment and settlement among countries (refer to figure 8).

Global electronic commerce tax hub (GetH), was designed to not only clarify a consumer and supplier's country jurisdiction in an attempt to curb tax loopholes, but also provide various services for global electronic commerce, while satisfying the consumer country's jurisdiction principle.

The standard processes in the GetH are described as follows:

(Process 1) Merchant registration to the taxation office: merchants used to register to their taxation office in accordance with their physical location (Country M).

(Process 2) Multilateral agreement for establishing the trusted third party (TTP): To set up the TTP for electronic commerce taxation, agreements need to be made in the various level of global, regional, and nation. Multilateral agreement can be viewed more effective measure than that of bilateral.

(Process 3) Merchant registration to the TTP: pursuant to the principle of the registration of non-residents to consumer jurisdiction country, the merchants register to the tax office of the consumer's country before any B2C transactions could occur. In this regard, TTP is required to hold business registration number or related information that are delivered by the supplier's taxation office.

Process 4, 5, and 6 are the same as the processes of 1, 2, and 3 of the EFT system of CPT.

(Process 7) The TTP captured the price and tax information of which countries merchant sell goods and services.

(Process 8) The TTP delivers related taxed to the taxation office of the consumer jurisdiction country, while at the same time, send the tax invoice to the consumer.

(Process 9) Tax report to send both of taxation offices to ensure tax settlement and clearance

Figure 9. Process of Trusted Third Party (TTP) in Cross-Border Electronic Commerce

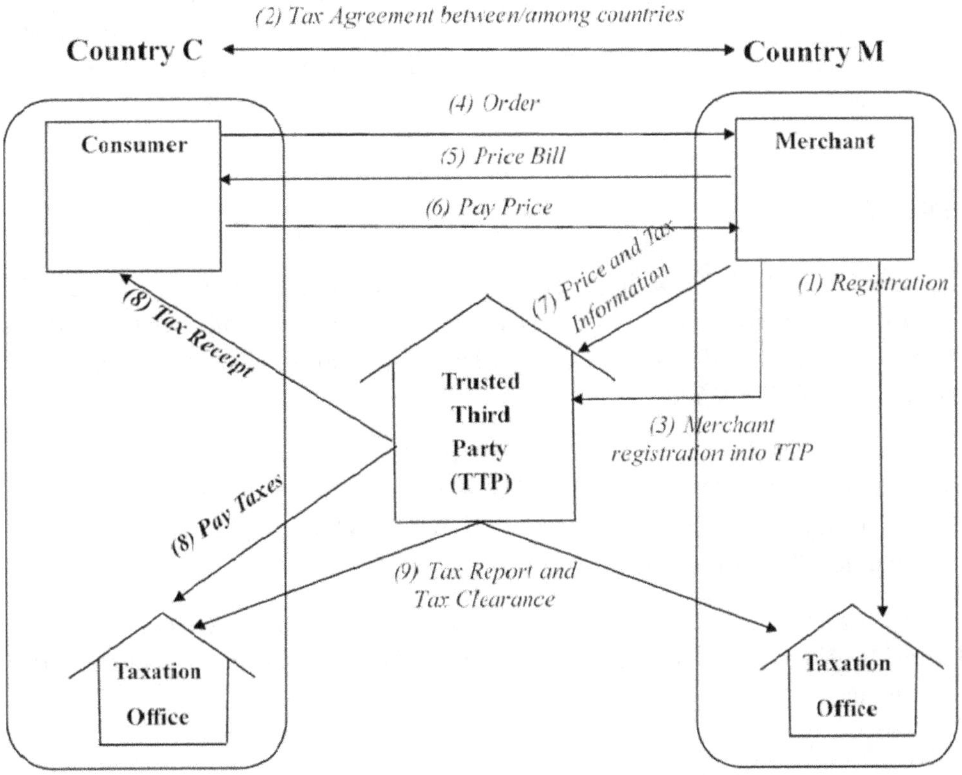

Technology components in the TTP models such as GETI and GetH are identified as (i) identification and authentication, (ii) tax calculation using database, (iii) electronic payment, (iv) tax reporting generation, and (v) tax auditing.

CONCLUSION

This chapter is aimed at conceptual design to develop the consumption tax system for the cross-border electronic commerce from the perspective of fintech enablers. The Consumer Payment Tax (CPT) system is accordingly excogitated to deal with the consumption taxes for global electronic commerce in compliance with the principle of the consumer country's jurisdiction principle. This chapter shows that the CPT has been proved to satisfy the seven (7) criteria – equitable system, simple system, confidence, minimizing tax evasion, avoiding economic distortion, reducing clearance cost, alignment of current tax system - to establish the consumption tax system of global electronic commerce. The CPT can be regarded as the integral system comprising the consumer delivered Sales (CDS) tax system, the global electronic tax invoice (GETI), and the global electronic commerce tax hub (GETI) that were previously designed and developed. The CPS system is based on (i) electronic funds transfer (EFT), (ii) credit card, (iii) electronic cash, and (iv) technologies needed for the trusted third party (TTP), so that consumers are able to pay the consumption taxes in a direct tax payment way using the enablers of fintech technologies.

In conclusion, the CPT can improve the financial and fiscal inclusiveness of government in the country level by (i) preventing dominant electronic commerce suppliers from evading associated consumption taxes, (ii) increasing the government revenues for consumer located countries, particularly developing countries, (iii) replacing indirect tax payment by direct tax payment, enhancing consumer's awareness on his or her consumption tax, and thereby preventing a tax shifting and unfair consumption taxes, and (iv) streamlining the consumption taxes collection process and minimising tax collection cost that reduce the consumer's burden.

REFERENCES

EU. (2000). *Directive 2000/31/EC of the European Parliament and of the Council of 8 June 2000 on certain legal aspects of information society services, in particular electronic commerce, in the Internal Market ('Directive on electronic commerce')*. Retrieved from https://eur-lex.europa.eu/legal-content/EN/TXT/HTML/?uri=CELEX:52003DC0702&from=EN

Financial Action Task Force (FATF). (2020). *Draft updated Guidance for a risk-based approach to virtual assets and VASPs, FATF/PDG(2020)19/REV1*. Retrieved from https://www.fatf-gafi.org/media/fatf/documents/recommendations/March%202021%20-%20VA%20Guidance%20update%20-%20Sixth%20draft%20-%20Public%20consultation.pdf

HM Revenue & Customs. (2020). *Guidance Businesses selling goods in the UK using online marketplaces*. Retrieved from https://www.gov.uk/guidance/vat-overseas-businesses-using-an-online-marketplace-to-sell-goods-in-the-uk

Hwangbo, Y. (2004). Establishing Trusted Third Party for Taxing Global Electronic Commerce: System Architecture of Global Electronic Tax Invoice (GETI). *International Review of Public Administration, 9*(1), 33–40. doi:10.1080/12294659.2004.10805037

Hwangbo, Y. H., & Kifle, H. (2011). Overcoming barrier to move forward to Transactional Stage of e-Government for Brunei Darussalam. *CSPS Strategy and Policy Journal, 2*, 73–90.

J&T Express. (2020). *Understanding the e-Commerce Tax Regulation in Southeast Asia*. Retrieved from https://www.jtexpress.sg/insights/understanding-the-ecommerce-tax-regulations-in-south-east-asia-2020

Lee & Hwangbo. (n.d.). Cyberconsumption Taxes and Electronic Collection Systems: A Canonical Consumer-Delivered Sales Tax. *International Journal of Electronic Commerce, 4*(2), 61-82.

Li, F. (2017). Research on Customs Administration to Cross-Border Electronic Commerce Importation under Taxation Measurement. *American Journal of Industrial and Business Management, 7*(5). doi:10.4236/ajibm.2017.75043

McNally, C. A. (2020). *The DCEP: Developing the Globe's First Major Central Bank Digital Currency*. Retrieved from https://www.chinausfocus.com/finance-economy/the-dcep-developing-the-globes-first-major-central-bank-digital-currency

Nakamoto, S. (2008). *Bitcoin: A Peer-to-Peer Electronic Cash System*. Retrieved from https://bitcoin.org/bitcoin.pdf

Nazarov, M. A. (2019). *Digital Economy: Russian Taxation Issues*. Retrieved from https://www.elibrary.ru/item.asp?id=39181878

OECD. (1997). *Dismantling the Barriers to Global Electronic Commerce, Turku (Finland)*. Retrieved from https://www.oecd-ilibrary.org/science-and-technology/dismantling-the-barriers-to-global-electronic-commerce-turku-finland_236647320075

OECD. (1998). *OECD Ministerial Conference on global electronic commerce*. Retrieved from https://cordis.europa.eu/event/id/10900-oecd-ministerial-conference-on-global-electronic-commerce

OECD. (2001). *Consumption Tax Aspects of Electronic Commerce*. Retrieved from https://www.oecd.org/tax/consumption/Taxation%20and%20eCommerce%202001.pdf

Papis-Almansa, M. (2019). VAT and electronic commerce: the new rules as a means for simplification, combatting fraud and creating a more level playing field? *ERA Forum, 20*, 220-221. doi: 10.100712027-019-00575-9

Salameh, Fatafta, & Shawawreh. (2021). The Possibility of Applying the Tax Accounting System and its Effectiveness on Electronic Commerce in Jordan. *Academy of Accounting and Financial Studies Journal, 25*(1), 4–5.

Schwinn, R., & Teo, E. G. S. (2018). Inclusion or Exclusion? Trends in Robo-advising Financial Investment Services. Handbook of Blockchain, Digital Finance, and Inclusion, 2, 481-492.

Setiawan, S. (2018). E-commerce Taxation and Fiscal Policy Perspective: The Case of Indonesia. *Research in Business and Social Science, 7*(3), 7–8. doi:10.20525/ijrbs.v7i3.900

Chapter 12
Crafting Strategies of Security Breaches:
How Financial Technology Business Modela Work in Data-Centric Approaches

Heru Susanto
https://orcid.org/0000-0002-1823-357X
University of Technology Brunei, Brunei & National Research and Innovation Agency, Indonesia & Tunghai University, Taiwan

Nurul Mardhiah
Department of Management, School of Business, University of Technology Brunei, Brunei

Alifya Kayla Shafa Susanto
Department of Information Security, School of Computing and Informatics, University of Technology Brunei, Brunei

ABSTRACT

In recent years, the number of financial technology players and users have increased at a significant rate due to the rapid technological advancement in financial technology. While smart devices are providing more useful features to users, they have also made it possible for cyber threats to migrate from desktops to smart devices. Thus, it is important for smart device users to be aware that their device could be exposed to cyber threats and that users could protect their devices by employing data-centric cyber security measures. This study reveals how financial technology business model responded to the breach phenomenon by employing data-centric protection approaches. The result is very interesting. Data-centric security is very needed as it is capable of protecting data as a whole. It provides a gapless protection, meaning to say, the data are encrypted and classified wherever it moves. With persistent protection and cross-platform operability, data-centric security will eliminate gaps and keep data protected.

DOI: 10.4018/978-1-7998-8447-7.ch012

INTRODUCTION

Technology is playing a major role in every aspect of a human being; financial technology, shopping, online transaction, business, study, social to name a few, which means that almost all of an individual's personal information has become digitalized. At the same time, securing this information from data breaches has become one of the biggest challenges to many governments and agencies. Cyberattack and Cybercrime such as Phishing, cyberbullying, blackmailing and online fraud are some examples of cyber threats, which will undoubtedly increase along with the growth of technology and development of social media. Therefore, protecting or preventing cyber threats from happening is vital and to some extent, it is becoming a priority for some country. In recent years, media attention to cyberattack is increasing as a number of cyberattacks are growing. Thus, it gives the impression that it has happened frequently and becoming more dangerous. Besides, as stated by PwC (2020), about 50 per cent of the respondents across global reported an incident of fraud and economic crime in the past 24 months, which led to losing US$42 billion excluding the brand damage, and market share. On top of that Cybercrime is at the second-place fraud that the respondents experienced with 34 per cent, with this statement it shows that cyberattack is more dangerous.

Financial technology industries frequently deal with hacking and information theft. According to the Symantec (a cyber security firm) Internet Security Threat Report 2019 (2019) every month there are more than 4,800 websites compromised with formjacking code, and more than 3.7 million formjacking attacks in 2018 being blocked by the firm. Moreover, according to McAfee in 2017, the global economy has been affected about $600 billion due to Cybercrime. According to Rajeyyagari and Alotaibi (2018), the nation's growth more impacted by cybercrimes such as hacking of accounts, blackmail, defamation and with the impact of cybercrimes every year, the organizations are losing billions of money and reputation leading to loss of future business. Cyber threats and cyber security are interconnected. Whenever we think about cyber security, the first thing that comes into our mind is its threat. In this digital platform, especially during this Pandemic COVID-19 as most of the businesses and organizations allowed their employees to work from home and without secure Internet access could lead to data breaches as all of our devices and network can be reached by a hacker. The mindset that "it will never happen to us" has to change. Individuals and organizations need to be aware of what to look out for and how to protect themselves and their institutions against cyber threats. As cyber threat involves everyone, there are several ways to protect individuals or organizations from becoming a victim on this digital platform. Therefore, it is necessary for a country to develop the law and awareness that are needed to protect internet users within their countries.

In addition, speaking on the digital impact of Pandemic COVID-19, the Ministry of Transport and Infocommunications minister said pandemic has accelerated digital transformation and connectivity in Brunei, it has also increased cyber security threats. Cyber security threats and incidents have become more obvious with irresponsible actors launching cyber security attacks to disrupt critical services and systems. Malicious activities such as phishing and scams during COVID-19 have also increased, making the public anxious and uncertain of the situation." (Rasidah, 2020). Cyber security plays an important role along with the development of information technology (IT). Recently, securing information has become one of the biggest challenges to many governments and agencies as well as society due to the growing cyberattack and threats. Hence, many governments, and agencies are taking several approaches to prevent cyber threats. In the case of Brunei, the government and agencies are taking several approaches such as by forming a National cyber security agency, stated cyber security on Digital Economy Masterplan

2025, collaboration with universities as well as sharing and educate people through awareness programs, social media, websites, radio and television on Internet safety and information security.

This study focuses on several approaches and policy in related with financial technology business model towards cyber security threats. In other hand, comparative studies between selected ASEAN Countries was conducted to reveal cyber security readiness policy. It also focuses on several ways to protect individuals or organizations from becoming a victim on this digital platform, and cyber threats include types and impact.

Problem Statement

In financial technology industries, cyberattack and cybercrime such as Phishing, cyberbullying, blackmailing and online fraud are some forms of cyber threats, which will undoubtedly increase along with the growth of technology and development of social media. Almost all of an individual's personal information has become digitalized, securing this information from data breaches has become one of the biggest challenges to many governments and agencies, as the victim's personal data can be used by actors to commit fraud such as phishing attacks, online stalking as well as hacking attempts, and the organizations direct factors and costs of data breaches are financial theft, and operation disruption. In financial technology business model, the indirect factors and costs from the data breaches include losing reputation leading to loss of future business and losing billions of moneys due to financial theft and also time spent on recovery can lead to increased expenses. However, this study aims to reveal approaches in creating a cyber-secure among financial technology industries. This research goals include: (i) To enhance knowledge in cyber security and cyber threats within financial technology industries; (ii) To reveal government and agency approaches to cyber threats in selected ASEAN Countries; (iii) To educate society on how to prevent unauthorized access or use towards information through data-centric protections; (iv) To propose a data-centric framework to securing IT applications (apps) in nowadays emerging ICT.

Significance of the Study

To enhance knowledge in cyber security and cyber threats, to study governments and agency measure to cyber threats in selected ASEAN Countries as well as to educate society on how to prevent unauthorized access or use towards information as world is moving towards digital life such as financial technology, shopping, online transaction, business, study, and social means that almost all of an individual's personal information has become digitalized and if, not protected will led to data breaches. This research is significance as the findings will be in great use for society to refer to how to prevent unauthorized access or use towards information and get to know measures taken by organizations towards protecting the nation, in many vary areas especially within financial technology industries through data-centric protection approaches.

LITERATURE REVIEW

Information security and data privacy are facing risks as the world is driven more on social networks, online transactions, and stored information through internet and automated processes performed through the use of IT systems (Bendovschi, 2015). If the information is leaked, that organization may lose money and business opportunities therefore information is important to be protected, secure and managed appropriately (Kritzinger and Smith, 2008). Nowadays in the business environment, technologies such as cloud computing, social computing, and next-generation mobile computing are basically changing how organizations use information technology for sharing information and performing electronic commerce (Sharma, 2012). Development of new technologies influences changes on the use of the internet and other IT systems (Szumski, 2018). According to Szumski (2018) also due to emerging technologies, it is impossible to protect our personal information in a very effective way as technologies are present in almost every aspect of our life and also nowadays cyber threats are increasing day by day. Rapid growth of information security management put the world into the new form of threat and protection models (Szumski, 2018)

Moreover, with the development of technology, cybercrime time after time increases in terms of number of attacks and level of damage caused to its victims. Developing new ways to gain unauthorized access to data, networks, and also systems, actors aim to compromise the confidentiality, integrity and availability of information, basically their targets are from individuals to small or medium sized companies and even largest businesses (Bendovschi, 2015).

Of all the developments in technology, the Internet is one of the most significant inventions to date (Hunton, 2011). Over the years there is no doubt that the Internet has developed immensely, providing billions of individuals and organizations across the world with digital communication (Livingstone and Helsper, 2007). Hence individuals and organizations are more dependent on it, as individuals use it for shopping and online transactions and organizations use the Internet to support their business process.

However, even though the Internet offers various advantages, it is always threatened by many risks such as cybercrime (Riem, 2001). Cyber criminals use the Internet as a platform to grow (Selwyn, 2008) and it is easy for them to go unpunished because of the difficulties involved in tracing the origins of such crime (Huston, 2011). The main reason for cybercrime is the exploitation of personal information. (De Joode, 2011). Therefore, Internet users are at the risk having their personal information leaked. Most of the Internet users are unaware of the concept of protecting information. (Thomson, Von Solms, and Louw, 2006) and they often behave in an insecure manner which makes them easily become the targets. According to Grobler, Dlamini, Ngobeni, and Labuschagne (2011) Internet users not only pose a threat to themselves, but also to national security.

The risks that may be faced by an individual and organizations will be stated at below;

i. Identity Theft

Technology, especially internet is playing a major role in every aspect of human beings such as shopping, online transactions, business, study, and social media. This means that almost all of an individual's personal information has become digitalized, which leads internet users to become victims of identity theft. According to Marshall, and Tompsett (2005) cyber actors may use the information to commit fraud for example buying products using the stolen identity. Therefore, one of the impact from identity theft for an individual is financial loss (Brody, Mulig, and Kimball, 2007). There are several forms to obtain personal data in cyberspace such as phishing. Phishing refers to sending out emails which are meant to lure the recipients into revealing their personal information. These emails usually seem important and sent in the hope that the recipients will find the email is important and be lured into giving out their personal information. Unfortunately, even though there are many incidents and awareness about this, there is always someone who is likely to take the bait (Brody, Mulig, and Kimball, 2007)

ii. Cyber Bullying

Cyber bullying is a new form of traditional bullying, as an extension of traditional bullying into the virtual world. Cyber bullying involves the use of technology such as the internet purposely to cause harm to others. The victims will be threatened through text messages, emails, phone calls, instant messages for example WhatsApp, and also social media platforms such as Instagram, Facebook as well as Twitter. These mediums make cyber bullying even more harsh than traditional bullying as the actors can easily reach the victims at any time and anywhere (Swartz, 2009).

iii. Cyber Stalking

According to Mullen, Pathe and Stuart (1999) stalking refers to a behavior involving an effort to forcefully contact or communicate with an unwilling person. This behaviour often threatens and makes considerable fear to the victims (Mullen, Pathe, and Stuart, 1999). There is no difference between cyber stalking and traditional stalking, cyber stalking also forces unwanted communication in a forceful manner that makes fear in the victim. However, the difference between traditional and cyber stalking is the use of medium communication. Cyber stalking is using technology such as email as its communication mediums (Philips, and Morrissey, 2004). According to Ogilvie (2001) there are several forms of cyber stalking including internet stalking, email stalking and computer stalking.Internet stalking, where the actor tracks the victim's activities online, following the victims while online from one site to another. Moreover, the victim will receive false information from the actor in order to scare them. This form of stalking always comes with traditional stalking such as threatening mail, phone calls and even physical assaults. Email stalking as the name itself is using email as the main medium used for communicating. The actor will send threatening emails and send amounts of junk mails to the victim. According to Ogilvie (2001) computer stalking uses the internet to gain unauthorized control of the victim's computer where the actor expects to have direct communication with the victim.

iv. Cybercrime

Cybercrime is an internet-based criminal activity (Gorge, 2007). According to Davis, Golinelli, Beckman, Cotton, Anderson, Bamezai, and Steinberg (2008) there are three types of cybercrime that can be done against organizations including cyberattack, cyber theft and other computer security incidents. Cyberattack, where computer systems are targeted by viruses like Worms, Trojan Horses, and Denial of Service (DoS) attacks which prevents customers from accessing specific services on the internet.

While, cyber theft is used to steal money and valuable information through computer systems to commit fraud. Other computer security incidents involve hacking into company systems and accessing confidential information.

iv. Cyber Threat

What is the definition of cyber threat? Computer Security Resource Centre, National Institute of Standard and Technology defined cyber threat as any circumstance or event that potentially to influence organizational operations including mission, functions, image, or reputation, individuals, organisations, and the Nation through an information system through unauthorized access, destruction, disclosure, modification of information, and denial of service. According to Okutan, and Cebi (2019) common types of Cybercrimes include;

Table 1.

Type	Details
Identity Theft	Gains access to somebody else' information to steal money, access confidential information, health insurance fraud and many more. The actors may do this by finding out internet user's passwords through hacking, retrieving personal information from social media, and also through phishing.
Cyber Stalking	Involves using electronic means, including the Internet to stalk people. Cyberstalking includes blackmailing, slander, defamation and many more.
Cyber Bullying	A form of bullying through the Internet.
Malware	Software that performs a malicious task on a target device or network.
Phishing	An email-borne attack that involves tricking the email recipient into disclosing confidential information for example passwords, or downloading malware by clicking on a hyperlink in the message.

The International Institute for Strategic Studies (2015) defined Cyber security as a body of technologies, processes, and practices designed to protect networks, computers, programs and data from attack, damage or unauthorised access. According to Cybersecurity and Infrastructure Security Agency (2009) Cyber security is the art of protecting networks, devices, and data from unauthorized access or criminal use and the practice of ensuring confidentiality, integrity, and availability of information. Thakur, Qiu, Gai and Ali (2015) defined cyber security as the integration of policies, security measures, approaches to risk management, protocols, technologies, process and training which can be used in securing the organization and cyber setup along with user assets. Cyber security is the activity of protecting networks, computers, databases, data centres and applications with appropriate procedural and technologies security measures (Tonge, Kasture, and Chaudhari, 2013).

A study by Thakur, Qiu, Gai and Ali (2015) three important factors of cyber security include the methods of protecting Information Technology (IT), the data itself, the data being processed and transmitted together with physical and virtual setup, the level of protection obtained by applying such measures and the professional aspects associated. This paper includes cybersecurity workforce, vulnerability scanning, email virus filtering, personal information protection, prevention of cybersafety, and firewall services. The authors conclude that it was found that most of the previous studies are conducted on email security, firewalls, and vulnerabilities. However, not many studies from the perspective of password security. Therefore, there is a need for more studies in terms of techniques and models to ensure that passwords are protected. A study by Tonge, Kasture, and Chaudhari (2013) software like firewalls and antivirus are important but not enough to ensure the safety of personal information and computer networks. Cyber

Ethics, Cybersafety, and Cybersecurity issues need to be integrated in the educational process beginning at an early age. Cyber Security plays an important role in the development of information technology as well as Internet services. Whenever we heard about cybercrime our first thought is usually on national cybersecurity, how good is our infrastructure for handling it. This paper has examined the significance of privacy for individuals as a fundamental human right. Violations of human rights arise from the unlawful collection and storage of personal data, the problems associated with inaccurate personal data, or the abuse, or unauthorized disclosure of such data. In this paper the authors also include the current threats, issues, challenges and measures of the IT sector in society.

There is no single answer for success, but by collaborating with public and private organizations and agencies, and also by advancing security measures particularly looking into mission-critical systems, processes and applications that are connected into cyberspace, businesses will be able to work towards a future environment that is both open and secure. (Sharma, 2012). In view of the risks that accompany along with the increasing reliance on the Internet, certain safety and security measures have been taken. Many developed countries, such as the United States (US), the United Kingdom (UK) and others, have established and implemented a number of cyber security measures including awareness and education initiatives. This is due to the fact that lack of knowledge is viewed as a factor that contributes to insecure online behaviour by Internet users.

DISCUSSION

In this chapter will present the findings from the interview made with AITI and also present a comparative analysis on cyber security approaches in terms of technical, and management including Legal, Organizational, Education and Awareness as well as collaboration approaches. Besides Brunei, the countries to be analysed include Indonesia, and Malaysia. These countries have been chosen because as neighbors, both of them have somewhat similar culture with Brunei.
The analysis will based on as follow;

(i) Legal Measures

This part aims to identify each country's law towards cybercrime.

Brunei

It is important for Brunei to enhance cyber security, to ensure national security and stability in Brunei as it moves towards *Wawasan 2035*. Findings from the interview is the participant mentioned that the new cybersecurity laws are currently in progress. However, specific legislation on cybercrime has been presented as follows; (Authority for Info-communications Technology Industry of Brunei Darussalam, 2018).

Table 2.

Type of Offences	National Law
Distributing, selling or advertising obscene things	Penal Code, Chapter 22
Seditious Intention	Section 4 of Sedition Act, Chapter 24
Distributing False Information	Public Order Act, Chapter 148
Broadcasting issues not in compliance with the broadcasting and internet codes	Internet Code of Practice Notification Broadcasting Act, Chapter 180
Defamation	Defamation Act, Chapter 192
Unauthorized access of computer material and other related matters	Computer Misuse Act, Chapter 194

Indonesia

According to International Telecommunication Union (2015) Indonesia has specific legislation on cybercrime regarding Electronic Information and Transaction, namely Law of The Republic of Indonesia Number 11 of 2008 (Articles 29-37). However, according to Rizal, and Yani (2016), there are several laws that support the implementation of cyber security including Law No. 8 of 1999 which is for Consumer Protection, Law No.2 of 2002 State Police of the Republic of Indonesia, Law No.25 of 2009 which is on Public Service and others.

Malaysia

According to the National Cyber Security Agency (2021), several cyber laws in Malaysia include Computer Crime Act 1997 (Act 563) which highlighted offences relating to the misuse of computers, Digital Signature Act 1997 for secure online transactions via the use of digital signatures, Personal Data Protection Act 2010 is to control the processing of personal data in commercial transactions, Electronic Commerce Act 2006 for legal detection of electronic messages in commercial transaction, Electronic Government Activities Act 2007 legal detection of electronic messages dealings between the the public and government, and others.

(ii) Technical Measures

This part aims to identify whether each country has their own one stop portal against cybercrime which provides information directly to the public, framework of cyber security standards as well as whether there is a guidance for Small Medium Enterprise to protect their company data from cybercrime.

Brunei

Findings from the interview, the participant mentioned that all information regarding the latest cyber incidents can be found through Brunei Computer Emergency Response Team (BruCERT) website, and also through Secure Verify Connect for any news and advice regarding the use of the Internet such as social media platforms, protect the computer from any viruses and others.

Moreover, the participant also mentioned that under Secure Verify Connect provides training for the public especially senior citizens on digital skill. While, in order to reduce the risk of cyber threats in organizations, the National Cyber security framework has been implemented as a set of standards and guidelines to fight against data breach.

Indonesia

In Indonesia, Ministry of Communication and Informatics (MCI) under the supervision of both Directorate General of Informatics Applications, and Directorate General of Resources and the Postal and Informatics are responsible for policy formulation and implementation as well as providing technical guidance such as by providing training, monitoring and evaluation that are related to their areas (Persadha, Waskita and Yazid, 2015). Furthermore, Indonesia has also implemented frameworks related to cybersecurity including Ministerial Regulation No.82 of 2014 about regulation that involve guidelines on cyber defence under Indonesian National Armed Forces (TNI) as a reference for both the Ministry of defence and the TNI (United Nations Institute For Disarmament Research, 2021).

Malaysia

There are several frameworks that have been implemented by Malaysia in related to cyber security standards such as Malaysia Smart City Framework to strengthen policies that are related to cybersecurity as well as personal data. The Public Sector Cybersecurity Framework provides guidance to the government organizations to protect information on cyberspace. Malaysian Public Sector Management of Information and Communications Technology Security Handbook to provide guidelines to the government organizations on ICT security management in terms of legal, technical and also operational related to international standards (United Nations Institute For Disarmament Research, 2021).

Moreover, Malaysia also has a one stop portal which provides public alert and advisory on the latest cyber incidents under Malaysia Computer Emergency Response Team website, and also through the National Cyber Security Agency website.

(iii) Organizational Measures

This part aims to identify Brunei, Indonesia and Malaysia National strategies and Master Plan of Cyber security, and agencies that are responsible for cybersecurity in each country.

Brunei

There are several government organizations and agencies that involved in cyber security in Brunei, which are the Authority for Info-communications Technology Industry (AITI), Cyber Security Brunei (CSB), Brunei Computer Emergency Response Team (BruCERT) and also IT Protective Security Services Sdn Bhd (ITPSS). Moreover, other related organizations include the Ministry of Defence, the Royal Brunei Armed Forces dealing with cybercrime intelligence and cyber law enforcement, and also Attorney General's Chambers in terms of legislation. The Authority for Info-communications Technology Industry (AITI) was formed in January 2003 as telecommunications regulator, national radio-frequency spectrum manager and developer of ICT industry in Brunei. AITI has a specific unit that handles cyber security namely, Data Protection Office. This unit is currently under developing regulation for Personal data protection. Cyber Security Brunei (CSB) was formed in August 2020 under the Ministry of Transport and Infocommunications (MTIC) to monitor and coordinate national efforts to combat cyber security threats and cyber crime in Brunei by enhancing awareness of cyber threats to the public as well as organizations. Even Though CSB is still new, however, the country's major cyber security services such as BruCERT, Cyberwatch Centre and National Digital Forensic Laboratory are already operating under ITPSS in collaboration with the Internal Security Department as an acting cyber security centre (Bakar, 2020). Meanwhile, Brunei Computer Emergency Response Team (BruCERT) was formed in May 2004 has become Brunei's most trusted one stop portal dealing with computers related to security incidents with the vision to enhance security of ICT in Brunei through proactive prevention and effective response. IT Protective Security Services Sdn Bhd (ITPSS) was formed in 2003 as an information security solutions and provide specialised information security and physical security services such as penetration testing, digital forensics, secure event management and training in terms of IT security. Furthermore, the Digital Economy Master Plan framework has been launched in 2020 with the objectives to transform Brunei into a smart nation. One of the strategies under this framework is to focus on implementing cyber security initiatives and digital data policy that will provide governance as well as framework of data protection and sharing.

Indonesia

According to Rizal, and Yani (2016) Information Security Coordination Team, Directorate of Information Security, and Indonesia Security Incident Response Team on Internet Infrastructure are organizations that are related with cyber security in Indonesia. The Information Security Coordination Team is responsible to coordinate cyber security, focus on the expertise and training in the area of information and technology. Meanwhile, the Directorate of Information Security function is to formulate and implement such as related to training, monitoring, evaluation and reporting in the area of information security governance. Lastly, Indonesia Security Incident Response Team on Internet Infrastructure responsible to handle security that is taking place in internet infrastructure. Furthermore, aside from the public sector there are other organizations that are involved with cyber security in Indonesia include Indonesia Communication Emergency Response Team and also Indonesia Academic Computer Security Incident Response Team. Indonesia Communication Emergency Response Team (ID-CERT) is a supporting organization that works with the public sector in special cases in order to support the development of cyber security in Indonesia. Meanwhile, Indonesia Academic Computer Security Incident Response Team is the organization responsible for the universities that wanted to focus on the development of security in Indonesia. The Government-Computer Security Incident Response Team was also established to handle evaluation and emergency response that related to information security. Indonesia also has a special agency responsible for securing national confidential data called Lembaga Sandi Negara (Lemsaneg), responsible to coordinate with other government organizations such as Indonesian National Police, Indonesia National Army, and also the Ministry of Defense. In law enforcement and handling cybercrime, Indonesian National Police have a special unit responsible to handle cyber crime (Persadha, Waskita, and Yazid, 2015).

Malaysia

From the public sector, there are several organizations that are responsible to handle cyber threats including the Ministry of Science, Technology and Innovation (MOSTI), Ministry of Communications and Multimedia Malaysia, and also National Cyber Security Agency. MOSTI is responsible to design a framework involving the national policy of ICT. They are also used to supervise a Malaysia Computer Emergency Response Team (MyCERT). Malaysian Communications and Multimedia Commissions is responsible to monitor and regulate communication and multimedia activities in Malaysia such as regulation and supervision of telecommunication, broadcast, Internet Service Provider (ISP) and others. They also has the authority to shut down websites that contents of pornography, and also fraud (Persadha, Waskita, and Yazid, 2015). Meanwhile, the National Cyber Security Agency is responsible to develop and implement national cyber security policies and strategic, protecting Critical national Information Infrastructures (CNII), and also responsible in addressing cyber threats such as through organizing cyber security awareness, capacity-building programmes, and shared resources among other agencies. Malaysia also has their own Computer Emergency Response Team known as Malaysia Computer Emergency Response Team (MyCERT), responsible for dealing with computer security incidents for the public such as providing emergency response to home users and organisations on cyber security incidents for example cyber harassment, viruses, hack attempts, and also data breaches (under Cyber999 Help Centre). Moreover, they are also responsible for security breach alerts for example on security incidents or malware outbreak and provide advisories such as advice and recommendation from the expert. Cyber Security Malaysia is an agency under MOSTI responsible to provide technical services such as programmes and initiatives for example outreach and capacity building in order to reduce the vulnerability of digital systems, and at the same time strengthen Malaysia's cyberspace. In addition to the organization above, under the Royal Malaysian Police (RMP) there is one department that is responsible to conduct Investigation of Cybercrime and Multimedia Unit called Commercial Crime Investigation Department. Malaysia also formed a Computer Forensic Laboratory responsible to train police officers and computer forensics (Persadha, Waskita, and Yazid, 2015).

Furthermore, there are several strategies and plans related to cyber security in Malaysia include Malaysia Cyber Security Strategy 2020-2024, Malaysia Smart City Framework, National Policy on Industry 4.0, National Security Policy, National Security Council Directive No.24: National Cyber Crisis Management Policy and Mechanism, and also National Cyber Security Policy. Malaysia Cyber Security Strategy 2020-2024 contains five strategic pillars including effective governance and management; strengthening legislative framework and enforcement; catalysing world class Innovation, Technology, R&D and Industry; enhancing capacity and capacity building, awareness and education and also strengthening global collaboration (United Nations Institute For Disarmament Research, 2021). One of the strategies under Malaysia Smart City Framework is to strengthen policies which are related to cyber security and personal data. In addition, the National Policy on Industry 4.0 provides guidelines on cyber security and IoT security for Industry 4.0 as the development of cybersecurity capabilities. Meanwhile, National Security Policy has included the following such as maintaining cyber security and Defence, and also ensuring a secured cyber environment through comprehensive risk management as one of the strategies to be pursued. National Security Council Directive No.24: National Cyber Crisis Management Policy and Mechanism mentioned strategy that will be taken for cyber crisis mitigation and response between Malaysia's Critical National Information Infrastructure with the collaboration between public and private sector. While, National Cyber Security Policy is to address the threats to the Critical National Information Infrastructure (CNII) involving the networked information systems across critical sectors.

(iv). Education and Awareness

This part aims to identify any cyber security education and awareness held by organizations and agencies of each country.

Brunei

In Brunei, to increase the awareness in terms of Internet safety and information security among Bruneian, various training and program had been held by several organizations and agencies as follow;

ITPSS offers training on IT Security awareness among executive management, and also end users, which is adapted from the National Institute of Standards and Security and SANS Institute (USA). They also held workshops on basic information security. Moreover, ITPSS also organized an annual hacking competition namely 'Cyber Battle: Capture the Flag Competition' with the aim to inspire the young generation to pursue careers in IT particularly related to cybersecurity such as digital forensics, cryptography and many more. In addition, BruCERT also takes an initiative by organizing an awareness program namely Secure Verify Connect among the public by giving education, seminars as well as workshops with the objectives of increasing the awareness in terms of Internet safety and information. They also collaborate with RTB's Pilihan FM in terms of Internet safety and also Information security awareness called Cyber Safe. Furthermore, BruCERT has launched its awareness website to provide the public with easy access to information related to online threats and also provide best practices to protect from IT related security risks.

Indonesia

In Indonesia, to increase the awareness related to cyber security, various training and program had been held by several organizations and agencies can be found as follow;

According to Setiadi (2012) the Ministry of Communication and Information Technology (MCIT) has created a program namely Health and Safe Internet program in order to enhance information security in cyberspace through education and public awareness. MCIT also launched an annual program called Information Security Index (KAMI Index) aims to map the maturity stage of information security among the public service providers. Moreover, MCIT has collaborated with several organizations including the Ministry of Research and Technology, IGOS Center and PC LINUX by designing a software called Internet Devices Health and Safe for Children Indonesia (Perisai), in order to protect and educate the children from negative content.

Malaysia

There are several initiatives that are taken by organizations and agencies in Malaysia to promote awareness among the public and organizations including CyberSAFE, CyberGURU, and also one stop portal. CyberSAFE educates and enhances cybersecurity awareness and also promotes a safe digital world to the public with the aims that online users could protect their devices and information. Meanwhile, in order to increase the number of competent and certified cyber security professionals in Malaysia, one of services under Cyber Security Professional Development namely CyberGURU have been formed. CyberGURU works as a platform for sharing sessions between local and international experts as well as academicians.

Malaysia also has a one stop portal which provides public alert and advisory on the latest cyber incidents under Malaysia Computer Emergency Response Team website, and also through the National Cyber Security Agency website.

(v). Sharing and Collaboration

This part aims to identify local and international cooperation related to cyber security of each country.

Brunei

For International cooperation related to cyber security, Brunei is a member of ASEAN Defence Minister's Meeting-Plus (ADMM-Plus), ASEAN Network Security Action Council, International Telecommunication Union (ITU), Forum of Incident Response and Security Teams (FIRST), Asia Pacific Computer Emergency Response and Security (APCERT), Asia-Pacific Telecommunity (APT) and also, Organization of the Islamic Conference-CERT (OIC-CERT). Brunei participated in several cyber security activities such as ASEAN-JAPAN Information Security, APT Cybersecurity Forum, APCERT Incident Drill, ADMM-Plus, and many more.

Indonesia

Indonesia has collaborated with several international organizations related to cyber security. According to Setiadi (2012) for International cooperation, Indonesia has become a member of ASEAN Network Security Action Council, ITU, APCERT, OIC-CERT, and also member of Cybersecurity Alliance for Mutual Progress (CAMP). For local cooperation, Indonesian National Armed Forces has cooperate with some organizations who are experts in the area of information technology such as with Institut Teknologi Del (IT Del) in order to develop human resource skills to deal with cyber security (Rizal, and Yani, 2016) Moreover, Indonesia is also doing bilateral and multilateral cooperation such as with Japan, the United Kingdom, and other countries, Australia with Indonesia Cyber Policy Dialogue as well as Indonesia with Russia Cyber Bilateral Dialogue. Indonesia also participated in ASEAN-JAPAN Information Security, APT Cybersecurity Forum, APCERT Incident Drill, ADMM-Plus, and many more, in terms of cyber security activities.

Malaysia

For International cooperation, Malaysia has become a member of ASEAN Network Security Action Council, ITU, APCERT, OIC-CERT, CAMP, ADMM-Plus, APT, FIRST and also Global Forum on Cyber Expertise (GFCE). Malaysia participated in many cybersecurity activities including ASEAN-JAPAN Information Security, APT Cybersecurity Forum, Octopus Conference which cooperation against cybercrime, APCERT Incident Drill, ADMM-Plus and many more. Furthermore, Malaysia is also doing trilateral cooperation such as trilateral meeting on security between Indonesia, Malaysia and Philippines. This agreement involve the spread of terrorism related content particulary in social media.

Data Centric Information Security: Financial Technology Business Model

Implications of the effects of data breach, especially within financial technology business model, may lead to the affected as follows, **Reputational Cost,** As seen from the table, regardless of the types of organization, data breach incident can contribute to reputational cost. In both sectors, due to the organization's failure to make sure the consumers data are safe and secure, consumers may lose trust in the company, and it will take time for the company to regain their trust back. **Business Continuity Cost,** almost organizations are affected with business continuity cost. For some, these costs include, deactivating the affected features on their website and shutting down the whole system or website temporarily or permanently. Because of this, it forces the employees and consumers to stop using the website or the system which therefore, reduces productivity and thus especially for business organization, it may lead to have lower or negative profit margin. **Competitive Advantage Cost,** in business sector, while some of their features or website need to be shut down temporarily, users or consumers that had been using the website or the feature will go to the company competitors as an alternative of the company service. While in healthcare, they could lose their competitive advantage as deactivating their system will lead them to be unable to work efficiently and thus, makes the operation and administration process within the organization slower. **Investigation Costs,** in every data breach regardless types of sector, they need to contact some parties such as IT researchers to investigate the cause of the data breach and who is behind the attack. This could be a cost for the company because in investigation, the researchers will need to inspect the system and the employees which consume a lot of time. Furthermore, as the system was inspected, the employees cannot proceed with their work and thus, reduce the productivity of the organization. **Contractual Costs**, looking at the nature of the data breach case which shows that the breach was actually originated by their IT vendor, it can be seen that, data breach occurred in healthcare sector does not really impacted their partners or other parties compare to data breach occurred in business sector. This consequence may have a high cost as it can make their partners or clients to lose trust in them and eventually lose ties with the business. **Notification Costs**, notifying users or consumers is actually one of the requirements whenever an organization faced a cyberattack which includes data breach. Failed to do so may lead to regulatory costs and litigation costs. As seen from the table, almost both sectors immediately contacted their users about the breach. This could be a cost because preparing emails in a short period of time to be sent to all the individual involved can takes a lot of work and time of the employees while they can spend it on other things such as focusing on the organization's main service. **Regulatory Costs,** regardless of the sector, every organization found guilty of failed to take the appropriate action once data breach incident occurred may be charged to pay legal expenses such as civil penalties or fines. **Litigation Costs,** as for this cost, there are no solid evidence in the news obtained stating clearly that the affected consumers had filed a lawsuit against the organization for failing to protect their data. However, if any of the organizations were to received this cost, this cost usually involve a huge amount of money as the number of individuals involved from the organization are huge in amount as well.

However, few things organization should learn from their mistakes and improve on them such as; creating and implementing a proper guideline on how to handle a data breach, improving their security on the personal data hold, creating a team specialized in searching for vulnerabilities in system before those vulnerabilities are misused by malicious entities, rebuilding user's trust by being honest and transparent to users, strengthening security and policy regarding user's data, provide an intensive training and courses for employees especially IT staff on data breach particularly on the importance of data breach and identifying the phishing emails.

Here, data centric security is an approach that uses various methods to protect sensitive data itself regardless of the location of the data from potentially being stolen, breached or misused by malicious entities. It is a different approach compared to traditional security strategy. In traditional security strategy, it focuses on protecting data stored in specific locations, server or network only and this will cause a problem because when the data moves somewhere else, another security solution must be implemented or the data will be left unprotected. Data centric security solves this problem as it focuses on protecting individual files containing sensitive information and administer appropriate security protection in order to safeguard the data wherever the data goes. There are various ways of protecting data using data centric security strategy such as: **(1) Encryption,** countermeasures can protect data from being accessed by unauthorized users and it can also protect data from being accessed illegal ways by authorized parties or personnel. In implementing encryption, there should be a set of rules to adhere to ensure the whole process is clear to users and thus creates a better user experience to them. There are various types of encryptions that the organization can choose from and some of it are: *transparent data encryption* – it has fastest route for implementation as transparent encryption can be performed without altering the database of the system or the application code. This type of encryption provides the best protection for structured data kept within data stores or unstructured data located in files. *Application Layer Encryption or Tokenization* - it has the highest degree of protection where the application of this encryption which requires the modification to either database or application code, and provides protection of data whenever it is in motion and at stationary. **(2) Strong Encryption Key Management,** when an organization made a decision to implement encryption, they should take into account a system that allows authorized users to decrypt data and use it for specific needs or jobs while ensuring unauthorized users can't get access to it. The process of managing encryption key is known to be complex but with the rise of advancing technology and innovation nowadays, new technology such as automated cryptographic key management has greatly reduced the inefficient manual way.

Beneficiary of Data Centric Security

Protecting data on the perimeter using firewalls, antivirus software and access controls may always be needed but it will not help to protect the data stored in the cloud or that shared via email against the data breaches. Data centric security is an approach in protecting data as a whole and the data can defend itself. *Security must be able to protect data wherever it is being used, viewed or saved* Therefore, it is vital for businesses to focus on their data through implementing or developing data centric security strategy to help everyone understand the power of data and how it can benefit the business and customers. Data centric security of an organisation also helps to protect sensitive data or information in the files and database that contain it, and where the data moves while being protecting and - are control and review by only the authorized user. The data cannot easily be manipulated and change without being detected. By doing so the company can take advantage of cloud computing, mobile technology, and others without leaving the company in danger such as leaking data. Moreover, corporates, governments and organizations are continually being attacked by cyber criminals for which these criminals are involved in the stealing of critical-business data, customer data and third-party information. Almost all companies or organizations store data such as customer personal information, product information, financial data and valuable asset data. When protecting data, customer's data should be put as top priority in handling them. This is why companies should shift their security to a more data-centric approach.

Data-Centric Security is very much needed as it is capable of protecting data as a whole. It provides a gapless protection, meaning to say, the data are encrypted and classified wherever it moves. With persistent protection and cross-platform operability, data-centric security will eliminate gaps and keep data protected either if it is shared or not. With that being said, the importance of data-centric Security would be a guaranteed protection of data. By implementing it, it will focus on the control of a company's or an organisation's central network. Although it is automatic, it provides coverage for the entire network on a single organisation without spaces in between those data and if the organisation evolves, it evolves as well. Other than protecting the central data, it can also prevent risks of rogues' application from coming through the network boundaries or through the cloud network. Even if there is a breach, it can only attack whatever is left unguarded. Meaning to say, it can minimise the risks of losing sensitive data and the small part that is affected can be detained and quarantined or even removed.

Wall Between Data and Hackers

Human intervention can be a factor of vulnerability of data protection. It is important to consider user data security awareness at all levels of the organization. Traditional security such as Firewalls and endpoint protections are not effective anymore in the incident of a data breach. Individual or employee will be the front line of defence when it comes to the security of the company's data as these individuals are the ones that can either be the one handling them with care or be the one that is the cause of a data breach. Employees/Individuals act as a defensive wall that stand between hackers and data. Enterprises need to begin focusing users' actions and activities on their interaction with data specifically sensitive data because if the users are not educated on the correct procedures given, data can be vulnerable to criminal attacks. However, training and focusing on employees are sensible solutions as they are the one who is handling the data every day. By focusing on monitoring users' actions/behaviours, companies can effectively engage in the fight to protect the data. A training program can be introduced to help the employees of an organisation to prepare themselves against those types of attacks, especially those employees who have access to a highly classified data. At the same time, informing customers about their best practises when it comes to data security. Those who are already trained in data security can ensure the company's safety so that the company can focus on the goals the company is trying to achieve and can change the environment of the company itself without the fear of any attacks.

Employees / Individual always need to be aware of the storage of sensitive data. By means of installing an anti-malware software, keeping an up-to-date operating system, ensuring that every device and files that has sensitive data is encrypted and is protected with authentication. When it comes to handling sensitive data, users must make sure that they are connected to a corporate or a secured wireless connection only, not doing their office work in a public place or using a public Wi-Fi. Additionally, preventing a thief gaining physical control over a corporate device or data is also very important. Such negligence can cause data to be kept by a thief or irresponsible individual. Moreover, the devices used for handling and storing the data should be equipped with strong passwords. For example, using a password that contains at least one lowercase letter, one uppercase letter, one numeric digit and one special character with a minimum of 12 characters. Not only that, devices should be automatically locked when left unused for a certain amount of time - when devices are left unused for 30 seconds the device will automatically be locked to prevent unauthorized users to access the devices.

Data-Centric Security Strategies: Centralized Management Control

A centralized management control is essential on possessing complete control over sensitive data from the moment it was created. It is a crucial method for Data Loss Protection (DLP) where it identifies, monitors and protects data. Organizations are able to keep track of all the activities on data and logged it for auditing and reporting. Not only that, organization can revoke or grant access to protect data anytime to protect against mistakes that leads to data loss and misuse by insiders. Data cannot be protected when it is untraceable. Identifying data with the use of automation system in processing and handling data will lessen human error or the jeopardize of data. This automation is possible with the use of a data discovery technology where it continuously monitors file activities such as finding data no matter where it is located either in a cloud, mobile, external devices. Data is continuously moving and is fractious. By encrypting data, it will protect the data from unauthorized users from accessing the data in authorized ways or places. An effective data encryption provides full integrated encryption that utilizes data tagging that protects data wherever it goes; storage devices, back-up storage or email attachments. *Data Classification*, a data classification decides what kind of data to protect and how it will be protected. Data classification tools facilitates the separation of valuable information from the less valuable ones. It is used to improve in the handling of sensitive data. *Access Control*, data access should be based on roles of the individual in the organization with specific permission and privileges. Rules shall be applied based on the roles, places that are allowed to access the data and type of devices that are permitted. Access control mechanism will determine who has the rights to access data after is has left an entity. *Data Backup*, security is important, but if you have a strong security already but there is no backup for the data kept, the company will certainly lose it all. Every company should ensure that data is properly backed up. This can be done either monthly, weekly or even daily. Backup testing are practiced to ensure the data can be recovered when needed.

Data-Centric Protection and Policies

Organizations or businesses should make every effort in raising business consequences of data breaches. A clear and effective implementation of a data protection policy should be communicated throughout the departments. Violating the policy grounds for termination or a disciplinary act by the administration. A data protection policy may contain: **WHO** can use the data? Specific individuals or the position of the individual should be placed for which these individuals only can handle certain types of data. There should be only few people that is given access to sensitive data. For example, a part-timer or an intern if they were placed on that department, they are allowed to access to only certain data that does not contain any sensitive information or something safer, they are not granted access to any type of information. This should be considered because they are short-term employees. **WHAT** can each person/role/rank do with the data? Each person or employee have access to certain files or data. Depending on the position, a low-tier employee usually handles a smaller amount of data for their scope of work. While an employee with a higher position usually will have access to more type of data because of large scope of work for decision making. **WHEN** data can be used? Data cannot be accessed anywhere or anytime. Data should be handled or used in a secure environment or secured network. Data will be at risk if done in public areas or using a public and unsecured network. **WHERE** can the data be used? Data should be used in an office or when using a corporate network. When in a public place, data should be handled carefully, because eyes are everywhere and the risk is very high especially theft.

BYOD Policies

Most organizations or businesses nowadays allows their employees to bring their own devices to increase productivity and reduce costs. Accessing sensitive information on personal devices means that data is travelling outside of the company's network. Implementing BYOD policies create a governance and compliance of device usage. The policies include; what type of devices can be used and the type of data that can be used on their personal devices. *Implementing Two-Step Security when Employees are Away,* an employee of a company should be trained up to a certain level of awareness to prevent data breaches in their respective companies. With that knowledge, companies can also customize their own data banks to a fully encrypted one just because hackers are everywhere and hackers are getting better and more dangerous in today's society. By doing so, if, let's say, there is a company retreat, the data is already safe from attackers. *Employee Leaving Strategy,* if the employee is terminated or dismissed, companies need to implement employee leaving strategy, so all the data stored on their devices should be removed or erase, to prevent misuse of certain data. Additionally, a statement must be signed by the employee that is leaving that contains some agreement; the employee must not intrude in the use of the company's data once they left the company, the employee will not leak any information learned while they were working in the company and also any data or information used in their personal devices must be terminated before they leave the company.

CONCLUSION

ICT growth has given impact to the increasing cyber threats within financial technology industries. selected ASEAN Countries has tried to address these problems by making policies and regulations, developed technical and procedures, formed an organization related to cyber security, and also conducted international cooperation. Aldo, those, showed selected ASEAN Countries, initiatives to protect cyberspace.

In other hand, almost all companies or organizations store data such as customer personal information, product information, financial data and valuable asset data. When protecting data, customer's data should be put as top priority in handling them through data-centric approach. Data-Centric Security is very much needed as it is capable of protecting data as a whole. It provides a gapless protection, meaning to say, the data are encrypted and classified wherever it moves. With persistent protection and cross-platform operability, data-centric security will eliminate gaps and keep data protected either if it is shared or not. With that being said, the importance of data-centric Security would be a guaranteed protection of data

REFERENCES

Authority for Info-communications Technology Industry of Brunei Darussalam. (2018). *Content Regulation*. Retrieved from https://www.aiti.gov.bn/SitePages/Content-Regulation.aspx

Bendovschi, A. (2015). Cyber-Attacks – Trends, Patterns and Security Countermeasures. *Procedia Economics and Finance*, *28*, 24–31. doi:10.1016/S2212-5671(15)01077-1

Blackmailer receives two-year jail time, one caning. (2020, April 24). Retrieved April 29, 2021, from https://borneobulletin.com.bn/blackmailer-receives-two-year-jail-time-one-caning/

BruCERT. (2021). *Services*. Retrieved April 30,2021, from https://www.brucert.org.bn/services

Chuchu, F., & Gafur, M. (2018). Cyber Crime in Brunei Darussalam Viewed from Sociological Perspective. *Proceedings of the 7th International Conference on Multidisciplinary Research*, 354-361. 10.5220/0008885103540361

Cybersecurity and Infrastructure Security Agency (CISA). (2009, May 6). *What is cybersecurity?* Retrieved from https://us-cert.cisa.gov/ncas/tips/ST04-001

Gade, N. R., & Reddy, U. G. J. (2014). *A Study of Cyber Security Challenges and Its Emerging trends on Latest Technologies*. Retrieved from https://www.researchgate.net/publication/260126665_A_Study_Of_Cyber_Security_Challenges_And_Its_Emerging_Trends_On_Latest_Technologies

Hong, K. S., Chi, Y. P., Chao, L. R., & Tang, J. H. (2003). An integrated system theory of information security management. *Information Management & Computer Security*, *11*(5), 243–248. doi:10.1108/09685220310500153

Hunton, P. (2011). A rigorous approach to formalising the technical investigation stages of cybercrime and criminality within a UK enforcement environment. *Digital Investigation*, *7*(3-4), 105–113. doi:10.1016/j.diin.2011.01.002

International Telecommunication Union. (2015). *Global Cybersecurity Index & Cyberwellness Profiles*. Retrieved from https://www.itu.int/dms_pub/itu-d/opb/str/D-STR-SECU-2015-PDF-E.pdf

ITPSS. (2018, July 17). *Career in Cybersecurity*. Retrieved fromhttps://www.itpss.com/News/2018/17072018.html

ITPSS. (2020). *Training*. Retrieved April 30,2021, from https://itpss.com/TrainingOverview.html

Kortjan, N. (2013). *A Cyber Security Awareness and Education Framework for South Africa*. Retrieved from https://core.ac.uk/download/pdf/145053774.pdf

Kritzinger, E., & Smith, E. (2008). Information security management: An information security retrieval and awareness model for industry. *Journal of Computer Security*, *27*(5-6), 224–231. doi:10.1016/j.cose.2008.05.006

Livingstone, S., & Helsper, E. J. (2007). Taking risks when communicating on the Internet: The role of offline social-psychological factors in young people's vulnerability to online risks. *Information Communication & Society*, *2001*(3), 619-644. doi:10.1080/13691180701657998

National cyber security agency begins operations. (2020, October 13). Retrieved January 20, 2021, from https://thescoop.co/2020/10/13/national-cyber-security-agency-begins-operations/

National Cyber Security Agency (NACSA). (2021, April 27). *Malaysian Cyber Laws*. Retrieved from https://www.nacsa.gov.my/legal.php

National cyber security agency to be formed, says MTIC minister. (2020, January 10). Retrieved from https://thescoop.co/2020/01/10/national-cyber-security-agency-to-be-formed-says-mtic-minister/

National Institute of Standards and Technology. (2012). *Cyber Threat*. Retrieved from https://csrc.nist.gov/glossary/term/Cyber_Threat

Net threat: Morphing pictures for revenge. (2015, July 8,). Retrieved April 29, 2021, from https://timesofindia.indiatimes.com/city/chandigarh/Net-threat-Morphing-pictures-forrevenge/articleshow/47981141.cms

Okutan, A., & Cebi, P. D. Y. (2019). A Framework for Cyber Crime Investigation. *Procedia Computer Science*, *158*, 287–294. doi:10.1016/j.procs.2019.09.054

Persadha, P. D., Waskita, A. A., & Yazid, S. (2015). Comparative Study of Cyber Security Policies Among Malaysia, Australia, Indonesia: A Responsibility Perspective. *2015 Fourth International Conference on Cyber Security, Cyber Warfare, and Digital Forensic*, 146-150. 10.1109/CyberSec.2015.36

Rajeyyagari, S., & Alotaibi, A.S. (2018). A study on cyber-crimes, threats, security and its emerging trends on latest technologies: influence on the Kingdom of Saudi Arabia. *International Journal of Engineering & Technology, 7*(2.3), 54-58. doi:10.14419/ijet.v7i2.3.9969

Reim, A. (2001). Cybercrimes of the 21st Century. *Computer Fraud & Security*, *2001*(3), 13–15. doi:10.1016/S1361-3723(01)03015-9

Rizal, M., & Yani, Y. M. (2016). Cybersecurity Policy and Its Implementation in Indonesia. *Journal of ASEAN Studies*, *4*(1), 61–78. doi:10.21512/jas.v4i1.967

Selwyn, N. (2008). A Safe Haven for Misbehaving? An Investigation of Online Misbehaviour Among University Students. *Social Science Computer Review*, *26*(4), 446–465. doi:10.1177/0894439307313515

Setiadi, F. (2012). Am Overview of the Development Indonesia National Cyber Security. *International Journal of Information Technology & Computer Science*, *6*. Retrieved from http://docshare01.docshare.tips/files/27192/271922656.pdf

Sharma, R. (2012). Study of Latest Emerging Trends on Cyber Security and its challenges to Society. *International Journal of Scientific & Engineering Research, 3*(6). Retrieved from https://www.ijser.org/researchpaper/Study-of-Latest-Emerging-Trends-on-Cyber-Security-and-its-challenges-to-Society.pdf

Sharma, R. (2012). Study of Latest Emerging Trends on Cyber Security and its challenges to Society. *International Journal of Scientific & Engineering Research, 3*(6). Retrieved from https://www.ijser.org/researchpaper/Study-of-Latest-Emerging-Trends-on-Cyber-Security-and-its-challenges-to-Society.pdf

Susanto, H. (2018). Smart mobile device emerging Technologies: an enabler to Health Monitoring system. In *High-Performance Materials and Engineered Chemistry* (pp. 241–264). Apple Academic Press. doi:10.1201/9781315187860-8

Susanto, H., & Almunawar, M. N. (2015). Managing Compliance with an Information Security Management Standard. In *Encyclopedia of Information Science and Technology* (3rd ed., pp. 1452–1463). IGI Global. doi:10.4018/978-1-4666-5888-2.ch138

Susanto, H., & Almunawar, M. N. (2016). Security and Privacy Issues in Cloud-Based E-Government. In *Cloud Computing Technologies for Connected Government* (pp. 292–321). IGI Global. doi:10.4018/978-1-4666-8629-8.ch012

Susanto, H., & Almunawar, M. N. (2018). *Information Security Management Systems: A Novel Framework and Software as a Tool for Compliance with Information Security Standard.* CRC Press. doi:10.1201/9781315232355

Susanto, H., Almunawar, M. N., Leu, F. Y., & Chen, C. K. (2016). Android vs iOS or Others? SMD-OS Security Issues: Generation Y Perception. *International Journal of Technology Diffusion*, *7*(2), 1–18. doi:10.4018/IJTD.2016040101

Susanto, H., Ibrahim, F., Nazmudeen, S. H., Mohiddin, F., & Setiana, D. (2020). Human-Centered Design to Enhance the Usability, Human Factors, and User Experience Within Digital Destructive Ecosystems. In *Global Challenges and Strategic Disruptors in Asian Businesses and Economies* (pp. 76–94). IGI Global.

Susanto, H., Leu, F. Y., Caesarendra, W., Ibrahim, F., Haghi, P. K., Khusni, U., & Glowacz, A. (2020). Managing Cloud Intelligent Systems over Digital Ecosystems: Revealing Emerging App Technology in the Time of the COVID19 Pandemic. *Applied System Innovation*, *3*(3), 37. doi:10.3390/asi3030037

Susanto, H., Yie, L. F., Rosiyadi, D., Basuki, A. I., & Setiana, D. (n.d.). Data Security for Connected Governments and Organisations: Managing Automation and Artificial Intelligence. In Web 2.0 and Cloud Technologies for Implementing Connected Government (pp. 229-251). IGI Global.

Susanto, H., Yie, L. F., Setiana, D., Asih, Y., Yoganingrum, A., Riyanto, S., & Saputra, F. A. (2020). Digital Ecosystem Security Issues for Organizations and Governments: Digital Ethics and Privacy. In Web 2.0 and Cloud Technologies for Implementing Connected Government (pp. 204-228). IGI Global.

Szumski, O. (2018). Cybersecurity best practices among Polish students. *Procedia Computer Science*, *126*, 1271–1280. doi:10.1016/j.procs.2018.08.070

Thakur, K., Qiu, M., Gai, K., & Ali, M. L. (2015). An Investigation on Cyber Security Threats and Security Models. *2015 IEEE 2nd International Conference on Cyber Security and Cloud Computing*, 307-311. 10.1109/CSCloud.2015.71

The International Institute for Strategic Studies. (2015). Evolution of The Cyber Domain: The Implications for National and Global Security. Author.

Tonge, A. M., Kature, S. S., & Chaudhari, S. R. (2013). Cyber security: Challenges for society- literature review. *IOSR Journal of Computer Engineering*, *12*(2), 67–75. www.iosrjournals.org. doi:10.9790/0661-1226775

UNIDIR. (2021, April). *UNIDIR Cyber Policy Portal.* Retrieved from https://unidir.org/cpp/en/states/malaysia

UNIDIR. (2021, April). *UNIDIR Cyber Policy Portal.* Retrieved from https://unidir.org/cpp/en/states/malaysia

Warning of scam syndicate. (2020, August 25). Retrieved April, 29, 2021, from https://borneobulletin.com.bn/warning-of-scam-syndicate-2/

Yie, L. F., Susanto, H., & Setiana, D. (2020). Collaborating Decision Support and Business Intelligence to Enable Government Digital Connectivity. In *Web 2.0 and Cloud Technologies for Implementing Connected Government* (pp. 95–112). IGI Global.

Compilation of References

AAVE. (2021). *The Liquidity Protocol*. Available at https://aave.com/

Abbasi, K., Alam, A., Du, M. A., & Huynh, T. L. D. (2021). FinTech, SME efficiency and national culture: Evidence from OECD countries. *Technological Forecasting and Social Change*, *163*, 120454. Advance online publication. doi:10.1016/j.techfore.2020.120454

Abdullah, N., Redzuan, F., & Daud, N. A. (2020). E-wallet: Factors influencing user acceptance towards cashless society in Malaysia among public universities. *Indonesian Journal of Electrical Engineering and Computer Science*, *20*(1), 67–74. doi:10.11591/ijeecs.v20.i1.pp67-74

Abu, S. T., & Tsuji, M. (2011). The Development of ICT for Envisioning Cloud Computing and Innovation in South Asia. *International Journal of Innovation in the Digital Economy*, *2*(1), 61–72. doi:10.4018/jide.2011010105

Abyan, M. A. (2018). *Konsep Penggunaan Financial Technology dalam Membantu Masyarakat Sub Urban di Indonesia dalam Melakukan Transaksi Finansial*. Research Gate. Retrieved from https://www.researchgate.net/publication/324386435_Konsep_Penggunaan_Financial_Technology_dalam_Membantu_Masyarakat_Sub_Urban_di_Indonesia_dalam_Melakukan_Transaksi_Finansial doi:10.13140/RG.2.2.36402.30404

Acar, O., & Çıtak, Y. E. (2019). FinTech integration process suggestion for banks. *Procedia Computer Science*, *15892019*, 971–978. doi:10.1016/j.procs.2019.09.138

Adam, A. (2017, April 28). Selamat tinggal generasi milenial, selamat datang generasi Z. *Tirto*. Retrieved from https://tirto.id/selamat-tinggal-generasi-milenial-selamat-datang-generasi-z-cnzX

ADB. (2015). *Asia SME Finance Monitor 2014*. Asian Development Bank.

Agrawal, A., Catalini, C., & Goldfarb, A. (2014). The simple economics of crowdfunding, innovation policy and the economy. *Innovation Policy and the Economy*, *14*(1), 63–97. doi:10.1086/674021

Ahad, A. D., Anshari, M., & Razzaq, A. (2017). Domestication of smartphones among adolescents in Brunei darussalam. *International Journal of Cyber Behavior, Psychology and Learning*, *7*(4), 26–39. doi:10.4018/IJCBPL.2017100103

Aji, H. M., Berakon, I., & Md Husin, M. (2020). COVID-19 and e-wallet usage intention: A multigroup analysis between Indonesia and Malaysia. *Cogent Business & Management*, *7*(1), 1804181. doi:10.1080/23311975.2020.1804181

Ajzen, I. (1991). The theory of planned behavior. *Organizational Behavior and Human Decision Processes*, *50*(2), 179–211. doi:10.1016/0749-5978(91)90020-T

Alam, M. M., Awawdeh, A. E., & Muhamad, A. I. Bin. (2021). Using e-wallet for business process development: challenges and prospects in Malaysia. *Business Process Management Journal*.

Ali, I., & Zhuang, J. (2007). *Inclusive Growth Toward a Prosperous Asia: Policy Implications*. Economics and Research Department Working Paper No. 97. Asian Development Bank.

Ali, I., & Son, H. H. (2007). Measuring inclusive growth. *Asian Development Review*, *24*(1), 11–31.

Allen, F., Demirguc-Kunt, A., Klapper, L., & Martinez Peria, M. S. (2016). The foundations of financial inclusion: Understanding ownership and use of formal accounts. *Journal of Financial Intermediation*, *27*(4), 1–30. doi:10.1016/j.jfi.2015.12.003

Al-Mudimigh, A., & Anshari, M. (2020). Financial technology and innovative financial inclusion. In *Financial technology and disruptive innovation in ASEAN* (pp. 119–129). IGI Global.

Ananta, Y., & Hastuti, R. K. (2019, July 17). Tak percaya bunga fintech setinggi langit? Ini buktinya! *CNBC Indonesia*. Retrieved from https://www.cnbcindonesia.com/tech/20190716204353-37-85447/tak-percaya-bunga-fintech-setinggi-langit-ini-buktinya

Andress, J. (2014). *The Basics of Information Security: Understanding the Fundamentals of InfoSec in Theory and Practice*. Syngress.

Andrew, J. V., Ambad, A. S. N., & Tan, K. E. (2019). A Model of Factors Influencing Consumers' Intention to Use e-Wallet System in Malaysia: A Systematic Review. *Malaysian Journal of Business and Economics*, *6*(2), 2289–8018.

Anshari, M., Almunawar, M. N., & Masri, M. (2020a). An overview of financial technology in Indonesia. *Financial technology and disruptive innovation in ASEAN*, 216-224.

Anshari, M. (2020, March). Workforce mapping of fourth industrial revolution: Optimization to identity. *Journal of Physics: Conference Series*, *1477*(7), 072023. doi:10.1088/1742-6596/1477/7/072023

Anshari, M., Almunawar, M. N., & Masri, M. (2020). An overview of financial technology in Indonesia. In M. Anshari, M. N. Almunawar, & M. Masri (Eds.), *Financial technology and disruptive innovation in ASEAN* (pp. 216–224). Information Science Publishing. doi:10.4018/978-1-5225-9183-2.ch012

Anshari, M., Almunawar, M. N., & Masri, M. (2020b). Financial Technology and Disruptive Innovation in Business: Concept and Application. *International Journal of Asian Business and Information Management*, *11*(4), 29–43. doi:10.4018/IJABIM.2020100103

Anshari, M., Almunawar, M. N., & Masri, M. (2022). Financial Technology Ecosystem in Promoting a Healthy Lifestyle. In *Emerging Ecosystem-Centric Business Models for Sustainable Value Creation* (pp. 159–169). IGI Global. doi:10.4018/978-1-7998-4843-1.ch007

Anshari, M., Almunawar, M. N., Masri, M., & Hamdan, M. (2019). Digital marketplace and FinTech to support agriculture sustainability. *Energy Procedia*, *156*, 234–238. doi:10.1016/j.egypro.2018.11.134

Anshari, M., Almunawar, M. N., Masri, M., & Hrdy, M. (2021b). Financial Technology with AI-Enabled and Ethical Challenges. *Society*, 1–7.

Anshari, M., Arine, M. A., Nurhidayah, N., Aziyah, H., & Salleh, M. H. A. (2021a). Factors influencing individual in adopting eWallet. *Journal of Financial Services Marketing*, *26*(1), 10–23. doi:10.105741264-020-00079-5

Antovski, L., & Gusev, M. (2003). *M-Payments*. Paper presented at the 25th International Conference of Information Technology Interfaces, Cavtat, Croatia.

Arjunwadkar, P. Y (2018). *FinTech: The Technology Driving Disruption in the Financial Services*. CRC Press, Taylor & Francis Group Industry.

Arner, D. (2016). *FinTech: Evolution and regulation.* Retrieved from: https://law.unimelb.edu.au/__data/assets/pdf_file/0011/1978256/D-Arner-FinTech-Evolution-Melbourne-June-2016.pdf

Arner, D. W., Barberis, J., & Buckley, R. P. (2015). The evolution of FinTech: A new post-crisis paradigm. *Georgetown Journal of International Law*, *47*, 1271. doi:10.2139srn.2676553

Arslanian, H., & Fischer, F. (2019). The Future of Finance: The Impact of FinTech, AI, and Crypto on Financial Services. Springer International Publishing. doi:10.1007/978-3-030-14533-0

ASEAN. (2015). *Asean Economic Community (AEC).* Jakarta: ASEAN Secretariat. Available at Error! Hyperlink reference not valid.

Aseng, A. C. (2020). Factors influencing generation z intention in using fintech digital payment services. *Cogito Smart Journal*, *6*(2), 155–166. doi:10.31154/cogito.v6i2.260.155-166

Asyifa, D. I. (2020). Exploring Indonesian gen z digital reading issues. In *Conference Proceeding UHAMKA International Conference on English Language Teaching (ELT) and Computer Assisted Language Learning (CALL) (UICELL).* Jakarta: Universitas Muhammadiyah Prof. Dr. HAMKA.

Authority for Info-communications Technology Industry of Brunei Darussalam. (2018). *Content Regulation.* Retrieved from https://www.aiti.gov.bn/SitePages/Content-Regulation.aspx

Autoriti Monetori Brunei Darussalam. (2016). *Brunei Darussalam financial sector blueprint, 2016-2025* [Slides]. AMBD. https://www.ambd.gov.bn/SiteAssets/financial-sector-blueprint/Final%20Sector%20Blueprint%202016%20-%202025%20FINAL.pdf

Au, Y. A., & Kauffman, R. J. (2008). The economics of mobile payments: Understanding stakeholder issues for an emerging financial technology application. *Electronic Commerce Research and Applications*, *7*(2), 141–164. doi:10.1016/j.elerap.2006.12.004

Ayyagari, M., Juarros, P., Peria, M., & Singh, S. (2016). *Access to Finance and Job Growth: Firm-Level Evidence across Developing Countries.* World Bank Policy Research Working Paper 7604.

Babajide, A. A., Adegboye, F. B., & Omankhanlen, A. E. (2015). Financial Inclusion and Economic Growth in Nigeria. *International Journal of Economics and Financial Issues*, *5*(3), 629–637. http: www.econjournals.com

Balan, R. K., Ramasubbu, N., & Tayi, G. K. (2006). *Digital wallet: Requirements and challenges.* Singapore Management University and SUNY at Albany.

Bangladesh Bank. (2019a). *Bangladesh Financial Intelligence Unit (BFIU) report 2019.* Retrieved from https://www.bb.org.bd/bfiu/bfiu_lawguidelist.php

Bangladesh Bank. (2019b). *Bangladesh Mobile Financial (MFS) Regulations.* Retrieved from https://www.bb.org.bd/bfiu/bfiu_lawguidelist.php

Bangladesh Bank. (2021a). *Mobile financial services statistics.* Retrieved from https://www.bb.org.bd/en/index.php/econdata/index

Bangladesh Bank. (2021b). *Overview of financial system of Bangladesh.* Retrieved from https://www.bb.org.bd/fnansys/index.php

Bangladesh Bureau of Statistics. (2014). *Bangladesh: Demographic and health survey 2014.* Retrieved from https://www.dhsprogram.com/pubs/pdf/FR311/FR311.pdf

Bangladesh Security and Exchange Commission. (2015). *Alternative investment rules, 2015*. Retrieved from https://www.sec.gov.bd/slaws/BSEC(Alternative_Investment)_Rules,_2015_22.06.2015.pdf

Bangladesh Telecommunication Regulatory Commission. (2020). *Licenses and Statistics*. Retrieved from http://btrc.gov.bd/license-statistics

Bank Indonesia. (2021). *Archipelago Report*. https://www.bi.go.id/id/publikasi/laporan/Documents/Laporan_Nusantara_April_2021.pdf

Barkhordari, M., Nourollah, Z., Mashayekhi, H., Mashayekhi, Y., & Ahangar, M. (2016). Factors influencing adoption of e-payment systems: An empirical study on Iranian customers. *Information Systems and e-Business Management*, *15*(1), 89–116. doi:10.100710257-016-0311-1

Bartik, A. (2020). *How Are Small Businesses Adjusting To Covid-19? Early Evidence From A Survey*. Nber Working Paper Series, No. 26989. Nber. https://www.nber.org/papers/w26989

Basher, S. A., Hassan, M. K., & Islam, A. M. (2007). Time-varying volatility and equity returns in Bangladesh stock market. *Applied Financial Economics*, *17*(17), 1393–1407. doi:10.1080/09603100600771034

Bassiouni, D., & Hackley, C. (2014). Generation z children's adaptation to digital consumer culture: A critical literature review. *Journal of Customer Behaviour*, *13*(2), 113–133. doi:10.1362/147539214X14024779483591

Bátiz-Lazo, B., & Wood, D. (2002). An historical appraisal of information technology in commercial banking. *Electronic Markets*, *12*(3), 192–205. doi:10.1080/101967802320245965

Beckers, K. (2015). *Pattern and Security Requirements: Engineering-Based Establishment of Security Standards*. Springer. doi:10.1007/978-3-319-16664-3

Belleflamme, P., Lambert, T., & Schwienbacher, A. (2013). Individual crowdfunding practices. *Venture Capital*, *15*(4), 313–333. doi:10.1080/13691066.2013.785151

Belleflamme, P., Lambert, T., & Schwienbacher, A. (2014). Crowdfunding: Tapping the right crowd. *Journal of Business Venturing*, *29*(5), 585–609. doi:10.1016/j.jbusvent.2013.07.003

Bendovschi, A. (2015). Cyber-Attacks – Trends, Patterns and Security Countermeasures. *Procedia Economics and Finance*, *28*, 24–31. doi:10.1016/S2212-5671(15)01077-1

BIBD. (n.d.). *BIBD NEXGEN wallet*. http://www.bibd.com.bn/personal/digitalbanking/nexgen-mobile/

Bidgoli, H. (2006). Handbook of Information Security: Threats, Vulnerability, Prevention, Detection, and Management. John Wiley & Sons Inc.

BIS & FSB. (2017). *FinTech Credit: Market Structure, Business Models and Financial Stability Implications*. Report prepared by a Working Group established by the Committee on the Global Financial System (Bank for International Settlements) and the Financial Stability Board.

Blackmailer receives two-year jail time, one caning. (2020, April 24). Retrieved April 29, 2021, from https://borneobulletin.com.bn/blackmailer-receives-two-year-jail-time-one-caning/

Blakstad, S., & Allen, R. (2018). *FinTech Revolution: Universal Inclusion in the New Financial Ecosystem*. Palgrave Macmillan. doi:10.1007/978-3-319-76014-8

Bofondi, M., & Gobbi, G. (2017). The big promise of FinTech. *European Economy*, (2), 107-119.

Bona, C., Koslow, L., Frantz, R., Nadres, B., & Ratajczak, D. (2020). *How Marketers Can Win with Gen Z and Millennials Post-COVID-19*. https://www.bcg.com/publications/2020/how-marketers-can-win-with-gen-z-millennials-post-covid

Booth, A., & McCawley, P. (Eds.). (1981). *The Indonesian Economy during the Soeharto Era*. Oxford University Press.

Boritz, J. E. (2005). IS Practitioners Views on Core Concepts of Information Integrity. *International Journal of Accounting Information Systems*.

Bottiglia, R., & Pichler, F. (2016). *Crowdfunding for SMEs: A European Perspective*. Palgrave Macmillan Studies in Banking and Financial Institutions, Springer Nature. doi:10.1057/978-1-137-56021-6

BPS - Statistics Indonesia. (2021a, January 21). *Berita resmi statistik no. 7/01/Th.XXIV concerning hasil sensus penduduk 2020*. Jakarta: Statistics Indonesia (BPS).

BPS - Statistics Indonesia. (2021b). *The Indonesian population census 2020 highlights*. A material presentation for United Nations Expert Group Meeting.

BPS. (2018). *Profil Industri Mikro dan Kecil 2017*. Badan Pusat Statistik.

Brandl, B., & Hornuf, L. (2020). Where did FinTechs come from, and where do they go? The transformation of the financial industry in Germany after digitalization. *Frontiers in Artificial Intelligence*, *3*(1), 1–12. doi:10.3389/frai.2020.00008 PMID:33733128

Broadbent, E., Gougoulis, J., Lui, N., Pota, V., & Simons, J. (2017). *Generation Z: Global citizenship survey*. The Varkey Foundation.

BruCERT. (2021). *Services*. Retrieved April 30,2021, from https://www.brucert.org.bn/services

Bruton, Garry, & Khavul, Siegel, & Write. (2015). New Financial Alternatives. In Seeding Entrepreneurship: Microfinance, Crowdfunding, and Peer To Peer Innovations. *Entrepreneurship Theory and Practice*, *39*(1), 9–26.

Buffington, C. (2020). *Measuring the Effect of COVID-19 on US Small Businesss: The Small Business Pulse Survey*. No. CES-20-16, US Census Bureau. https://www.census.gov/library/working-papers/2020/adrm/CES-WP-20-16.html

CAF. (2021). *World Giving Index 2021*. https://www.cafonline.org/about-us/publications/2021-publications/caf-world-giving-index-2021

Carlin, B., Olafsson, A., & Pagel, M. (2017). *Fintech adoption across generations: Financial fitness in the information age (No. w23798)*. National Bureau of Economic Research.

Carney, M. (2017). The promise of FinTech–something new under the sun. In *Speech at Deutsche Bundesbank G20 Conference, by Bank of England Governor Mark Carney*. Retrieved from https://www.fsb.org/wp-content/uploads/The-Promise-of-FinTech-%E2%80%93-Something-New-Under-the-Sun.pdf

Catalyst. (2021, March 2). Generations: Demographic trends in population and workforce (Quick take). *Catalyst*. Retrieved from https://www.catalyst.org/research/generations-demographic-trends-in-population-and-workforce/

Central Research Agency Indonesia. (2020). *Analysis of the Results of the Covid-19 Impact Survey on Business Actors*. https://www.bps.go.id/publication.html?Publikasi%5BtahunJudul%5D=&Publikasi%5BkataKunci%5D=dampak+covid&Publikasi%5BcekJudul%5D=0&yt0=Tampilkan

Chandler, N. (2020, July 27). *How digital wallets work*. HowStuffWorks. https://electronics.howstuffworks.com/gadgets/high-tech-gadgets/digital-wallet.htm

Chang, E., & West, M. (2006). Digital Ecosystems A Next Generation of the Collaborative Environment. *iiWAS, 214*, 3-24.

Chang, Y., Wong, S. F., Lee, H., & Jeong, S. P. (2016, August). What motivates Chinese consumers to adopt FinTech services: a regulatory focus theory. In Proceedings of the 18th annual international conference on electronic commerce: *E*-commerce in smart connected world (pp. 1-3). Academic Press.

ChapmanP. (2019). *Crowfunding*. https://www.elgaronline.com/view/edcoll/9781788979016/14_chapter3.xhtml doi:10.4337/9781788979023.00015

Chappell, G., Harreis, H., Havas, A., Nuzzo, A., Pepanides, T., & Rowshankish, K. (2018). *The lending revolution: How digital credit is changing banks from the inside*. https://www.mckinsey.com/business-functions/risk/our-insights/the-lending-revolution-how-digital-credit-is-changing-banks-from-the-inside

Chemmanur, T. J., Imerman, M. B., Rajaiya, H., & Yu, Q. (2020). Recent Developments in the FinTech Industry. *Journal of Financial Management. Markets and Institutions*, *8*(01), 2040002. doi:10.1142/S2282717X20400022

Chen, L., & Kimura, F. (2020). *E-commerce Connectivity in ASEAN*. Academic Press.

Chen, W., & Chen, X.H. (2021). Enabling Government and Efficient Market in FinTech Innovation-Evidence from China's net loan industry. *International Financial Research*, 27-36. doi:10.16475/j.cnki.1006-1029.2021.03.003

Chen, Y. C. (2020). Look at the comparative advantage of Internet finance from Ant Financial. *Modern Marketing*, *1*, 35-36. doi:10.19932/j.cnki.22-1256/f.2020.01.020

Chen, D., Lou, H., & Van Slyke, C. (2015). Toward an understanding of online lending intentions: Evidence from a survey in China. *Communications of the Association for Information Systems*, *36*(1), 17. doi:10.17705/1CAIS.03617

Chin, W. W. (1998). Issues and opinion on structural equation modeling. *Management Information Systems Quarterly*, (March), vii–xvi.

Choudhury, M., & Goswami, C. (2019). MSME Financing Gaps – Review of Literature for the Period 2005 To 2016. *Journal of Small Business and Entrepreneurship Development*, *7*(2), 50–60. doi:10.15640/jsbed.v7n2a5

Chuchu, F., & Gafur, M. (2018). Cyber Crime in Brunei Darussalam Viewed from Sociological Perspective. *Proceedings of the 7th International Conference on Multidisciplinary Research*, 354-361. 10.5220/0008885103540361

Clarke, I. (2001). Emerging value propositions for M-commerce. *The Journal of Business Strategy*, *18*(2), 133–149.

Coffie, C. P. K., Hongjiang, Z., Mensah, I. A., Kiconco, R., & Simon, A. E. O. (2020). Determinants of FinTech payment services diffusion by SMEs in Sub-Saharan Africa: Evidence from Ghana. *Information Technology for Development*, 1–22. doi:10.1080/02681102.2020.1840324

Cojoianu, T. F., Clark, G. L., Hoepner, A. G. F., Pažitka, V., & Wójcik, D. (2020). Fin vs. tech: Are trust and knowledge creation key ingredients in fintech start-up emergence and financing? *Small Business Economics*. Advance online publication. doi:10.100711187-020-00367-3

Compound Finance. (2021). Available at https://compound.finance

Copperwaite & Leifer. (2015). *Learning Flask Framework*. Packt Publishing Ltd.

CPC Central Committee & The State Council. (2019). *Support Shenzhen construction of socialism with Chinese characteristics the opinions of the demonstration zone*. http://www.gov.cn/zhengce/2019-08/18/content_5422183.htm

CPC Central Committee. (2020). *Proposal of the CPC Central Committee on Formulating the Fourteenth Five-Year Plan for National Economic and Social Development and the Long-Term Goals for the year 2035*. http://www.gov.cn/zhengce/2020-11/03/content_5556991.htm

Croutzet, A., & Dabbous, A. (2021). Do FinTech trigger renewable energy use? Evidence from OECD countries. *Renewable Energy*, *179*, 1608–1617. doi:10.1016/j.renene.2021.07.144

Cumming, D., & Hornuf, L. (2018). The Economics of Crowdfunding. Fintech and the Financing of SMEs and Entrepreneurs: From Crowdfunding to Marketplace Lending. doi:10.1007/978-3-319-66119-3

Cybersecurity and Infrastructure Security Agency (CISA). (2009, May 6). *What is cybersecurity?* Retrieved from https://us-cert.cisa.gov/ncas/tips/ST04-001

CYZone. (2018). *2018-2019 China FinTech Whitepaper.* https://oss.cyzone.cn/2019/0402/1382923a6a7e1b6c875f323f1c3a7b80.pdf

Dam & Lin. (1996). *Cryptography's Role in Securing the Information Society.* Committee to Study National Cryptography Policy, National Research Council.

Davis, F. D. (1989). Perceived usefulness, perceived ease of use, and user acceptance of information technology. *Management Information Systems Quarterly*, *13*(3), 319–340. doi:10.2307/249008

De Sartiges, D., Aparna, B., Justine, T., & Patrick, W. (2020, May 20). *Southeast Asian Consumers Are Driving a Digital Payment Revolution.* Boston Consulting Group (BCG). Retrieved from https://www.bcg.com/publications/2020/southeast-asian-consumers-digital-payment-revolutions

Deloitte, A. E. R. (2015). *SMEs Powering Indonesia's success.* https://www2.deloitte.com/id/en/pages/financial-advisory/articles/smes-powering-indonesia-success-report.html

Deloitte. (2020). *FinTech | On the brink of further disruption.* https://www2.deloitte.com/content/dam/Deloitte/nl/Documents/financial-services/deloitte-nl-fsi-FinTech-report-1.pdf

Demirguc-Kunt, A., Klapper, L., & Singer, D. (2017). Financial Inclusion and Inclusive Growth: A Review of Recent Empirical Evidence. *Financial Inclusion and Inclusive Growth: A Review of Recent Empirical Evidence.*

Demirguc-Kunt, A., Klapper, L., Singer, D., & Van Oudheusden, P. (2017). *The global findex database.* Retrieved from http://documents. worldbank. org/curated/en/187761468179367706/pdf/WPS7255. pdf

Demirgüç-Kunt, A., Klapper, L., Singer, D., Ansar, S., & Hess, J. (2018), The Global Findex Database 2017. International Bank for Reconstruction and Development.

Demirgüç-Kunt, A., Klapper, L., Singer, D., Ansar, S., & Hess, J. (2020). The global Findex Database 2017: Measuring financial inclusion and opportunities to expand access to and use of financial services. *The World Bank Economic Review*, *34*(Supplement_1), S2–S8. Advance online publication. doi:10.1093/wber/lhz013

Dev, S. M. (2006). Financial inclusion: Issues and challenges. *Economic and Political Weekly*, •••, 4310–4313.

Dewi, M. A. (2020). The Impact of FinTech on the Development of Financial Inclusion in MSMEs in East Java. *Gorontalo Accounting Journal*, *3*(2), 68–83. doi:10.32662/gaj.v3i2.973

Dhaka Tribune. (2021). *State-owned venture capital firm Startup Bangladesh sets sail.* Retrieved from https://www.dhakatribune.com/business/economy/2021/04/01/2021

Di Pietro, F. (2019). Deciphering Crowdfunding. In *Disrupting Finance FinTech and Strategy in the 21st Century.* Palgrave Studies in Digital Business & Enabling Technologies.

Diagnostic, C. (2016). *Building Digital Bangladesh: The Way Forward for Digitizing Payments.* Retrieved from https://btca-prod. s3. amazonaws. com/documents/278/english_attachments/BTC-Bangladesh-Diagnostic Web. pdf, 1480177392.

Diamantopoulos, A., & Siguaw, J. A. (2006). Formative versus reflective indicators in organizational measure development: A comparison and empirical illustration. *British Journal of Management, 17*(4), 263–282. doi:10.1111/j.1467-8551.2006.00500.x

Dimock, M. (2019, January 17). *Defining generations: Where millennials end and generation Z begins.* Pew Research Center. Retrieved from https://www.pewresearch.org/fact-tank/2019/01/17/where-millennials-end-and-generation-z-begins/

Ding, X., Ijima, J., & Ho, S. (2004). *Unique features of mobile commerce. Tokyo 152- 8552.* Graduate School of Decision Science and Technology, TITECH.

Dong, J. X. (2020). Analysis of Competitive Advantage of Internet Financial Platform Enterprises Based on Porter's Five Forces Model -- Taking Ant Financial as an Example. *Commercial Economy, 10,* 175-176. doi:10.19905/j.cnki.syjj1982.2020.10.072

Dranev, Y., Frolova, K., & Ochirova, E. (2019). The impact of fintech M&A on stock returns. *Research in International Business and Finance, 48*(February), 353–364. doi:10.1016/j.ribaf.2019.01.012

Drasch, B. J., Schweizer, A., & Urbach, N. (2018). Integrating the 'troublemakers': A taxonomy for cooperation between banks and fintechs. *Journal of Economics and Business, 100*(March), 1–17. doi:10.1016/j.jeconbus.2018.04.002

Drive the Country's Economic Progress. (n.d.). Retrieved from http://www.information

DS Research & AFPI. (2020). Evolving Landscape of FinTech Lending in Indonesia. https://dailysocial.id/research/evolving-landscape-of-FinTech-lending-in-indonesia-2020

DSInnovate. (2021). *Spectrums The Power of E-commerce Spectrums.* https://dailysocial.id/research/the-power-of-e-commerce-spectrums

DSResearch & Bank CIMB Niaga. (2020). *FinTech Report 2020: Maintaining Growth during Pandemic.* https://dailysocial.id/research/FinTech-report-2020

DSResearch & Mandiri Capital Indonesia. (2020). *SME Empowerment.* https://dailysocial.id/research/sme-empowerment-report-2020

DSResearch. (2020). *Evolving Landscape of FinTech Lending in Indonesia 2020.* https://dailysocial.id/research/evolving-landscape-of-FinTech-lending-in-indonesia-2020

Dwidienawati, D., & Gandasari, D. (2018). Understanding Indonesia's generation Z. *International Journal of Engineering & Technology, 7*(3.25), 245-252.

Economic Planning Unit. (2021). *Malaysia Digital Economy Blueprint.* https://www.epu.gov.my/sites/default/files/2021-02 malaysia-digital-economy-blueprint.pdf

Eldridge, D., Nisar, T. M., & Torchia, M. (2019). What impact does equity crowdfunding have on SME innovation and growth? An empirical study. *Small Bus Econ, 56,* 105–120. https://link.springer.com/article/10.1007%2Fs11187-019-00210-4

Emmanuel, C., Otley, D., & Merchant, K. (1990). *Accounting for management control.* Academic Press.

Ericlee, N. M., & Evanson, M. N. (2014). *Effectiveness of Mobile payment services among SMEs: experiences from SMEs in Ongata Rongai Township of Kajiando County in Kenya.* International Research Journal of Business and Management – IRJBM.

Esho, E., & Verhoef, G. (2018). *The Funding Gap and the Financing of Small and Medium Businesses: An Integrated Literature Review and an Agenda.* MPRA Paper No. 90153. University of Johannesburg. Available at: https://mpra.ub.uni muenchen.de/90153/MPRAPaperNo.90153

EU. (2000). *Directive 2000/31/EC of the European Parliament and of the Council of 8 June 2000 on certain legal aspects of information society services, in particular electronic commerce, in the Internal Market ('Directive on electronic commerce')*. Retrieved from https://eur-lex.europa.eu/legal-content/EN/TXT/HTML/?uri=CELEX:52003DC0702&from=EN

Evans, K. (2021, February 4). *Indonesia's 2020 census: A first glimpse*. The Australia-Indonesia Centre (AIC). Retrieved from https://australiaindonesia.com/aic/commentary/ indonesias-2020-census-a-first-glimpse/

EY Global FinTech Index. (2019). *Global FinTech adoption index*. Retrieved from https://www.ey.com/en_gl/ey-global-FinTech-adoption-indexbal

EY. (2019). *Global FinTech adoption index 2019*. https://www.ey.com/en_gl/ey-global-FinTech-adoption-index

Faul, F., Erdfelder, E., Lang, A.-G., & Buchner, A. (2007). G*Power 3. A flexible statistical power analysis program for the social, behavioral, and biomedical sciences. *Behavior Research Methods*, *39*(2), 175–191. doi:10.3758/BF03193146 PMID:17695343

Fenwick, M., McCahery, J. A., & Vermeulen, E. P. M. (2017) *Fintech and the Financing of Entrepreneurs: From Crowdfunding to Marketplace Lending*. TILEC Discussion Paper No. 2017-25, ECGI - Law Working Paper No. 369/2017, Lex Research Topics in Corporate Law & Economics Working Paper No. 2017-3. Available at https://ssrn.com/abstract=2967891 doi:10.2139/ssrn.2967891

Ferrari, R. (2016). FinTech impact on retail banking–from a universal banking model to banking verticalization. In S. Chishti & J. Barberis (Eds.), *The FinTech book: The financial technology handbook for investors, entrepreneurs and visionaries* (pp. 248–252). John Wiley & Sons. doi:10.1002/9781119218906.ch65

Financial Action Task Force (FATF). (2020). *Draft updated Guidance for a risk-based approach to virtual assets and VASPs, FATF/PDG(2020)19/REV1*. Retrieved from https://www.fatf-gafi.org/media/fatf/documents/recommendations/March%202021%20-%20VA%20Guidance%20update%20-%20Sixth%20draft%20-%20Public%20consultation.pdf

Financial Service Authority –Boston Consulting Group. (2020). *How MSMEs & Banking Can Succeed in the Era of Disruption, Economy & Digital, Joint Research*. https://www.ojk.go.id/id/data-dan-statistik/research/prosiding/Documents/Kajian%20Bagaimana%20UMKM%20dan%20Perbankan%20Dapat%20Sukses%20di%20Era%20Disrupsi%20Ekonomi%20dan%20Digital.pdf

Financial Service Authority. (2019). *National Financial Literacy and Inclusion Survey*. https://www.ojk.go.id/id/berita-dan-activities/publikasi/Pages/Survei-Nasional-Literasi-dan-Inclusion-Keuangan-2019.aspx

Financial Service Authority. (2021). *Statistics FinTech Lending*. https://www.ojk.go.id/id/kanal/iknb/data-dan-statistik/FinTech/Pages/Statistik-FinTech-Lending-Periode-April-2021-.aspx#

Financial Stability Board. (2016). *Financial Stability Board agrees 2017 work plan*. https://www.fsb.org/wp-content/uploads/Financial-Stability-Board-agrees-2017-workplan.pdf

Financial Stability Board. (2017). *Financial stability implications from FinTech*. https://www.fsb.org/2017/06/financial-stability-implications-fromFinTech/

Financial Stability Board. (2017). *FinTech credit: Market structure, business models and financial stability implications*. https://www.bis.org/publ/cgfs_fs b1.pdf

Fintech News Malaysia. (2021). *Malaysia FinTech Report 2021*. https://de.statista.com/statistik/studie/id/44591/dokument/fintech-report/

Foley, S., Karlsen, J. R., & Putnins, T. J. (2019). Sex, Drugs, and Bitcoin: How Much Illegal Activity Is Financed through Cryptocurrencies? *Review of Financial Studies*, *32*(5), 1798–1853. doi:10.1093/rfs/hhz015

Forme, S. (2014). *CSS: Basics - Professional*. Sparks Publications.

Foroughi, B., Iranmanesh, M., & Hyun, S. S. (2019). Understanding the determinants of mobile banking continuance usage intention. *Journal of Enterprise Information Management*, *32*(6), 1015–1033. doi:10.1108/JEIM-10-2018-0237

Francis, T., & Hoefel, F. (2018, November 12). *'True Gen': Generation Z and its implications for companies*. Academic Press.

Fry, R., & Parker, K. (2018, November 15). *Early Benchmarks Show 'Post-Millennials' on Track to Be Most Diverse, Best-Educated Generation Yet.* Pew Research Center. Retrieved from https://www.pewresearch.org/social-trends/2018/11/15/early-benchmarks-show-post-millennials-on-track-to-be-most-diverse-best-educated-generation-yet/

Gabor, D., & Brooks, S. (2016). The digital revolution in financial inclusion: International development in the FinTech era. *New Political Economy*, *22*(4), 423–436. doi:10.1080/13563467.2017.1259298

Gade, N. R., & Reddy, U. G. J. (2014). *A Study of Cyber Security Challenges and Its Emerging trends on Latest Technologies*. Retrieved from https://www.researchgate.net/publication/260126665_A_Study_Of_Cyber_Security_Challenges_And_Its_Emerging_Trends_On_Latest_Technologies

Gai, K., Qiu, M., & Sun, X. (2018). A survey on FinTech. *Journal of Network and Computer Applications*, *103*, 262–273. doi:10.1016/j.jnca.2017.10.011

Ganciu, M. R., & Andrei, N. (2019). Using technology acceptance model to adopt Intelligent Banking. *FAIMA Business & Management Journal*, *7*(4), 13–23. https:search.proquest.com/openview/56b6c5848dd1b5891876bc4cae0f856d/1?pq-origsite=gscholar&cbl=2037693

Gomber, P., Koch, J. A., & Siering, M. (2017). Digital Finance and FinTech: Current research and future research directions. *Journal of Business Economics*, *87*(5), 537–580. doi:10.100711573-017-0852-x

Google, Temasek, & Bain & Company. (2019). *e-Conomy SEA 2019: Swipe up and to the right: Southeast Asia's $100 billion internet economy*. Retrieved from https://www.blog.google/documents/47/SEA_Internet_Economy_Report_2019.pdfgov.bn/Publication%20listsPDF/Brunei%20Darussalam%20Newsletter/2020/BDN%20JUL%202020.pdf

Google, Temasek, & Bain. (2019). *e-Conomy SEA report 2019: Swipe up and to the right: Southeast Asia's $100 billion Internet economy*. https://www.thinkwithgoogle.com/intl/en-apac/consumer-insights/consumer-journey/e-conomy-sea-2020-resilient-and-racing-ahead-what-marketers-need-to-know-about-this-years-digital-shifts

Google, Temasek, & Bain. (2020). *e-Conomy SEA report 2020, Resilient and racing ahead — What marketers need to know about this year's digital shifts*. https://www.thinkwithgoogle.com/intl/en-apac/consumer-insights/consumer-journey/e-conomy-sea-2020-resilient-and-racing-ahead-what-marketers-need-to-know-about-this-years-digital-shifts/

Gourinchas, Kalemli-Özcan, Penciakova, & Sander. (2020). *Covid-19 And Sme Failures, Nber Working Paper Series.* National Bureau of Economic Research.

Gourinchas, P., & Kalemli-Özcan, S. (2020). *COVID-19 and business failures.* UC Berkeley. doi:10.3386/w27877

Government Office for Science. (2015). *Fintech futures: the UK as a world leader in financial technologies*. https://www.gov.uk/government/uploads/system/uploads/attachment_data/ file/413095/gs-15-3-fintech-futures

Griffiths, P. (2020). *The FinTech Industry: Crowdfunding in Context*. Advances in Crowdfunding. doi:10.1007/978-3-030-46309-0_11

Gundaniya, N. (2020, February 5). *Everything you need to know about QR code payments.* Digital Finance Solutions, Ewallet Payment System, Wallet App Development. https://www.digipay.guru/blog/everything-you-need-to-know-about-qr-code-payments/

Gupta, P., & Mandhy Tham, T. (2018). *FinTech: The New DNA of Financial Services.* Walter de Gruyter Inc. doi:10.1515/9781547400904

Haas, P., Blohm, I., & Leimeister, J. M. (2014). *An empirical taxonomy of crowdfunding intermediaries.* International conference on information systems, Auckland, New Zealand.

Hadad, M. D. (2010). *Developing a Financial Inclusion Strategy: The Case of Indonesia.* Presentation for the *2010 AFI Global Policy Forum*, Bali.

Haddad, C., & Hornuf, L. (2016). *The Emergence of the Global Fintech Market: Economic and Technological Determinants.* Available at: https://www.researchgate.net/publication/307957382

Hair, J. F., Hult, G. T. M., Ringle, C. M., & Sarstedt, M. (2014). *A Primer on Partial Least Squares Structural Equation Modeling (PLS-SEM).* Sage Publications.

Hair, J. F., Hult, G. T. M., Ringle, C. M., Sarstedt, M., & Thiele, K. O. (2017). Mirror, mirror on the wall: A comparative evaluation of composite-based structural equation modeling methods. *Journal of the Academy of Marketing Science, 45*(5), 616–632. doi:10.100711747-017-0517-x

Halim, N. A. R. A., Hashim, N. F. A., Alek, S. K. A., Asmali, K. N., Rosli, R., & Anshari, M. (2021). BeUsin: Savings and Investment Platform. In Handbook of Research on Innovation and Development of E-Commerce and E-Business in ASEAN (pp. 526-548). IGI Global.

Hamdan, M., & Anshari, M. (2020). Paving the Way for the Development of FinTech Initiatives in ASEAN. In *Financial technology and disruptive innovation in ASEAN* (pp. 80–107). IGI Global. doi:10.4018/978-1-5225-9183-2.ch004

Hamdan, M., Chen, C. K., & Anshari, M. (2020, November). Decision Aid in Budgeting Systems for Small & Medium Enterprises. In *2020 International Conference on Decision Aid Sciences and Application (DASA)* (pp. 253-257). IEEE. 10.1109/DASA51403.2020.9317018

Hamdan, M., Jaidin, J. H., Fithriyah, M., & Anshari, M. (2020, December). E-Learning in Time of Covid-19 Pandemic: Challenges & Experiences. In *2020 Sixth International Conference on e-Learning (econf)* (pp. 12-16). IEEE. 10.1109/econf51404.2020.9385507

Harris, P. (2018). *What Is HTML Code?* Power Kids Press.

Hasmawati, F., Samiha, Y. T., Razzaq, A., & Anshari, M. (2020). Understanding Nomophobia Among Digital Natives: Characteristics And Challenges. *Journal of Critical Reviews, 7*(13), 122–131.

Hayduk, L. A., & Littvay, L. (2012). Should researchers use single indicators, best indicators, or multiple indicators in structural equation models? *BMC Medical Research Methodology, 12*(159), 159. doi:10.1186/1471-2288-12-159 PMID:23088287

Hazair, H. (2018, November 18). *Local e-wallet BruPay banks on millennials, merchant-friendly features.* The Scoop. https://thescoop.co/2018/11/14/local-e-wallet-brupay-banks-on-millennials-merchant-friendly-features/

Hazik, M., & Hassnian, A. (2019). Blockchain, Fintech, and Islamic Finance. In Building the Future in the New Islamic Digital Economy. Publisher de Gruyter.

Henseler, J., Ringle, C. M., & Sarstedt, M. (2015). A new criterion for assessing discriminant validity in variance-based structural equation modeling. *Journal of the Academy of Marketing Science*, *43*(1), 115–135. doi:10.100711747-014-0403-8

Hidayat, S. E., & Rafiki, A. (2021). Comparative analysis of customers' awareness toward CSR practices of Islamic banks: Bahrain vs Saudi Arabia. Social Responsibility Journal. doi:10.1108/SRJ-05-2020-0174

Hill, H. (Ed.). (1994). *Indonesia's New Order: The Dynamics of Socio-economic Transformation*. Allen & Unwin.

Hill, J. (2018). FinTech in a Global Setting. In J. Hill (Ed.), *FinTech and the Remaking of Financial Institutions* (pp. 269–283). Academic Press. doi:10.1016/B978-0-12-813497-9.00014-7

HM Revenue & Customs. (2020). *Guidance Businesses selling goods in the UK using online marketplaces*. Retrieved from https://www.gov.uk/guidance/vat-overseas-businesses-using-an-online-marketplace-to-sell-goods-in-the-uk

Hong, K. S., Chi, Y. P., Chao, L. R., & Tang, J. H. (2003). An integrated system theory of information security management. *Information Management & Computer Security*, *11*(5), 243–248. doi:10.1108/09685220310500153

Hornuf, L., Klus, M. F., Lohwasser, T. S., & Schwienbacher, A. (2020). How do banks interact with FinTech startups? *Small Business Economics*, 1–22.

Hornuf, L., & Schwienbacher, A. (2017). Should Securities Regulation Promote Equity Crowdfunding? *Small Business Economics*, *49*(3), 579–593. doi:10.100711187-017-9839-9

Huang, Y. M. (2020). Evaluation on the effect of strategic transformation of Kingdee under the background of cloud era. *Modern Business*, *28*, 135–137.

Hunton, P. (2011). A rigorous approach to formalising the technical investigation stages of cybercrime and criminality within a UK enforcement environment. *Digital Investigation*, *7*(3-4), 105–113. doi:10.1016/j.diin.2011.01.002

Hwang, S.-S. (2014). *What We Need in the FinTech Craze*. http://www.lgcnsblog.com/technology/what-we-need-in-the-fiFinTech-craze/

Hwangbo, Y. (2004). Establishing Trusted Third Party for Taxing Global Electronic Commerce: System Architecture of Global Electronic Tax Invoice (GETI). *International Review of Public Administration*, *9*(1), 33–40. doi:10.1080/12294659.2004.10805037

Hwangbo, Y. H., & Kifle, H. (2011). Overcoming barrier to move forward to Transactional Stage of e-Government for Brunei Darussalam. *CSPS Strategy and Policy Journal*, *2*, 73–90.

IDC. (2020). *China's enterprise application SaaS market will outpace the trend*. https://www.idc.com/url.do?url=/getdoc.jsp?containerId=prCHC47172620&position=1&transactionId=111279551&term=5Lit5Zu95LyB5Lia57qn5bqU55So77yIRUHvvIlTYWFT5biC5Zy66Lef6Liq56CU56m25oql5ZGK&page=1&perPage=25

Idris, M. (2021, January 22). Generasi Z dan Milenial Dominasi Jumlah Penduduk Indonesia. *Kompas*. Retrieved from https://money.kompas.com/read/2021/01/22/145001126/generasi-z-dan-milenial-dominasi-jumlah-penduduk-indonesia?page=all

IFC. (2017). *MSME Finance Gap*. International Finance Corporation. Available at: https://www.smefinanceforum.org/sites/default/files/Data%20Sites%20downloads/MSME%20Report.pdf

ILO. (2020). *ILO Monitor: COVID-19 and the world of work*. https://gisanddata.maps.arcgis.com/apps/opsdashboard/index.html#/bda7594740fd40299423467b48e9ecf6

Imerman, M. B., & Fabozzi, F. J. (2020). Cashing in on innovation: A taxonomy of FinTech. *Journal of Asset Management*, *21*(3), 167–177. doi:10.105741260-020-00163-4

IMF Policy Paper. (2019). *FinTech the experience so far*. Retrieved from https://www.imf.org/en/Publications/Policy-Papers/Issues/2019/06/27/FinTech-The-Experience-So-Far-47056

Intan, N. (2021, June 25). OJK ungkap tujuh ciri pinjol ilegal dan rentenir online. *Republika*. Retrieved from https://www.republika.co.id/berita/qv8klw423/ojk-ungkap-tujuh-ciri-pinjol-ilegal-dan-rentenir-emonlineem

International Data Corporation. (2020). *DC FutureScape: Worldwide Digital Transformation 2021 Predictions*. https://www.idc.com/getdoc.jsp?containerId=US46880818

International Finance Corporation. (2017). *Assessment Of The Shortfalls And Opportunities In Financing Micro, Small And Medium Enterprises In Emerging Markets*. https://www.ifc.org/wps/wcm/connect/03522e90-a13d-4a02-87cd-9ee9a297b311/121264-WP-PUBLIC- MSMEReportFINAL.pdf?MOD=AJPERES&CVID=m5SwAQA

International Monetary Fund. (2017). *FinTech and financial services: initial considerations*. https://www.imf.org/~/media/Files/Publications/SDN/2017/sdn1705.ashx

International Monetary Fund. (2021). *World Economic Outlook Reports April 2021*. https://www.imf.org/en/publications/weo

International Telecommunication Union. (2015). *Global Cybersecurity Index & Cyberwellness Profiles*. Retrieved from https://www.itu.int/dms_pub/itu-d/opb/str/D-STR-SECU-2015-PDF-E.pdf

iResearch. (2020). *Dawn - 2020 China FinTech industry development research report*. http://report.iresearch.cn/report/202011/3687.shtml

Isnaini, I. H. (2021, June 24). Awas! Rentenir online gentayangan, kenali 7 ciri-cirinya. *SindoNews*. Retrieved from https://ekbis.sindonews.com/read/464934/178/awas-rentenir-online-gentayangan-kenali-7-ciri-cirinya-1624503982

ITPSS. (2018, July 17). *Career in Cybersecurity*. Retrieved fromhttps://www.itpss.com/News/2018/17072018.html

ITPSS. (2020). *Training*. Retrieved April 30,2021, from https://itpss.com/TrainingOverview.html

J&T Express. (2020). *Understanding the e-Commerce Tax Regulation in Southeast Asia*. Retrieved from https://www.jtexpress.sg/insights/understanding-the-ecommerce-tax-regulations-in-south-east-asia-2020

James, K. (2018, May 15). *Progresif launches brunei's first mobilwallet*. The World News. https://theworldnews.net/bn-news/progresif-launches-brunei-s-first-mobile-wallet

Jennifer, S. (2021). *Why Fintech Battles Ahead Are About More Than Banks*. https://www.bloomberg.com/news/articles/2021-03-02/why-fintech-battles-ahead-are-about-more-than-banks-quicktake

Jinjarak, Y., & Wignaraja, G. (2016). An Empirical Assessment of the Export—Financial Constraint Relationship: How Different are Small and Medium Enterprises? *World Development*, *79*, 152–163. doi:10.1016/j.worlddev.2015.11.012

Johng, Y. (2008). IBM System i Security: Protecting i5/OS Data with Encryption. IBM.

Joseph, S. (2019). *The Opportunity for Fintech in Indonesia's SME Financing Gap*. Technology. Available at https://www.brinknews.com/19646/

Junida, A. I. (2021, January 21). BPS: Penduduk Indonesia didominasi generasi Z dan milenial. *Antaranews*. Retrieved from https://www.antaranews.com/berita/1960808/bps-penduduk-indonesia-didominasi-generasi-z-dan-milenial

Juvo. (2021). *Building Financial Identities for 4 Billion People Globally*. Available at https://www.juvo.com/

Kang, J. (2018). Mobile payment in Fintech environment: trends, security challenges, and services. *Human-Centric Computing and Information Sciences*, *8*(1), 32. doi:10.1186/s13673-018-0155-4

Karashchuk, O. S., Mayorova, E. A., Nikishin, A. F., & Kornilova, O. V. (2020). The method for determining time-generation range. *SAGE Open*, *10*(October-December), 1–8. doi:10.1177/2158244020968082

Karavellas, T. (2013). *Towards a Universal Mobile Payments System* (Master's thesis).

Kark, K., Briggs, B., & Terzioglu, A. (2019). The future of work in technology. *Deloitte Insight*. https://www2.deloitte.com/us/en/insights/focus/technology-and-the-future-of-work/tech-leaders-reimagining-work-workforce-workplace.html

Kata Data. (2021). *Only 12.5% of MSMEs in Indonesia are Immune from the Covid-19 Pandemic*. https://katadata.co.id/agustiyanti/finansial/605d9f635fdf7/hanya-12-5-umkm-di-indonesia-yang-kebal-dari-pandemi-covid-19

Katz, J., & Lindell, Y. (2007). *Introduction to Modern Cryptography: Priniciples and Protocols*. Chapman and Hall / CRC. doi:10.1201/9781420010756

Kim & Mirusmonov. (2010). *An empirical examination of factors influencing the intention to use mobile payment*. doi:10.1016/j.chb.2009.10.013

Kim, C., Tao, W., Shin, N., & Kim, K.-S. (2010). An empirical study of customers' perceptions of security and trust in e-payment systems. *Electronic Commerce Research and Applications*, *9*(1), 84–95. doi:10.1016/j.elerap.2009.04.014

Kim, Y., Choi, J., Park, Y. J., & Yeon, J. (2016). The adoption of mobile payment services for "Fintech". *International Journal of Applied Engineering Research: IJAER*, *11*(2), 1058–1061.

Kirui, O. K., Okello, J. J., Nyikal, R. A., & Njiraini, G. W. (2013). Impact of mobile phone-based money transfer services in agriculture: Evidence from Kenya. *Zeitschrift für Ausländische Landwirtschaft*, *52*(2), 141–162. doi:10.4018/jictrda.2012010101

Klassen, R. D., & Whybark, D. C. (1999). Environmental management in operations: The selection of environmental technologies. *Decision Sciences*, *30*(3), 601–631. doi:10.1111/j.1540-5915.1999.tb00900.x

Knudsen, L. R., & Robshaw, M. (2011). *The Block Cipher Companion*. Springer. doi:10.1007/978-3-642-17342-4

Kock, N., & Lynn, G. (2012). Lateral collinearity and misleading results in variance-based SEM: An illustration and recommendations. *Journal of the Association for Information Systems*, *13*(7), 546–580. doi:10.17705/1jais.00302

Kontan. (2021). *Bank Indonesia urges banks to lower loan interest rates and extend MSE credit*. https://keuangan.kontan.co.id/news/bank-indonesia-imbau-perbankan-terurunkan-bunga-kredit-dan-salurkan-kredit-umkm

Kortjan, N. (2013). *A Cyber Security Awareness and Education Framework for South Africa*. Retrieved from https://core.ac.uk/download/pdf/145053774.pdf

KPMG. (2019). *The pulse of FinTech 2018: biannual global analysis of investment in FinTech*. https://assets.kpmg/content/dam/kpmg/xx/pdf/2019/02/the-pulse-of-FinTech-2018.pdf

Kritzinger, E., & Smith, E. (2008). Information security management: An information security retrieval and awareness model for industry. *Journal of Computer Security*, *27*(5-6), 224–231. doi:10.1016/j.cose.2008.05.006

Krugman, P. (1994). The Myth of Asia's Miracle. *Foreign Affairs*, *73*(November-December), 62–78. doi:10.2307/20046929

Kumar, R. (2017). *Targeted SME Financing and Employment Effects: What Do We Know and What Can We Do Differently?* Jobs Working Paper No.3. Washington, DC: World Bank.

Ky, S., Rugemintwari, C., & Sauviat, A. (2019). *Is FinTech good for bank performance? The Case of Mobile Money in the East African Community*. Hal-02155077.

Lacasse, R. M., Lambert, B. A., Osmani, E., Couture, C., Roy, N., Sylvain, J., & Nadeau, F. (2016). A Digital Tsunami: Fintech and Crowdfunding. *Proceedings of International Scientific Conference on Digital Intelligence.*

Lai, H., Sun, S. R., & Sun, N. (2021). Enterprise risk research based on FinTech listed companies. *Science Technology and Industry, 21*(04), 145–149.

Lancaster, L. C., & Stillman, D. (2009). *When generations collide: Who they are. Why they clash. How to solve the generational puzzle at work.* HarperCollins.

Laucereno, S. F. (2021, June 29). Awas terjebak! Catat nih ciri-ciri rentenir online. *Detik.* Retrieved from https://finance.detik.com/fintech/d-5623866/awas-terjebak-catat-nih-ciri-ciri-rentenir-online

Lauer, J. (2017). Creditworthy: A History of Consumer Surveillance and Financial Identity in America. Columbia Studies in the History of U.S. Capitalism.

Lay, R. (2018). *Sentinel Chain - The World's First Global Marketplace for Financial Inclusion Services.* Available at https://infocorp.io/Cow-Token-A-Local-Blockchain-UseCase.pdf

Leboeuf, G., & Schwienbacher, A. (2017). *Crowdfunding as a New Financing Tool in The Economics of Crowdfunding Startups, Portals, and Investor Behavior.* Springer Nature.

Lee & Hwangbo. (n.d.). Cyberconsumption Taxes and Electronic Collection Systems: A Canonical Consumer-Delivered Sales Tax. *International Journal of Electronic Commerce, 4*(2), 61-82.

Lee, I., & Shin, Y. J. (2018). FinTech: ecosystem, business models, investment decisions, and challenges. *Business Horizons, 61*, 35–46. .09.003 doi:10.1016/j.bushor.2017

Lee, C. C., Li, X. R., Yu, C. H., & Zhao, J. S. (2021). Does FinTech innovation improve bank efficiency? Evidence from China's banking industry. *International Review of Economics & Finance, 74*, 468–483.

Lee, I., & Shin, Y. J. (2018). FinTech: Ecosystem, business models, investment decisions, and challenges. *Business Horizons, 61*(1), 35–46. doi:10.1016/j.bushor.2017.09.003

Lee, S. H., & Lee, D. W. (2015). FinTech-conversions of finance industry based on ICT. *Journal of the Korea Convergence Society, 6*(3), 97–102. doi:10.15207/JKCS.2015.6.3.097

Leong, K., & Sung, A. (2018). FinTech (Financial Technology): What is It and How to Use Technologies to Create Business Value in Fintech Way? *International Journal of Innovation, Management and Technology, 9*(2), 74–78. doi:10.18178/ijimt.2018.9.2.791

Lestari, N. P. M. (2019). Pemahaman generasi milenial berinvestasi di peer to peer lending. *Jurnal Manajemen Bisnis, 16*(3), 17–30. doi:10.38043/jmb.v16i3.2229

Leu, F. Y., Ko, C. Y., Lin, Y. C., Susanto, H., & Yu, H. C. (2017). Fall Detection and Motion Classification by Using Decision Tree on Mobile Phone. In Smart Sensors Networks (pp. 205-237). doi:10.1016/B978-0-12-809859-2.00013-9

Leu, F. Y., Liu, C. Y., Liu, J. C., Jiang, F. C., & Susanto, H. (2015). S-PMIPv6: An intra-LMA model for IPv6 mobility. *Journal of Network and Computer Applications, 58*, 180–191. doi:10.1016/j.jnca.2015.08.014

Li, F. (2017). Research on Customs Administration to Cross-Border Electronic Commerce Importation under Taxation Measurement. *American Journal of Industrial and Business Management, 7*(5). doi:10.4236/ajibm.2017.75043

Li, W., Badr, Y., & Biennier, F. (2012). Digital ecosystems. *Proceedings of the International Conference on Management of Emergent Digital EcoSystems - MEDES'12,* 118–119. https://www.researchgate.net/publication/262330068_Digital_ecosystems_Challenges_and_prospects

Lie & Bert. (1999). *Cascading Style Sheets, designing for the Web.* Addison Wesley.

Lightbourne, J. (2017). Algorithms & Fiduciaries: Existing and proposed regulatory approaches to artificially intelligent financial Planners. *Duke Law Journal*, *67*(3), 651–679.

Lim, A. S. (2007). Inter-consortia battles in mobile payments standardization. *Electronic Commerce Research and Applications*, *2*(2), 15–23.

Lin, M., & Viswanathan, S. (2015). Home bias in online investments: An empirical study of an online crowdfunding market. *Management Science*, *62*(5), 1393–1414. doi:10.1287/mnsc.2015.2206

Liu, J. C., Leu, F. Y., Lin, G. L., & Susanto, H. (2018). An MFCC-based text-independent speaker identification system for access control. *Concurrency and Computation*, *30*(2), e4255.

Liu, Y., & Tsyvinski, A. (2021). Risks and Returns of Cryptocurrency. *Review of Financial Studies*, *34*(6), 2689–2727. doi:10.1093/rfs/hhaa113

Livingstone, S., & Helsper, E. J. (2007). Taking risks when communicating on the Internet: The role of offline social-psychological factors in young people's vulnerability to online risks. *Information Communication & Society*, *2001*(3), 619-644. doi:10.1080/13691180701657998

Loukas, G., & Oke, G. (2010). Protection Against Denial of Service Attacks: A Survey. *The Computer Journal*, *53*(7), 1020–1037. doi:10.1093/comjnl/bxp078

Lyman, T., & Lauer, K. (2015, March 10). *What is digital financial inclusion and why does it matter?* Consultative Group to Assist the Poor (CGAP). Retrieved from https://www.cgap.org/blog/what-digital-financial-inclusion-and-why-does-it-matter

Lynn, T., Mooney, J. G., Rosati, P., & Cummins, M. (2019). Disrupting Finance: FinTech and Strategy in the 21st Century. Palgrave Studies in Digital Business & Enabling Technologies, 121-130. doi:10.1007/978-3-030-02330-0_8

Lyons, A. C., Kass-Hanna, J., & Fava, A. (2021). FinTech development and savings, borrowing, and remittances: A comparative study of emerging economies. *Emerging Markets Review.* doi:10.1016/j.ememar.2021.100842

Lyu, Q. (2014). Seven unsuccessful cases of Internet finance. *China Internet Weekly*, *4*, 26–29.

Mackenzie, A. (2015). The FinTech revolution. *London Business School Review*, *26*(3), 50–53. doi:10.1111/2057-1615.12059

Maier, E. (2016). Supply and demand on crowdlending platforms: Connecting small and medium-sized enterprise borrowers and consumer investors. *Journal of Retailing and Consumer Services*, *33*, 143–153. doi:10.1016/j.jretconser.2016.08.004

Mallat, N. (2007). Exploring consumer adoption of mobile payments – A qualitative study. *The Journal of Strategic Information Systems*, *16*(4), 413–432. doi:10.1016/j.jsis.2007.08.001

Mallat, N., Rossi, M., & Tuunainen, V. K. (2006). The impact of use situation and mobility on the acceptance of mobile ticketing services. *Proceedings of the 39th Hawaii international conference on system sciences.* 10.1109/HICSS.2006.472

Manyika, J., Lund, S., Singer, M., White, O., & Berry, C. (2016). *Digital finance for all: Powering inclusive growth in emerging economies.* McKinsey Global Institute.

Marini, Linawati, & Putra. (2020). The Role of FinTech on Financial Inclusion in South Tangerang MSMEs. *Sustainability: Journal of Management and Journal of Accounting, 5*(2), 91-104. doi:10.32493/keberlanjutan.v5i2.y2020.p91-104

Martin, C. A., & Tulgan, B. (2006). *Managing the generation mix: From urgency to opportunity.* HRD Press.

Ma, Y., & Liu, D. (2017). Introduction to the special issue on Crowdfunding and FinTech. *Financial Innovation*, *3*(1), 8. doi:10.118640854-017-0058-9

McCann, F., & Myers, S. (2020). *COVID-19 and the transmission of shocks through domestic supply chains. Financial Stability Notes, No. 3*. Central Bank of Ireland.

McCrindle, M., & Fell, A. (2019). *Understanding generation Z: Recruiting, training and leading the next generation.* McCrindle Research Pty Ltd.

McDougal, A. (2018). *Fun with Flowcharts*. The Rosen Publishing Group, Inc.

McKinsey. (2016). *What's next for China's booming FinTech sector?* https://www.mckinsey.com/industries/financial-services/our-insights/whats-nextfor-chinas-booming-FinTech-sector

McNally, C. A. (2020). *The DCEP: Developing the Globe's First Major Central Bank Digital Currency*. Retrieved from https://www.chinausfocus.com/finance-economy/the-dcep-developing-the-globes-first-major-central-bank-digital-currency

McWaters, R. (2015). *The future of financial services: How disruptive innovations are reshaping the way financial services are structured, provisioned and consumed.* World Economic Forum.

Metwaly, A. H. W., & Metwaly, A. W. (2021). *Stake Hodler Capitalism: Blockchain and DeFi*. Decentralized Finance.

Mohd Thas Thaker, M. A., Allah Pitchay, A. B., Mohd Thas Thaker, H. B., & Amin, M. F. B. (2019). Factors influencing consumers' adoption of Islamic mobile banking services in Malaysia: An approach of partial least squares (PLS). *Journal of Islamic Marketing*, *10*(4), 1037–1056. doi:10.1108/JIMA-04-2018-0065

Mollick, E. R. (2014). The Dynamics of Crowdfunding: An Exploratory Study. *Journal of Business Venturing*, *29*(1), 1–16. doi:10.1016/j.jbusvent.2013.06.005

Morgan, P. J., & Trinh, L. Q. (2019). *Fintech and Financial Literacy in the LAO PDR*. ADBI Working Paper Series No.933. Asian Development Bank Institute.

Mujeri, M. K., & Azam, S. E. (2018). *Interoperability of Digital Finance in Bangladesh: Challenges and Taking-Off Options*. Retrieved from http://inm.org.bd/wp-content/uploads/2018/06/Working-Paper-54.pdf

Mukhtar, H. (2018). *KriptografiuntukKeamanan Data*. Deepublish Publisher.

Mulasiwi, M. C., & Julialevi, O. K. (2020). Optimization of Financial Technology (FinTech) on Increasing Financial Literacy and Inclusion of Purwokerto Medium Enterprises. *Performance*, *27*(1), 12–20. doi:10.20884/1.jp.2020.27.1.2284

Mulyani, M. A., Razzaq, A., Ridho, S. L. Z., & Anshari, M. (2019b, October). Smartphone and Mobile Learning to Support Experiential Learning. In *2019 International Conference on Electrical Engineering and Computer Science (ICECOS)* (pp. 6-9). IEEE. 10.1109/ICECOS47637.2019.8984501

Mulyani, M. A., Razzaq, A., Sumardi, W. H., & Anshari, M. (2019a, August). Smartphone Adoption in Mobile Learning Scenario. In *2019 International Conference on Information Management and Technology (ICIMTech)* (Vol. 1, pp. 208-211). IEEE. 10.1109/ICIMTech.2019.8843755

Musari, K. (2021, June 23). Ketika ekonom rabani 'generasi z' Jawa Timur menyambut era digital. *Kempalan*. Retrieved from https://kempalan.com/2021/06/23/ketika-ekonom-rabani-generasi-z-jawa-timur-menyambut-era-digital/

Muthukannan, P., Tan, B., Tan, F. T. C., & Leong, C. (2021). Novel mechanisms of scalability of financial services in an emerging market context: Insights from Indonesian FinTech Ecosystem. *International Journal of Information Management*, *61*. doi:10.1016/j.ijinfomgt.2021.102403

Muzdalifa, I., Rahma, I. A., & Novalia, B. G. (2018). The Role of FinTech in Improving Financial Inclusion in MSMEs in Indonesia (Islamic Finance Approach). *Home, 3*(1). Advance online publication. doi:10.30651/jms.v3i1.1618

Naik, G. S. (2019). *Mastering Python Scripting for System Administrators*. Packt.

Nakamoto, S. (2008). *Bitcoin: A Peer-to-Peer Electronic Cash System*. Retrieved from https://bitcoin.org/bitcoin.pdf

National Bureau of Statistics. (2020). *Zhang Min, a statistician from the trade and foreign economy department of the National Bureau of Statistics, interprets October's retail sales data*. http://www.stats.gov.cn/tjsj/sjjd/202011/t20201116_1803215.html

National Cyber Security Agency (NACSA). (2021, April 27). *Malaysian Cyber Laws*. Retrieved from https://www.nacsa.gov.my/legal.php

National cyber security agency begins operations. (2020, October 13). Retrieved January 20, 2021, from https://thescoop.co/2020/10/13/national-cyber-security-agency-begins-operations/

National cyber security agency to be formed, says MTIC minister. (2020, January 10). Retrieved from https://thescoop.co/2020/01/10/national-cyber-security-agency-to-be-formed-says-mtic-minister/

National Institute of Standards and Technology. (2012). *Cyber Threat*. Retrieved from https://csrc.nist.gov/glossary/term/Cyber_Threat

Nazarov, M. A. (2019). *Digital Economy: Russian Taxation Issues*. Retrieved from https://www.elibrary.ru/item.asp?id=39181878

Net threat: Morphing pictures for revenge. (2015, July 8,). Retrieved April 29, 2021, from https://timesofindia.indiatimes.com/city/chandigarh/Net-threat-Morphing-pictures-forrevenge/articleshow/47981141.cms

Nexus Mutual. (2021). *Get covered against smart contract failure & exchange hacks*. Available at https://nexusmutual.io/

Ng, A. W., & Kwok, B. K. B. (2017). Emergence of FinTech and cybersecurity in a global financial center: strategic approach by a regulator. *Financial Regulation and Compliance, 25*(4), 422–434. doi:10.1108/JFRC-01-2017-0013

Ng-Kruelle, G., Swatman, P. A., Rebme, D. S., & Hampe, J. F. (2002). The price of convenience. Privacy and mobile commerce. *Quarterly Journal of Electronic Commerce, 3*(3), 273–285.

Nguyen, C. V., Ali, M. M., & Islam, A. M. (2011). *The current state of the financial sector of Bangladesh: An analysis*. AIUB Bus Working Paper Series, No 2011-03. Retrieved from https://core.ac.uk/download/pdf/6323449.pdf

Nguyen, T. A. N. (2017). Financing Constraints on SMEs in Emerging Markets: Does Financial Literacy Matter? *Review of Socio-Economic Perspectives, 2*(2), 53–65.

Nicoletti, B. (2017). *The Future of FinTech*. Springer International Publishing. doi:10.1007/978-3-319-51415-4

North, D. C. (1989). Institutions and Economic Growth. *World Development, 17*(9), 1319–1332.

Nurohman, Y. A., Kusuma, M., & Narulitasari, D. (2021). Fintech, Financial Inclusion, and Sustainability: A Quantitative Approach of Muslims SMEs. *International Journal of Islamic Business Ethics, 6*(1), 54–67. doi:10.30659/ijibe.6.1.54-67

Nur, T., & Panggabean, R. R. (2021). Factors influencing the adoption of mobile payment method among generation z: The extended utaut approach. *Journal of Accounting Research, Organization, and Economics, 4*(1), 14–28.

Obe, O. O., & Balogu, V. F. (2007). Practice, trends and challenges of mobile commerce in Nigeria. *Information Technology Journal, 6*(3), 448–456. doi:10.3923/itj.2007.448.456

Oblinger, D., Oblinger, J. L., & Lippincott, J. K. (2005). *Educating the net generation.* Brockport Bookshelf. Retrieved from https://digitalcommons.brockport.edu/bookshelf/272

Oblinger, D. G., & Oblinger, J. L. (Eds.). (2005). *Educating the net generation.* Educause.

OECD. (1997). *Dismantling the Barriers to Global Electronic Commerce, Turku (Finland).* Retrieved from https://www.oecd-ilibrary.org/science-and-technology/dismantling-the-barriers-to-global-electronic-commerce-turku-finland_236647320075

OECD. (1998). *OECD Ministerial Conference on global electronic commerce.* Retrieved from https://cordis.europa.eu/event/id/10900-oecd-ministerial-conference-on-global-electronic-commerce

OECD. (2001). *Consumption Tax Aspects of Electronic Commerce.* Retrieved from https://www.oecd.org/tax/consumption/Taxation%20and%20eCommerce%202001.pdf

OECD. (2010). *The G-20 Toronto Summit Declaration June 26 – 27, 2010.* Toronto: G20.

OECD. (2020). OECD Economic Outlook. OECD Publishing. doi:10.1787/0d1d1e2e-en

Office of the CPC Central Committee & The State Council. (2019). *The Implementation Plan for the Pilot Comprehensive Reform of Shenzhen Pilot Demonstration Zone for Building Socialism with Chinese Characteristics (2020-2025).* http://www.gov.cn/zhengce/2020-10/11/content_5550408.htm

Oh, E. Y., & Rosenkranz, P. (2020). *Determinants of Peer-to-Peer Lending Expansion: The Roles of Financial Development and Financial Literacy.* ADB Economics Working Paper Series, No.613. Manila: Asian Development Bank.

OJK. (2020). *Perkembangan Fintech Lending [Development of fintech lending]. Department Pengawasan IKNB 2A.* Otoritas Jasa Keuangan.

Okutan, A., & Cebi, P. D. Y. (2019). A Framework for Cyber Crime Investigation. *Procedia Computer Science, 158,* 287–294. doi:10.1016/j.procs.2019.09.054

Omarini, A. E. (2018). *FinTech and the future of the payment landscape: the mobile wallet ecosystem. A challenge for retail banks?* Academic Press.

Ondrus, J., & Pigneur, Y. (2006). Towards a holistic analysis of mobile payments: A multiple perspectives approach. *Electronic Commerce Research and Applications, 5*(3), 246–257. doi:10.1016/j.elerap.2005.09.003

Ouyang, L. (2021). Opportunities and challenges of FinTech innovation. *Economic Research Guide, 464,* 53–55.

Ozili, P. K. (2018). Impact of digital finance on financial inclusion and stability. *Borsa Istanbul Review, 18*(4), 329–340. doi:10.1016/j.bir.2017.12.003

Papis-Almansa, M. (2019). VAT and electronic commerce: the new rules as a means for simplification, combatting fraud and creating a more level playing field? *ERA Forum, 20,* 220-221. doi: 10.100712027-019-00575-9

Parker, K., & Igielnik, R. (2020, May 14). *On the cusp of adulthood and facing an uncertain future: what we know about gen Z so far.* Pew Research Center. Retrieved from https://www.pewresearch.org/social-trends/2020/05/14/on-the-cusp-of-adulthood-and-facing-an -uncertain-future-what-we-know-about-gen-z-so-far-2/

Patwardhan, A., Singleton, K., & Schmitz, K. (2018). *Financial Inclusion in the Digital Age. CreditEase.* International Finance Corporation, the Stanford Graduate School of Business. https://responsiblefinanceforum.org/wp-content/uploads/2018/03/FinancialInclusionintheDigitalAge.pdf

PBOC. (2020). *The Opinions on Financial Support for the Development of the Greater Bay Area.* http://www.pbc.gov.cn/goutongjiaoliu/113456/113469/4023428/index.html

People's Bank of China. (2017). *The People's Bank of China set up a FinTech Committee.* http://www.pbc.gov.cn/goutongjiaoliu/113456/113469/3307529/index.html

People's Bank of China. (2019). *The People's Bank of China has launched a pilot program to regulate FinTech innovation.* http://www.pbc.gov.cn/goutongjiaoliu/113456/113469/3933971/index.html

People's Bank of China. (2019). *The People's Bank of China issued the Financial Technology Development Plan (2019-2021).* http://www.pbc.gov.cn/goutongjiaoliu/113456/113469/3878634/index.html

Persadha, P. D., Waskita, A. A., & Yazid, S. (2015). Comparative Study of Cyber Security Policies Among Malaysia, Australia, Indonesia: A Responsibility Perspective. *2015 Fourth International Conference on Cyber Security, Cyber Warfare, and Digital Forensic*, 146-150. 10.1109/CyberSec.2015.36

Pinochet, L. H. C., Diogo, G. T., Lopes, E. L., Herrero, E., & Bueno, R. L. P. (2019). Propensity of contracting loans services from FinTech's in Brazil. *International Journal of Bank Marketing*.

Popescu AD. (2020c). Transitions and concepts within Decentralized Finance (Defi) Space. *Research Terminals In The Social Sciences.*

Popescu, A. D. (2019). Empowering Financial Inclusion through FinTech. *Social Sciences and Education Research Review*, *6*(2), 198–215.

Popescu, A. D. (2020a). Decentralized Finance – The Lego of Finance. *Social Sciences and Education Research Review*, *7*(1), 321–348.

Popescu, A. D. (2020b). *Financial Technology (FinTech) as a Driver for Financial Digital Assets.* Ovidius University Annals, Economic Sciences Series.

Pradiatiningtyas, D., Dewa, C. B., Safitri, L. A., & Kiswati, S. (2020). The effect of satisfaction and loyalty towards digital payment system users among generation Z in Yogyakarta special region. *Journal of Physics: Conference Series*, *1641*(012110), 1–6. doi:10.1088/1742-6596/1641/1/012110

Pranata, N. (2019). The Role of Digital Payments Fintech in Accelerating the Development of MSMEs in Indonesia. In N. Nemoto & N. Yoshino (Eds.), *Fintech for Asian SMEs*. Asian Development Bank Institute.

Pryanka, A. (2021, January 21). BPS: Gen Z dan Milenial Dominasi Penduduk Indonesia. *Republika.* Retrieved from https://www.republika.co.id/berita/qna4mf457/bps-gen-z-dan-milenial-dominasi-penduduk-indonesia

Pukuh, N., & Widyasthika, H. F. (2017). When Growth is Inclusive in Indonesia? *Jurnal Perencanaan Pembangunan: The Indonesian Journal of Development Planning*, *1*(3), 195–209. doi:10.36574/jpp.v1i3.19

Putra, Y. S. (2016). Theoritical review: Teori perbedaan generasi. *Among Makarti*, *9*(2), 123-134.

Putri, A. S. (2020, January 8). Jumlah Kabupaten dan Provinsi di Indonesia. *Kompas.* Retrieved from https://www.kompas.com/skola/read/2020/01/08/150000469/jumlah-kabupaten-dan-provinsi-di-indonesia?page=2

PwC. (2017). *Summary of the 2017 global FinTech survey in China.* https://www.pwccn.com/zh/fifinancial-services/fiFinTech/global-fiFinTech-survey-china-summary-2017.pdf

Qiancheng Research Institute of Internet Finance. (2019). *2018 National Online*. Lending Bulletin.

Quartey, P., Turkson, E., Abor, J. Y., & Iddrisu, A. M. (2017). Financing the growth of SMEs in Africa: What are the constraints to SME financing within ECOWAS? *Review of Development Finance*, *7*(1), 18–28. doi:10.1016/j.rdf.2017.03.001

Rafie, B. T. (2021, June 25). Simak ciri pinjol ilegal: Penawaran lewat SMS, bunga mencekik. *Kontan.* Retrieved from https://keuangan.kontan.co.id/news/simak-ciri-pinjol-ilegal-penawaran-lewat-sms-bunga-mencekik

Rahaman, M. M. (2011). Access to Financing and Firm Growth. *Journal of Banking & Finance*, *35*(3), 709–723. doi:10.1016/j.jbankfin.2010.09.005

Rajeyyagari, S., & Alotaibi, A.S. (2018). A study on cyber-crimes, threats, security and its emerging trends on latest technologies: influence on the Kingdom of Saudi Arabia. *International Journal of Engineering & Technology, 7*(2.3), 54-58. doi:10.14419/ijet.v7i2.3.9969

Rauniyar, G., & Kanbur, R. (2010). Inclusive growth and inclusive development: A review and synthesis of Asian Development Bank literature. *Journal of the Asia Pacific Economy*, *15*(4), 455–469. doi:10.1080/13547860.2010.517680

Razzaq, A., Samiha, Y. T., & Anshari, M. (2018). Smartphone habits and behaviors in supporting students self-efficacy. *International Journal of Emerging Technologies in Learning*, *13*(2), 94. doi:10.3991/ijet.v13i02.7685

Rehman, Z. U., & Shaikh, F. A. (2020). Critical Factors Influencing the Behavioral Intention of Consumers towards Mobile Banking in Malaysia. *Engineering, Technology &. Applied Scientific Research*, *10*(1), 5265–5269.

Reim, A. (2001). Cybercrimes of the 21st Century. *Computer Fraud & Security*, *2001*(3), 13–15. doi:10.1016/S1361-3723(01)03015-9

Reinhardt, A., & Dufrasne, B. (2019). *IBM DS8880 Encryption for data at rest and Transparent Cloud Tiering (DS8000 Release 8.5).* IBM.

Report, M. S. C. (2020). *Impact of COVID-19 on FinTechs: Indonesia.* https://www.microsave.net/wp-content/uploads/2020/09/Impact-of-COVID-19-on-FinTechs.pdf

Reuters. (2017). *World's first ATM machine turns to gold on 50th birthday.* Retrieved from https://www.reuters.com/article/us-atm-anniversary-idUSKBN19I166

Ringle, C., Wende, S., & Will, A. (2015). *SmartPLS 3.3.3.* http://www.smartpls.com

Ringle, C., Wende, S., & Will, A. (2018). Partial least squares structural equation modeling in HRM research. *International Journal of Human Resource Management*, *31*(1), 1–27.

Rizal, M., & Yani, Y. M. (2016). Cybersecurity Policy and Its Implementation in Indonesia. *Journal of ASEAN Studies*, *4*(1), 61–78. doi:10.21512/jas.v4i1.967

Roldán, J. L., & Sánchez-Franco, M. J. (2012). Variance-based structural equation modeling: Guidelines for using partial least squares. In M. Mora, O. Gelman, A. L. Steenkamp, & M. Raisinghani (Eds.), *Research methodologies, innovations and philosophies in software systems engineering and information systems* (pp. 193–221). IGI Global. doi:10.4018/978-1-4666-0179-6.ch010

Rosidi, A. (2017). Niat menurut hadis dan implikasinya terhadap proses pembelajaran. *Jurnal Inspirasi*, *1*(1), 39–50.

Rusdianasari, F. (2018). The Role of Financial Inclusion through FinTech Integration in Indonesia's Financial System Stability. *Journal of Applied Quantitative Economics*, 244-253. . doi:10.24843/JEKT.2018.v11.i02.p10

Russo, C. (2020). *The Defiant: Money Legos Aren't Fitting Right (But They Could).* Available at https://thedefiant.substack.com/p/money-legos-arent-fitting-right-but-ac9

Ryu, H. S. (2018). What makes users willing or hesitant to use Fintech?: The moderating effect of user type. *Industrial Management & Data Systems, 118*(3), 541–569. doi:10.1108/IMDS-07-2017-0325

Sachs, I. (2004). *Inclusive Development Strategy in an Era of Globalization.* Working Paper No. 35, Policy Integration Department, World Commission on the Social Dimension of Globalization. Geneva: International Labour Office.

Safouane, M. B., John, M., & Gergely, T. (2021). Current trends in and future potential of crowdfunding to finance R&D of treatments for neglected tropical diseases. *Drug Discovery Today.* doi:10.1016/j.drudis.2021.02.021

Sahoo, R., & Sahoo, G. (2016). Computer Science with Python. New Delhi: New Saraswati House (India) Pvt. Ltd.

Salameh, Fatafta, & Shawawreh. (2021). The Possibility of Applying the Tax Accounting System and its Effectiveness on Electronic Commerce in Jordan. *Academy of Accounting and Financial Studies Journal, 25*(1), 4–5.

Samiya, T. M. (2020, January). *A preview of digital ecosystem & engagement through gaming in the context of bangladesh, robi axiata ltd.* BRAC University. http://dspace.bracu.ac.bd/xmlui/bitstream/handle/10361/14008/15104161_BBA.pdf?sequence=1

Sandy, K. F. (2020, December 4). 7 ciri-ciri fintech ilegal, bunga tinggi dan petugas penagih tidak beretika. *iNews.* Retrieved from https://www.inews.id/finance/bisnis/7-ciri-ciri-fintech-ilegal-bunga-tinggi-dan-petugas-penagih-tidak-beretika

Saputra, R., Kartawinata, B. R., Wijayangka, C., & Moeliono, N. N. K. (2019). Analisis faktor investasi pada mahasiswa generasi Z. *Jurnal Ilmu Keuangan dan Perbankan (JIKA), 9*(1), 42-58.

Sari, P., & Rinofah, R. (2019). The Influence Of Financial Technology On Financial Satisfaction With Financial Achievements As A Mediation Variable. *Business Studies Widya Wiwaha College of Economics, 27*(2), 134–146. doi:10.32477/jkb.v27i2.56

Schindler, J. (2017). FinTech and Financial Innovation: Drivers and Depth. *Finance and Economics Discussion Series, 2017*(081).

Schueffel, P. (2016). Taming the beast: A scientific definition of FinTech. *Journal of Innovation Management, 4*(4), 32–54. doi:10.24840/2183-0606_004.004_0004

Schwinn, R., & Teo, E. G. S. (2018). Inclusion or Exclusion? Trends in Robo-advising Financial Investment Services. Handbook of Blockchain, Digital Finance, and Inclusion, 2, 481-492.

Scoop, T. (2019, September 10). *Calling all youths: 'We need your input for the national youth policy.'* The Scoop. https://thescoop.co/2018/12/20/calling-all-youths-we-need-your-input-for-the-national-youth-policy/#:%7E:text=According%20to%20the%20Department%20of,Youth%20Congress%20in%20February%202019

Selwyn, N. (2008). A Safe Haven for Misbehaving? An Investigation of Online Misbehaviour Among University Students. *Social Science Computer Review, 26*(4), 446–465. doi:10.1177/0894439307313515

Sen, A. (1999). *Development as Freedom.* Knopf.

Serrano-Cinca, C., Gutiérrez-Nieto, B., & López-Palacios, L. (2015). Determinants of default in P2P lending. *PLoS One, 10*(10), 1–22. doi:10.1371/journal.pone.0139427

Setiadi, F. (2012). Am Overview of the Development Indonesia National Cyber Security. *International Journal of Information Technology & Computer Science, 6.* Retrieved from http://docshare01.docshare.tips/files/27192/271922656.pdf

Setiawan, S. (2018). E-commerce Taxation and Fiscal Policy Perspective: The Case of Indonesia. *Research in Business and Social Science, 7*(3), 7–8. doi:10.20525/ijrbs.v7i3.900

Setkab - Cabinet Secretariat of the Republic of Indonesia. (2021, January 23). *Statistics Indonesia releases 2020 census results.* Office of Assistant to Deputy Cabinet Secretary for State Documents & Translation. Retrieved from https://setkab.go.id/en/statistics-indonesia-releases-2020-census-results/

Sharma, R. (2012). Study of Latest Emerging Trends on Cyber Security and its challenges to Society. *International Journal of Scientific & Engineering Research, 3*(6). Retrieved from https://www.ijser.org/researchpaper/Study-of-Latest-Emerging-Trends-on-Cyber-Security-and-its-challenges-to-Society.pdf

Shim, Y. W., & Shin, D. H. (2016). Analyzing China's FinTech Industry from the Perspective of Actor–Network Theory. *Telecommunications Policy, 40*, 168–181.

Shmueli, G., Sarstedt, M., Hair, J. F., Cheah, J. H., Ting, H., Vaithilingam, S., & Ringle, C. M. (2019). Predictive model assessment in PLS-SEM: Guidelines for using PLSpredict. *European Journal of Marketing, 53*(11), 2322–2347. doi:10.1108/EJM-02-2019-0189

Shneor, R., Zhao, L., & Flåten, T.B. (2020). *Advances in Crowdfunding: Research and Practice.* Palgrave Macmillan. doi:10.1007/978-3-030-46309-0

Shofawati, A. (2019). The Role of Digital Finance to Strengthen Financial Inclusion and the Growth of SME in Indonesia. *The 2nd International Conference on Islamic Economics, Business, and Philanthropy (ICIEBP),* 389–407. Available at https://www.researchgate.net/publication/332196655_The_Role_of_Digital_Finance_to_Strengthen_Financial_Inclusion_and_the_Growth_of_SME_in_Indonesia

Short, J. C., Ketchen, D. J. Jr, McKenny, A. F., Allison, T. H., & Ireland, R. D. (2017). Research on crowdfunding: Reviewing the (very recent) past and celebrating the present. *Entrepreneurship Theory and Practice, 41*(2), 149–160. doi:10.1111/etap.12270

Sia, S. K., Soh, C., & Weill, P. (2016). How DBS Bank Pursued a Digital Business Strategy. *MIS Quarterly Executive, 15*(2).

Siddik, N. A., & Kabiraj, S. (2020). Digital Finance for Financial Inclusion and Inclusive Growth. In Digital Transformation in Business and Society. Palgrave Macmillan. doi:10.1007/978-3-030-08277-2_10

Silbert, S. (2015). *How Mobile Payments Will Grow in 2016.* Retrieved June 13, 2021, from www.fortune.com

Simangunsong, E. (2018, June). Generation-Z buying behaviour in Indonesia: Opportunities for retail businesses. *MIX: Jurnal Ilmiah Manajemen, 8*(2), 243–253. doi:10.22441/mix.2018.v8i2.004

Sitorus, L. (2015). *Algoritma dan Pemrograman.* CV Andi Offset.

Spinelli, R. (2017). What is Blockchain Technology, Cryptocurrency Bitcoin, Ethereum and Smart Contracts? In Blockchain for dummies. Smashwords.

Sprulock, J. (2013). *Bootstrap.* O'Reilly Media.

State Council. (2011). *Decision on Accelerating the Cultivation and Development of Strategic Emerging Industries.* http://www.gov.cn/zwgk/2010-10/18/content_1724848.htm

Statista. (2021). *Bangladesh: Age structure from 2009 to 2019.* Retrieved from https://www.statista.com/statistics/438190/age-structure-in-bangladesh/

Statista. (2021). *Number of fintech startups worldwide from 2018 to 2021, by region.* Retrieved from https://www.statista.com/statistics/893954/number-fintech-startups-by-region/

Statistics Canada (2012). *Catalogue No. 98-311-X2011003 Census in Brief, Generations in Canada: Age and sex, 2011 Census.* Ottawa: Authority of the Minister responsible for Statistics Canada, Minister of Industry.

Stefani, U., Schiavone, F., Laperche, B., & Burger-Helmchen, T. (2020). New tools and practices for financing novelty: A research agenda. *European Journal of Innovation Management*, *23*(2), 314–328. doi:10.1108/EJIM-08-2019-0228

Stemler, A. (2013). The jobs act and crowdfunding: Harnessing the power and money of the masses. *Business Horizons*, *56*(3), 271–275. doi:10.1016/j.bushor.2013.01.007

Stewart, H., & Jürjens, J. (2018). Data security and consumer trust in FinTech innovation in Germany. *Information & Computer Security*, *26*(1), 109–128. doi:10.1108/ICS-06-2017-0039

Sugiantoro, B., Anshari, M., & Sudrajat, D. (2020, June). Developing Framework for Web Based e-Commerce: Secure-SDLC. *Journal of Physics: Conference Series*, *1566*(1), 012020. doi:10.1088/1742-6596/1566/1/012020

Sukmana, Y. (2019, February 28). Ketua OJK: Sekarang rentenir sudah online. *Kompas*. Retrieved from https://ekonomi.kompas.com/read/2019/02/28/155407326/ketua-ojk-sekarang-rentenir-sudah-online

Sulaeman. (2021, January 21). Per 2020, Penduduk RI Didominasi Generasi Z. *Merdeka*. Retrieved from https://www.merdeka.com/uang/per-2020-penduduk-ri-didominasi-generasi-z.html

Supratman, L. P. (2018). Penggunaan media sosial oleh digital native. *Jurnal Ilmu Komunikasi*, *15*(1), 47–60. doi:10.24002/jik.v15i1.1243

Susanto, H., & Almunawar, M. N. (2015). Managing Compliance with an Information Security Management Standard. In Encyclopedia of Information Science and Technology (3rd ed., pp. 1452–1463). IGI Global. doi:10.4018/978-1-4666-5888-2.ch138

Susanto, H., Yie, L. F., Rosiyadi, D., Basuki, A. I., & Setiana, D. (n.d.). Data Security for Connected Governments and Organisations: Managing Automation and Artificial Intelligence. In Web 2.0 and Cloud Technologies for Implementing Connected Government (pp. 229-251). IGI Global.

Susanto, H., Yie, L. F., Setiana, D., Asih, Y., Yoganingrum, A., Riyanto, S., & Saputra, F. A. (2020). Digital Ecosystem Security Issues for Organizations and Governments: Digital Ethics and Privacy. In Web 2.0 and Cloud Technologies for Implementing Connected Government (pp. 204-228). IGI Global.

Susanto, H. (2018). Smart mobile device emerging Technologies: an enabler to Health Monitoring system. In *High-Performance Materials and Engineered Chemistry* (pp. 241–264). Apple Academic Press. doi:10.1201/9781315187860-8

Susanto, H., & Almunawar, M. N. (2016). Security and Privacy Issues in Cloud-Based E-Government. In *Cloud Computing Technologies for Connected Government* (pp. 292–321). IGI Global. doi:10.4018/978-1-4666-8629-8.ch012

Susanto, H., & Almunawar, M. N. (2018). *Information Security Management Systems: A Novel Framework and Software as a Tool for Compliance with Information Security Standard*. CRC Press.

Susanto, H., Almunawar, M. N., Leu, F. Y., & Chen, C. K. (2016). Android vs iOS or Others? SMD-OS Security Issues: Generation Y Perception. *International Journal of Technology Diffusion*, *7*(2), 1–18. doi:10.4018/IJTD.2016040101

Susanto, H., Ibrahim, F., Nazmudeen, S. H., Mohiddin, F., & Setiana, D. (2020). Human-Centered Design to Enhance the Usability, Human Factors, and User Experience Within Digital Destructive Ecosystems. In *Global Challenges and Strategic Disruptors in Asian Businesses and Economies* (pp. 76–94). IGI Global.

Susanto, H., Leu, F. Y., Caesarendra, W., Ibrahim, F., Haghi, P. K., Khusni, U., & Glowacz, A. (2020). Managing Cloud Intelligent Systems over Digital Ecosystems: Revealing Emerging App Technology in the Time of the COVID19 Pandemic. *Applied System Innovation*, *3*(3), 37. doi:10.3390/asi3030037

Suwana, F., Pramiyanti, A., Mayangsari, I., Nuraeni, R., & Firdaus, Y. (2020). Digital media use of gen z during covid-19 pandemic. *Jurnal Sosioteknologi, 19*(3), 327–340. doi:10.5614ostek.itbj.2020.19.3.2

Sydney, M., & Vildana, H. (2021). *Wall Street Asks If Bitcoin Can Ever Replace Fiat Currencies.* https://www.bloomberg.com/news/articles/2021-06-13/wall-street-asks-if-bitcoin-can-ever-replace-fiat-currencies

Synthetix. (2021). *The Derivatives Liquidity Protocol.* Available at https://synthetix.io/

Szumski, O. (2018). Cybersecurity best practices among Polish students. *Procedia Computer Science, 126*, 1271–1280. doi:10.1016/j.procs.2018.08.070

Taher, S. A., & Uddin, M. K. (2018). *Use of big data in financial sector of Bangladesh – A review.* Retrieved from https://www.econstor.eu/bitstream/10419/190348/1/A6_3_Taher-and-Uddin.pdf

Talom, F. S. G., & Tengeh, R. K. (2020). The impact of mobile money on the financial performance of the SMEs in Douala, Cameroon. *Sustainability, 12*(1), 183. doi:10.3390u12010183

Tambunan, T. T. H. (2011). *Overview of Financial Framework for Supporting MSMEs in Indonesia.* Presentation for The Third Country Training Programme on Micro Finance for African Region: Managing Micro Finance Institution, the Non-Aligned Movement Centre for South-South Technical Cooperation (NAM CSSTC) and the Japan International Cooperation Agency (JICA). Jakarta: NAM Centre Building.

Tambunan, T. T. H. (2009). *SME in Asian Developing Countries.* Palgrave Macmillan Publisher. doi:10.1057/9780230250949

Tambunan, T. T. H. (2015). Financial Inclusion, Financial Education, and Financial Regulation: A Story from Indonesia. *ADBI Working Paper 535.* Asian Development Bank Institute. doi:10.2139srn.2641734

Tambunan, T. T. H. (2018). MSMEs and Access to Financing in a Developing Economy: The Indonesian Experience. In A. Woldie & B. Thomas (Eds.), *Financial Entrepreneurship for Economic Growth in Emerging Nations.* IGI Global. doi:10.4018/978-1-5225-2700-8.ch008

Tambunan, T. T. H. (2019). The impact of the economic crisis on micro, small, and medium enterprises and their crisis mitigation measures in Southeast Asia with reference to Indonesia. *Asia & the Pacific Policy Studies, 6*(1), 1–21. doi:10.1002/app5.264

Tambunan, T. T. H., Santoso, W., Busneti, I., & Batunanggar, S. (2021). The Development of MSMEs and the Growth of Peer-to-Peer (P2P) Lending in Indonesia. *International Journal of Innovation, Creativity and Change, 15*(2), 585–611.

Tan, L. J. (2020). Economics and Math of Token Engineering and DeFi: Fundamentals of Token Economics. Economics Design.

Tech in Asia. (2019, November 5). *The future of Southeast Asia's mobile wallets. Tech in - Connecting Asia's Startup Ecosystem.* https://www.techinasia.com/future-southeast-asias-mobile-wallets

Teigland, R., Siri, S., Larsson, A., Puertas, A.M., & Bogusz, C.I. (2018). The Rise And Development Of FinTech: Accounts Of Disruption From Sweden And Beyond. *Routledge International Studies In Money And Banking*, 88 – 90.

Teixeira, R., Frey, W. H., & Griffin, R. (2015). *States of change: The demographic evolution of the American electorate.* Academic Press.

Telles, M. A. (2008). *Python Power! The Comprehensive Guide.* Thomson Course Technology.

Thakur, K., Qiu, M., Gai, K., & Ali, M. L. (2015). An Investigation on Cyber Security Threats and Security Models. *2015 IEEE 2nd International Conference on Cyber Security and Cloud Computing*, 307-311. 10.1109/CSCloud.2015.71

Thani, F. A., & Anshari, M. (2020). Maximizing Smartcard for Public Usage: PDCA and Root Cause Analysis. *International Journal of Asian Business and Information Management, 11*(2), 121–132. doi:10.4018/IJABIM.2020040108

The 51st AMM and related meetings. (2018). *ASEAN*. Retrieved from https://asean.org/wp-content/uploads/2018/08/PM-Remarks-Transcript.pdf

The Daily Star. (2020). *FinTech to boost stocks*. Retrieved from https://www.thedailystar.net/business/news/FinTech-boost-stocks-1825978

The Financial Express. (2016). *ICT in Banking Industry*. Retrieved from https://thefinancialexpress.com.bd/views/ict-in-banking-industry

The Financial Express. (2020). *Vision 2025 launched to create startup and VC-friendly ecosystem in BD*. Retrieved from https://thefinancialexpress.com.bd/trade/vision-2025-launched-to-create-startup-and-vc-friendly-ecosystem-in-bd

The Hinrich Foundation & AlphaBeta. (2019). *The digital Komodo Dragon: How Indonesia can capture the digital trade opportunity at home and abroad*. https://alphabeta.com/our-research/the-digital-komodo-dragon-how-indonesia-can-capture-the-digital-trade-opportunity-at-home-and-abroad/

The International Institute for Strategic Studies. (2015). Evolution of The Cyber Domain: The Implications for National and Global Security. Author.

The Jakarta Post. (2020). *Fintech's role in financial inclusion rises but infrastructure, literacy challenges loom*. Business. Available at: https://www.thejakartapost.com/news/2020/09/24/fintechs-role-in-financial-inclusion-rises-but-infrastructure-literacy-challenges-loom.html

The US Financial Stability Board. (2020). *Financial innovation and structural change*. Retrieved from https://www.fsb.org/work-of-the-fsb/financial-innovation-and-structural-change/fintech/

The Washington Post. (2016). *Generation Z: What it's like to grow up in the age of likes, LOLs, and longing*. New York: Diversion Books.

Tilley, J. (2017). *Automation, robotics, and the factory of the future*. https://www.mckinsey.com/business-functions/operations/our-insights/automation-robotics-and-the-factory-of-the-future

Tomczak, A., & Brem, A. (2013). A conceptualized investment model of crowdfunding. *Venture Capital, 15*(4), 335–359. doi:10.1080/13691066.2013.847614

Tonge, A. M., Kature, S. S., & Chaudhari, S. R. (2013). Cyber security: Challenges for society- literature review. *IOSR Journal of Computer Engineering, 12*(2), 67–75. www.iosrjournals.org. doi:10.9790/0661-1226775

Towers-Clark, C. (2019). *Big Data, AI & IoT Part Two: Driving industry 4.0 one step at a time*. Retrieved from https://www.forbes.com/sites/charlestowersclark/2019/02/20/big-data-ai-iot-part-two-driving-industry-4-0-one-step-at-a-time/#597a782f23a0

Tracxn. (2021). *FinTech startups in Bangladesh*. Retrieved from https://tracxn.com/explore/FinTech-Startups-in-Bangladesh

Treiblmaier, H., & Clohessy, T. (2020). *Blockchain and Distributed Ledger Technology Use Cases: Applications and Lessons Learned*. Springer International Publishing. doi:10.1007/978-3-030-44337-5

Uhl, M. W., & Rohner, P. (2018). Robo-Advisors versus Traditional Investment Advisors: An Unequal Game. *The Journal of Wealth Management, 21*(1), 44–50. doi:10.3905/jwm.2018.21.1.044

UNCTAD. (2019). *Bangladesh rapid eTrade reediness assessment*. Retrieved from https://unctad.org/system/files/official-document/dtlstict2019d6_en.pdf

UNIDIR. (2021, April). *UNIDIR Cyber Policy Portal.* Retrieved from https://unidir.org/cpp/en/states/malaysia

Uniswap. (2021). *Uniswap Protocol - Swap, earn, and build on the leading decentralized crypto trading protocol.* Available at https://uniswap.org/

Unsworth, A. (2012, December 12). *First m-banking platform in brunei.* Mobile Payments World. https://www.mobilepaymentsworld.com/first-m-banking-platform-in-brunei-2/

van der Westhuizen, P. (2016). *Bootstrap for ASP.NET MVC.* Packt Publishing Ltd.

Venture, E. (2021). *Digital Competitiveness Index 2021: Momentum Of Acceleration Of Digital Economic Transformation, Mapping of Digital Competitiveness in 34 Provinces and 25 Cities in Indonesia.* https://east.vc/dci/#form

Wang, Q. X. (2021). The impact of Insurtech on Chinese insurance industry. *Procedia Computer Science, 187*, 30–35.

Wang, R., Liu, J., & Luo, H. (2021). FinTech development and bank risk taking in China. *European Journal of Finance, 27*, 4–5, 397–418. doi:10.1080/1351847X.2020.1805782

Wardhani, N. K. (2020). *How fintech can help Indonesia's small and medium enterprises survive the COVID-19 pandemic.* The University of Queensland. Available at https://research.uq.edu.au/article/2020/11/how-fintech-can-help-indonesia%E2%80%99s-small-and-medium-enterprises-survive-covid-19-pandemic

Warning of scam syndicate. (2020, August 25). Retrieved April, 29, 2021, from https://borneobulletin.com.bn/warning-of-scam-syndicate-2/

Wasil, W. (2020, April 18). Brunei moving closer towards smart nation, digital economy – the bruneian. *The Bruneian News.* https://www.thebruneian.news/brunei-moving-closer-towards-smart-nation-digital-economy

Wewege, L., & Thomsett, M. C. (2019). *The Digital Banking Revolution: How Fintech Companies Are Transforming the Retail Banking Industry Through Disruptive Financial Innovation.* De Gruyter. doi:10.1515/9781547401598

White, O., Madgavkar, A., Sibanda, T., Townsend, Z., & Ramírez, M. J. (2021). *COVID-19: Making the case for robust digital financial infrastructure.* McKinsey Global Institute.

Whitman, M. E., & Mattord, H. J. (2009). *Principles of Information Security* (3rd ed.). Course Technology.

Wojcik, D., & Ioannou, S. (2020). COVID-19 and finance: Market developments so far and potential impacts on the financial sector and centres. *Tijdschrift voor Economische en Sociale Geografie, 111*(3), 387–400.

Wong, A. (2018, December 15). *BIBD introducing brunei's first NFC mobile payment in january.* Biz Brunei. https://www.bizbrunei.com/2018/12/bibd-nexgen-wallet-introducing-bruneis-first-nfc-mobile-payment-in-january/

Wong, A. (2019, November 3). *BruPay launches: No transaction or registration fees.* Biz Brunei. https://www.bizbrunei.com/2018/11/brupay-launches-no-transaction-registration-fees/

Wong, A. (2020, November 13). *Scan and pay: BIBD QuickPay enables cashless payment using QR codes.* Biz Brunei. https://www.bizbrunei.com/2018/08/scan-and-pay-bibd-quickpay-enables-cashless-payment-using-qr-codes/

World Bank Group. (2018). *The Global Findex Database – Measuring Financial Inclusion and the FinTech Revolution.* Available at https://globalfindex.worldbank.org/

World Bank. (1993). *The East Asian Miracle: Economic Growth and Public Policy, Summary.* Oxford University Press.

World Bank. (2019). *Fintech: The experience so far- executive Summary.* https://documents.worldbank.org/curated/en/130201561082549144/Fintech-The-Experience-so-Far-Executive-Summary

World Economic Forum. (2017). *Beyond FinTech: A Pragmatic Assessment of Disruptive Potential in Financial Services.* https://www3.weforum.org/docs/Beyond_FinTech_-_A_Pragmatic_Assessment_of_Disruptive_Potential_in_Financial_Services.pdf

World Economic Forum. (2020). *The Next Chapter for FinTech in China.* https://www3.weforum.org/docs/WEF_The_Next_Chapter_for_FinTech_in_China_2021.pdf

Yakoboski, Hasler, & Lusardi. (2018). *Millennial Financial Literacy and Fin-tech.* Academic Press.

Yao, Y. H., Li, J. P., & Sun, X. L. (2021). Measuring the risk of Chinese FinTech industry: evidence from the stock index. *Finance Research Letters, 39.* doi:10.1016/j.frl.2020.101564

Yao, F. (2020). A Brief Analysis of Opportunities and Challenges of FinTech Based on Solow Economic Growth Model. *Journal of Contemporary Accounting, 2021*(02), 70–72.

Yearn Finance. (2021). Available at https://yearn.finance

Yie, L. F., Susanto, H., & Setiana, D. (2020). Collaborating Decision Support and Business Intelligence to Enable Government Digital Connectivity. In *Web 2.0 and Cloud Technologies for Implementing Connected Government* (pp. 95–112). IGI Global.

Yin, R. H., & Chen, X. Y. (2021). Risk analysis and regulatory response strategies for FinTech companies — A case study of Ant Group. *Rural Finance Research, 03*, 69–78.

Yovanda, Y. R. (2021, June 24). 7 ciri rentenir online yang harus dihindari agar tidak terjebak bayar bunga gila-gilaan. *Tribunnews.* Retrieved from https://www.tribunnews.com/bisnis/2021/06/24/7-ciri-rentenir-online-yang-harus-dihindari-agar-tidak-terjebak-bayar-bunga-gila-gilaan

Zavolokina, L., Dolata, M., & Schwabe, G. (2016). The FinTech phenomenon: Antecedents of financial innovation perceived by the popular press. *Financial Innovation, 2*(1), 1–16. doi:10.118640854-016-0036-7

Zemke, R., Raines, C., & Filipczak, B. (2000). *Generations at work: Managing the clash of boomers, gen xers, and gen yers in the workplace.* Amacom.

Zhejiang Development and Reform Commission. (2019). *Special Plan for the Construction of Hangzhou International FinTech Center.* http://zjjcmspublic.oss-cn-hangzhou-zwynet-d01-a.internet.cloud.zj.gov.cn//jcms_files/jcms1/web149/site/attach/0/0c5407d88303477e87f691fd19e58a7d.pdf

Zhejiang Digital Economy Development Leading Group. (2019). *The Action Plan for the Construction of Zhejiang Emerging Financial Center.* http://zjjcmspublic.oss-cn-hangzhou-zwynet-d01-a.internet.cloud.zj.gov.cn//jcms_files/jcms1/web2701/site/attach/0/4ac81a8c611f489fae4b609bf87b55ad.pdf

Zhejiang University. (2020). *Global FinTech Hub Report 2020.* http://upload.xinhua08.com/2020/0911/1599789773612.pdf

Zin, A. (2020, July 27). *Cashless payments straight out of your pocket – the bruneian.* The Bruneian News. https://www.thebruneian.news/cashless-payments-straight-out-of-your-pocket

About the Contributors

Muhammad Anshari is Senior Assistant Professor at School of Business and Economics, Universiti Brunei Darussalam (UBDSBE) and currently he is also serving as Deputy Director, Institute of Policy Studies, Universiti Brunei Darussalam. He received his Bachelor Management Information Systems (Honours) from International Islamic University Malaysia (IIUM), his Master of IT (E-Business) from James Cook University Australia, and his PhD programme from Universiti Brunei Darussalam. His professional experience started when he was IT Business Analyst at Astra International and Adjunct Professor Departmet of Informatics, Universitas Islam Negeri Sunan Kalijaga Yogyakarta, Indonesia. Dr Anshari was research fellow at National Taiwan University funded by The Government Republic of China (Taiwan). He was also research fellow at King Saud University, Kingdom of Saudi Arabia in 2009. He has collaborated actively with researchers in several other disciplines of Business Information Systems, E-Health & Mobile Health, Digital Marketplace, FinTech, Big data in business, ICT & Area Studies, and ICT in Education.

Mohammad Nabil Almunawar is currently an associate professor at the School of Business and Economics, Universiti of Brunei Darussalam (UBDSBE), Brunei Darussalam. He was the former dean of UBDSBE. He received his bachelor's degree in 1983 from Bogor Agricultural University, Indonesia, master's degree (MSc) from the Department of Computer Science, University of Western Ontario, London, Canada in 1991, and PhD in Computer Science/Information Systems from the University of New South Wales in 1998. Dr. Almunawar has published more than 100 papers in refereed journals, books, book chapters, encyclopedias, and international conference proceedings. He has more than 30 years of teaching experience in the area of information systems and e-business/e-commerce. His overall research interests include applications of IT in management, e-business/commerce, digital marketplace/platform, digital business ecosystem, health informatics, information security, and cloud computing. Currently, he focuses his research on digital transformation, digital marketplace, digital platform, and digital business ecosystem.

Masairol Masri earned his Ph.D. in Business Administration from Manchester Business School, University of Manchester, UK. He joined Universiti Brunei Darussalam in 2001 as a Tutor before pursuing his Master in Business Administration in 2002 at International Islamic University, Malaysia. Prior to that, he worked as an Audit Assistant at Deloitte & Touche, Brunei Darussalam from 1999. His research interests are in the performance measurement, financial reporting, Islamic accounting and finance with particular reference to small and medium enterprises. While in Universiti Brunei Darussalam, he has held various administrative position such as the Deputy Director for Office of Studies and Administration at the School of Business and Economics and the Accounting Programme Coordinator. He was also a member of the Brunei Darussalam Accounting Standard (BDASC) working committee for Non-Public Interest Entities. He has been a member of the Brunei Darussalam Public Accountant Oversight committee (PAOC) under Ministry of Finance and Economics since 2018. He is currently the Dean of the Universiti Brunei Darussalam School of Business and Economics.

* * *

Noraini Abdullah was a Senior Lecturer in the Mathematics and Economics Programme in the Faculty of Science and Natural Resources, Universiti Malaysia Sabah. She obtained her Bachelor of Science degree from Universiti Kebangsaan Malaysia (1999), Master of Science in Industrial Mathematical Modelling from Loughborough University of Technology, United Kingdom (2003) and obtained her doctorate (PhD) in Mathematics with Economics from Universiti Malaysia Sabah (2013). She was the vice-chairman of the Mathematical and Statistical Application Research Group (MASA) of Universiti Malaysia Sabah. Her research interests would include Multiple Regression Models, Multiple Binary Logistics Models, and Parameter Estimation besides Mathematics with Economics.

Sheikh Abu Taher currently holds associate professor position in the department of Finance and Banking, Jahangirngar University, Bangladesh. He completed BS in Finance from University of Dhaka, Bangladesh and MS and PhD from University of Hyogo, Japan (with Japanese Government Scholarship recipient). His research interest mainly focuses on digital economy, digital finance and modeling of future finance industry. He publishes papers in Telematics and Informatics (Elsevier), International Journal of Innovation in the Digital Economy (IGI Global), International Journal Applied Behavioral Economics (IGI Global), Informatica Economica, Springer Medical Lecture Series and so on. He has been nominated for several best papers award namely, O.S. Braunstein Best Student Paper Award (Pacific Telecommunication Council, USA) and International Telecommunication Society Best Student Paper Award (ITS Biennial Conference, Japan).

Akbari Indra Basuki received a BSc in Electronic and Instrumentation, and an MSc in Computer Engineering. Currently, He is a researcher at Research Center for Informatics, the Indonesian Institute of Sciences and a part time lecturer. His research interests include Software Defined Networking, Network Security, IoT, and Blockchain applications.

Zuozhang Chen is an Associate Professor at Dongwu Business School of Soochow University. His research interests include financial technology, Sino-Japanese economy, public private partnership, and Chinese business.

Sutan Emir Hidayat is currently the Director of Islamic Economy Supporting Ecosystem at the National Committee for Islamic Economy and Finance (KNEKS), the Republic of Indonesia. He is the working group member of: Sustainability Working Group of CIBAFI; Working Group FAS 1 of AOIFI; Advisory Board, IFN Red-Money; Editorial Advisory Board, International Journal of Islamic and Middle Eastern Finance and Management, Emerald; and Editorial Advisory Board, Journal of Economic Cooperation and Development, SESRIC. He was recognized by ISFIN as one of the top influential 500 personalities on a global scale since 2015.

Yeoul Hwangbo is currently a senior fellow of Asian study society as well as a professor of Tashkent University, Uzbekistan. He has experienced in working as (i) a senior adviser for Prime Minister's Office, a director general of Brunei Economic Development Board (BEDB) and a professor of e-Government Innovation Centre of Universiti Brunei Darussalam (UBD) in Brunei and (ii) a professor of e-Government innovation Centre of Korea Advanced Institute of Science and Technology (KAIST) in the Republic of Korea (ROK). Meanwhile He conducted the government services in the area of e-Government and e-Business promotion as an international consultant of Asian Development Bank (ADB) and governments advisers. His working areas include science & technology innovation (STI) policy, e-Business, and e-Government. He received his bachelor degree of public administration and minored in Physic from SungKyungKwan (SKK) university in 1985, master degree of public administration from Seoul National University (SNU) in 1987, and Ph.D. in management information system from Korea Advanced Institute of Science and Technology (KAIST) in 1999.

Nelson Lajuni serves as a senior lecturer at the Faculty of Business, Economics and Accountancy. He has been teaching finance, banking and business related courses for almost 20 years. He earned his DBA in Management (Finance) at the MARA University of Technology Malaysia. He is also a member of Certified Financial Planner (CFPTM) under the Financial Planning Association of Malaysia (FPAM) since February 2017 and a member of the Malaysian Institute of Management since June 2020. His research of interests includes, but are not limited to Financial Management, Financial Planning, Financial Literacy, FinTech, Behavioural Finance, Consumer Finance, and PLS-SEM.

Chenghai Li is an independent researcher. Her research interests include FinTech, finance and Chinese economy.

Khairunnisa Musari is currently an Assistant Professor at Department of Islamic Economics, Postgraduate Program and Faculty of Islamic Business Economics (FEBI), Kiai Haji Achmad Siddiq State Islamic University (UIN KHAS), Jember, Indonesia. She is a member of the Indonesian Association of Islamic Economist (IAEI) and a Lead Independent Associate Ambassadors of VentureEthica. She has experience as a Senior Specialist for Islamic Finance of UNDP Indonesia. She was listed as the Top 150 Most Influential Women in Islamic Business & Finance 2020 by Cambridge-IFA.

Salumah Nain currently serves as a senior lecturer at the Department of Business Management. She has been teaching accounting, finance, and business-related courses for almost 15 years. He earned his MBA at the Universiti Malaysia Sabah. Her research interests include but are not limited to Management Accounting, Taxation, Financial Management, Financial Statement Analysis, Fintech, and PLS-SEM.

Andrei Popescu is Co-Founder of SCX Holdings and Seasoned FinTech/DeFi/Blockchain Tech Start-Ups Investor/Advisor. PhD candidate and a vision-driven entrepreneur/executive with career-long record of business growth and innovation. Andrei helped in building great companies in Singapore, Austria, Italy and Romania with extraordinary people, while seeking continuous intellectual stimulation through a broad set of experiences in dynamic, challenging, and high-intensity environments. He has been engaged on helping organizations that evolve in challenging markets to break down the barriers that prevent them from reaching their potential, which operate in Scandinavia, Eastern Europe, China and Asia-Pacific. Andrei is an active participant in the FinTech sphere, Crypto & Alternative Assets

Class Ecosystems and the Blockchain/DLT communities in Southeast Asia, Europe and the USA; who attends meetups regularly, speaks at the conferences and advises on Blockchain/DLT/IoT/AI/Alternative Investments & FinTech Projects. As an Alternative Asset Class management, Andrei is bridging new FinTech instruments, with traditional world's best corporate and institutional investors, where alternative FinTech assets are still in an early, immature, evolving stage of their existence. Andrei believes that the introduction of Alternative FinTech Assets into the financial services sector, will not only stabilize the investment landscape, but will radically disrupt old-school ways of the financial world. Thanks to the increasing offer of FinTech solutions, the segment of alternative investments is opening up the trading sphere to assets that, until now, could not be traded quickly and easily, also will enable us to create faster and more cost-effective financial instruments. His focus and interest are on Strategic Investments in Disruptive Technologies & Innovations, FinTech, Financial Innovations, Financial Digital Assets, Blockchain, DLT, Crypto Asset Trading Systems, Decentralized Finance (DeFi), dApps, Digital Markets & Trading Platforms, Data Science, Data Capital, Artificial Intelligence (ANI, AGI, ASI, ML, DL) Applications, AI based Automated Trading Strategies, Business Strategy Implementations via AI systems.

Didi Rosiyadi received the Ph.D. degree in Computer Science and Information Engineering from National Taiwan University of Science and Technology (NTUST), Taiwan, in 2013. Currently, He is a researcher in Research Center for Informatics, Indonesian Institute of Sciences (LIPI) and also a lecturer in any universities in Indonesia. His research interests include digital image watermarking, steganography and cyber security. He has published more than 50 research papers.

Michael Sampat is an independent researcher working in a number of different disciplines including Sociology, Political Science, Ethics, and Biblical Studies.

Desi Setiana received a BSc and MSc in Psychology Behavior of Information Technology, respectively from University of Indonesia and University of Brunei. She is researcher at the Ministry of Law and Human Right, Republic of Indonesia. Her research interests are in the areas of Psychology of Information Security, User Behaviour toward Cyberbullying, IT Emerging Technology for Psychology Education. She is now in-pipeline to pursuing Ph.D in IT Psychology for Cyberbullying and Security Protection for Prisoners.

Heru Susanto is currently Researcher at Research Center for Informatics, the Indonesian Institute of Sciences. At present he is an Honorary Professor, Department of Information Management, College of Management, Tunghai University, Taichung, Taiwan, and also Visiting Scholar at School of Business, University Technology of Brunei. Dr. Susanto has worked as an IT professional in several roles, including Web Division Head of IT Strategic at Indomobil Group, and Prince Muqrin Chair for Information Security Technologies. His research interests are in the areas of Information Security, 5G Technologies, Grid Application, Big Data, Business Process Re-engineering, and e-Marketing. Dr. Susanto received a BSc in Computer Science; an MBA in Marketing Management; an MSc in Information Systems; and a PhD in Information Security, from IPB University, King Saud University and Tunghai University, respectively. Nowadays, Dr. Heru Successfully authoring more than 35 books published by Francis & Taylor Group; including 8 full authored books and 30 book chapters, and more than 60 international publication in peer review journal and high impact journal; Scopus, Science Direct, Springer, ISI, and Global Indexed, such as: Information Security Management Systems, Business Process Reengineering

An ICT Approach, The Emerging Technology of Big Data, Human Capital through ICT, Chemical Technology and Informatics in Chemistry with Applications.

Masatsugu Tsuji is Ph.D. Faculty of Economics, Kobe International University, and Professor Emeritus of Osaka University. Received B.A. from Kyoto University in 1965; M.A. from Osaka University in 1967; and Ph.D. in Economics from Stanford University, US. in 1976. He is currently professor of Kobe International University. His serves include visiting professors of Carnegie Mellon University, US and National Cheng Kung University, Taiwan; Board of Director, International Telecommunications Society; Editorial Board, Journal of International Society of Telemedicine and eHealth, and Smart Homecare Technology and TeleHealth; coordinator of e-Health Economics, ISfTeH. He has over 200 publications. Current research focuses on economic evaluation of telemedicine and e-Health using econometric methods, and the applications of ICT such as 5G mobile, AI and robot for innovation in medicine, telecommunications, and other industry. He has been consulting the Japanese Government and local governments for implementing telemedicine projects.

Avnner Chardles Wellfren is a postgraduate student at Universiti Malaysia Sabah's Centre for Post Graduate Studies. He earned a Bachelor of Business (Financial Management and Banking) degree with First Class Honours in 2021. He also received a BMC (Bloomberg Market Concept) qualification as part of his interest in finance. Avnner's current research focuses on subjects such as investment, financial behaviour, fintech, and millennials.

Poshan (Sam) Yu is a Lecturer in Accounting and Finance in the International Cooperative Education Program of Soochow University (China). He is also an External Professor of FinTech and Finance at SKEMA Business School (China), a Visiting Professor at Krirk University (Thailand) and a Visiting Researcher at the Australian Studies Center of Shanghai University (China). Sam leads FasterCapital (Dubai, UAE) as a Regional Partner (China) and serves as a Startup Mentor for AIC RAISE (Coimbatore, India). His research interests include financial technology, regulatory technology, public-private partnerships, mergers and acquisitions, private equity, venture capital, start-ups, intellectual property, art finance, and China's "One Belt One Road" policy.

Index

Premier Reference Source
Emerging GIS Applications for Emergency and Disaster Management

Premier Reference Source
Managerial Strategies and Green Solutions for Project Sustainability

Premier Reference Source
Comparative Approaches to Using R and Python for Statistical Data Analysis

Premier Reference Source
Solutions for High-Touch Communications in a High-Tech World

www.ingramcontent.com/pod-product-compliance
Lightning Source LLC
LaVergne TN
LVHW062155300926
849161LV00010B/2668
9781799884477